W9-CMB-322

CHERUBINI

Da Capo Press Music Reprint Series

GENERAL EDITOR

FREDERICK FREEDMAN

VASSAR COLLEGE

CHERUBINI

*Memorials Illustrative of his
Life and Work*

By Edward Bellasis

DA CAPO PRESS · NEW YORK · 1971

A Da Capo Press Reprint Edition

This Da Capo Press edition of
Cherubini is an unabridged republication
of the new edition published in London in 1912.

Library of Congress Catalog Card Number 70-138497
SBN 306-70071-9

Published by Da Capo Press, Inc.
A Subsidiary of Plenum Publishing Corporation
227 West 17th Street, New York, N.Y. 10011
All Rights Reserved

Manufactured in the United States of America

MEMORIALS OF CHERUBINI.

[*After Ingres*, 1842.

CHERUBINI:

MEMORIALS ILLUSTRATIVE OF HIS LIFE AND WORK.

'(Imagination) round him flew,
(Music) led him by the hand,
Instructed him in all she knew,
And gave him absolute command.'

———

'The most rarefied mental, or
spiritual music.'
THOMPSON,

BY

EDWARD BELLASIS

Honorary Member of the Florentine Cherubini Society

NEW   EDITION

BIRMINGHAM
CORNISH BROTHERS LIMITED
39 NEW STREET
1912

' Un grand homme s'endort, mais il ne meurt jamais.'—*Emile Deschamps* on Cherubini.

' The most accomplished musician, if not the greatest genius of the 19th century.'—*Ulibicheff*.

' A colossal and exceptional nature, an existence full of days, of master-pieces, and of glory.'—*Miel*.

' A vast, powerful, and complex genius.'—*Pougin*.

' The last and noblest Roman in the purely classical style of art.'—*Baillot*.

' One hundred years hence it will remain to be as new as the organ-music of Bach, as the choral fugues of Handel, as the melodies of Mozart are now.'—*Chorley* on *Médée's* orchestration.

' The inimitable author of *Démophon, Lodoïska, Elisa* and *Médée.*'—*Méhul*.

' The greatest dramatic composer of his time.'—*Haydn*.

' One may well be pardoned, for forgetting that any school of music ever existed but that of which they form so bright and enduring an ornament.'—*Grove* on the overtures.

Cipriani Potter: 'Who is the greatest living composer, yourself excepted?' *Beethoven:* 'Cherubini.'

' Old Cherubini ! there's a matchless fellow.'—*Mendelssohn*.

' Whom I often feel tempted to compare to Dante.'—*Schumann*.

' We can never say enough of such masterpieces.'—*Weber* (after hearing the *Water Carrier*).

' It was that opera that gave me the first impulse to composition.'—*Spohr*.

' It would be difficult to answer them if they now came amongst us, and asked in what respect we had improved on their mode of musical procedure.'—*Wagner* on Cherubini, Méhul and Spontini.

' If Palestrina had lived in our day, he would have been a Cherubini.'— *Adolphe Adam*.

' The greatest composer of sacred music in this [the 19th] century.'—*Hiller*.

' Imperishable works of art.'—*Riehl*.

' The ancient and the modern style unite to form the most perfect whole that can possibly be imagined.'—*Fétis*.

' Cherubini, by his veiled imperceptible melody, has known how to reach the most mysterious depths of Christian meditation.'—*Berlioz*.

' He possessed a remarkable aptitude for rendering sensible, for inter-preting religious truths.'—*Fr. Girod, S.J.*

' Your Mass is golden.'—*Hummel*, to Cherubini (after hearing the *Mass in A*).

' The severe simplicity of style to be found in much of his sacred music seems admirably in keeping with the services of the Church. . . . In his most jubilant work, the great Coronation *Mass in A*, we never lose the impression that it is *sacred* music to which we are listening.'—*Prout*.

' Dear son, you are worthy to sing the praises of God.'—*Cardinal Caprara*, Papal Legate at Paris (after hearing the *Mass in F*.)

' The Masses of . . . Cherubini and others are choice and serious compositions and are far from being unbecoming the holiness of the Church.'—*Cardinal Bartolini*, late Prefect S.C.R.

' Where the religious song is accompanied by musical instruments, these must serve solely for adding to its force, so that the sense of the words penetrate deeper into the hearts of the faithful, and their spirit being roused to the comtemplation of spiritual things, be elevated towards God and the love of divine objects.'—*Pope Benedict XIV*.

' The Church has always recognized and favoured the progress of the arts, admitting to the service of the cult everything good and beautiful discovered by genius in the course of ages,—always, however, with due regard to the liturgical laws, consequently modern music is also admitted in the Church since it, too, furnishes compositions of such excellence, sobriety and gravity that they are in no way unworthy of the liturgical functions.'—*Pope Pius X*.

INSCRIBED TO

JOHN FRANCIS BARNETT, ESQ.,

NEPHEW OF THE COMPOSER OF

'THE MOUNTAIN SYLPH,'

AND HIMSELF THE COMPOSER

OF

'THE ANCIENT MARINER,'

OF

' PARADISE AND THE PERI,'

AND OF

'THE RAISING OF LAZARUS,'

ETC.

PREFACE

TO NEW EDITION.

M Y main idea, compiling these *Memorials* in 1874, was to collect facts about Cherubini in pamphlets, periodicals and dictionaries, more or less inaccessible; besides giving some fresh material; printing a Catalogue of Works, long out of print; correcting a few errors; citing views on the value of his life's work; and where, so far as I knew, little had been said, venturing on some opinions of my own. Such an undertaking really supplied, no doubt imperfectly enough, a want in English at the time, but had Pougin's articles in the *Ménéstrel*, translated later on in the columns of the *Musical World*, appeared earlier and in English book-form, there would have been little call for *Memorials*.

As to the discussion of Operas and Masses, this has much invaded the continuity of biographical narrative; Hazlitt somewhere tells us, if we wish to see 'the force of human genius,' to read Shakespeare; if 'the futility of human learning,' then—'his commentators.' Especially with music does expression of its inner meaning escape us in verbal analysis—even with illustrations in aid, at best inadequate, but better than nothing, and designed to whet the appetite for more in a study of the works themselves. With regard to criticism at second-hand, there has been more 'précis,' and curtailment. It is, however, always interesting to know in full what the Great Masters thought of one another. In other respects, musical criticism is only too liable to become either amateur commonplaces to the professional, or scientific 'caviare to the general,' or dreary philosophical disquisitions, on a subject-matter, in its essence immaterial and elusive, so subtle, so indefinable is that divine art, with its 'inexhaustible evolution and disposition of notes, so rich yet so simple, so intricate yet so regulated, so various yet so majestic,' as Cardinal Newman writes, 'with its mysterious stirrings of heart, and keen emotions, and strange yearnings after we know not what, and awful impressions from we know not whence.'[1] *Lodoïska, Médée, Les Deux Journées,* the *Masses,* the *Requiems,* the *Regina Cœli,* the *8-part Credo,* of this 'vast powerful, and complex genius,'[2] are easier to listen to than to talk about. Nevertheless, a composer's life is intimately bound up with his works. The one cannot be separated from the other, and some notices, more or less specific, of the chief works have been given.

I subjoin a list of authorities, some of which, when done with, were placed in the British Museum.

L. Cherubini (anonymous), E. W. Fritzsch, 12mo, with lengthened critique on *Les Deux Journées.*

Luigi Cherubini: Seine Kurze Biografie und ästhetische Darstellung seiner Werke (anonymous); 1809, Erfurt, 8vo, by Dr. Ignaz E. F. Arnold (1774-1812), with notices of *Lodoïska, Elisa, Médée, Les Deux Journées, Anacréon, Faniska* and *La Cintura d'Armida.* Along with other notices it was re-printed under the title *Gallerie der berühmtesten Tonkünstler des achtzehnten und neunzehnten Jahrhunderts, 1816,* Erfurt.

Alexander E. Choron (1771-1834) and François J. M. Fayolle (1774-1852). *Dictionnaire Historique des Musiciens.* 1810-11-17, Paris; with information about Cherubini, furnished by the composer.

Biographie des Hommes vivants. 1816-17, Paris; with notice of Cherubini signed A.

Biographie Nouvelle des Contemporains. 1821-22, Paris; with notice, etc.

The Harmonicon for 1825. London; with notice, and list of operas, etc.

Chapelle-Musique des Rois de France, 1832, Paris.

Dictionnaire de la Conversation. 1834, Paris; with notice, etc., by François H. J. Castil-Blaze (1784-1857).

Biographie Universelle et Portative des Contemporains. 1834, Paris; with notice, etc.

Encyclopédie des Gens du Monde. 1835, Paris; with notice, etc., by Edme. F. A. M. Miel, of the French Institute (1775-1842), who wrote its *Annals.*

---

[1] *Oxford University Sermons,* 346-7.
[2] Pougin.

Also his *Notice sur la Vie et les Ouvrages de Chérubini.* 1842, Paris, 8vo., 1st published in the *Moniteur Universel* for 24, 25, 29 Aug. 1842, the author consenting to its publication in a separate form at the request of a number of artists, who had heard him deliver it as a lecture. It also forms part of a history of French art, closing a chapter on the Conservatoire.

Louis L. de Loménie (1818-78). *Contemporains Illustres,* 10 vols., with notice, etc., identical, I believe, with that published separately by the author, an Academician, under the title of *Chérubini, par un Homme de Rien ;* (a pseudonym). 1841, Paris, 12mo.

Charles Place. *Essai sur la Composition Musicale. Biographie et Analyse Phrénologique de Chérubini avec notes et plan cranioscopique.* 1842, Paris, 8vo. This was read at the 'séance' of the Phrenological Society of Paris 27 May, 1842. Place was a phrenological doctor, exiled at Brussels after the 'Coup d'Etat' of 1851, and is so taken up with his examination of Cherubini's cranium, that he leaves little room for biography, in great measure derived from that of M. Adam, in the journal *La France Musicale,* while, for several communications, he is indebted to MM. A. Gourdin, Boieldieu the younger, and Pilati. Place endeavours to show that the organs of veneration, affection, courage, breadth, melody, order, firmness, construction, esteem of oneself, &c., were strongly developed in Cherubini ; those of colour, form, language, destructiveness, love of country, &c., less so ; whilst there was an almost total absence of idealism, justice, and benevolence ! No idealism !

Luigi Picchianti (1786-1864). *Notizie sulla Vita e sulle Opere di Luigi Cherubini,* 1843, Milano ; 1844, Firenze. The author, a guitarist, writes that he obtained his facts from lives issued in France and Italy, during the lifetime and after the death of Cherubini, through persons connected with the composer's family, and by means of personal investigations at Florence. Among the lives mentioned is a translation from the French in the *Rivista Musicale* of Florence for April 1842, of a life in the *Revue et Gazette de Paris* of the previous March.

Cherubini. *Notice des Manuscrits Autographes de la Musique composée par feu M.L.C.Z.S. Chérubini, ex-surintendant de la Musique du Roïə Directeur du Conservatoire de Musique, Commandeur de l'Ordre Royale de la Legion d'Honneur, Membre de l'Institut de France, etc. etc. etc. ; Catalogu, Général par ordre chronologique des ouvrages composés par moi Marie-Louis-Charles-Zenobi-Salvador-Cherubini, né à Florence le 14 Septembre de l'année 1760.* 1843, Paris, 8vo. Edited by A. Bottée de Toulmon (1797-1850), librarian of the Conservatoire, and published with the sanction of Cherubini's family, who were about to dispose of the composer's MSS. Here we have a faithful record, by Cherubini himself, of nearly all his compositions, dating from 1773 to 1841. A supplement is added of works not in the catalogue, of duplicate MSS. mostly in the composer's own handwriting, and of copies by him of works of various composers. Following upon the mention of many pieces are notes by their author. Collations with one or two smaller lists in MS. placed at Pougin's disposal by the family, give some 6 more pieces.

Michaud. *Biographie Universelle Ancienne et Moderne.* 1844, Paris, art. Cherubini, and list of chief works, by J. A. L. de Lafage, of the French Institute (1801-62).

Jacques F. F. E. Halévy (1799-1862). *Etudes sur la Vie et les Travaux de Chérubini,* that 1st appeared in the *Moniteur des Arts,* of 23, 30 March ;

18 May 1843, under the title of *Etudes sur Chérubini.* He divides his life into 4 unequal parts, never living to complete his work. M. Léon Halévy remarks that this is the less to be regretted, since, while the 1st portion throws a vivid light on the least-known phase of Cherubini's life, his early career in his native country, the other intended parts, giving the later facts, would only have been telling us what we already know. Still, Pougin deplores not having the disciple's opinion on the great works of the master. ' It is certain that the pages of Halévy . . . are precious in more than one respect ; . . . they are an eloquent pleading in favour of the master's genius, at times misunderstood.' Also his *Derniers Souvenirs et Portraits,* 1863.

Cherubini's *Treatise on Counterpoint and Fugue,* translated by Mrs. Cowden Clarke. 1854, London, with notice, etc.

Castil-Blaze. *Théâtres Lyriques de Paris. L'Académie Impériale de Musique. Histoire Littéraire, musicale, chorégraphique . . de 1645 à 1855.* 2 vols., 1855, Paris, 8vo.

Fr. Louis Girod, S.J. *De La Musique Religieuse.* A defence of modern church-music. 1859, Namur, 8vo. with notice, etc. in the last chapter.

Nouvelle Biographie Générale. 1856, Paris, with notice, etc., by René D. Denne-Baron (1804-65). Also his *Mémoires Historiques d'un Musicien. Cherubini sa Vie, ses Travaux, leur Influence sur l'Art.* 1862, Paris, 8vo. ; to some extent from Miel.

Raoul Rochette. *Notice historique sur la Vie et les Ouvrages de M. Cherubini,* the 'Eloge' of Cherubini delivered at the Institute by its secretary, Oct., 1843, at the annual public 'séance,' and printed in *Institut Royal de France. Séance, etc., de l'Académie des Beaux Arts,* of which the writer was secretary. 1843, Paris, 4to.

Adolphe C. Adam (1803-56). *Derniers Souvenirs d'un Musicien.* 1859, Paris, 12mo. with notice, etc.

Antoine A. E. Elwart (1808-77). *Histoire de la Société des Concerts.* 1860, Paris, with notices, etc.

Dr. John Hullah (1812-84). *History of Modern Music.* 1862, London, with notice, etc.

The Musical World. 1862, London ; (*M. W.*) with notice, etc., chiefly a translation from the German, by J. V. Bridgeman, from the *Niederrheinische Musik-Zeitung* (*N.M.Z.*), citing A. von Ulibicheff (1795-1858) in his *Nouvelle Biographie de Mozart,* etc.

Abbé Théodule E. X. Normand, otherwise Théodore Nisard. *Cherubini,* etc. 1857, Paris ; 1867, Le Mans, 4to.

F. J. Fétis (1784-1871). *Biographie Universelle des Musiciens.* 1867, Paris, 8vo, 8 vols. Much of art. Cherubini in this well-known work is in Fétis' *Des Manuscrits autographes de L. Cherubini,* a series of articles in *La Revue et Gazette musicale,* 1843, cited by Pougin and others.

Félix Clément (1822-85). *Musiciens Célèbres.* 1868, Paris, 8vo, with portrait and notice, etc. by a former chapel-master of the Sorbonne ; also his *Dictionnaire Lyrique, ou l'Histoire des Operas,* etc. 1869, Paris.

Baldassarre Gamucci. *Intorno alla Vita e delle Opere di Luigi Cherubini, Fiorentino, ed al monumento ad esso innalzato in Santa Croce. Cenni biografici.* 1869, Firenze, 8vo. Gamucci, pupil of Picchianti, gives a minute account of the raising of the monument to Cherubini at Florence.

Imperial Dictionary of Biography, with notice by Dr. George A. Macfarren (1813-87).

Dr. Ferdinand Hiller (1811-85). *Cherubini,* an appreciation, translated from the German into *Macmillan's Magazine,* July 1875, (then under the editorship of the late Sir George Grove), and placed also in his *Musikalisches und Personliches ;* 1873, Leipsic.

La Mara (a pseudonym). *Luigi Cherubini,* 8vo, chiefly after Denne-Baron for facts ; but 'full of interest and overflowing with ingenious views' (Pougin), and appearing in the authoress's 2nd volume of *Musikalische Studienskopfe,* 1876, Leipsic, and in pamphlet form. An Italian translation, originally in the *Rivista Europea* for May 1877, has also appeared separately. The authoress, Frau Lipsius of Leipsic, consulted Mme. Rosellini, the composer's younger daughter, at Liszt's request, conveyed through Mme. Laussot (afterwards Mme. Hillebrand) foundress of the Cherubini Society at Florence : so the latter informed me.

Sir George Grove. *Dictionary of Music and Musicians,* 4 vols., small 4to ; 1880, London, with notice, etc. of 5½ columns, by A. Maczewski, but without mention of the D minor Mass, and no list of works in 1st or 2nd ed. as the late Sir George intended in note to myself 23 Feb. 1880. A reference is since given to such list in *Quellen Lexicon,* the above omission is rectified, and the notice duly revised, however, in 1904, ed. J. A. Fuller-Maitland.

Henri L. Blanchard (1778-1858). *Cherubini,* originally appearing as articles in Parisian Journals, and published separately (not seen).

Arthur Pougin. *Cherubini : His Life, his Works, and the Part played by him in Art,* a series of articles, originally appearing in *Le Ménestrel,* Paris, and translated in successive numbers of the *Musical World (M. W.)* between 28 Jan. 1882, and 15 March 1884, that adds vastly to our knowledge from information at 1st hand, corrects many errors, and by publishing private letters, repairs the scant justice hitherto done to the noble, albeit austere personal character of the composer. Also his supplement to Fétis, 2 vols. 1881.

Dr. Hugo Riemann. *Dictionary of Music,* translated from the German by Mr. F. S. Shedlock, a succinct, and, I believe, valuable work : art. Cherubini.

Luigi Cherubini, a notice appended to the posthumous works of the composer as issued by Ricordi, Milano, small 4to.

G. T. Ferris. *Great Musical Composers,* with chapter on Méhul, Spontini, and Cherubini ; New York ; and F. J. Crowest's *Cherubini,* London, 1890, are apparently, for the most part, compilations, as to facts, from *Memorials,* 1st ed.

Rev. E. L. Taunton. *History and Growth of Church Music,* small 8vo., 1887, London.

Encyclopædia Britannica, with notices, etc., extended in new ed. by Mr. D. F. Tovey.

Many other works are referred to in *Memorials,* citing views on Cherubini, by Haydn, Beethoven, Weber, Hummel, Spohr, Mendelssohn, Schumann, Burney, Carpani, Gerber, Nohl, Jahn, Schindler, Krehbiel, Ritter, Naumann, Ramann, Frimmel, Kastner, Chorley, Ella, Riehl, Hauptmann, Moscheles, Dannreuther and Wagner.

Among Novello's popular *Primers of Biography* appears *Luigi Cherubini,* by Mr. Joseph Bennett, while the late Professor Ebenezer Prout's various publications show his knowledge and appreciation of the great Florentine.

In France, the land of his adoption, Cherubini, diligent Director of the Conservatoire, taught a skilful 'technique' to French music which it had never known before his time, but has retained ever since. If this teacher of Boieldieu, Auber and Halévy was strict as a teacher, this strictness worked for good inasmuch as Cherubini was a moderating force amid a period of change and freedom. As a composer he is for all time, but not all his music. There is great wealth in his sacred, a more moderate income in his secular music, as to melody. A competent critic once told me that in variety of accompaniment he equals Wagner, and such variety is seen in *Lodoïska,* an opera of massive calibre, written at 30, with no knowledge of his great contemporary, Mozart. As a composer then, he contributed, along with, but independently of, Mozart to the innovations in opera completed by Wagner : and he is a great composer partly because he suffered. It was not all sunshine, during Revolutions and Restorations, for the protégé of Louis XVI. and Marie Antoinette, the servant of the Republic, the opponent of Napoleon, the chapel-master of Louis XVIII. and Charles X., and the subject of Louis Philippe. A strong will made order dominate his life and work. The latter's mathematical forms did not extinguish the 'glimpse divine,' conferred by neither Conservatoires nor degrees. There is a slow prodigality of output, of unequal merit, during the course of 81 years. The profusion of a Schubert, who died at 31, is an Eden's luxuriance, Cherubini's partly a Leasowes, partly a Dutch garden. Ella deemed that of all the Great Masters Cherubini had the 'least fancy.' The known canons and the less known occasional pieces in private collections show that fancy was within his gift. His Italian tunefulness appears in contributions to Italian opera, and in *Pimmalione,* that pleased Napoleon, who liked Italian music. Cherubini, says Castil-Blaze, 'skilfully navigates his barque between Gluck and Piccinni,' for he has two styles, one Italian, another German, and at times a composite style, but never really a French style ; a style, with a presage in the *Water Carrier,* of the romantic, of which Weber took note. It is certain that separate items, such as the duet from *Epicure,* the scene from *Le Crescendo,* the Jason and Medea duet of warring song, the once familiar excerpts from *Anacréon* and *Les Abencérages,* heard in the concert-room, could hold their own to-day, just as the glorious *Medea, Water Carrier, Anacréon* and other overtures continue to do. Perhaps suspecting the fate of Cimarosa and his school, Cherubini in 1788 entered the road that Handel and Gluck combined to make ; which Mozart and himself extended, and Beethoven trod. The wonder, however, is that any of his operatic music has survived the books that conspired, along with 'a certain absence of scenic instinct,'[3] to weigh down so noble a muse.[4] Outrun in opera on these accounts, at the two-mile course, even despite the tremendous *Médée,* he takes a better place at the hundred yards with the exquisite *Water Carrier.* He shortened the former for his Viennese audience, but the latter needed no shortening and, if criticized in detail for its text, has Goethe's approval of the plot, and Spohr's, Weber's and Mendelssohn's for the music. Herein he sustains our musical interest from first to last.

In Hiller's view he reigns supreme in sacred music during the last century, given imaginative and devotional expression along with modern tonality, in his case informed by a Sarti's learning. That music ranges from the immense D minor Mass, taking over

---

[3] Fétis.

[4] As if to come to *Lodoïska's* rescue, an air and two entr'actes were added to the score at Vienna in 1805, and a scene and aria for Mme. Milder at Count Bruhl's request, by Weber, at Berlin in 1816. With regard to *Faniska,* it ' is rather a symphony with songs than a dramatic lyrical work.'—*C. M. von Weber,* tr. 1865, i. 401 ; ii. 377-8.

an hour, to the brief B flat Mass only 20 minutes
long, while the *Regina Coeli*, the *Confirma Hoc* and
the Communion Prelude for Charles X.'s coronation,
crown of his sacred work, show his greatness in hymn,
offertory and instrumental composition, the Prelude,
according to Berlioz, being ' mystical expression in all
its purity, contemplation, and Catholic ecstasy ! '

And coming to a personal matter, youth generally
sees no faults in its hero ; but if age comes to see
spots in the sun, the sun still shines. While citing
what great composers and professional critics have said,
I have also ventured, though but an amateur, on some
impressions of my own, gained after 50 years' love and
admiration. And my hero is no puppet of a day's
fair. If Cherubini is still not enough known, the loss
is especially theirs who might, but do not, know him
as they should. Cherubini, indeed, appears so great
for high art and science, sustained in a perfect balance seen
over and over again, that herein his modern compeers
seem few. 'Cherubini,' wrote the late Lord Coleridge to
me, in a kind and encouraging letter, 'is, to my mind, a
very great man, who has never, in this country, at any
rate, quite had his proper place granted him.' In the
combination of exceeding order and genius displayed, I
had almost said, he is unique among composers ; as
also in a sustention and gradual development of powers
that make his last work, written at 76, for many, in some
respects at least, the greatest work of all.

Writing little or nothing for drawing or concert-
rooms apart from his overtures and larger Masses, he
never can be known as Beethoven is known. But though
neither of them be Bœotians, we can regard both as a
sort of second Epaminondas and Pelopidas, inseparable
Generals of forces in Opera and Mass: here they stand or
fall together. Add some hymns, 4tets, canons, and
the cradle song on occasion of the Count de Chambord's
baptism, and Cherubini's field of action is fairly recon-
noitred as known to-day. Two pieces, indeed, one

secular, the other sacred, have attained a general
popularity ; the canon *Perfida Clori,* so beautiful as to

be set over here to words beginning 'God Save Victoria;'
and the *Ave Maria* with 'everything that is touching

and lovely and loving in the prayer.'[5]

The amount of new music tends to oust much
of the old, so with only 6 days in the week for work
—some would make them 7—there is less room for the
Florentine than there used to be. His masterpieces
from *Lodoïska* in 1791 to the male voice *Requiem* in
1836, give him his classic place, that is—one not now
gainsaid. His art is sincere ; no mere 'trick, or game,
or fashion of the day without meaning,'[6] and founded
on the twin canons of eternal truth and beauty that
emanate from one who was an Italian by birth, French
by adoption, German by inclination, and who contrived
to please three very different audiences—in Turin, in
Paris and in Vienna.

Theatres, Churches, Festivals and Musical Societies
in Germany, England and other countries, have long
given his best works, and to the honour of his profession Cherubini's sincerest admirers have been found
among his own rivals. And Seyfried's record of what
Beethoven thought of him, narrated, too, by Schindler, as

---

[5] Fr. Girod, S.J.   [6] Cardinal Newman. *Idea of a Univ. disc.* iv.

the ' most admirable ' among his contemporaries, may become ' the voice itself of posterity.' [7]

Cherubini's sun—or star shall I call it ?—will shine so long as music is music and not mere science and noise. It is no flickering flame or faint twinkle. After over a century it gives a steady light still. This reputedly cold man can subdue us to tears or shake us with fear. *Médée* is full of deepest sentiment. When real masterpieces of his begin, like the latter, or the *Water Carrier* or the two *Requiems*, we feel their power ; we have to listen, and ' the mariner hath his will.'

My readers must not expect to find in the following simple pages that fulness of description, and that scientific treatment in detail, essential to any thoroughly adequate review of compositions so elaborate and magnificent, for all their simplicity, as Cherubini's. Of necessity on divers grounds, the works had to be considered with a brevity cousin german to inadequacy. But may these *Memorials*, as re-arranged, from published and unpublished material, claim along with their old enthusiasm, increasing as time goes on, a reasonable measure of accuracy, and even a completeness in essentials ? And may it all be some compensation for present amateurism, and an absent professionalism ? To do justice to such a master would require, I know well, a highly equipped writer and musician, along with such large sympathies as one would fain ask of some who are still cold in regard to Cherubini ; sympathies not incommensurate with the genius illustrated in a momentous era of the world's history—one not less so for music.

In conclusion, let me thank those friends who encouraged me in my task, helped me in divers translations, and supplied me with information that I could not otherwise have obtained.

[7] Miel.

CONTENTS.

SECULAR MUSIC.

CHAPTER I.

ITALY, FRANCE AND ENGLAND.

1760—1788.

' Submissive to the might of verse,
And the dear voice of harmony,
By none more deeply felt than thee.'
WORDSWORTH.

CHAPTER II.

FRANCE.

1788—1791.

' For terror, joy or pity,
Vast is the compass and the swell of notes :
From the babe's first cry to voice of regal city,
Rolling a solemn sea-like bass that floats
Far as the woodlands.'
WORDSWORTH.

CHAPTER III.

FRANCE.

1791—1797.

' The generations were prepar'd ; the pangs,
Th' internal pangs were ready, the dread strife
Of poor humanity's afflicted will
Struggling in vain with ruthless destiny.'

' How oft along thy mazes,
Regent of sound, have dangerous Passions trod.'

WORDSWORTH.

CHAPTER IV.

FRANCE.

1797—1800.

' Point not these mysteries to an Art
Lodg'd above the starry pole ;
Pure modulations flowing from the heart
Of divine Love, where Wisdom, Beauty, Truth
With Order dwell, in endless youth?'

WORDSWORTH.

CHAPTER V.

FRANCE AND GERMANY.

1800—1806.

'. . . men endowed with highest gifts,
The vision and the faculty divine.'

WORDSWORTH.

SACRED MUSIC.

CHAPTER I.

FRANCE AND BELGIUM.

1806—1809.

' Break forth into thanksgiving,
Ye banded instruments of wind and chords ;
Unite, to magnify the Ever-living,
Your inarticulate notes with the voice of words ! '
WORDSWORTH.

CHAPTER II.

FRANCE AND ENGLAND.

1809—1816.

' I cannot of that music rightly say,
Whether I hear or see or taste the tones ;
O ! what a heart subduing melody ! '
NEWMAN.

CHAPTER III.

FRANCE.

1816.

' Hosannas pealing down the long drawn aisle,
And Requiems answered by the pulse that beats
Devoutly.'
WORDSWORTH.

Contents.

CHAPTER VII.

FRANCE.

1835—1842.

' A Voice to Light gave Being ;
To Time and Man his earth-born chronicler,
A Voice shall finish doubt and dim foreseeing,
And sweep away life's visionary stir.'

WORDSWORTH.

CHAPTER VIII.

FRANCE.

1842.

'. . . Then in melodious swell
Inviting Requiems for the faithful dead. . . .
O Sanctuary rare of all creation . . .
Soothing the soul with hope . . .'

CASWALL.

APPENDICES.

INDEX.

LIST OF ILLUSTRATIONS.

PART I.

—

SECULAR MUSIC.

SECULAR MUSIC.

CHAPTER I.

ITALY, FRANCE AND ENGLAND.

1760—1788.

> ' Submissive to the might of verse,
> And the dear voice of harmony,
> By none more deeply felt than thee.'
>
> WORDSWORTH.

Cherubini's parentage and birth at Florence—He is taught music by his father and the 2 Felicis, Bizzarri and Castrucci—Early compositions—3 Masses—A pension from Leopold II. to study under Sarti—Anthems in Palestrina's style—Airs in Sarti's operas—*Il Quinto Fabio* his 1st opera at Alessandria — *Armida* at Florence — *Adriano in Siria* at Leghorn—*Il Messenzio* at Florence—*Il Quinto Fabio*, No. 2, at Rome —*Ninfa crudele* canon, and Padre Martini—*Lo Sposo di Tre, Marito di Nessuna* at Venice—*L'Idalide* at Florence —*Alessandro nell' Indie* at Mantua—To Paris and London—Musician to the King's Theatre—*La Finta Principessa*—Return to Paris—Introduction to Queen Marie Antoinette—Airs in Italian Opera—Return to London—Introduction to the Prince of Wales—*Giulio Sabino*—Airs in Italian Opera—Residence in Paris—*Amphion*—*Circe*—*Ifigenia in Aulide* at Turin.

MARIA LUIGI CARLO ZENOBI SALVADORE CHERUBINI, ' the last and noblest Roman in the purely classical style of art '[1]—' the most accomplished musician, if not the greatest genius, of the nineteenth century '[2]—was born at Florence, one minute after 12, in the morning of the 8th day of September, 1760—a year and a half after Handel's death, when Mozart was aged 4, and 10 years before the birth of Beethoven. On the 15th following he was baptized at the Basilica of St. John the Baptist, and duly registered at the Baptistery of Sta. Maria del Fiore, opposite the Duomo or Cathedral.[3]

[1], Baillot.

[2] von Ulibicheff.

[3] See Appendix I. for register from the Baptistery at Florence, and history of birth date discrepancies. The register does not say Salvatore, as might be expected.

Cherubini's father, Bartholomew Cherubini, son of Mark Cherubini, was 'maëstro al clavicembalo,' or harpsichord accompanist at the Pergola Theatre, Florence, and lived in a modest cottage on the Via Fiesolana in the quarter of San Pier Maggiore, which bears on its door the street number of 22, and formerly had the district number of 6886.[4]

Cherubini's mother was Verdiana, daughter of one Philip Bosi. She died at the age of 40, when her son was between 4 and 5 years old. Both parents were by birth Florentines, and he was the 10th child of a family of 12, all of whom he survived, although so weakly at birth that little hope was entertained of rearing him. From his earliest childhood he showed a quick and superior intelligence; but nothing specific is known about him until his 7th year. Whether he discovered discords from his cradle, or sang beautifully at the age of 3, cannot be ascertained.

In the notice at the head of his catalogue, he writes: ' I began to learn music at the age of 6, and composition at the age of 9; the 1st taught me by my father, Bartholomew Cherubini, professor of music; my 1st 2 masters in the 2nd being Bartholomew Felici and his son Alexander. After their death, I had for masters Peter Bizzarri and Joseph Castrucci.[5] About the year 1777 or 1778, I obtained a pension from the Grand Duke Leopold to continue my studies, and perfect myself under the celebrated Joseph Sarti, with whom I worked for 3 or 4

---

[4] Cherubini wrote to his daughter, Mme. Rosellini 5 Feb. 1830: 'If when walking about Florence you are anxious to know the house wherein I was born, know that it is the 3rd, on entering, from the *via delle Carretti*, *via Fiesolana*. I think that, as my father bought the house after I left Florence, and had it rebuilt, it no longer looks the same as when I was born; but this has not changed its site, and Nesti, who knew it, will tell you what it was like then, supposing you go to see the place of my cradle with him.' *cit.* Pougin, *M.W.*, 1883, 752. I visited his birth-place 8 Jan. 1878, and 3rd May, 1881, and on the way thereto, 30 March, 1881, ' made the tour of the Grand Opera House (Paris), to see that Cherubini's bust appeared thereon, among a number of inferior geniuses.'

[5] *N.M.Z.*, *M.W.*, 1862, and the Monday Popular Concert Programmes omit this sentence. Fétis, Clément and others incorrectly say that Cherubini learnt music from his father before he was 6.

years. By the counsels and lessons of that great master, I mastered counterpoint and the elements of dramatic music. At his side he put me to compose, as exercises for myself, as well as to relieve him in his own labours, all the airs of the 2ndary parts in the operas he composed. These pieces, that have not appeared under my name, are not to be found in the present catalogue, and I possess none of them; they are to be found among my master's various scores.'[6]

In his musical teaching, Bartholomew Cherubini, according to Picchianti, was attached to old forms, and an observer of the ancient scholastic discipline. Yet, despite disadvantages thence accruing, young Cherubini was able in 3 years, from the age of 6 to that of 9, to acquire a fair knowledge of solfeges and accompaniment of figured basses, as well as of playing the harpsichord. It is told of him that he found at home an old violin, and amused himself by scraping on it, until one evening at the Pergola, a player being absent from the orchestra, he quietly took his place and played the part well. Indeed, all that Nardino, the conductor, had to find fault with was a certain timidity and hesitation, natural at 1st under the circumstances. In the meantime Cherubini did not neglect some mathematics and languages, although, as to the latter, he never seems to have spoken, beyond Italian, other than somewhat broken French, sometimes incorrectly spelt. Looking at his refined music, you would say:—here is possibly a scholar outside his art! but he never was a Gluck; and few of the Great Masters were. At length, being considerably advanced, for his age, in musical studies, he was placed by his father under 'old Felici,' so called to distinguish him from his son Alex-

---

[6] Remarking on Cherubini's uncertainty as to the year in which he went to Bologna, Fétis (*Biog. Univ.* ii. 204) adds that Cherubini left for that city toward the end of 1777, and obtained his pension in 1778. If so, the latter year would seem the more likely one wherein Cherubini would go to Bologna. All his works up to 1778, exclusively, are marked in the Catalogue 'Florence'; and in a note to the section for that year, he writes: 'At this time I was at Bologna.'

ander, also an artist of merit.　Old Felici's works, ' alla
cappella ' were a model of clearness and ingenuity.　He
was deemed the best Tuscan professor of his day, while
his school enjoyed no mean reputation.[7]　' At this time, the
art of counterpoint was lost in a multitude of rules and
observations, each of which, being drawn from particular
cases, and not from general principles, gave rise to a 1,000
exceptions.　To master all these rules, and their innumerable limitations, long and wearisome labour had to be
undergone.　Thus we can appreciate Cherubini's rapid
intelligence, which in 4 years under the Felicis could
master, in boyhood, those contrapuntal studies wherein it
was not given every one to succeed, though he employed
double the time.　Moreover, he knew through a just
criterion—through his genius and exquisite taste—how to
draw from those dry exercises the greatest profit—how to
form his artistic individuality.　And, in fact, besides the
elegant and original forms, the clearness and purity of
style, always employed by him even in his most trifling
and least important pieces, there ever appeared something
of an antique caste, whence he derives an absolute speci-
alty, which may be deemed the most precious result of
his early scholastic studies.[8] '

　　　Cherubini began to compose when he was 12 years
old.　In 1773, a Mass of his writing pleased his father,
its performance exciting some interest.　To this succeeded
an ' intermezzo ' for a ' théâtre de société ' in Florence ;
in 1774, a 2nd Mass, a cantata, ' La Pubblica Felicità,'
executed in a side chapel of the Cathedral or Duomo, on
occasion of a ' fête ' in honour of the Grand Duke, and a
psalm ; in 1775, a 3rd Mass, a psalm, an ' intermezzo '
' Il Giuocatore,' and a ' Magnificat ; ' in 1776, 2 Lamentations of Jeremiah, a ' Miserere,' a rondeau, a duet, and
an ' aria buffa ; ' in 1777, a motet, an oratorio, the name
not known, but executed at St. Peter's, Florence, and a

[7] He was born about 1730 (Pougin thinks a little earlier), and opened a
school of counterpoint at Florence (Fétis).
[8] Picchianti, 14.

'Te Deum;' in 1778, 17 antiphons, 'alla' Palestrina; in 1779, Litanies,[9] works that announced the appearance of a new star in the musical firmament, one destined to shine over 3 quarters of a century—and beyond, to future ages.

These 36 compositions may be called his youthful productions, followed by secular compositions till the eventful turn in his history, in the year 1808.

Picchianti tells us that the Florentine's force of intellect might be seen in the above. The MSS. of most of them are lost. Cherubini concealed such as remained with care. After his decease, Halévy could not resist the desire of perusing them. He did so, and tells us: 'In going over them, I understood how it was from a sort of self-respect and caution . . . that he withdrew them from all eyes. Everything there anounced the intelligent child, brought up in a good school, reared on good precepts; but there was nothing to indicate the genius that was to reveal itself later on.'

A composer in Italy learns to sing before writing foi the voice, and Cherubini now took vocal lessons from Bizzarri. From him he went on to Castrucci, under whom he mastered the organ and harpsichord. His progress was rapid. His compositions pleased the public and the 'connoisseur.' He was pointed at in the streets of Florence as a prodigy, but he was no spoilt child. He wanted to travel through Italy, so as to perfect himself in his art, and become personally known to musicians—a wish that his father's friends advised should be acceded to.[10] But Bartholomew Cherubini had no means of maintaining away from home a lad between 15 and 16 years of age. Peter Leopold II., Grand-Duke of Tuscany, afterwards Emperor of Austria, however, had noticed young Cherubini, and admired his talent; and,

---

[9] Yet Hiller deems it 'extremely doubtful' whether 'a single note of Cherubini's, during his life, was ever performed in that splendid city.'

[10] De Lafage writes that, from information which he obtained at Florence, he believes that Cherubini travelled with Disma Ugolini (1755—1828), a student like himself under the Felicis, and master of Picchianti.

hearing that he was the son of poor but respectable
parents, offered, at his own expense, to send him to study
at Bologna. Such was the generosity that enabled young
Cherubini to seek out the great Joseph Sarti, pupil of
Padre Martini, and his celebrated school at Bologna.
Haydn greatly admired Sarti, whose reputation at this
time through Italy stood high ; by whom Cherubini
was cordially welcomed ; and who perceived, on examining him, that he needed but practice to be able to
compose dramatic music. And Cherubini's rapid intelligence soon made him the favourite pupil of all. Under
Sarti, he had to abandon Leo and Durante for Palestrina.
Sarti was an enthusiastic disciple of the latter, whereas
Cherubini, at this time, had little liking[11] for him. Indeed,
it was not till years afterwards that the latter fully realized
how important it was for composers of church-music to
study him. Still, he now obeyed his master in everything,
even writing 20 anthems in the style of the old Roman
master. Sarti had a notion about an ideal style in music,
as Palestrina before him, and, to further this among his
pupils, made them imitate his own custom of composing
at night in a large unfurnished room, with a lamp suspended from the ceiling, that shed only a glimmering light.
Another feature in Sarti's teaching was to write out works
of the old composers, a method that Cherubini kept up
through life, leaving over 3000 pages of MS. of this nature.
Sarti soon reposed such confidence in Cherubini's ability
as to let him practice himself in dramatic music by
interpolating airs or recitatives, in his own 'Le Sirol,'
'Achille in Sciro,' 'Giulio Sabino,' and other operas,
represented under their composer's direction, with the
help of Cherubini, at Bologna, Venice, Florence, Milan,
and Turin. Sarti made his pupils thus compose in opera,
to obtain experience in writing for the public, and gain,
under cover of their master's name, an applause as
encouraging as it was useful. 'These scores contain a

[11] Fr. Girod says so, but cites no authority.

crowd of beauties by Cherubini,'[12] and their insertion was
the beginning of a custom that Cherubini continued till
1792, of putting music of his own in the Italian operas
and 'pasticcios' of Cimarosa and his school: many fine
pieces thus became allied to works that no longer live. If
a work proved heavy for the public taste, Cherubini had to
make it light, whereas if a work cannot stand on its own
merits, the sooner it falls the better.

In 1779, Fioroni, chapel-master of Milan Cathedral,
died, and Sarti, being chosen for the vacant post, moved
with Cherubini to Milan, where, in 1780, the latter inter-
mitted, some say ended, regular studies, that after 11 years
resulted in making him, at the age of 19, one of the most
learned musicians of Italy. Certainly he had worked long
and well before there were short roads to proficiency, to
acquire that thorough knowledge, which he, if any one,
possessed. It may be questioned whether Bach knew
more of the science of music than Cherubini, while neither
was a pedant for all their science. They often mastered
it; it seldom mastered them. Yet it is rather Cherubini's
industry than his lengthy studies that calls for notice. An
Italian musical education in the middle of the 18th century was necessarily a slow progress, and 11 years would
not be needed at the present day for a clever pupil to
gain all the knowledge that Cherubini acquired. Fétis
reckons that, with the analytic method, and progressive
exercises, half that time would be sufficient; but the
method of analysis was then unknown in the musical
schools of Italy. The masters furnished the pupil with
model compositions, without being able to explain either
the origin of, or the reasons for, the rules prescribed. 'To
the questions and objections of their pupils they knew but
one reply: the authority of the school. . . . Taught by
them Cherubini was only able to acquire, after long
practice, his marvellous knowledge of all the points
relating to form, style, tonality, rhythm and modulation.

[12] Denne-Baron.

Himself a perfect master, yet when showing by an example the application of a precept, he could seldom find
an explanation of the precept itself, and woe to the pupil
who did not understand him by a half-word.'[13] In fact
we are asked to believe that, in teaching, neither Cherubini
nor his masters could explain why this or that was so;
but they knew that it ought to be so. In 1780, Sarti
procured for Cherubini a commission to write an opera
at Alessandria, where, at the autumnal fair, he brought
out the 3-act 'Il Quinto Fabio.' He writes: 'This is my
1st opera; I had then completed my 19th year.'[14] It had
no particular success, and Cherubini returned to Milan,
writing 5 airs for an opera given there, as well as a motet
for Marchesi, a celebrated singer, and another entitled
'Nemo gaudeat' for 2 choirs and 2 organs. From Milan
he proceeded to Venice, where he was to have written
another opera, but on arrival found that the manager engaging him had become bankrupt ; 2 numbers only of the
intended work had been composed. He returned to
Florence, and in 1782 produced there 'Armida,' a 3-act
opera, given during the carnival at the Pergola. His
wonderful style, studied and complicated harmonies, as
displayed in his operas, were not to the taste of the
Italians, who were accustomed to light melodies and
simple accompaniments. People were afraid that the
originality displayed in his compositions might work
havoc with their beloved 'cantilene' and 'fioriture.'[15]

In the spring appeared from him another 3-act opera,
'Adriano in Siria,' performed at the opening of a new
concert-hall at Leghorn, with an added air for Crescentini,
who sang in the work.[16]

[13] Fétis.
[14] Catalogue. Fétis, and *N.M.Z.*, *M. W.* 1862, think 'dix-neuf' ought
to be 'vingt,' and rightly if *Il Quinto Fabio* was produced on or after
14 Sept. 1780.
[15] *L. Cherubini*, Fritzch. 6.
[16] Fétis (*Biog. Univ.* ii. 390) writes that he sang in Cherubini's *Artaserse,*
but no such work appears in the Catalogues.
Mistakes easily occur in vast compilations like those of Fétis. They
are only noted here lest they live on. Some, I fear, can criticize him,

The judgment of the people of Leghorn was : this music is ' too learned.' Dr. Hiller tells us that being curious to know something about these early operas, Cherubini lent him ' Armida ' and ' Adriano,' with this note : ' I fear these scores will not interest you much, for they are the productions of a mere lad, fresh from school, and written in the style then in vogue. If the one does not please you, leave the other unread.' Dr. Hiller found nothing of the school-boy about them, but all the marks of a most able pen, but admits their resemblance to the operas—German and Italian—of the day.

Returning to Florence, Cherubini wrote 10 nocturns, 6 of which were 1st printed in London, in 1786, with this dedication, in Italian, to Signor Corsi, a Florentine noble-man, Marquis of Caiazzo, Lord of Dugenta, Millazzano, and Raiano of Castelle, and Chamberlain to the Grand Duke and Duchess of Tuscany : ' In case this slight work of mine, which I take the liberty of offering to you, should possess sufficient merit to be kindly received by your generous mind, and further, to meet with sincere approval from your most refined taste, I shall have reason to flatter myself that it may appear not wholly unpleasing in the eyes of the public, which knows too well your mastery of the fine arts, especially of music, not to conform its judg-ment to yours. But howsoever it may please you, noble sir, to judge me, I shall at least have the satisfaction affor-ded me by my work of a favourable opportunity for showing you, so far as I can, the sincere and most just esteem which I entertain for the amiable qualities that render you very dear to all, and at the same time be able, in the face of the world, to glory in being, with all the respect which I profess, your devoted servant, L. CHERU-BINI.'[17] Such was the dedicatory style of the period.

Another 3-act opera, ' Il Messenzio,' was given with success 8 Sept. Cherubini was known to our countryman,

while forgetting the debt they owe him, which I here take the opportunity of acknowledging for myself.

[17] From a copy in the British Museum.

George Nassau Clavering, 3rd Earl Cowper,[18] an amateur, in Italy at this time, for whom he wrote 2 duets with accompaniment for 2 'cors d'armour.'[19]   An air for Babbini, the singer, in a 'pasticcio' called 'Semiramide,' performed at Florence, closes the list of Cherubini's noteworthy works in 1782.   In Jan. 1783, by agreement in the previous year, he composed at Rome a 2nd 3-act 'Il Quinto Fabio,' brought out there at the Argentina.[20] This was followed by the canon of 'Ninfa Crudele,' that owed its origin to the jealousy of several learned musicians, who were foolish enough to doubt whether Cherubini could solve a musical problem.   This at their request, he did, and did it so well that the piece assured him the reputation of being one of the 1st harmonists of his day.[21]   A canon for solution had been chosen by the celebrated Padre Martini, who now made Cherubini's acquaintance for the 1st time.   'Lo Sposo di Tre, Marito di Nessuna,' a 2-act opera-buffa, was represented Nov. 1783, at St. Samuel's Theatre, Venice.   The Venetians thought highly of Cherubini, and the 'Indice Teatrale' for 1784 advised them to call him 'il cherubino,' adding, 'Toccante meno al suo nome, dalla dolcezza dei suoi canti'

[18] He died 22 Dec. 1789.   He is represented, in a picture by Zoffany (exhibited at South Kensington in 1867), as listening with evident enjoyment to a musical performance by members of his family, one of whom, a lady, plays the harpsichord, while his father-in-law, Mr. Francis Gore, leads or accompanies on the violoncello.

[19] They were otherwise called 'amorshorn' —a kind of horn, invented about 1760, by Kölbal, a Russian musician, the improvments in which consisted of valves, and a semi-circular cover upon the opening.   This idea of a valve-horn, was not pursued further, because the 'inventions-horn,' introduced shortly afterwards, was a step towards the end obtained in the 'ventil-horn.'—*M.W.,* 1862, 500.

[20] Fétis thinks that this *Quinto Fabio* was merely an improved version of the 1st, and another writes that *Quinto Fabio* was 'repeated' in Rome. —*L. Cherubini,* Fritzch.   Cherubini does not indicate this himself.   It is a separate MS.   Denne-Baron writes that Cherubini, after his engagement at Rome, returned to Florence to give *L'Idalide* there, and then went to Venice for *Lo Sposo di Tre;* but *L'Idalide* was not brought out till after *Lo Sposo.*

[21] Some state that Cherubini wrote 'Ninfa Crudele' on his way to Florence from Venice, or after arriving there from Venice ; in both cases after the production of *Lo Sposo di Tre ;* but it is mentioned in Cherubini's catalogue before that opera ; hence it may be concluded that it was composed at Florence, before *Lo Sposo* and the visit to Venice.

CHERUBINI

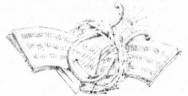

(less as in any allusion to his name than because of the sweetness of his songs), or was it, as Clément suggests, that the Venetians called him ' il cherubino,' more in allusion to his handsome face and frizzly hair, than to the angelic grace of his songs ? adding, 'we have known charming portraits of Cherubini when young ; his features were delicate and pleasing. Later on, intense application, the habit of study, and, it must be said, the cares of strife, profoundly modified the expression of his countenance.' [22]

From Venice Cherubini, in 1784, undertook his last journey to Florence. A patched-up oratorio, made up of sundry pieces from his operas, with a new tenor air and 2 choruses, was performed for the benefit of the Jesuit Fathers at their church there.[23]

This was quickly followed by 2 operas, ' L'Idalide,' the last work Cherubini wrote for his native city, given at the Pergola ; and ' Alessandro nell' Indie,' represented during the spring fair at Mantua ; [24] both in 2 acts.

From Mantua, Cherubini went to Milan to see Sarti again, to whom he ascribed whatever successes he had achieved.[25] His affection for him, as we shall see, was life-long.

They saw each other for the last time at Parma, and

---

[22] Clément, 249.

[23] The Society of Jesus could not exist as such between 1769 and 1814, but members of it may have lived at Florence as secular priests. The late Rev. W. Maher, S J., thought that Cherubini was their chapel-master at Naples and Palermo ; but when had he time to be such ?—unless it were merely an honorary post.

[24] He wrote, also, ' the comic opera of *I Viaggiatori Felici.'—L. Cherubini,* Fritzch. This is the only authority for Cherubini having written such work. Moreover, when he mentions the latter's 4tet, ' Car da voi dipende,' inserted in *I Viaggiatori Felici,* ' by different authors' (writes Cherubini), Anfossi, Piccinni, aud Parenti, he again call that work Cherubini's, which leads me to suppose his whole statement erroneous.

[25] According to Denne-Baron, Cherubini once more placed himself under Sarti, writing excellent fragments of religious music, to be found among his works. That Cherubini rejoined Sarti whenever he could do so, is asserted by 1 or 2 biographers, and may be believed. There are the positive assertions of Castil-Blaze and Miel, that Cherubini had not broken with Sarti when producing his 1st opera—a statement supported by the fact of Cherubini returning to Milan after *Il Quinto Fabio* had been brought out, though studies, during such snatch visits, must have been prosecuted desultorily.

quitted Italy simultaneously, Sarti for Russia.　By means of the latter's connection with England, where his operas at this period found acceptance ; and conceivably through Lord Cowper's influence ; [26] thanks also to a reputation already spreading, Cherubini had received an invitation to visit London.　He was to be musician for 2 years to the King's Theatre in the Haymarket,[27] and he tells us that he left for England Sept. 1784.　On his way thither he passed through Turin, where the committee of the Royal Theatre asked him to write an opera for them, and this he promised to do so soon as his engagement in England was over.

The state of English music there, at this time, was hardly re-assuring.　Handel had been dead some 25 years. Pre-eminent in oratorio, and more than holding his own against Buononcini in opera, despite Swift's epigram, yet after death his influence declined, and not till now, 1784, did a notion of a Festival or Commemoration in his honour take practical shape.　Italian music had resumed the ascendant, in London after 1759, as, when Gluck left, it did in Paris.　No doubt Cimarosa and Paisiello were better than Buononcini and Porpora ; but native talent was not encouraged by the ascendency in question, which is seen in the circumstance of Cherubini's own engagement.

On arriving in London as composer for the King's Theatre, he wrote 6 pieces for a 2-act 'pasticcio,' ' Il Demetrio,' successfully performed 22 Jan. 1785, which, sung by Babbini and Crescentini, were well received, though the 1st-named, according to Parke, was never very popular in England as a singer.　He adds that Cherubini's

[26] So *M. T.,* March 1908, suggests.
[27] He was not, *M. T.* points out, King's Musician, as Picchianti, whom I followed, wrote.　With Choron and Fayolle, Pougin seems to have thought him King's composer, and this a post that led Cherubini to write for the King's Theatre.—*M. W.,* 1882, 237.
The late Sir G. Grove, wrote (Progr. Crystal Palace Concerts, Overt. *Medea*) that Cherubini assisted at the Handel Commemoration in Westminster Abbey, in July, 1784.　Cherubini writes that he left Turin about the autumn (Sept.).　Two years later would do, but even in 1786 he left in July for Paris.

overture, and duet in the 3rd act, gave promise of future greatness.[28] Cherubini subsequently brought out 'La Finta Principessa,' a 2-act opera buffa, in the Haymarket, with applause. 'Most of the music is pretty . . . ' wrote the 'Public Advertiser' of 2 April, 1785, 'the 1st, and yet more the 2nd air of Franchi, are as fanciful—excel in the power of pleasing—more than anything since the time of Sacchini.' It was repeated during the season.[29]

Returning to Paris in July, he made the acquaintance of Viotti,[30] one of the best friends he ever had, with whom he kept up a correspondence while in England; who presented him to Queen Marie Antoinette, and probably induced him to compose for the Sacred Concerts an instrumental piece and 3 Italian airs, sung by Babbini, that appear on the bills for 8 Sept. 1785.[31] These, however, were not very favourably received, and he returned Oct. to London.

In 1786, Cherubini inserted 6 airs in Paisiello's ' Il Marchese Tulipano,' wherein Babbini and Sestini appeared; and this he conducted himself, and ' the greatest praise that can be given to these pieces is to say that the pieces interpolated sustained without any loss the vicinity of the admirable melodies of Paisiello.'[32] Babbini was applauded in Cherubini's beautiful air ' Madamina,' sung to English words, ' For tenderness form'd,' by Mrs. Crouch.[33]

Cherubini's reputation admitted him to the society of the Prince of Wales, afterwards George IV., who was delighted with his talent and agreeable voice. The Prince was fond of singing, and the composer sang at the royal amateur's réunions, as well as at those of William, 4th

[28] *Musical Memoirs,* 1784-1830. I. 49-50. The overture was not Cherubini's, and there were 2 acts. He may refer to the subsequent opera.
[29] *cit. M.T.,* March, 1908.
[30] Some say, without apparent authority, that this acquaintance sprang up during Cherubini's 1st visit to Paris, on his way to London. Cherubini's notice to de Beauchesne states it as above.—*Cit.* Pougin, *M. W ,* 1882, 237.
[31] *Mercure de France,* cit. Pougin *M.W.,* 1882, 238. These do not appear in the catalogue, but may have been old pieces.
[32] De Lafage.
[33] *M.T.,* March, 1908.

Duke of Queensberry, who had a particular affection for our composer.

In a 2nd 2-act work produced at the King's Theatre, Haymarket, 30 March, 1786, with 'libretto' by Metastasio, Marchesi made his London 'début.'[34]   Dr. Burney remarks: 'His opera of "Giulio Sabino" was murdered in its birth, for want of the necessary support of the capital singers in the principal parts. Babbini, the tenor, being elevated to 1st man, and the Ferraresi to 1st woman, were circumstances not likely to prejudice the public in favour of the composer.'[35]   Cherubini was annoyed at the failure of his serious opera, and the theatrical season of 1786 being over, writes: ' I quitted England about the period of the month of July in this year ; I came to Paris and established myself there.'[36]   He was accompanied by Babbini.

At Paris he composed the cantata ' Amphion,' written, but not performed, for the ' Loge Olympique,' a Society patronized by the Queen, who gave it an apartment at the Tuileries for its concerts. He had meant to rejoin his family in Italy, but, being urged by Viotti to remain in Paris, and persuaded into the belief that artists had there a higher position and a better field for action, he took up permanent residence there with his friend, till 1791.

Queen Marie Antoinette, who had been struck by Cherubini's superior manner and bearing, wished to hear some of his music at the concerts she gave at Versailles. Halévy writes of Cherubini : ' It was a happy era for him, for success flattered him. He had then seen 28 years. A portrait, painted a little while after this period, by Mdlle. Dumont, and preserved in his family, shows him to us graceful and neat in person, gifted with a noble and expressive countenance, and with a persuasive air. The world liked him, and he liked the world. He was for a moment all the rage, and became a lion.' He

---

[34] *Harmonicon*, 1825.
[35] *General History of Music*, 1789, iv. 527.   The Ferrarese del Bene's real name was Francesca Gabrielli.
[36] Catalogue.

Cherubini

à Vienna presso Gio. Cappi.

[After Le Dru.

might, indeed, have exclaimed, with Wordsworth's recluse :

'Society became my glittering bride,
    And airy hopes my children.'

Viotti introduced him to the highest society of the capital;
to Madame de Polignac, Madame D'Etioles, Madame de
Richelieu, and to bright assemblies where Garat and
Azevedo sang; to Florian the author, on whose tale of
'Estella' Cherubini wrote in 1787 18 romances; to the
Abbé Morellet, the brilliant Piccinnist; and lastly, to
Marmontel, whom he 1st got to know at Morellet's
house, and who gave him 'Démophon' to set to music.
Viotti, further, introduced him to the 'Société Academique
des Enfans d'Apollon,' an association for concerts, founded
in 1741. Cherubini prized, above all the other guilds
joined, his membership in that society, as reminding him,
when Viotti was no more, of the kindness of a very
true friend in days gone by. At one of the 'Concerts des
Amateurs,' he heard a symphony of Haydn that pleased
him so much that he began the same evening to study
that master's works. In him, we are told, he recognised
his own power. 'He learned from Haydn how to
combine depth with lightness, grace with power, jest with
earnestness, toying with dignity.' [37]

Dr. Burney writes of 1787 : 'Cherubini, the nominal
composer in this year at the opera, was a young man of
genius, who had no opportunity while he was here of
displaying his abilities, but previous to his arrival he had
frequently been noticed in his own country, where he is
now travelling fast to the Temple of Fame.' [38]   He adds

[37] *L. Cherubini*, Fritzch.
[38] Has this statement about Cherubini being 'nominal composer' for
1787 misled me, De Lomenie, &c., into stating that he again returned to
England? The 2 years' engagement, was, of course, for 1785-6.   How it
extended 'nominally' I do not know, but Cherubini's own note, *cit.*
Pougin, *M. W.* 1882, 436, nowise suggests any return to England in 1787.
Denne-Baron refers to Cherubini's (alleged) return from London to Paris in
1787, and Nisard objects : 'For this circumstance to be exact, the
illustrious composer must have already come to the French capital.'
Well, he had come once to Paris before, while passing through to England
for the 1st time in 1784, and twice again from London in 1785 and 1786.

that a comic opera, ' Giannina e Bernadone,' by Cimarosa, was produced 13 Jan. 1787, with additional songs by Cherubini. Paisiello's ' Gli Schiavi per amore ' was also brought out.

Cherubini at length bethought him of his promise at Turin ; so, leaving Paris Oct. 1787, he worked hard in the Piedmont capital, and at the carnival of 1788 produced there his brilliant 3-act opera of ' Ifigenia in Aulide,' the last work written in Italy.[39] Its success was so great that Marchesi made choice of it for singing in, during the autumn season, at La Scala, Milan, where he made no little effect with the air, ' A voi torno Sponde amate.' ' The music, now sublime, now tender, but invariably energetic and attractive, produced almost unheard of effects. The Court, even, could not resist the general enthusiasm ; our princes, who do not usually applaud performances, applauded a good deal.'[40] ' Ifigenia ' was also performed at Florence and Parma, and always, if we are to believe the journals of the day, with success. We may be glad that it was so : that Cherubini left Italy for good and all in sunshine. Yet, though he had nearly reached the years allotted to Schubert, he had hitherto done little or nothing great. Had he died at this period, he would be a rather obscure name in Fétis' immense dictionary. His genius, like that of Gluck, developed slowly. A short life would have been fatal to the renown of both. What would not Mozart, Beethoven, Schubert, and Mendelssohn have done had they lived so long as either ? And yet, in this last work written for Italy, Halévy detects something auguring future greatness. ' This opera,' he writes, ' differs in style from Cherubini's preceding works. He is already more nervous; there peeps out, I know not exactly how much force and

[39] De Lomenie erroneously supposes that *Ifigenia* was brought out at Turin before Cherubini went to London a 2nd time *(sic)* in 1787.

[40] *Calendrier Musical,* 1789, *cit.* Pougin, *M.W.,* 1882, 257. Dr. Riemann, I believe erroneously, states that Cherubini brought out his *Didone abbandonata* at Brescia in the winter of 1787-8. The Catalogues give no such work.

virility, of which the Italian musicians of his day did not know, or did not seek the secret. It is the dawn of a new day. Cherubini was preparing himself for the combat. Gluck had accustomed France to the sublime energy of his masterpieces. Mozart had just written " Le Nozze di Figaro " and " Don Giovanni." He must not lag behind ; he must not be conquered ; in the career he was about to dare enter, he would meet 2 giants.' 'We especially remark in this opera of " Ifigenia " an admirable trio . . . . filled with an expression very deep and very true, of sadness and pity. . . . I am inclined to believe that when writing it, Cherubini was under the influence of real sorrow. Perhaps, in this sweet and noble piece of inspiration, he was addressing a last farewell to his native country . . . it was never his lot to see Italy again.'[41] I have now come to the end of the earliest stage of Cherubini's life, with details only too scanty, and, it is to be feared, dry and uninteresting.

Cherubini returned definitively to Paris, where he lived and died ; where he was to influence, as the author of ' Alcestis ' had done before him, the taste of a people, and to pass through a brilliant, if somewhat chequered career.

[41] *Cit.* also Pougin (*M. W.*, 1882, 257) who asks : When did Cherubini become a naturalized Frenchman ? He is called such, about 1797-8, in the *Dictionnaire Néologique,* by Le Cousin Jacques. Fétis, *Biog. Univ.* Supplement, Pougin, i. 177.

CHAPTER II.

FRANCE.

1788—1791.

' For terror, joy or pity,
    Vast is the compass and the swell of notes :
From the babe's first cry to voice of regal city,
    Rolling a solemn sea-like bass that floats
        Far as the woodlands.'

WORDSWORTH.

Cherubini's and Vogel's *Démophons* in Paris—Marmontel—The Loge Olympique—J. B. Rousseau's *Circe*—The Bouffons at the Tuileries—Cherubini made Director of Italian Opera there—Writes pieces in Italian Opera—Two styles—*Marguerite d'Anjou*—Trials during the Revolution—He has to leave the Tuileries—Opening of the Feydeau Theatre—*Mirabeau à son lit de mort*—Cherubini's and Kreutzer's *Lodoïskas*—Musique d'effet.

WHEN Cherubini arrived in Paris from Turin in 1788, 2 operas called ' Démophon ' were close upon completion, one by Vogel, the other by Cherubini, who had begun to work on Marmontel's story while in England. Vogel was already known to the public as the composer of the ' Toison d'Or,' and according to Fétis, had previously been offered Marmontel's libretto, but, being a dilatory man, had kept the managers of the opera waiting 2 years without finishing the music, so the poem was given to Cherubini; but according to Pougin, Vogel had never anything to do with Marmontel's ' Démophon,' but only with a libretto on a similar subject by Desriaux. His fault was a preference for filling a wine-glass to keeping an engagement; and he died 28 June 1788, of a fever. Both operas had been written for the Royal Academy of Music, but, wisely enough, were not brought out at one and the same time. Lays, the singer, wished Vogel's ' Démophon ' to come 1st, but Cherubini contrived to obtain for his opera priority of performance. This excited some enmity against Cherubini, and when Vogel's work appeared it was cried up. Desriaux's libretto was better than Marmontel's. The latter had followed Metastasio too servilely, and had duly brought in the 2 pairs of lovers, 'always so essential in Italian opera.' 'There was then a mania for doubling these lovers, as well as for bringing forward 2 works in succession, composed on one given subject. By this means a saving was made in cloth, and the make-up of a collection of costumes; while the same decorations served for both dramas.'[1] Cherubini's 'Démophon' appeared 5 Dec. 1788, conducted by the composer himself; that of Vogel 22 Sept. 1789. Neither was successful, though Vogel's overture became popular. Cherubini's in C is a vigorous composition, and an effective piece, too seldom heard.

Of 'Démophon,' Fétis observes: 'It produced little effect, and the public received it with coldness. . . . Compare the scores of this opera with "Ifigenia." . . . In this latter melody abounds. . . . "Démophon," on the other hand, offers us nothing but a dryness in the airs, a number of faults as regards rhythm and symmetry of phrasing, and, what is worse than all, a languid monotony in the general tone of the work. . . . Whence did an embarrassment that so cramped Cherubini's genius arise? It was clearly produced by the requirements of the French stage, hitherto unknown to the composer, . . . that did not afford him the cadenced rhythms of his native tongue. . . . From time to time you perceive the beginning of a felicitous melody—for instance, in the air, "Faut il enfin que je déclare?" and in "Au plaisir de voir tant de charmes," etc.; but the detestable sham lyric verses of Marmontel soon come to dissipate the melodious essence. . . . Poor Cherubini did not know what to do with these verses of every dimension, sometimes forcing him to make his phrase of 5 measures, at other times allowing him only one of 2. . . . .' Halévy wishes he had been advised 'not

[1] Castil-Blaze.

to break away brusquely and entirely from his beautiful
Italian school. . . . All hitherto had gone well. . . .
The world, the poet, the theatre, seconded his dearest
wishes. Marmontel had handed him the poem for the
opera; it was a " Démophon." Everything smiled on
Cherubini; . . . seemed likely to succeed with him.
Everything, in fact, did succeed—except " Démophon " '
(performed 8 times). Halévy deplores that Cherubini
fell in with Morellet and Marmontel instead of Sedaine,
author of 'Richard Cœur de Lion,' who would have made
him a good musical drama, helpful to inspiration.

In 'Démophon,' observes Picchianti, setting a truer
store by this remarkable work, 'Cherubini exhibited a
more elaborate workmanship, more grandeur of form; and
so suddenly perfected his style, that he rose above the
ordinary and popular intelligence of the time. . . . so
great were the masculine beauties that appeared in this
Spartan. These, however, ... were not thought sufficient to compensate for the want of colour and dramatic
interest, faults . . . . to be assigned more to the poet
than to the musician.' Halévy, too, sees 'great merit in
the instrumentation,' 'beautiful choruses,' 'the founda-
tions of a new school and a new style,' and that 'these
qualities could not be appreciated by the public.' But when
he says 'inspiration was lacking,' and Fétis, after some
praise, that 'there is nothing but dryness in the airs,' and
'nothing remarkable even in the harmony,' naught of this
really applies, as I shall easily show, to large portions of
'this feeble production.' But 'Démophon' was a 1st
attempt at French verse, with a Marmontel who was no
Racine, and with a somewhat sombre subject, requiring
for its music, at least, good poetry to escape being at
times wearisome. It seems, however, to have more
opportunities for contrast than Hoffmann's 'Médée,' and
as many as Loreaux's 'Lodoïska.' The 1st act, before the
Temple of Apollo, opens with a most beautiful duet of
soprani, with a 4-part chorus, 'Père d'Orphée,' wherein
Fétis' 'melodious essence' at once 'exhales itself' as in the

opening of ' Médée;' or take the haunting phrase for the
2 soprani later on with a gentle, rhythmic accompaniment.

In the 2nd scene Lygdamus, high-priest and people listen
to the Oracle's announcement that the Thracian people's
troubles will cease when force yields to weakness, etc.
Sc. 3.—Lygdamus declares that King Demophon and
family should be included when the lots are drawn!
Sc. 4.—Dirce declares that if she discovers her own secret
marriage to Osmides, the King's son, she will expose
him to Demophon's anger, herself to death, and their
son to danger.
Sc. 5.—An elabo-
rate scena between
Osmides and
Dirce. The final
' allegro ' is concise
and brilliant.

Sc. 6 and 7.—Osmides is praising Dirce, when Adrastus announces the King's arrival. Sc. 8.—Demophon altercates with Astor, Dirce's father, and, Sc. 9, prays that a worthy sacrifice be chosen. The beautiful 7-part chorus of youths, maidens, women and old men, succeeds, praised by Fétis for 'the merit of the instrumentation, the texture of the vocal portion, and the robustness

of the style,' and is prolonged as an 8-tet into Sc. 10.— The maidens fly for protection to their parents for fear lest the lot fall on any of themselves. Sc. 11.—Osmides enters, and demurs to the King's plan that he should marry Princess Ircile, daughter of the Phrygian monarch, thereby uniting the 2 dominions. Ircile arrives at the port to brilliant strains, and, Sc. 12, a joyously melodious chorus, thus accompanied, succeeds. What dryness is there here?

Act II.—The port of Perinth. Ircile complains to Neades, Osmides' brother, of the latter's cold reception of her. Neades avows his affection in 'Faut il enfin que je declare;' Ircile is much troubled. The burden of a future crown is added to this fresh sorrow of discarded love. Sc. 2.—Osmides, avowing that he is a husband and a father, suggests that his brother Neades be affianced to Ircile in his place, singing 'Au plaisir de voir tant de charmes,' etc. Ircile is at 1st naturally rather overcome at this proposal. Sc. 3.—Dirce, Astor and Osmides confer. Osmides is for defence, Astor for flight. Sc. 4.—A duet between Osmides and Dirce, bewails their lot, but will not listen to any separation. This 1st section is in C, and the rest in C minor, but with the same main theme, and the pathos in both keys is there despite Marmontel and his verse, and the whole a fine conception. Sc. 5.—A ship attends Astor and Dirce for Lemnos, and they are about to depart, when, Sc. 6, Osmides is arrested by Adrastus, and Sc. 7,—in a 'scena,' that Wagner might have signed, he gives way to despair at Dirce and his son's impending fate. What elaborate accompaniments are herein displayed by this composer of 28 years, with no Mozart known by him to show the way!

Act III. The Palace vestibule. Sc. 1.—Osmides pleads for Dirce and Astor to Demophon, and avows his own prior alliance with the former. Sc. 2 and 3.—The incensed King now makes Osmides' prior suggestion, that Néades should take his place as spouse of Ircile, with succession to the throne, his own proposal, but Osmides'

ready acquiescence nowise appeases Démophon's wrath.
Sc. 4.—A superb trio in A, between Néades, Osmides
and the King, follows. What virile force is here! At an

acceleration of the time, note the King's bold entry:
'Va donc périr avec elle,' while the others continue

their appeal in Osmides' behalf, 'A son père il est fidéle,'
and 'Que son roi le rappelle,' the orchestra sweeping
the gamut with semi-quavers in ascending and descending
scale, a vastly effective and extended 'coda,' dramatically
closing with the King's abrupt departure. Sc. 5.—Ircile
asks Neades not to abandon his brother Osmides. Sc. 6.—
Dirce, arrayed for sacrifice, surrounded by guards, crosses
the palace vestibule for the temple. What dryness
is there here? There is no more beautiful march or
effective recitative in Cherubini's operas.

 The interior of Apollo's temple. Ircile
now speaks to Dirce, the crowd retiring. The
latter has no hope left, but confides her son to
Ircile's care. Sc. 7.—Then follows a brief
chorus, 'mäestoso,' of Handelian simplicity,
'Le plus beau sang,' unlike anything in the

opera, and sung at 1st by priests (tenors, 1 and 2; and basses) and preluded, like the 'Hailstone,' with a few simple chords; the voices entering at the ƒ p below:

and then a new subject enters, the whole ending in a close already heard at the outset, with the voices in unison on G.

The march's opening is then given, and the priest-
esses, behind the scenes, give out a stately theme to a
moving bass that recalls the more
beautiful march at the close of the
2nd act of 'Les Deux Journées.' Sc.
8.—This is afterwards given in full
unison by all the female voices, and
then in 3 separate parts. What dryness is there here?

Dirce is about to be slain, when, Sc. 9, Osmides,
Astor and soldiers rush in, and Lygdamus declares against
the sacrifice of Lodoïska. Sc. 10.—The temple is full of
soldiers, with Osmides defiant. Sc. 11.—Demophon enters
in anger against him. Osmides bids him take his life, and
announces that Dirce is his wife, and that if she and her
child are sacrificed, heaven will have no hand in it.

In the final grand scene, Demophon relents, and the
opera ends with a magnificent 'Allegro vivace,' to ceaseless
triplet accompaniment, and supported later on by a 4-part
chorus, 'A ses autels que tout s'unisse pour célèbrer un si
beau jour,' expressive of the universal happiness in broad,
simple strains, worthy of Haydn,

whether it be at the opening theme, or in the persistent
canonic forms throughout the 9-part succeeding 'ensemble,'

or at the pendant˙ strain, that, like a peal of bells, rings out merrily.

Cherubini never wrote broader, freer, more spontaneous music. There is nothing better of its kind in 'Les Deux Journées.' 'Démophon,' curtailed, would be a fine opera on any stage, almost in spite of Marmontel, who, a Piccinnist himself, had scarcely caught the right man to continue Piccinni's school. 'Si des mots font un opéra,' said a wag, ' "Démophon" est un opéra.' It remains an opera on other grounds.

Cherubini's 1st French opera at least brought him into notice: some drawing-rooms even ventured at applause. Among the small fry of Italian composers, this big 'Démophon' drama could only have fallen like a bomb-shell. Such a work, for them merely scientific and noisy, was something very new, but, at present, Cherubini determined to write no more tragic music.

For the concerts of the 'Loge Olympique' Cherubini now wrote another cantata to 'Circe,' according to Miel, ' one of the masterpieces of French lyric drama,' by J. B. Rousseau. J. Rousseau 1st sang in it, and again at a concert ' given in the Pantheon for Mme. Todi's benefit

At the Tuileries, too, in 1789, this lady-rival of Mara sang the 'scèna' 'Sarete alfin contenti,' written expressly for her by Cherubini. In putting 'Circe's' 84 lines, praised by La Harpe, to music, Cherubini must have had all his work cut out for him. Did he rise to the occasion? For example:

> ' Sa voix redoutable
> Trouble les Enfers ;
> Un bruit formidable
> Gronde dans les airs ;
> Un voile effroyable
> Couvre l'univers ;
> La terre tremblante
> Frémit de terreur ;
> L'onde turbulente
> Mugit de fureur ;
> La lune sanglante
> Recule d'horreur ! ' [2]

In 1789 Léonard Autié, commonly called Léonard, perfumer to the Queen, and a man of great wealth, obtained, through her influence, a licence to open a theatre for Italian opera, and sent Viotti to Italy to obtain the best singers. Viotti returned, having engaged Viganoni, Mengozzi, Revedino, the fine actor Raffanelli, M. and Mme. Mandini, and Mesdames Morichelli and Banti. Mme. Baletti, already in Paris, and Mesdames Barchielli, Raffanelli, Galli, Mlle. Nebel, and MM. Scalzi and Simoni, were also engaged. For Baletti, who 1st appeared at one of the 'Concerts Spirituels' Nov. 1788, Cherubini wrote the 'scena' and air, 'Ma che vi fece, oh stella.' 'Her voice was sweet, her vocalization perfect, her expression touching.' [3] The whole company was placed under the patronage of Monsieur, Comte de Provence, afterwards King Louis XVIII. The 'Théâtre de Monsieur' was temporarily opened in the hall of the Tuileries 26 Jan. 1789; and the 'Troupe de Monsieur,' or the 'Bouffons,' as they were called, began such a series of performances of the best operas of Cimarosa and his school as could not be excelled anywhere else. [4]

---

[2] *cit.* Framery and Ginguene's 'Musique' in *Encyclopédie Méthodique.*
[3] Fétis, *Biog. Univ.* i. 229.
[4] Fétis writes : ' The Troupe made its " début " in a kind of booth,

Pougin shows, in elaborate detail, what great work Cherubini did between 1789 and 1792 for this old Italian school. As director of the company, at a salary of 4000 francs, he had to discharge the delicate duty of assigning parts to singers, besides arranging works for representation; and so untiring was his zeal, that his friends at one time feared for his health. He required from others the same exactnesss practised by himself, and would lose patience and become severe if any of the singers were deficient in attention at rehearsal, or inability for their respective parts;[5] another account remarking, on the other hand, how 'he had the happy art of gaining over the singers to his views by a suavity of manner and a conciliatory mode of address, not always possessed by one of his talent and profession.'[6] He could be, no doubt, both strict and kind; there is evidence of this, as we shall see later on. Cherubini sometimes, but Mestrino as a rule, led in the orchestra; and the latter, dying Sept. 1790, was succeeded by Puppo, the violinist. To bring out further the merits of the singers, and as part of his agreement with Viotti, Cherubini inserted some 40 airs in the Italian operas put on the stage, all of them exciting general attention, among them the trio, 'Son tre, sei, nove,' in Cimarosa's 'Italiana in Londra;' the 4tet, 'Non ti fidar,' in Gazzaniga's 'Don Giovanni Tenorio;' the superb 4tet, 'Cara da voi dipende,' much applauded, in 'I Viaggiatori Felici,' by divers authors; and the 9 airs in Paisiello's 'La Molinara,' given in 1789, and admired by Louis XVI.

De Lafage remarks, 'that Cherubini had now 2 distinct styles, one allied to Paisiello and Cimarosa by the grace, elegance, and purity of the melodic forms; the other, to the school of Gluck and Mozart, more harmonic than

called "Le Théâtre de la Foire St. Germain," forgetting it was not till afterwards that they removed thither. Elsewhere he says: 'Cette compagnie débuta en 1789 aux Tuileries;' thus correcting himself and confirming Halévy, Pougin and other authorities. Compare *Biog. Univ.* ii. 265, and viii. 362.

[5] Picchianti.

[6] *Harmonicon,* 1825.

melodious, rich in instrumental details. This manner was 'then the unappreciated type of a new school, destined to change all the forms of art.'[7] Cherubini's present popularity, however, was owing to his 1st style. 'The Italian melody had always a great many admirers among persons of education and good taste ; and Cherubini, by his beautiful compositions, the grace of his songs, and the delightful manner of his pianoforte playing, was everywhere welcomed and admired.'[8] There is not, perhaps, 'another example of a composer writing at one and the same time in 2 different manners,'[9] and I suppose this is quite true. Not till the 'Bouffons' left Paris was Cherubini quit of Italian influences, and freer to follow his 2nd manner.

Meanwhile an opera—' Marguerite d'Anjou '—was actually begun for Louis XVI., at the Tuileries ; but the events of 1789 stopped its progress, and Cherubini retired for a time to Breuilpont in Normandy.

When the Revolution broke out, Cherubini's hopes became almost as clouded as those of the Monarchy. Hitherto his connection had distinctly been with the aristocracy, and now they were fleeing in all directions, or else mounting the scaffold. His livelihood became precarious, and he suffered in many ways, especially during the 1st 5 years of anarchy. Forced to live in seclusion, he passed his time in studying music, the physical sciences, drawing, and botany, and, wisely enough, limited his circle of acquaintances to a few trustworthy friends, mostly musicians like himself, such as Lesueur. His knowledge of the violin became the means of once saving his life. To stir out of doors was more or less of a risk, because numerous and reckless mobs paraded the streets night and day ; and during an occasion of more than ordinary excitement, Cherubini fell into the hands of a band of ' sansculottes,' who were roving about the city seeking musicians to con-

---

[7] Fétis.   [8] Picchianti.   [9] Raoul Rochette.

duct their chants. It was a special satisfaction for them
to compel the talent that had delighted Royalty and
Nobility to administer to their own gratification. On
Cherubini firmly refusing to lead them, a low murmur ran
through the crowd, and the fatal words, ' The Royalist!
the Royalist ! ' resounded on all sides. At this critical
juncture, one of Cherubini's friends, a kidnapped musician
too, seeing his imminent danger, thrust a violin into his
unwilling hands, and succeeded in persuading him to head
the mob. The whole day these 2 musicians accompanied
the hoarse and overpowering yells of that revolutionary
assemblage ; and when at last a halt was made in a public
square, where a banquet took place, Cherubini and his
friend had to mount some empty barrels and play till the
feasting was over.

Another annoyance for Cherubini was enrolment as
a member of the National Guard, entailing the custody of
prisoners, and escorting them to the scaffold. He would
gladly have quitted such scenes of horror ; but there were
difficulties in the way. In the 1st place, he was engaged
as leader of the Italian Theatre till 1792, with an obliga-
tion by his agreement therewith to produce 2 original
operas, neither of which had yet appeared ; 2ndly, it was
no easy task to elude the vigilance of officials in any
attempt at escape from French territory ; 3rdly, the value
of French notes, reduced in France to a 15th of their
proper value, was almost nominal in other countries, and
of gold Cherubini had little ; lastly, he had promised his
hand to Anne Cécile, the beautiful and accomplished
daughter of M. Tourette, a musician of the old 'Chapelle
Royale,' and husband to one of the ladies-in-waiting to the
Princesses Adelaide, and Victoria, aunts to the King.

When Louis XVI. arrived in Paris from Versailles,
the ' Bouffons ' had to leave their quarters in the Tuileries,
and take refuge in the Nicolet Hall, near the fair of St.
Germain, until Léonard's new opera-house was ready for
them in the Rue Feydeau.

A French company now joined the Italian Troupe,

already strengthened by the acquisition of Garat; and on the opening of the Feydeau Theatre, the 1st work there performed was Persuis' 'Nuit Espagnole;' the 2nd, given 18 July 1791, was Cherubini's 'Lodoïska,' one of the 2 works, long preparing, that formed part of his agreement. Several numbers of it had been given 2 months earlier, 24 May, set to what M. Pougin terms 'a very moving little drama,' entitled 'Mirabeau à son lit de mort.'

'Lodoïska' was greeted at once with enthusiasm, in France and Germany. Mme. de Justal created the title 'rôle.'[10]

As there had been 2 'Demophons,' so there were 2 'Lodoïskas,' Kreutzer's, with its overture and other themes (partially known still in the ball-room), appearing 6 weeks earlier than Cherubini's at the Favart.

'Cherubini's overture to "Lodoïska" has something of mannerism in the 2nd movement, compared with the 2nd movement of "Anacreon"—not in the notes, but in the style of the passage—but which may be excused from the peculiar novel effect. Good modulations are to be found in the movement to which I allude, particularly the passage begun in A minor, after repeated in A major; and that part where a succession of chords begin upon D, in which the composer has altered the usually received rules for accent, by placing it, for bars in succession, upon the 2nd part of the bar. Our author's tact appears to lie in that ingenious distribution of particular detached passages to the several instruments he employs, which so much distinguished the great Mozart. . . .'[11]

In the subject of the 'libretto,' somewhat similar to the books of 'Fidelio' and Grétry's 'Cœur de Lion' combined, Cherubini was at last fortunate. It was taken by Fillette Loreaux from Louvet's then popular romance of 'Le Chevalier de Faiblas.' The text, however, according to the 'Journal de Paris,' was 'below mediocrity.'

---

[10] It was an error to give Mme. Scio as 1st creator of the part as she took it up only in 1792. I followed Denne-Baron. See Pougin, *M. W.,* 1882, 532, for account of her.

[11] F. W. N., *Quarterly Musical Magazine.*

The plot is this: Lodoïska is imprisoned in the castle of a tyrant Dourlinski, who endeavours in vain to obtain her acceptance of his hand. Her lover Floreski gains admittance to the castle, and under pretence of being her brother, comes to claim her on the part of her mother. Floreski, having obtained Dourlinski's leave to stay the night previous to his return to Warsaw, is subsequently discovered attempting to effect Lodoïska's escape by giving the guards drugged wine. At this point the castle is stormed by the friendly Titzikan, leader of the Tartars, and Lodoïska rescued. The opera's success was immense, the audience rising to their feet and applauding every number. Decorators and machinists were called before the curtain at the close of the performance, got up with a splendour unusual in a 2nd-class theatre, and only seen at Grand Opera—costumes, scenery, orchestra, interpretation, all alike were magnificent, the final scene including the destruction of a palace.[12]

'We also called for the author of the music,' wrote one journal: 'it is Monsieur Cherubini, a young artist, known by several works that have already placed him in the 1st rank of composers.'

Act I.—The opening, with a Tartar chorus led by Titzikan, 'Concertons notre vengeance,' at once indicates

[12] See Pougin, *M. W.,* 1882, 532, for full details.

the massive calibre of the whole opera. The accompaniment of quavers and semi-quavers prevails throughout, save where the 1st phrase occurs. Sc. 2.—Titzikan has a grandiose air, expressive of the text, 'Triomphons,' etc., but he will be open and above board in attacking this tyrant Dourlinski. Sc. 3.—Varbel, Floreski's attendant, in his air, 'Voyez la belle besogne,' rallies his master on thus foolishly seeking out Lodoïska at the present juncture. Sc. 4 is a superbly accompanied 4-tet. Two examples in illustration of the instrumental forms, 1 from the

No. 2.

opening of the scena, are subjoined. Titzikan, supported by a Tartar soldier, and neither at first recognized as a friend, finally bids Floreski and Varbel surrender their arms, and exercise prudence in their enterprise. Sc. 5 is a bright and broad terzetto, 'Jurons,' between the above 3, and a 3-part male chorus, advocating alliance and conciliation, while vowing, if needs be, to contend to the last. Sc. 6 is a brilliant polonaise, accompanying solos and duet of

Varbel and Floreski. Sc. 7.—Finale, wherein Varbel
appears before the castle, and after a beautiful dialogue
between him, Floreski, and Lodoïska (within), is challenged
by Altamor.   Floreski states their request to be conducted
to the master of the castle, the male chorus bidding them
fear the place.   A splendid 6-tet succeeds, Floreski avowing that he will risk all for his love, and the rest sounding
a note of warning.   The opening strain, 'Maëstoso,' of
this section, begins and ends a truly grand page of
Cherubini.

Act II., Sc. 8, contains Lodoïska's beautiful lament
(recit., 'allegro' and air, 'larghetto,') 'Que dis-je o cièl'
over her own captivity and Floreski's risk in coming to her.

Sc. 9 is the duet, 'A ces traits je connais ta rage,' to restless strings between, Lodoïska adjuring him, and Dourlinski threatening her, subsequently altered by the composer. Sc. 10 is the grand 4-tet and 'scena,' where Dourlinski orders Lodoïska to be separated from her attendant Lysinka, and where the chorus of soldiers, in noble accents, come in 'sotto voce,' sympathizing with the heroine, and entreating Dourlinski to leave her, 'ce faible secours:' finally, when the tyrant orders Lysinka to be forcibly separated from her mistress, they still implore his clemency. Sc. 11 is a trio, wherein Floreski avows his jealousy, Dourlinski his irritation, and Altamor his sense that Floreski's secret as assailant is out. Sc. 12 is Floreski's air, 'Rien n'égale sa barbarie,' with brilliant

accompaniment, given only to the violins (themselves accompanied by the other instruments), that precedes Sc. 13

and 14, the 'finale' of the 2nd act, where Floreski and his servant Varbel drug the guards. Floreski is afraid, since the guards are watching him attentively. Nothing can be more masterly; the music, without being disjointed, brings out all the 'asides.' The guards retire; the drug is mixed with the wine. They cannot resist the subsequent offer to imbibe, and fall down. At this point Dourlinski appears; opprobrious epithets are interchanged; the chorus again warn Floreski, and the whole ends in 4-tet soli and 3-part male chorus, 'Saisissez ce témeraire,' that fairly carries the listener away, and closes probably one of the greatest Finales in French opera.

Act III., Sc. 15.—Dourlinski's air of triumph at Floreski's capture is emphasized in one section by an

je suis mai _ tre de son sort de son sort

extended phrase, forcibly expressive of his satisfaction. Sc. 16.—Lodoïska sings her expressive air, 'Tournez sur moi votre colère.' Then, in Sc. 17, we have a powerful 4-tet. Floreski begins the scena 'Quoi? t'unir à ce barbare,' and Lodoïska adds that she would rather die. Dourlinski as rival, and Altamor as onlooker, bewail the tragic outlook. Sc. 18.—The Finale opens with dialogue and considerable symphony of unrest and alarm, and begins vocally at the moment where Dourlinski's poignard is turned aside from Floreski by Titzikan's dramatic entry. Floreski calls upon the seemingly lifeless Lodoïska. To Dourlinski, now a prisoner, and his question as to what ransom is required for him, Titzikan replies, 'Captivity;' and here the Poles and Tartars join in with a male 4-part chorus supporting a 6-tet soli, with 4-part male chorus, 'Notre fureur est légitime.'

In one year 'Lodoïska' was performed 200 times, and at short intervals 200 more representations took place. This record of 400 representations survives to tell the tale, not of an ephemeral popularity for a 2nd rate production, but of the success of one out of some half-a-dozen masterpieces, whereof we can say, with Fétis, that whether now performed or no (for a sensational taste not necessarily true or healthy art), the scores remain for 'connoisseurs,' attached to their studies, the objects of a sustained, or rather increasing admiration. 'Lodoïska' was again brought out 5 June 1819 at the Feydeau Theatre. Its popularity lasted longer in Germany. Weber, when Director of the Theatre Royal, analyzed it in the 'Dresdener Zeitung,' and produced it in the Saxon capital 13 July 1817. In 1818 it was played at Berlin. Cherubini, as we have seen, did not escape opposition. Some said, 'He enchains the actor to the orchestra.' He and his followers were stigmatized as mathematical composers, because they worked out their ideas carefully and systematically on a principle ; but the tide had completely turned against the old Italian composers. 'Lodoïska,' it was said, came to console people for Mozart's premature death, and, perhaps, marks the zenith in French classical opera.

About 1789 music, like everything else, was in a state of disturbance and transition, and an Italian is here seen renouncing his beautiful Italian style, and upsetting that of his countryman Cimarosa and his school. They had been reigning long. I once heard Cimarosa's 'L'Astuzie Femminili,' 18 July 1871, at Covent Garden, London; and his 'Il Matrimonio Segreto' lives on. But where are Paisiello, Guglielmi, Gazzaniga, Anfossi, and Parenti now ? A cause of decadence with some, if not all, was defective musical training. Contrast, too, Cherubini—probably the most learned musician of genius that ever lived—and Rossini, unacquainted with double counterpoint, but wanting no more lessons. There may be still Gluckists and Piccinnists, lovers of German, lovers of Italian music, but is not Italy's greatest glory, in the later days, to have produced a Cherubini, who could equally please Turin with ' Ifigenia,' Paris with ' Les Deux Journées,' and Vienna with ' Faniska,'—very different audiences? Anyway, Mozart in Germany, and Cherubini in France, were independent instruments of the change that was coming, with a Beethoven to follow, in all

departments of his art. In England Handel's influence
had waned before Cimarosa and his school, although in
the year 1784 people bethought them of his Commemoration in the Abbey; but this no way affected opera. In
Germany, Bach was hardly appraised everywhere at his
true worth as now, since Mendelssohn's time, while Gluck,
in both France and Germany, had advanced beyond
Rameau. Meanwhile the ' il mio tesoro ' style was ill-
fitted for stirring times. In politics, music and literature,
a new spirit was rising. If the dramas of Racine and the
operas of Lulli were akin, the poetry of a Schiller had its
counterpart in the music of a Beethoven. And mark
Ulibichiff's, Hiller's, Dannreuther's and Wagner's words.
They had no interest as Germans in crying up an Italian,
but they felt it due to a remarkable composer to say what
they did. 'We can easily understand,' the 1st writes,
'how Mozart's popularity must have thrown the Italian
masters of the transition period into the background.
But there was another rival element still more terrible
and destructive to them, viz., the contemporaneous rise
of the true dramatic music of the 19th century—the
music founded by the great masters of the French school
—Cherubini, Méhul, and Spontini. [13] What could com-

---

[13] Méhul's ' Euphrosine et Coradin,' ' new and daring in character,'
deemed his masterpiece by Berlioz, brought out a year before ' Lodoïska,'
4 Sept. 1790, began the great revolution in style, perfected by the greater
Italian. So thinks Pougin, but taking 'Ifigenia' and especially 'Démophon'
(1788) as the 1st manifestations of the new school, we can say with Clément :
' There is every evidence to show that Cherubini, in writing the operas of
" Démophon" and " Lodoïska," opened the way for Méhul, Lesueur, and
Spontini. (*Dictionnaire Lyrique*, 406). Space should be afforded for a
counter-criticism, now a curiosity. ' The success and vogue which his opera
of " Lodoïska " obtained in 1791 at the Feydeau Theatre, made an epoch in
that style of which it would be possible to regard him as the inventor had
not Méhul already made use of it, but with more reserve, taste, and felicity.
It was at that time thought the proper thing to prefer the learned "Lodoïska"
of the Feydeau to that of M. Kreutzer at the Favart Theatre, which was
more interesting and less pretentious. This last, however, since the union
of the 2 theatres, has kept the stage ; the other has disappeared from the
"répertoire" even before the musical revolution effected in France by
Della Maria. . . . The other works of M. Cherubini, in spite of the ephemeral success of some of them—in spite of the scientific merit which
"dilettanti" can recognise in various portions of his compositions—are
nearly forgotten nowadays ; they lack essentially verve, variety, and

posers who continued to work on a worn-out system do
against such works as "Lodoïska," "Les Deux Journées,"
"Faniska," "Joseph," and "Die Vestalin," which Europe
received with enthusiasm, and in which it recognized
itself ? . . . If, on the other hand, Gluck's calm and
plastic grandeur, and, on the other, the tender and
voluptuous charm of the melodies of Piccinni and Sacchini,
had suited the circumstances of a state of society sunk
in luxury, and nourished with classical exhibitions, this
could not satisfy a society shaken to the very founda-
tions of its faith and organization. The whole of the
dramatic music of the 18th century must naturally have
appeared cold and languid to men whose minds were
profoundly moved with troubles and wars; . . . "languor"
will, perhaps, best express generally that which no longer
touches us in the operas of the last century. . . . What we
require for the pictures of dramatic music is larger frames,
including more figures, more passionate and moving song,
more sharply marked rhythms, greater fulness in the vocal
masses, and more sonorous brilliancy in the instrumentation. All these qualities are to be found in " Lodoïska "
and "Les Deux Journées," and Cherubini may be regarded
not only as the founder of modern French opera, but also
as that musician who, after Mozart, has exerted the
greatest influence on the general tendency of the art. An
Italian by birth and the excellence of his education, . . .
—a German by his musical sympathies, as well as by the
variety and profundity of his knowledge,—and a Frenchman by the school and principles to which we owe his
finest dramatic works,—Cherubini strikes me as being the
most accomplished musician, if not the greatest genius, of
the 19th century.'[14] Another German writer adds: 'Cherubini's services as the reformer of French, or modern, opera

originality. "Les Deux Journées" is an exception,' &c. (*Biog. Univ. et
Port,* 1834.) After quoting the contemporary, *Almanach général des Spectacles,* Pougin voices the more general view, that 'we do not find in [Kreutzers'
work] a single piece that can come up to the fine pages of Cherubini's
"Lodoïska."'—*M. W.,* 1882, 532.

[14] *cit. N.M.Z., M.W.,* 1862. Mozart is not excepted from ' languor.'

are appreciated, especially in Germany, but by no means
sufficiently so, because they date from the same period as
Mozart's transformation of opera. . . . People still talked
and wrote a great deal about Gluck. . . . Cherubini
effected just as much as Gluck, in the blending of the
music with the poetry, and the characteristic representation
of the dramatic situation, though with far greater wealth
of musical fancy, because he employed in his harmonic
combinations a much richer store of instrumental resource
and knowledge, and raised the music above the nervous
interpretation of the words without sacrificing the psychical
truth of expression in the melody.   At the same time he
developed the received forms, and created . . . perfectly
new ones, distinguished for a scope never before known.
. . . Such a finale as that in " Lodoïska," and that in
" Les Deux Journées," were without parallel upon the
French operatic stage ; . . . Spontini . . . enjoyed the
advantage of Mozart's example, . . . while it was impossible that Cherubini could have known anything about
Mozart's masterpieces when composing " Lodoïska,"
" Elisa," " Medea," and " Les Deux Journées." '[15]   But
' there is no doubt, that Cherubini followed his own inspirations ; . . . a comparison of his style with that of his
illustrious predecessor proves it to demonstration.'[16]   This
is confirmed by Hiller, who, observing that Gluck ' lacked
power of development and grandeur of construction,' and
that 'Mozart united all the great qualities, but at the period
in question had hardly made his mark even in his own
country . . . .' then surveys the 'truly astonishing' scores

[15] *N.M.Z., M.W.,* 1862. Mozart's 'Figaro' was 1st brought out
1 May 1786 ; 'Don Juan' 29 Oct. 1787 ; 'Zauberflöte' 30 Sept. 1791. An
unsuccessful attempt was made to introduce 'Figaro' to Paris 20 March
1793. With Da Ponte and Beaumarchais adapted by Notaris, and music
ill-executed, the 5th night's performance was the last. 'Figaro' was not
known to France till after 'Lodoïska' had appeared ; the 'Zauberflöte'
came out after 'Lodoïska ;' a mangled version of 'Don Juan' was given in
Paris in 1805, when nearly all Cherubini's operatic masterpieces had
appeared, and its 1st performance there entire was not till 1811. There is
no proof that Cherubini studied Mozart's scores, or that they reached Paris
before, say, 1800.
[16] Fétis.

of ' Lodoïska,' and 'Médée,' with their ' wealth of characteristic themes, varying with the sense of the words,
the characters, and the changes of situation;' adding,
'despite all this life and movement, they constitute a style
of music almost architectural in the beauty and clearness
of its outlines. The harmonies and modulations, even
when most unusual, develop themselves with the natural
logical sequence and ease that always distinguish a Great
Master, and seem . . . to proceed from the independent
life of the separate parts, as with the old composers of the
strict polyphonic style. To Cherubini he ascribes many
effects 'so much used by the romantic school of Germany,
and so much abused by less gifted writers ; ' *i.e.*, 'the long-
sustained harmonies carrying rhythmical figures—the
"pedal points," so called—that keep the hearer in suspense,
until the return of the key-note acts like a release ; the
single sustained notes on the horn or clarinet, so exciting
to the imagination ; the mysterious resonance of some
weird melody in the veiled lower strings of the violas, the
frequent pauses, producing effects only possible in music
of this class, and so on.' Conservative and classical as
Cherubini may seem now, yet here a share in modern
romanticism is allowed him. While Sir Hubert Parry
calls him (only as teacher ?) ' the representative of all
that was old-fashioned and conventional in art,'[17] Hiller, as
composer of 'Médée,' and 'Les Deux Journées' overtures
alone, calls him ' the father of Beethoven, Weber, Schumann
and Wagner.' This is supplemented by Ulibicheff
when using the phrases, ' so picturesque, so poetic, so full
of warmth and effect,' in regard to the overtures to
' Lodoïska,' ' Médée,' ' Les Deux Journées,' ' Faniska,' and
'La Chasse du Jeune Henri.' One, too, avers that 'the
great works of Cherubini, though "Opéras comiques" in
name, are, in style, much more nearly allied to the German
Romantic opera.' In fact, according to another, Cherubini ' marks the transition point between the regular

[17] *Studies of Great Musical Composers*, 376.

symmetry of the style of Mozart, and the coming disturbance of form effected by Beethoven,'[18] Hence, possibly, this falling between 2 styles and periods may have militated against him. His opera is not exactly Comic, nor exactly Romantic. It glances at both. Hiller continues: 'Musical historians are fond of saying that Cherubini took the Germans for his teachers and examples. My conviction is that the Germans learnt far more from him than he did from them.'[19] Could a German say more ? Lastly M. Dannreuther remarks : 'All that can by any possibility be accomplished in the musical drama from the musician's point of view, and without taking the poet into consideration, was accomplished by Gluck's successors, Cherubini, Méhul and Spontini. They have widened, without destroying, the musical forms to the utmost; they maintained the traditional arrangement of the " aria ; " they rendered the recitative, and the connecting links between it and the " aria," more expressive ; and, what is of especial importance, they allotted the execution of the airs to more than one person, according to dramatic necessities,[20] . . . monologue, hitherto essential to all operas, was got rid of. Of course " duetti " and " terzetti " had been in use long before . . . but . . . they rendered these, which had formerly been mere slight modifications of the solo aria, subservient to the higher purpose of dramatic musical " ensemble," . . . . " and it would be difficult," remarks Wagner, " to answer them, if they now perchance came amongst us, and asked in what respect we had improved on their mode of

---

[18] F. H. Jenks, *Grove* ii. 522 ; H. J. Lincoln, *ib.* 622.

[19] He and Méhul, too, anticipate Rossini's more commonplace ' crescendos,' and abandon the rule of the 2nd subject in the dominant, and then the original key.—H. J. Lincoln, *Grove* ii. 622. Wagner, of course, develops the whole school's principles to their utmost capacity.

[20] In corroboration of this, Denne-Baron writes that in ' Les Deux Journées' Cherubini 'assigned a part to each instrument, as to a personage who has his own language and accent, at times establishing between them intelligent dialogues, or combining their different tones in harmonious groups, so as to unite them in energetic masses. In short, everywhere, on the stage as in the orchestra, amplitude and power of development, and, agreeably to the necessities of the drama, delicacy and elegance in the

musical procedure." '[21] Cherubini, for instance, anticipated Wagner's 'leit motif.' In 'Lodoïska' and 'Les Deux Journées' we find indications of it; that is, giving a certain set musical phrase to each character. Thus I recall an observation of Castil-Blaze to the effect that he knew Armand was concealed in Mikeli's water-cart through the playing of a flute. Without denying, then, that an unoperatic Bach and an operatic Gluck preceded a Cherubini; or that Handel vocally has not been surpassed, say, in his trio: 'The flocks shall leave their mountains,' and chorus 'Wretched Lovers' in 'Acis and Galatea,' for dramatic power and contrast, still 'Lodoïska' did originate on the operatic stage in France what has been called 'musique d'effet,' which found followers there in Méhul, Steibelt, Lesueur, Berton, Boieldieu, Halévy, Auber, even Meyerbeer and Rossini; but Cherubini is not held 'responsible for the direction that "effect-music" pursued, especially in our own time, through the instrumentality of Meyerbeer.'[22] Nor, let me add, for the din of cymbal and gong, and padding to follow, of Rossini, to which Cherubini lent himself in his later 'Ali Baba,' with its 'tumult and crash,' as Mendelssohn regretted. What effect-music really was, let one sentence sufficiently explain: 'While Cherubini carried out, in the melody, the fundamental law of dramatic truth, the agreement of the music with the situations in the drama, and their poetic expression, as laid down by Gluck, he exhibited greater depth of intention, fuller and bolder harmony, and a style of instrumentation which, by its richness and the characteristic

outlines, vigour in the "ensemble," effect as a whole, and ever purity and elevation of style, nobility in the choice of ideas, and sagacious and judicious disposition of all the parts.' Could praise go higher?

[21] *Wagner : His Tendencies and Theories,* 28.

[22] *N.M.Z., M.W.,* 1862. 'Cherubini,' writes the unfriendly critic of 1834 already cited, of the new style, 'has not become worthy of being placed beside the Paisiellos, the Guglielmis, and the Cimarosas, his contemporaries, for though often directing the orchestra of this theatre (de Monsieur), he never dared to risk there any whole opera in his own style— not even one of those which he had composed in Italy. Since it is easier to produce harmonies and noise, effects of purely theoretical calculation, than to create song, M. Cherubini, renouncing the Italian method, requiring

employment of the wind instruments especially, in conformity with the peculiar quality of their sound, introduced the orchestra in a brilliant manner, not only as the foundation for the vocal portion, but also as its necessary adjunct, and its equal in bringing about the theatrical effect as a whole.' [23]

'In nothing that Cherubini wrote do we come across aught that is not noble, far less upon aught that is low— the noblest feeling prevades his style, ... mere sensuous charm in his melodies he despises. The melodies frequently flow on in astonishing simplicity, but are mostly sustained by artistic harmonies, in the combinations of which he equals the greatest composers. The musical ideas and "motivi," moreover, are characterized by wonderful sharpness; nothing is vague or obscure; everything is clear, distinct, and firmly drawn.' [24] This is absolutely true.

With all this merit, then, why, for example, to use Clément of the Sorbonne's language, is not 'Lodoïska,' with its 'noble sustained style, admirable and profound harmonies, rich and varied modulations that prevent its getting old,' oftener performed? If the true cause of any abandonment of works such as these was, in Miel's opinion, 'a mediocre execution that ill-suited works so full and crowded,' this is no reason in a day that manages works far more 'full and crowded.' It is a truism that a masterwork must be done well. Do 'Fidelio' badly and will any work suffer more? Where Cherubini's best is done well, as when Mendelssohn took 'Les Deux Journées' in hand, enthusiasm runs like wildfire. It is always so. Cherubini's operas, however, have been accused of want of

imagination and fecundity, allies himself to the German manner, in substituting for an expressive melody the noisy and often unnatural effects of instrumental profusion.' This is just what was said of Gluck, Beethoven, Wagner, of every innovator. It sounds ludicrous now, applied to Cherubini's classicism replete with melody as well as science, as in "Lodoïska," but no doubt deemed very extravagant in 1791.

[23] *N.M.Z., M.W.,* 1862.

[24] *Ib.*

melody! Fétis replies: 'There is a copiousness of melody
in Cherubini, especially in "Les Deux Journées;" but such
is the richness of the accompanying harmony, and the
brilliant colouring of the instrumentation, considering the
period when the work appeared ; such, above all, was the
inability of the readers of the public taste to appreciate at
that time the combination of all these beauties, that the merit
of the melody was not appreciated at its just value. . . .
The same critics, . . . who hardly know what they are
talking about, assert that the author of "Elisa" and
"Médée" wants originality, while originality is precisely
one of the most remarkable qualities of the melodies that
have been cited [the duet in the "Epicure," the grand
scena in "Pimmalione," the air "Suspendez à ce mur,"
in "Les Abencérages," that of "Anacréon," "Jeunes
filles," and the chorus "Dors, noble enfant," in "Blanche
de Provence"] ; since, although full of charm, the forms
are absolutely new.' Fétis' contention here is not disputed
now. But the admiring Hiller thinks 'there is a great
lack of vitality in his operas, as compared with "Don
Giovanni," "Fidelio," or "Der Freïschutz," and in many
respects even with Gluck's, though, as lyric dramas, these
last are far behind Cherubini's.' His notion is this:
'Cherubini did not possess a sufficient flow of independent
beautiful melody. No one can say that his music is not
melodious; it is more correct to say that everything in it
sings.'

In the part of Constance in 'Les Deux Journées,'
expressing 'the same self-sacrificing conjugal love so nobly
embodied in "Fidelio,"' he finds only 'a few impassioned
phrases.' It may be so, and I can cite in the 1st act's
Finale in 'Lodoïska' an instance, I suppose, of what he
means, where Floreski and Lodoïska have the same short
beautiful phrase in succession, and then repeat it a note
lower. But does the comparative lack of 'concrete melodies,' seen to such profusion in Cherubini's Italian manner,
before and after 1788; in detached songs, and of course in
his church-music—and lengthy melodies too, as witness the

canon in 'Faniska,' and the 'Quoniam' of the Mass in D;—
does this want of detachable songs, à la Bellini and
Donizetti, available for drawing-room tea-parties, and such
as 'cannot well be separated from the character,' militate
against 'Lodoïska'? Save the canon, what separate songs
to be sung at concerts do we hear from 'Fidelio?' I have
never heard any, and the 'Prisoners' Chorus' can be
deemed heavy enough by not a few, if we take that for
an excerpt. Brevity of phrase, making much out of little,
but that little good, is a marked characteristic in
Beethoven and most great Masters. Schubert, on the
other hand, I believe, through want of complete training,
too often makes little out of much. The reverse process
is often a quality in the best music. If Mozart has more
tunes to hum, that is not deemed the only merit in an
opera-writer now. Do Weber or Spohr, very different
witnesses, hint at aught amiss in 'Les Deux Journées?'
Take the 3 acts, general, military, or pastoral, with melodious contrasts of every kind, so that you are never wearied,
the whole full of sparkling life, variety of accompaniment,
and exquisite harmonies. The dramatic merit is great in
'Lodoïska,' as also in 'Démophon' and 'Médée,' but there
is little contrast. A contemporary journal (not, for a
wonder, cited by Pougin) wrote of 'Lodoïska' as 'a reproach,' that it was 'too beautiful.' A strange way of
putting it, but the explanation follows. 'All the pieces,
worked out with infinite care and all equally worked out,

do not give the listener time to breathe; by being forced to admire, you end by being fatigued with this too continued beauty; you would prefer from time to time simpler pieces on which to take your repose.' This is the fault, then, not so much lack of melody as of contrast. Hiller also refers to Cherubini's dislike of leaving a piece until he had given it ' the very utmost finish, a habit whereby he often weakened the interest of his work, especially in dramatic music.' This was recognized by Cherubini himself when he shortened ' Médée ' for his Viennese audience. And even the admiring Fétis refers to 'a certain absence of scenic instinct, that makes itself conspicuous in the most beautiful works of his genius. Almost always the 1st inspiration is happy; but Cherubini, too prone to develop his idea by the merit of an admirable workmanship, forgets the requirements of the action; the scene extends under his hand; music alone preoccupies the musician, and the situations become tedious.' There is need, also, in tragedy's luggage, for accompanying hand-bags of comedy, while the poverty of libretti must have conduced to prolixity. We see this tendency in 'Médée,' but not in 'Les Deux Journées;' in the D minor Mass, but not in the male-voice Requiem. Dismissing, then, Hiller's lack of ' depth of feeling ' in Cherubini, written before Pougin's pages had told a different tale, and with, say, the 1st act of 'Elisa,' to indicate otherwise, I may admit with Ella, that ' imagination rather than fancy is Cherubini's dominating characteristic;' admit that he has not always the radiancy of Mozart, the Raphael of music; admit that he is oftener intense with Dante, than genial as Shakespeare. Finally, given noble or ignoble theme, Cherubini would incline, with Beethoven, to the former. One and the same great moral action of self-sacrifice is seen in ' Lodoïska,' ' Elisa,' ' Les Deux Journées,' ' Faniska,' and 'Fidelio.' No one ever listened to these and were not the better for so doing. As much cannot be said of Mozart's 'Il Seraglio,' 'Così fan Tutte,' ' Le Nozze di Figaro ' and parts of ' Don Giovanni,' whose exquisite music merited better books.

CHAPTER III.

FRANCE.

1791—1797.

'The generations were prepar'd; the pangs,
Th' internal pangs were ready, the dread strife
Of poor humanity's afflicted will
Struggling in vain with ruthless destiny.'

'How oft along thy mazes,
Regent of sound, have dangerous Passions trod.'

WORDSWORTH.

The Parisian Theatres—Flight of Viotti and the Bouffons—Refuge in Normandy—*La Libertà—La Palinodia à Nice—Kourkourgi—Elisa* —Foundation of the Conservatoire—Appointment as an inspector— Solfeges—Pupils—Republican Hymns—Foundation of the French Institute—Marriage to Anne Cécile Tourette—Notice of Cherubini's family—*Médée.*

THE number and variety of works produced at Paris between 1790 and 1800 are, indeed, astonishing. For order, authority, and religion, that decade was dreadful; for music, glorious: 25 theatres existed in Paris, many of them time-honoured buildings, where a century and more before had been heard the quiet music of Lulli, and the stronger strains of Rameau.[1] During the Republic,

---

[1] 1. Opéra National (Grand Opera), at the Porte St. Martin, which has changed its name so often, according to the different governments that succeeded each other in France, at one time being called Théâtre des Arts, at other times Théâtre de la République et des Arts, Théâtre Impérial de l'Opéra, Académie Impériale, Académie Royale, &c.
  2. Théâtre Français, at this period Théâtre de la République, at the Palais Royal.
  3. Théâtre de la Nation, at the Odéon, afterwards Théâtre Francais.
  4. Opéra Comique National, at the Salle Favart.
  5. Théâtre Feydeau, Rue Feydeau.
  6. Théâtre de la Montagne, or Montansier, at the Palais Royal.
  7. Théâtre National, Rue Richelieu.
  8. Théâtre du Marais.

E

Consulate, and Empire, the number of theatres never rose above 44. In 1807 there were 33; an Imperial decree reduced them to 8. At the Restoration there were 14, and in 1847, 33.[2] At the period we are treating, as stars of the 1st and 2nd magnitude were shining Cherubini at the Feydeau, and Méhul at the Favart. Boieldieu, Steibelt, Dalayrac, were beginning to be seen as secondary lights rising, while Philidor, Monsigny, Gossec, and Grétry were luminaries setting in the Parisian musical firmament. The year 1792, however, witnessed the departure of the ' Troupe de Monsieur,' alarmed at the turn political events were taking, and Viotti fled to England.[3]

The crisis came in 1793; the storm burst in all its fury, and when the King mounted the scaffold Cherubini had already taken refuge at La Chartreuse de Gaillon, near Rouen, once a Carthusian monastery, but at this time the country residence of his friend Louis, an architect, whose wife was a good musician and composed dramatic music. Here, living in comparative tranquillity and safety, he wrote ' La Libertà,' and ' La Palinodia à Nice, canzoni di Metastasio,' on which a critic observes : ' These duets of one of the most able of our modern composers are in

9. Théâtre des Amis de la Patrie, at the Salle Louvois.
10. Théâtre du Lycée des Arts, Rue St. Honoré.
11. Théâtre de l'Ambigu Comique, Boulevard du Temple.
12. Théâtre du Vaudeville, Rue de Chartres.
13. Théâtre des Variétés Amusantes, Boulevard du Temple.
14. Théâtre de la Gaîté, Boulevard du Temple.
15. Théâtre des Délassements Comiques, Boulevard du Temple.
16. Théâtre Patriotique, Boulevard du Temple.
17. Théâtre sans Prétention, Boulevard du Temple.
18. Théâtre Molière, Rue St. Martin.
19. Théâtre de la Cité.
20. Théâtre Lyrique et Comique, afterwards des Jeunes Artistes, at the corner of the Boulevard and Rue de Lancry.
21. Théâtre des Sans-Culottes.
22. Théâtre de la Rue St. Antoine.
23. Théâtre du Doyen, Rue de Nazareth.
24. Théâtre des Jeunes Elèves, Rue Dauphine.
25. Théâtre des Victoires Nationales. Rue du Bac.

[2] Aicard's *Patria*, 2350.
[3] Michaud's *Biog. Univ.* i. 97.

the same style as those of Clari, Steffani, and Handel, . . . in the answers and imitations between the parts, and in the modulations and frequent use of chromatics. The melodies are generally of a grave and sedate character, those in the triple time being frequently elegant. The slow movements are, perhaps, the best, and these have frequently much tenderness and pathos. We may name the 1st and 8th as instances. The 9th is a very happy adaptation of the words, but requiring great delicacy of execution. Indeed, the duets are not easy. We consider, then, these compositions in the light of antidotes to the disorders of the modern school, and capable of giving such a training to the mind as will prepare it for the relish of the beauties of that severe but true style in which passion, not surprise, is the object. They require, and therefore will lead to, musical knowledge and judgment; but their graceful elegance will very soon reconcile even a vitiated appetite to the admiration of their true beauties.'[4]

The 3-act opera of 'Kourkourgi,' composed at this period, 1793, would have been ready for representation in 1794, but could not be executed owing to the disorders of the anniversary of the 10th of August, and thus the overture was never written, nor the last part of the finale. The opera, put aside into a portfolio, was long afterwards brought out again, being to some extent incorporated in 'Ali Baba,' and, according to Place, in 'Faniska.' All that I have been able to ascertain about the libretto is that it was a very poor one, by Duveyrier Mélesville the elder, and that Kourkourgi, the hero, was a mandarin, a miser, and a coward.

News of his father's death at Florence, 10 Sept. 1792, aged 72, reached Cherubini at Chartreuse de Gaillon. The funeral expenses necessitated the sale, at Florence, of a little cottage, poorly furnished, belonging to the Cherubinis. His paternal inheritance left to him now consisted of a small house on the Fiesole road, where he had been born, the rent whereof, added to other sums of money,

[4] *Quarterly Musical Review.*

etc., for a long time sufficed to support one of his younger
sisters till her death, when the property reverted to the
generous brother.   But Cherubini, having fallen into want
himself, had at last to part with even this small estate.   It
was when suffering under this blow from the news of
his father's death that he began the moving opera of
'Elisa.'

Cherubini returned to Paris in 1794, and married,
12 April, Anne Cécile Tourette, faithful companion to
him through life, who bore him 3 children—a son and 2
daughters: Salvador, born in 1801, an artist of repute,
and inspector of the 'Beaux-arts,' who accompanied
Champollion on his scientific tour to Egypt, and died just
before the war between France and Germany, leaving 2
sons, Louis and Maxime; Victoire, the elder daughter,
who married, 9 March 1816, at St. Vincent de Paul,
Paris, M. Turcas, military commissary of Paris, and died
May 1875, aged 79; Zénobie, the younger daughter,
who married, 1827, the celebrated artist Hippolyte Rosellini, and lived at Pisa, and they had a son Giovanbattista.
A daughter of M. Turcas, Cécile Antoinette Clémentine,
married M. Duret, a sculptor and member of the Institute,
and she was the mother of the late Juliette, Mme. Cot,
on whom, and her daughter, I had the honour of calling
in 1899, and she graciously presented me with some
original sketches in colours of the great composer; and I
take this opportunity of recording this, her singular kindness to a total stranger, albeit a disinterested admirer of
her illustrious great-grandfather.   Madame Cherubini died
at Neuilly, 1 July 1864.

On 13 Dec. 1794, 'Elisa,' or 'Les Glaciers du
Mont St. Bernard,' with words by Révéroni St. Cyr,
appeared at the Feydeau, with Madame Scio as Elisa.
The general judgment on the work was, that it was 'too
learned, too German.'   It was one of the most touching
and beautiful works of the Master.   Having lost his
father, he began it with this sense of bereavement.   There
is a directness and simplicity about it worthy of Haydn.

Heart predominates over head.　I wonder if Mendelssohn ever heard it!

In both acts the scene represents the Mont St. Bernard Pass.　After the beautiful overture, too rarely performed in England,[5] the scene opens with the celebrated Introduction, where the Prior of the monastery and his attendant monks, bearing lanterns and pick-axes, are seen searching in the early morning for any travellers lost in the snow.　This begins picturesquely with the strings

alone, and then with supporting voices, 'O ciel! daigne exaucer nos vœux.'　Then soon succeeds, in striking contrast, a dramatic passage, that Denne Baron must have had in his mind, when he said, 'This music makes me shiver.'　Subsequently the chorus come in, as accompaniment to the violins in the 1st subject, exclaiming, 'O ciel! daigne exaucer nos vœux;' and on the entry of

---

[5] It was given in 1868 by the London Philharmonic Society, and has often formed an item in the Paris Conservatoire Concerts.

the 2nd subject the gloom lifts, and bells ring at ' Ah! la

belle journée' que l'air est pur'; the Prior's simple
accents at the traveller's danger following :

'S'il est au fond de ces abîmes
Quelques malheureuses victimes
Des frimats, des vents désastreux';

and finally comes a repetition of the 1st subject, 'Daigne
exaucer nos vœux.' The beauty and reality of this
chorus seem equal to anything of Cherubini, at this his
period of true operatic greatness. Sc. 2.—Florindo, un-
heroic hero, enters, with a servant Germain, and sings a
fine air, 'Lieux sauvages, tristes climats.' Its smooth

accents are again contrasted with an instrumentation
vividly descriptive of the chill, barren scene, the whole
dying away on a pedal point. An air follows, wherein
Germain descants on the fidelity of his master's love. A
symphonic interlude, descriptive of all the monastery bells
ringing out over the snowy waste at the 6 o'clock Angelus,
precedes the entry—Sc. 3 and 4—of Michel, the Savoyard
letter-carrier, in alarm, and with a note for Florindo,
wherein he is informed that Elisa has been betrothed to

his rival Sarti. In a long and impassioned recitative,
Florindo gives vent to his sorrow and despair. Sc. 5.—
Finale : the Prior enters, and seeing Florindo in distress,
endeavours to console him. Here is a duet, the Prior
entreating Florindo to enter the hospice, since it is getting
dusk, the effect being heightened by the monastery bell

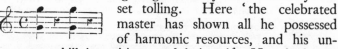 set tolling. Here 'the celebrated
master has shown all he possessed
of harmonic resources, and his un-
common skill in uniting modulations.'[6] Here is the art
concealing art, with manifest feeling. The horns sound
octaves in the 1st and 3rd beats in every bar to the
close, along with the bell. Sc. 6.—(with horn solo 'ad
libitum ')—Elisa and Laura, her maid, appear with
a guide. Elisa faints with fatigue. At sight of the
attendants of the hospice, the subject of the Introduction re-appears, and the monastery is blest as 'l'asile
des coeurs sincères,' and 'le temple de l'humanité.' At
the 'Larghetto' a lovely strain succeeds, and Elisa is

carried to the hospice. On this act, Miel well observes :
' C'est peut-être ce que la scène a du plus pathétique.'

The 2nd Act opens with 2 bright Savoyard choruses
with canonic forms, divided by an air for the guide, ' Vive
la France! ' and ' Partons, allons pour Paris,' with allusion
to the passage of the French over the Mont St. Bernard.
The 2nd chorus, particularly, has all the vocal grace and
suavity to be admired in Act I.

⁶ Denne-Baron.

Sc. 2.—The Prior and Elisa converse. Florindo is at the hospice. Her expressive 'cantabile' air, 'Je vais revoir tout ce que j'aime,' follows. Sc. 3.— Germain enters, and Elisa asks after Florindo, who, it appears, has left, leaving a letter to say that, having been betrayed, he knows how to die. A grand trio, 'Il veut périr,' succeeds, despair following dismay. The voices of Elisa, Laura, and the Prior die away, and the instruments, too, till those wonderful violas of Cherubini alone show sign of life. Sc. 4 and 5.—A storm; Florindo and Michel descend the path. The tempest's fury increases; a bridge they had crossed over, gives way.

Sc. 6 is very dramatic. Elisa and Laura hurry in, and approach the precipice : ' Grands dieux (*sic*), c'est Florindo ; ' he replies : ' Sauve-moi.' An avalanche hastens the dénouement, and Florindo is lost to sight. A chorus, in strains of great breadth and simplicity above, and one below in the chasm (how did it get there ?)

answer one another. Florindo, buried in the snow, re-appears before the foot-lights. The usual raptures and happy ending precede a final chorus.[7]

Such is a brief sketch of 'Elisa,' with a somewhat thin libretto, scarcely worthy of the music, at least in the 2nd Act, but an undoubted musical masterpiece. The libretto's plot is, at least, comprehensible, and I trust 'Elisa,' so near to being revived in London in 1815, will one day re-appear on our stage.

In 1795 the Paris Conservatoire was founded. After 14 July 1789, Sarrette, captain on the staff of the National Guard at Paris, had collected together 45 musicians, as a nucleus for the performance of the music of the Guard. In May 1790, the municipality took this body under their charge, and raised the number of musicians to 70. On 9 June, in the same year, a decree was issued for the formation of an 'Ecole gratuite de Musique de la Garde Nationale.' By his zeal, Sarrette came more immediately under the notice of the government ; and 8 Nov. 1793, a decree of the Convention created an 'Institut National de Musique,' consisting of 115 artists and 600 students, for the purpose of 'celebrating musically the national festivals.' The place for the Institute was situated in the Rue St. Joseph, the site being subsequently occupied by baths. By a law of 3 Aug. 1795, the National Convention suppressed the 'Musique de la Garde Nationale.' The same day, however, on the report of one Joseph Chénier, measures were taken for founding a Conservatoire of Music, that at length resulted in its establishment 25 Oct. 1795. Sarrette was appointed Director, with 5 inspectors, Lesueur, Grétry, Gossec, Méhul, and Cherubini, the 3 latter teaching counterpoint. The classes were opened for students a little more than a year afterwards, 30 Oct. 1796. The Conservatoire engaged correspondents abroad, such as Salieri and Haydn at Vienna, Paisiello at Naples, Winter

---

[7] Steibelt's Pianoforte Concerto, *Le Voyage au Mont St. Bernard,* takes its idea, and even details, from Cherubini's *Elisa,* Grove iii. 704[b].

at Munich, and Zingarelli at Rome. A special commission, consisting of Berton, Catel, Cherubini, Eler, Framery, Gossec, Lacépède, Langlé, Lesueur, Martini, Méhul, Provy, Rey, and Rodolphe, was appointed to compile a treatise on harmony for the school, and assembled 22 Dec. 1801. Several meetings having been dedicated to the consideration of various systems of harmony, the commission finally agreed to accept that of Catel 29 Feb. 1802. Méhul 'reported progress,' and the resolutions passed by the Conservatoire de Musique with respect to the adoption of Catel's 'Treatise on Harmony' were drawn up and signed by Sarrette as president. Prizes were eventually given to successful pupils, who were even sent to Italy for purposes of study at the expense of the State. In 1806, a separate department of 'déclamation' was formed, composed of 18 of the most talented pupils, 12 being men and 6 women; and for each man there was a gift of 1000, and for each woman 900 francs. Such an institution as the Conservatoire, that continues to flourish exceedingly, soon brought out a number of distinguished instrumentalists and vocalists. [8]

In the year of his appointment as an inspector of the Conservatoire, Cherubini commenced writing solfeges, the MSS. of which are in the Conservatoire Library. His labours as a teacher now began, and the assiduous pupil of Sarti became the master of Kuhn, Tariot, Auber, Berton, Baillot, Batton, Carafa, Leborne, Halévy, Boieldieu, Vaucorbeil and Zimmermann, to more than one of whom he imparted his own nobility of style. [9] Of these, Batton, in 1817, carried off the 'grand prix' for composition, given by the Institute. Halévy, composer of 'La Juive,' for 5 years Cherubini's pupil, took it in 1819, and Leborne

---

[8] *N.M.Z., M.W.*, 1862.

[9] Fétis denies that Boieldieu was ever Cherubini's pupil, but Halévy writes: 'Boieldieu went and placed himself under Cherubini's direction, . . . and asked him the secret of rendering the musical idea more copious, the thought more complete, the form more living and salient. The disciple, worthy of the master, returned strengthened and animated with a more powerful inspiration; the beautiful works which he has written since are a testimony to that.' *Notice sur A. Adam*, 15.

in 1820. Cherubini made his pupils do what he had himself done under Sarti—copy out, at times, works by other composers; for he said, although such works might be mediocre, yet they served this purpose, 'to learn from them how not to go wrong.' The effects of his teaching will be considered later on.

Cherubini being now a Government official, we can see how he came to write Republican hymns: 4 of them in 1795-6, after his appointment as one of the inspectors of the Conservatoire ; while as early as June 1794, Cherubini was called to fulfil official functions as professor at the 'Ecole de Musique de la Garde Nationale.' This was the time for patriotic songs, and Cherubini, forced by straitened circumstances to accept more than one civic post, could hardly avoid writing something for the Mountain. Clément deems these compositions the more excusable in a foreigner, in that he had no special tie binding him to the French monarchy; [10] but when, according to the 'Moniteur' of 26 Jan. 1796, he, 'the ancient "protégé" of Marie Antoinette,' is found presiding at a musical party to celebrate the anniversary of the death of Louis XVI., and directing the execution of a chorus, wherein may be heard the 'oath of hatred to royalty,' De Loménie deems such proceeding less defensible.

Cherubini writes: 'These pieces, of each of which I have not the exact date, were composed at different periods of the revolution, counting from this year (1795) up to the year 1798.' Clément, who tells us more about them, states that the year 1793 saw the 1st hymn. At least, I suppose he is right herein. He omits, however, the 'Hymn to the Pantheon,' which Cherubini 1st mentions. The Ode for the anniversary of 10 Aug. 1792, written by Lebrun of the Institute, made some stir. 'The expression of the most violent passions in the text contrasts with the harmonious charm of this composition. The accompaniment is formed by clarinets, horns, and bassoons, that play during the burden of the song an interesting march.' [11]

[10] Denne-Baron.   [11] Clément.

This, in 1795, was preceded by the 'Hymn to Fraternity,' to words by Désorgues, sung in the gardens of the Tuileries 22 Sept. 1793; the 'Salpêtre Républicain,' sung Jan. 1794, at the fête for the opening of works for extracting saltpetre; the 'Ode on the 18th Fructidor,' the day of the Conspiracy of poignards, 4 Sept. 1797. The 'Hymn and Funeral March (or "Pompe funèbre") for the Death of General Hoche,' was sung in the Champ de Mars 1 Oct. 1797, at the state funeral, in honour of that distinguished soldier, whose sudden death so distressed the nation, and Rochette thought the music 'a strikingly expressive piece, containing beauties of the highest order.'

> 'Du haut de la voûte éternelle,
> Jeune héros, reçois nos pleurs !

The words by M. J. Chénier, given in full by Pougin, are in 4 stanzas of 8 lines each; the action being 'a sort of pantomime, a nullity as regards dramatic merit.'[12] 'This composition, which the key of G minor renders so mournful, has every beauty.'[13] It was subsequently represented at the Grand Opera and the Feydeau as a 1-act piece, under the title of 'Pompe Funèbre,' with additional instrumentation, 11 Oct. 1797, but did not draw as a stage piece, though the music had made 'a prodigious impression on the people of Paris.'[14] The 'Hymn for the Fête de la Jeunesse,' to words by Parny, 30 March 1798, was followed by the 'Hymn for the Fête de la Reconnaissance,' to words by Mahérault, 29 May 1798; the accompaniment of the latter being treated in 'the most melodious manner.'[15]

Rouget de Lisle's 'Chant de l'Armée du Rhin' (the 'Marseillaise'), Méhul's 'Le Chant du Départ,' 'Le Chant de Victoire,' and 'Le Chant de Retour; Gossec's 'La Ronde du Camp,' the 'Hymn to Reason,' the 'Hymn for

[12] *Verités à l'ordre du jour* (an vii), 133, *cit.* Pougin, *M. W.* 1882, 661.
[13] Clément.
[14] Raoul Rochette, 46-7.
[15] Clément.

the Festival of the Supreme Being ;' and Gaveaux's 'Le Reveil du Peuple,' are like works of the period.[16]

The Institute was founded 25 Oct. 1795, and the 3 places assigned to musicians were bestowed on Gossec, Grétry, and Méhul. Cherubini, as an Italian, could hardly be placed before 3 famous French composers, and, indeed, generously supported Monsigny's nomination in preference to his own on the death of Grétry in 1813. In 1816, Louis XVIII. increased to 6 the number of places reserved for musicians.

'Lodoïska' had been somewhat gay. After a 3 years' interval appeared 'Elisa,' a work of a graver cast, to be followed by 'Médée,' the severest of all Cherubini's secular works, and where, among his operas, he is most in earnest. The 1st representation took place at the Feydeau, 13 Mar. 1797. Boieldieu's 'La Famille Suisse' running for 20 nights along with it alternately. By the contemporary accounts, it was well staged, well played, and well received. At the fall of the curtain, Gaveaux (Jason) recited some verses in Cherubini's honour. Mme. Scio as Medea 'was not only a great singer,' but she gave her 'verse often well turned and finely sonorous' like 'a skilful tragic actress.' 'She was truly admirable in the part, which set the seal upon her reputation, and all Paris flocked to the Feydeau to see her in a work wherein she was in turn touching and impassioned, harrowing and arrogant, wild and timid to a degree that baffles description.'[17]

The fiery and pathetic overture in F minor is deemed by Prout Cherubini's finest, though I should be disposed to put it 2nd, 'Les Deux Journées' 1st, and 'Anacréon' 3rd. The 'Médée' overture is indeed, perfect, fore-

---

[16] It has been strangely asserted that 'although the change produced in men's ideas by the revolution exerted a deep influence on [Cherubini's] style, it is a characteristic fact that the patriotic enthusiasm, which at that period seized even upon musicians, and impelled them to compose revolutionary songs, etc., did not affect Cherubini. He wrote nothing of the kind,'—but he wrote these Hymns, the early editions of which are among the chief rarities in Cherubini literature.—*M.W.*, 1862.

[17] Pougin, *M.W.* 1882, 621.

shadowing the whole sad story in a pathetic manner.
Mark the breadth, the 'momentum' of the opening, the

rolling, as it were, of the tide of human passion.   Contrast
with this the 2nd subject, so simple, yet so full of feeling,

with its pendant, where the emotion seems to swell with

the intensity of grief, and then that sorrowful passage,
the violoncellos opening with the 2nd subject, and the
violins following with a haunting melody, until the silence

of settled despair has come, broken only by the sobs of
the instruments.

Herr Greiner told Schindler that 'at an eating house
near the Josephstadt, Vienna, there was a clock that played
overtures and airs from good operas, and Beethoven
(possessor of the full score) was wont to place himself
quite close to it, that he might hear his favourite piece,
the overture to "Médée."'[18] Grove remarks, and I
gladly record this generous appreciation by a true lover
of the best in music: 'Though a most effective composition, and as an orchestral piece of music full of beauties, it

---

[18] Schindler Pougin, *M. W.,* 1883, 57. What has become of this musical
box? It played, also, a *Fidelio* trio.

appears to the writer to belong more to the region of pure music—of the overtures to the " Zauberflöte " and " Cosi fan Tutti "—than to those more romantic and picturesque compositions of which Beethoven gave the world the earliest examples in his " Coriolan " and " Leonora," and which Mendelssohn continued in the " Hebrides " and " Melusina," and other grand and delightful compositions of this class. With all its power and skill, Cherubini's mind was too conservative and classical to permit of his entering on this path in the orchestra. But his overtures are so pure, so free from everything petty and common-place, and so abounding in beauty, that while listening to them one may well be pardoned for forgetting that any school of music ever existed but that of which they form so bright and enduring an ornament.[19] The contemporary critic found the 1st act ' too long,' with ' a great deal of mere spectacle.' The 2nd act ' more dramatic and close.' The 3rd ' full of action.' Lastly, ' the music is broad, expressive, majestic and terrible.' The choruses were perfectly given ; the costumes were rich and correct.[20]

Two admirable criticisms by H. F. Chorley and E. Prout have appeared in English, the 1st written on occasion of a performance under Herr Guhr, to please Mendelssohn, Aug. 1844, at Frankfort, and I refer all lovers of Cherubini to both for interesting views and details.[21]

No. 1.—' Médée ' opens with a chorus, ' Tendre hymen,' exquisitely scored, for Dirce's attendants, with this

[19] *cit.* Macfarren also praises highly *Les Deux Journées,* but elsewhere writes : ' Notwithstanding the great merit of his overtures, this appears to have been the result of momentary inspiration rather than of mastery in that style of writing ; for he was manifestly deficient in the principles of construction, and instrumental music was therefore a department in which he was unqualified for success.'—*Imp. Biog.,* i., art. Cherubini, 1013. Such an opinion is a curiosity now. If anyone ever had a perfect mastery here, it was Cherubini, though I do not say that *L'Hôtellerie Portugaise* (which supports Macfarren in appearance) shows this. The New York Philharmonic Society's 1856-7 season gave the overture to *Médée,* and there are good notices of most of the others in the Crystal Palace Concert programmes signed G (Grove), cited above.

[20] *Le Journal d'Indications, cit.* Pougin. *M.W.* 1882, 611.

[21] *Modern German Music,* ii., 222, *et seq. M.T.* Feb., Mar., Ap. 1905.

delightful figure retained throughout, and I well recall
its exceeding beauty as heard in 1870 at Covent Garden,
followed by an air for Jason's bride herself, 'Je cede à ta

voix consolante,' brilliantly accompanied.   No. 2.—
Créon (Dessaules), the priest, Jason, and the chorus are
introduced in a stately march.   No. 3.—Jason's air to

Dirce, 'Eloigné pour jamais d'une éspouse cruelle,' is elaborately conceived, but 'weak.'   'What composer,' Chorley
asks, 'has been able to make the false lover in opera
interesting?' but adds: 'There are few things . . . finer
in music of any age' than the recitative 'solo,' and prin-
cipals and chorus, wherein Créon invokes a nuptial
blessing.   No. 4—Medea is here threatened by Créon,
Dirce, and the chorus in support.   No. 5.—When they

are gone, she appeals to Jason in this pathetic 'larghetto,'
'Vous voyez de vos fils la mére infortunée,' and its
abrupt cry, 'ingrat.' The act closes with their grand
duet, No. 6, 'Perfides ennemis,' 'one of the most
highly wrought and thoroughly sustained explosions of
passion existing in opera, . . . yet, where relief is needed,
subsiding into large continuous phrases. . . . The

O Fa - ta - le toi - son,

orchestra is treated with a fire, an amplitude, an ever
increasing animation and interest, the remembrance of
which arrests the breath. . . . The close of this 1st act
of " Medea " is one of the marvels of music ; almost in
opera what one of Lear's great scenes is in tragedy ! ' [22]
    No. 7.—'The opening bars of the magnificent intro-
duction to the 2nd act show how much contrast and
colour can be obtained by the simplest means. The score
looks almost like a row of empty staves, and yet how
masterly the effect of a very few notes.' [23] This leads to
No. 8, an 'Ensemble' with Créon, Medea, and Neris, her
attendant, with here, as elsewhere, the chorus in support
and contrast. No. 9.—An air for Neris, 'Ah, nos peines
seront communes,' wonderfully accompanied, as usual,
follows, and No. 10, yet another wild duet between Jason
and Medea, wherein our critic notes ' one of the earliest
and finest specimens of the "tremolando"—that expedient
since so vulgarized by misuse, here called into play to
picture the fever of wretchedness, suspense, dismay in the
deserted Medea, and of cowardly shrinking in her false
lover.' [24] No. 11.—A religious march, ' worthy of all
honour and study,' preludes the bridal scene.

[22] Chorley.
[23] Prout's *Orch.*, ii., 10.
[24] Chorley.

The unisonal choral hymn, 'Fils de Bacchus,' with the instruments 'in antiphony, contrast, and lastly, in support of it,' suggests to our excellent critic that 'all that is known and conjectured of the Greek modes was obviously familiar to Cherubini,' but, compared, with

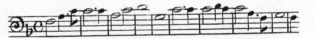

Gluck in the Greek religious marches, the 'sentiment of beauty is far stronger and sweeter' in the latter, not to say cloying?—which Cherubini could not be. 'Cherubini is comparatively antique, remote, in some measure cold,'[25] —possibly, but anyhow virile. The great storm prelude, No. 12, beginning the 3rd act, follows this bridal scene. Medea, with spoken ejaculation to 'sinister' accompaniment, 'reminds us that there is present at the banquet a

un poco piu moto.

[25] 'Greek art seems to be seated in the study-rooms of Méhul and Cherubini, as well as in the studios of David.'—Halévy's *Derniers Souvenirs.*

Fury, who has come thither unbidden.' Now, she is everywhere dealing destruction around her in two 'scenas,' Nos.
13 and 14, an 'aria,' and a finale, 'Eh quoi! je suis Médée,'
'on the grandest scale.' . . . 'The orchestration,'—[the
opera closing with 56 bars of symphony,]—Chorley deems
'has a "verve," a variety, and a might which, at the period
when Gluck wrote, were undiscovered. There is nothing in
Beethoven's "Fidelio" worthier of close study and fervent
admiration. 100 years hence it will remain to be as
new as the organ-music of Bach, as the choral fugues of
Handel, as the melodies of Mozart are now.'

A fault, in his view, is a strain on the physical endur-
ance in the title 'rôle.' Denne-Baron observes that
Cherubini's melodies 'were always perfectly suited to the
subject, and written within the compass of the human
voice.' Yes, often suited to the subject-matter, but not to
the voice, as being too much in the heights of that compass. With regard to 'Médée,' it was not any want of
knowledge to write vocally, but a too sudden revulsion to
Cherubini's 2nd manner in a tragic subject, treated in a
troubled period. The libretto by François Bénoit Hoffmann is not concise, although Prout thought it 'well-laid
out' for treatment, and 'the verses are at least respectable.'
A more serious complaint by Maczewski, Pougin and
Chorley,[26] is majestic monotony, as I should term it,
perhaps inseparable from the subject, relieved, it is true, by
the chorus, as in Greek tragedy, which also might be, in all
probability, monotonous to modern audiences. When all
is said, we know that no work of Cherubini so 'powerfully'
impressed Prout; that Auber called it 'la musique bien
faite;' and that it was a favourite with Schubert. Moscheles
wrote shortly before his own death: 'It was a great undertaking, but I have at last realized my desire to hear
Cherubini's "Medea" with Franz Lachner's Recitatives;
but the intense interest with which I followed every note
was too much for me.'[27]

[26] *Grove,* i., 345, *M. W.,* 1882, 621.
[27] *Life of Moscheles,* ii., conclusion, tr. A. D. Coleridge.

'Médeé,' with translated text by Herklotz, was performed 17 April 1800, at Berlin, with Mme. Schick as
Medea; in 1809 at Vienna, with 500 bars left out by
Cherubini himself.[28] In 1814, Mme. Milder-Hauptmann
undertook the part in Vienna. It was a great part, Chorley
notes, both with her and with Mme. Stöckl Heinefetter;
Mme. Cruvelli, and Mme. Schröder-Devrient were suited
for it. Mme. Materna and Frau Marianne Brandt
might have done it justice.[29] It was given in Italian
6 June 1865, at Her Majesty's, Haymarket, London, with
recitatives by Arditi, Mlle. Tietjens as Medea, and Sir C.
Santley as Créon; and her appearance therein, I can
recall personally, 3 Dec. 1870, at Covent Garden.
'Médée' was again announced in the bills for 1876, but
the great 'prima donna' died shortly afterwards. She
was in some respects admirable as Medea, but 'otherwise,'
as I noted at the time, 'the performance was not
satisfactory.'

A journal called the 'Censeur' made the following
remark on the opera: 'Cherubini's music is often melodius, and sometimes manly, but you find reminiscences
and imitations of Méhul's manner.' This was too much
for Méhul, who replied: ' O censor! you do not know this
great artist. But I, who know him, and who admire him
because I know him well,—I say, and can prove to all
Europe that the inimitable author of " Démophon," of
" Lodoïska," of " Elisa," and " Medea," has never had
need of imitating in order to be by turns elegant or full of
feeling, graceful or tragic—to be, in a word, the Cherubini
whom some persons would accuse of being an imitator,
but whom, unfortunately, they do not fail to imitate themselves on every possible occasion. [This is excellent.] This
artist, justly celebrated, can find one " Censor " to attack
him ; he will have, however, for defenders, all who admire

---

[28] The curtailments and variations are seen in Peters' edition, and
include 46 bars omitted from the 1st duet, 44 from the 2nd duet between
Jason and Medea, and 65 from Neris' air.
[29] Prout.

him, that is to say, all those who are made for feeling and appreciating grand talent.' When in 1810 some persons spread a report about Méhul being jealous of Cherubini, Méhul wrote a public letter, stating that he deemed Cherubini the greatest composer in Europe.

Cherubini thus dedicated 'Médée' to Méhul : 'Receive, my friend, from the hands of Friendship the homage she delights in paying to a distinguished artist. Your name, placed at the head of this work, will lend it a merit it did not possess, namely, that of appearing worthy of being dedicated to you, and this will serve it as a support; may the union of our 2 names everywhere attest the tender sentiments that bind us to each other, and the respect I entertain for real talent.—Cherubini.' Méhul, in return, inscribed his ' Uthal ' to Cherubini.

Hérold wrote to a friend in Paris in 1813: 'I have read in the papers the sorry success of the new [" Médée et Jason " by Fontenelle] whom I deem very audacious to come and show herself, when she knows she has an elder sister the very remembrance of whom is sufficient utterly to confound her.' [30]

After the fatigue of bringing out ' Médée,' Cherubini again went to his friend Louis at Chartreuse de Gaillon.

[30] Pougin, *M. W.* 1882, 621, who notes that a parody on the great work called *La Sorcière* appeared 27 March 1797 at the Théâtre de la Cité Variétés, written by Sewrin.

CHAPTER IV.

FRANCE.

1797—1800.

'Point not these mysteries to an Art
Lodg'd above the starry pole ;
Pure modulations flowing from the heart
Of divine Love, where Wisdom, Beauty, Truth
With Order dwell, in endless youth?'

WORDSWORTH.

Cherubini's first relations with Napoleon—*Hymne et Marche Funèbre pour
la Mort du Général Hoche*—*L'Hôtellerie Portugaise*—*La Punition*—*La
Prisonnière*, by Boieldieu and Cherubini—*Les Deux Journées,* otherwise
the *Water Carrier,* otherwise the *Escapes,* by Attwood.

BEFORE Napoleon had become 1st Consul, he had been
on familiar terms with Cherubini. One evening, when an
opera of the latter's was being performed, and the two
were present in the same box, Napoleon said : ' My dear
Cherubini, you are certainly an excellent musician ; but
really your music is so noisy and complicated, that I can
make nothing of it ; ' and Cherubini replied : ' My dear
general, you are certainly an excellent soldier ; but, in
regard to music, you must excuse me if I don't think it
necessary to adapt my compositions to your comprehen-
sion.' This is said to have been the beginning of their
estrangement.[1]

In 1797, Napoleon returned from Italy and directed
the musical taste of the capital by his admiration of the

[1] Some biographers state that if Napoleon wanted Cherubini, he had
always to go in search of him, the composer showing his indifference to the
conqueror by never taking the initiative and seeking out Napoleon. This
seems a rather ridiculous complaint ; Cherubini knew that Napoleon did not
like his music, save ' Pimmalione,' and outside his art was unable to help
the latter. The greater man sends for the lesser, and the lesser finds out
the greater, *if either wants the other,* but not otherwise.

Italian composers. He had brought with him from Italy a
march of Paisiello, composed expressly for him, and wished
it to be performed. He accordingly sent it to the Conservatoire. Sarrette, the director, thought this occasion a
good opportunity for letting Napoleon hear something
really 1st-rate as well as Paisiello's poor march; and also
for showing him what the newly-founded Conservatoire
could do in the way of a performance, and the progress
made by the students. Accordingly, Cherubini's Hymn
and Funeral March for the death of General Hoche, previously written on commission and performed at the Grand
Opera and the Feydeau, were settled upon for performance 28 Dec. before the Conservatoire, Napoleon, and
his Ministers. Every one about Napoleon highly praised the
work. But, whether vexed at a performance that did not, it
is said, go off well, or at another hero being praised, or at
the originality of music having so little in common with
his beloved Paisiello, Napoleon came up to Cherubini after
the concert, and without saying a word about his work,
launched forth into exaggerated praises of his favourite,
whom he styled the best composer of the age; and to
deprive Cherubini of the honour of a 2nd place among
living composers, he asserted that, after Paisiello, Zingarelli
was the only one who knew how to compose beautiful
music, whereupon Cherubini replied disdainfully, 'Be it so,
as to Paisiello, but Zingarelli!'[2] This, said in a low tone,
somewhat startled Napoleon, and it seems likely that he
did not forget Cherubini's reply.

On the eve of Napoleon's departure for Egypt in the
beginning of the summer of 1798, happening to be with

[2] I have followed Raoul Rochette and all the best accounts, including
Pougin, in the above. Picchanti says Cherubini did not reply to Napoleon
at all, but on this point nearly all the biographers are against him. Fétis
agrees with the account in the text in one place (*Biog. Univ.* ii. 266), but in
another (vi. 464) along with de Lafage (Michaud's *Biog. Univ.* i. 97), states
that the General put to competition a march for Hoche; but this is most
unlikely. Elwart says that Napoleon heard at the Conservatoire laudatory
pieces on himself, by Lesueur, Méhul, and Cherubini, and that when the
General made critical remarks on the latter's work, Cherubini replied :
'General, you only consult your genius when you make a plan of battle.'
Cherubini, however, mentions composing no march in honour of Napoleon.

Cherubini, he began bestowing high praises on the Italian composers, adding some strange remarks on Cherubini's own works, whereupon the latter is said to have replied : ' Citizen-general, occupy yourself with battles and victories, and allow me to treat according to my own talent an art of which you know nothing.'   Napoleon was at that time only a military chief, and turned away. A year and a half later, when he had become 1st Consul, such words might have been dangerous ; yet Cherubini, as we shall see, had collisions with Napoleon even when the Republic and Equality had passed away.

Cherubini produced the 1-act opera, ' L'Hôtellerie Portugaise,' with a libretto by St. Aignan, at the Feydeau. This little work was afterwards remembered for a trio, ' Que faire ô ciel,' and the light overture in F, the only important part of which is the mysterious introduction. After a few grand chords, reminding us of some ecclesiastical chant, in no way connecting with the rest of the work, the subject enters softly, at 1st given out in a low

register by the 1st violins : the other instruments, in imitation, following. It must be this portion to which de Lafage alludes when he speaks of the counterpoint founded upon ' Les Folies d'Espagne,' whatever that work may be. ' It is impossible to imagine,' he writes, ' anything where the artifices of science have been employed with more taste, grace, and felicity.' The ' allegro,' on the other hand, is composed of a number of themes, the effect of which is a certain patchiness seen oftener in ' Semiramide ' and like work, than in Cherubini. The chief characters were

Rodrigo, Rosello, Gabriela, and Ines. 'The opera performed yesterday achieved half a success. . . . The music was very good,' and there was a 'call for Citizen Cherubini, but he did not respond to it.'[3] No one liked the very poor libretto, and in 1803 it was performed in Vienna with as little applause as, later on, in Berlin.[4] The words were unworthy of the music.

Cherubini brought out, 23 Feb. 1799, another 1-act opera, 'La Punition,' with a libretto by Desfaucherets, at the Feydeau, the public applauding the music and hissing the book, which 'had to be cut down and remodelled;'[5] and 12 Sept. 1799, in conjunction with Boieldieu, 'Emma, or La Prisonnière' at the Montansier. This 1-act comedy in prose by Jouy, Longchamps, and St. Just, with 'ariettas' interspersed, according to a contemporary account, 'still draws large numbers, . . . not that it is very good, but it contains some comic situations, and some touches of wit by the authors of the pretty Vaudeville "Comment Faire?" The public hear music by Cherubini and Boieldieu, and see Brunet, the inimitable Brunet.'[6]

Cherubini's 'Les Deux Journées,' or the 'Water-Carrier,' was represented for the 1st time, 16 Jan. 1800 (26 Nivose an viii) at the Feydeau, with the following cast :—

Count Armand, President of the Parliament in Paris, pursued by the emissaries of Cardinal Mazarin	Citizen Gaveaux.
Constance, wife of Armand	Mme. Scio.
Mikeli, a Savoyard water-carrier in Paris, who befriends the Count	Citizen Juliet.
Daniel, his aged father	Citizen Platel.
Antonio, son of Mikeli	Citizen Jausserand.
Marcellina, daughter of Mikeli	Mlle. Rosette.
Sémos, Farmer at Gonesse	Citizen Prévost.
Angelina, his only daughter, affianced to Antonio .	Mlle. Desmares.

[3] *Courrier des Spectacles, cit.* Pougin, M.W., 1882, 661. I once heard the overture at the Crystal Palace Concerts under Mr Manns, who produced there *Lodoïska, Médée, Les Deux Journées, Faniska, Les Abencérages, Ali Baba* and the 1815 overtures.

[4] *L. Cherubini,* Fritzsch.

[5] Pougin. *M.W.,* 1882, 677.

[6] *ib. M.W., ib.* Picchianti errs in saying that Boieldieu and Cherubini worked together in *La Punition.*

First Commandant,	Italians in	.	.	Citizen Dessaules.
Second Commandant,	Mazarin's pay	.	.	.	Citizen Georget.
First Italian Soldier .	.	.	.	.	Citizen Darcourt.
Second Italian Soldier	.	.	.	.	Citizien Garnier.

An Officer of the Guard, a Sentinel, Guards and Soldiers,
Inhabitants of Gonesse.

Scene of Action, Acts 1 and 2, Paris; Act 3, Gonesse. Time, 1647.
Librettist, J. N. Bouilly.

The musical profession were well represented, and as at 'Lodoïska,' the audience rose and applauded every number. When the sublime transition on the words of thanksgiving to God, ' O celeste Providence,' in the finale

of the 1st act, rang through the theatre, enthusiasm knew no bounds. At the fall of the curtain, Cherubini was forced on to the stage, and the Conservatoire students, scaling the foot-lights, congratulated their master. Grétry, Martini, D'Alayrac, Gossec, Lesueur and Méhul followed in more leisurely fashion : and 200 representations did not satiate the enthusiasm of the Parisians. In Germany, and especially at Berlin and Frankfort, it was hailed with acclamation, and Beethoven eagerly studied it. His scanty library, at his death, was found to contain the score, while its 'terzetto' is in one of his fragmentary MS. sketch-books formerly in Herr Joachim's possession.[7] Riehl calls it 'emotion dramatized;' Schumann, whose 3rd symphony is thought to show the influence of Cherubini, somewhere styles it ' a masterly and intellectual work.' The melody is charming, yet united with the highest contrapuntal science, while the richness of the instrumentation may be compared to the colouring of a Paul Veronese. ' One of the best of the class of semi-serious opera ever written.

[7] *Grove*, i. 184-5. *Macmillan*, July 1875.

The subject is interesting, the treatment good, and the music incomparable.'[8] Some of Cherubini's friends wished the author to dedicate the score to Haydn, but he replied; 'No, as yet I have written nothing worthy of such a master.' The work was inscribed to Gossec and printed, we are told, ' at the express desire of Cherubini's friends.' Hiller and Hauptmann have waxed eloquent over the overture, and how it has affected them. The opening would have suited ' Médée,' better than the ' Water-carrier,' for 'I know no more striking effect of powerful imagination,' writes Ella, ' suggestive of the darkest imagery of tragic incidents than the whole of the introduction. After the opening— slow, lovely cadences of serene, placid harmony—["worth more," according to Mendelssohn, than all the 1834 Berlin repertory], come the double basses [and violon-cellos] in a grand figure of a vague character, reposing

on a deep pedal note. How touching are the bewailing

short melodic phrases, so tenderly expressed, with the penetrating cord of the augmented 5th in its simple

* *L. Cherubini*, Fritzsch.

structure! The mysterious "tremolo" of the violins, the
wailing effect of the flutes, the tragic responses of the
basses, and the terrific utterance of the horns on the 5th

of the dominant, until the grand climax of the "allegro"
are in the highest degree suggestive, and have served

Weber and Mendelssohn to good purpose.' Nor should
we pass over the thrice given affecting subject before the

'tremolando' begins. 'The rest of the overture, of a
highly imaginative description, symmetrical, varied in
effects, with subjects in bold contrast, is not easy, and
demands a vigorous execution. . . .'[9] Hiller adds: 'It has

---

[9] J. Ella's lecture on *Les Deux Journées* at the London Institution, and
Musical Sketches Abroad and at Home, 3rd ed. 20. The New York Philharmonic Society gave the overture twice in its season for 1866-7.

since been imitated and exaggerated 1000 times, but like
every truly grand and original work, is still full of freshness
and vigour.'[10]

The water-carriers of Paris were so pleased with his
touching representation of their calling in 'Les Deux
Journées,' that 12 of them called on Bouilly the morning
after the 1st performance and offered to supply his house
with water, free, for a year. While declining this offer,
he accepted some flowers, and drank their health, and
they his, with his best wine. The tale is, briefly, this. As
to the registration of certain edicts, Count Armand opposes
Cardinal Mazarin, who puts a price upon his head. His
various escapes, and especially Mikeli the Water-carrier's
good offices, form the staple of the plot. The varied incidents and the picture of a wife's devotion form good
material for illustration, although, from a literary point of
view, Bouilly is below the average.

'The libretto was suggested by the generous action of
a water-carrier towards a magistrate related to the author.
The spirit of this dramatic conception perfectly suited the
feeling and the tendencies of the public at that time, since,
after witnessing so many acts of cruelty, they felt the need
for returning to the pleasures of kindness and sensibility of
heart. . . . The old systems of the time, wherein the
dramas used to be composed almost exclusively of airs, were
beginning to be destroyed, whilst in this opera, save a duet
and a canzonet, the whole was composed of concerted
pieces and choruses, in a new style, full of vigour and charm.
. . . It need not fear comparison with the compositions
of the present day, when errors and negligence often re-

[10] 'F.W.H.' writes in the *Quarterly Musical Magazine*: 'There are
some uncommon modulations, brought about with simplicity, from A minor
to G with one sharp ; at the 26th bar of this movement from B to D (by the
7th upon A) ; and towards the end, where the 8-ve passage occurs, beginning upon B.'

G. A. Macfarren also observes that the overture alone, ' by the power
of its ideas, their admirable development, the peculiarity of its form, and the
vigour of its orchestration, gives Cherubini a foremost rank among musicians
in the estimation of all who set the highest value on the greatest order of
artistic productions.'—*Imp. Dict. Biog.*, i. 1012.

main concealed under the noise of an orchestra that deafens
the audience.   The magnificent "finale" of the 1st act
. . . possesses a truth of dramatic expression, and an en-
trancing variety of an appropriate colour impossible to
surpass.'[11]   The 2nd act's introduction, descriptive of the
awakening of Paris to a new day, is, on a very small scale,
forerunner to programme music like Elgar's 'Cockaigne,'
and is succeeded by a splendid soldier's chorus, 'Point de
pitié,' with 'rhythmical movements of the instruments, so
happily suited to the situation in the drama, as for instance
when the 2 officers [refer to] . . . Mazarin; [a contrast
to the chorus]—a kind of plain chant [thus closing]

 worked out in the form
of a march, and sup-
ported by chords of a
religious character, that
seem to recall the grave
functions of the Car-
dinal minister himself. . . .   Lastly, the chorus united
with the brilliant march presents, on account of the originality of the invention, the conduct, and exquisite taste of
the harmony, a true musical beauty.'[12]   The pastoral opening and chorus, 'Jeunes filles et bergerettes,' in the 3rd
act, afford a beautiful contrast to the foregoing.

Spohr writes : 'I recollect when the "Deux Journées"

---

[11] Picchianti.
[12] Picchianti : In 1808 Reicha, returning from Vienna, had performed
at the Conservatoire a fugal treatment of this march, which he dedicated to
Cherubini.   'He developed in this work,' says Miel, in his *Annals of the
Institute,* 'not only all the science which was characteristic of him, but also
a charm which it was not usual to find in the fugal style.'

was performed for the 1st time, how, intoxicated with
delight, and the powerful impression that the work had
made on me, I asked on that very evening to have the
score given to me, and sat over it the whole night, and
that it was that opera chiefly that gave me the 1st impulse
to composition.' Now hear Weber, to a friend, from
Munich, 30 June 1812 : 'Fancy my delight when I beheld
lying upon the table of the hotel the playbill with the
magic name " Armand." I was the first person in the
theatre, and planted myself in the middle of the pit, where
I waited most anxiously for the tones which I knew beforehand would again elevate and inspire me. I think I may
boldly assert that " Les Deux Journées " is a really dramatic and classical work. Everything is calculated so as
to produce the greatest effect ; all the various pieces are so
much in their proper place, that you can neither omit one
nor make any addition to them. The opera displays a
pleasing richness of melody, vigorous declamation, and all-
striking truth in the treatment of the situations, ever new,
ever heard and retained with pleasure. Trumpets have
been introduced in the overture, and I think they might
produce a good effect in the " allegro ; " but in the introductory " adagio," the single blasts on the horn alone are
indisputably better in the last all-powerful " crescendo,"
more effective, and more appropriate to lead up to the
grand climax, especially if the trumpets do not come in
before the E major. A part of the duet between Armand
and Constance was excellently given, but the commencement completely spoilt. I was most disagreeably surprised
by an attempt to improve the composition in the finale.
One of the most heavenly passages was, for reasons which
to me are perfectly incomprehensible, deprived of all its
éffect. After the quarrel of the water-carrier with Marcel-
line, whose opposition makes him angry, and when she
bursts into tears, the "fortissimo" ought to be followed by
a clarinet " quite alone," which should play the melody till
1st the bassoon and then the violoncello take it up, while
the brother, consoling and supplicating his sister, begins to

G

sing. This invariably produces the greatest effect. Here
not only did the oboe play it, but an accompaniment had
been added! The very difficult choruses in the 2nd act
went admirably. They were sung and played with precision and fire. Indeed, the 2nd act was more rounded
and spirited than the 1st. In the 3rd act I had again
occasion to regret some beautiful passages which had been
left out, especially the 2 or 3 words pronounced by the
farmer's daughter, "Ah, Antonio does not return;" by
the omission of which the musical passages clash with a
total absence of plan. If I have chattered, my dear friend,
so much about this opera, remember that we can never
say enough of such masterpieces, and so ardent a lover of
art as myself can count upon your indulgence.'[13]

Writing to an 'impresario,' 5 Feb. 1834, Mendelssohn, too, gives a very interesting account of the opera, as
conducted by himself: 'We are now rehearsing the
"Wasserträger," and every note calls to my mind
Edouard Devrient; for it is just as if written expressly for
you. Tell me why you have never sung it. Is it because
he has a son who gets married? In that case, I quote
Rokko. Or is the music out of fashion? Jesting apart,
you should think over the part and adapt it, of course re-
translating it for performance; get up the choruses and
action, and take the credit of having done a good thing.
The 1st 3 bars of the overture are worth more than your
entire répertoire, "Prince Riguet" included in the bargain.
Why, you must remain in the opera, if only for the sake
of having a piece of fun such as this every once and

a while, and of letting others share in it.'[14]   And to his
father, 28 March 1834 : ' The week before the " Wasserträger " was given was most fatiguing ; every day 2 great
rehearsals, often from 9 to 10 hours altogether, besides the
preparations for the church music this week, so that I was
obliged to undertake the regulation of everything—the
acting, the scenery, and the dialogue—or it would all have
gone wrong.   On Friday, therefore, I came to my desk
feeling rather weary ; we had been obliged to have a
complete general rehearsal in the forenoon, and my right
arm was quite stiff.   The audience, too, who had neither
seen nor heard of the "Wasserträger" for the last 15 or 20
years, were under the impression that it was some old forgotten opera, which the committee wished to revive, and
all those on the stage felt very nervous.   This, however,
gave exactly the right tone to the 1st act ; such tremor,
excitement, and emotion prevaded the whole, that at the
2nd piece of music the Dusseldorf opposition kindled into
enthusiasm, and applauded, and shouted, and wept by
turns.   A better Water-carrier than Günther I never saw;
he was most touching and natural, and yet with a shade
of homeliness, too, so that the " noblesse " might not appear too factitious.   He was immensely applauded, and
twice called forward.   This rather spoiled him for the 2nd
performance, when he over-acted his part and was too
confident ; but I wish you could have seen him the 1st
time.   It is long since I have had such a delightful evening
in the theatre, for I took part in the performance like one
of the spectators, and laughed, and applauded, and shouted
" Bravo ! " yet conducting with spirit all the time ; the
choruses in the 2nd act sounded as exact as if fired from
a pistol.   The stage was crowded between the acts, every
one pleased, and congratulating the singers.   The orchestra played with precision, except some plaguey fellows,
who, in spite of all my threats and warnings, could not be
prevailed on to take their eyes off the stage during the

---

[14] Devrient's *Recollections of Mendelssohn*, 171.

performance and to look at their notes. On Sunday it was given again, and did'nt go half so well, but I had my full share of enjoyment the 1st time, though the house on this occasion was far more crowded, and the effect the same. I write you all these details, dear father, as I know you are interested in this opera, and in our provincial doings. We really have as much music, and as good music, as could be expected during my 1st winter here.'[15]

The 'Water-carrier,' with a subject approved by Goethe and Mendelssohn, is brightness personified. ' The words and music,' says Miel, ' are in perfect accord.' ' I cannot,' said Goethe, ' enjoy an opera unless the story is as perfect as the music, so that the 2 may keep pace one with another. If you ask what opera I think good, I would name the " Wasserträger " (Water-carrier), for here the subject is so perfect that if given as a mere drama without music it could be seen with pleasure. Composers either do not understand the importance of a good foundation, or they have not intelligent poets who know how to assist them with good stories.'[16]

The fastidious Mendelssohn, writing to Mr. Planché on the subject of a 'libretto,' remarks: 'As you ask me to name a model, I should say a subject between " Fidelio " and " Les Deux Journées " of Cherubini would suit me most—more like the 1st with regard to the internal plot —to the development of passion ; and like the 2nd in the historical basis—the activity of the choruses and the serene atmosphere which breathes throughout the whole, notwith-standing all the perils and the narrow escapes which occur

[15] Mendelssohn's *Letters,* 1833-47 ; *tr.* Lady Wallace, new ed. 1867, 27.
[16] *Conversations with Eckermann,* 333, Bohn's Library, 1875. Clément is hostile ' The author of the libretto,' he writes, ' has so multiplied the incidents that the interest is divided, and cannot be centred on any one character of the piece. There is neither unity of time, nor of place, nor of action. The beautiful music of the Florentine master could not save such a poem.' For those who think the libretto too simple, the '*Athenæum*' well remarked in 1872 :' The tale is not more simple than that of *Fidelio.* In the two books the persecution and adventures of a married couple form the mainspring of interest ; the escapes of the French count and countess are as exciting as those of Leonora and Florestan—in both the devotion of a wife is vividly exemplified.' See Clément's *Dictionnaire Lyrique.*

in it. In short, could you find me a subject in which some
virtuous heroical deed was celebrated, which represented
the triumph of some noble striving feeling equally known
to every one of the hearers, who knows at all any feeling,
and who could then see his own internal life on the stage,
but more concentrated—in short, translated into poetry;
and if that same story happened in a country, or time, and
a people which could give a lively background to the
whole (be it dark or not), which, in reminding us of history, could in the same time "remind us of our present
time" (as, for instance, the dark figure of Cardinal Mazarin
forms a background in the "Deux Journées;" but it could
be more prominent still), and if every act of the opera had
its own effects, its own poetical point which comes to issue
in the "finale" (as also in "Les Deux Journées," at least
in the 1st and 2nd acts)—if you could find such a subject,
that would be the one I wish for; and if ever I can succeed, I should be sure to do it with such a subject.'[17]

The 'Escapes,' by Attwood, founded on the 'Water-
carrier,' was given, I feel almost sorry to record, 'with the
greatest applause,' at Covent Garden, London, 14 Oct.
1801, as a 'Musical Entertainment,' with Incledon as
Armand; and although not too much of 'Les Deux Journées' appears, I come at last upon the theme of Cherubini's beautiful pastoral chorus, 'Jeunes filles et bergerettes'
in the 3rd act, set to words beginning, 'Flowers around

strewing, hair loosely flowing,' followed by this march, with
words, 'Towards the green I see thee marching,' sung by

[17] J. R. Planché's *Recollections and Reflections*, ii.   M. Jules Barbier
turned Bouilly's mediocre prose into verse, and M. Carvalho 'intends,'
writes Pougin, 'reviving the opera thus completed,' along with the air for
Mme. Todi, 'agreeing admirably therewith.'—*M. W.*, 1882, 692.

Sémos. The 'terzetto,' 'O mon libérateur,' succeeds. Cherubini's music, however, is everywhere altered and mangled. The composer produced his beautiful opera in Vienna before an enthusiastic audience 30 July 1805. Weber also brought it out in Oct. 1813 at Prague, and it was given 12 Nov. 1824 at Covent Garden, London. The admirable performance that took place at Drury Lane in 1872, for the 1st time in England on the Italian stage, contrasts favourably enough with the above. The Italian dialogue, translated by Zaffira, was set to recitative by Sir Michael Costa, who led the performance. In place of the brief finale of the 3rd act, the sublime section ending the 1st, with ' O celeste Providence,' was repeated. It was, I think, an admirable representation, but one that was not repeated.[18] Mme. Tietjens, so admirable as Leonora, had here, in Constance, a like part, on a lesser scale: it was well suited to her fine gift. She pleased one and all. The year 1875-6 also saw admirable performances of the ' Water-carrier,' by the Carl Rosa Opera Company, at the Princess' and Lyceum, London, beginning at the former 27 Oct. 1875, and ending at the latter theatre 2 Dec. 1876. I heard it 6 times with ever-increasing pleasure, and vented amateur enthusiasm by calling it 'a gem of the purest lustre,' which is just what it is. Mme. Torriani was Constance, Sir Charles Santley, Mikeli, and admirable in the part, while in 1886

---

[18] Perhaps it was too much of an 'Opera Comique' for a theatre more suited to Grand Opera. The following was the cast : Armand, Sig Vizzani ; Michael, Sig. Agnesi ; Daniel, Sig. Zoboli ; Antony, Sig. Rinaldini ; Sémos, Mr. A. Howell ; 1st officer, Sig. Foli ; 2nd officer, Sig. Balesca ; Constance, Mdlle. Tietjens ; Marcellina, Mdlle. Marie Roze ; Angelina, Mdlle. Bauermeinster ; a peasant, Mdlle. Rita.

the pupils of the Royal College of Music, led by Sir Villiers Stanford, gave it most creditably at the Savoy, London, before King Edward VII., then Prince of Wales, and every one was delighted, as usual, particularly Sir George Grove, then Principal, as Spohr, Weber and Mendelssohn were before them.

If 'Les Deux Journées' has not since been heard over here, the causes may be sought in the multiplicity of works, new and old, and to the predominance of Wagner, who illustrates in fullest development, with greater dramatic genius, and superior books, principles 1st enunciated by Cherubini. Still, as ' Die Zauberflöte' and ' Der Freischutz ' are at times given, so ' Les Deux Journées ' should be. Great is a libretto's power over an opera's fate, sometimes causing its semi-banishment from the stage, or burying it in oblivion. Bouilly is no ideal librettist,[19] but neither is Schikaneder, and Bouilly's plot has the approval of Goethe.

Many descriptions of ' Les Deux Journées ' have appeared, among others, from Castil-Blaze, Arnold, and Emilio Cianchi ; that of the latter being, according to Gamucci, a well-worked-out analysis, read at the annual public assembly of the ' Corpo Accademico del Regio Instituto musicale ' of Florence, in the hall of the ' Buon Umore,' 17 May 1863, and subsequently printed in the minutes of the Academy. No detailed notice has been attempted here of the best known of Cherubini's operas, but I may note, in conclusion, that the modern edition of the full score, issued by the firm of Peters, of Leipsic, is a sort of testimony to the fact that in Germany such genius as Cherubini's is never likely to be forgotten.

---

[19] Clément singles out for reprobation the lines in the 2nd Act's chorus :

' Meritons la bienveillance
Du célèbre Mazarin ;
Surveillons et servons bien
Son Eminence.'

CHAPTER V.

FRANCE AND GERMANY.

1800—1806.

'Men endowed with highest gifts,
The vision and the faculty divine.'
WORDSWORTH.

Cherubini's and Méhul's *Epicure*—Napoleon again—Varied activities
—Paisiello and Lesueur Consular chapel-masters—*Anacréon*—*Les
Arrets*—Mozart's Requiem—*Achille à Scyros*—Visit to Berlin—Sarti's
family—Arrival in Vienna—With Haydn, Beethoven, Hummel—Introduction to the Emperor Francis II.—*Le Mystère*—Operas produced—
Conducts concerts for Napoleon at Schonbrunn—A commercial speculation—*Fidelio*—*Faniska*—Return to Paris.

WHILE Cherubini was effecting his operatic reforms at the
Feydeau by his 'Lodoïska,' 'Elisa,' 'Médée,' and 'Les
Deux Journées,' he was being ably seconded at the Favart
(whose company, about 1802, joined that of the Feydeau)
by Méhul, who produced there his 'Mélidor,' and elsewhere his 'Euphrosine' and 'Stratonice.' Shortly after the
appearance of 'Les Deux Journées' the two composers
wrote a work together. This was the 3-act opera of
'Epicure,' with words by Dumoustier, given at the Favart
14 March 1800, and reduced to 2 acts at the 3rd performance 20 March. It is now remembered, if at all, for an
exquisitely beautiful duet of Cherubini, 'Ah, mon ami, de
notre asile,' and the overture, which 'came to be considered in Germany as one of Cherubini's classical works,
and was imbued with such extravagance that it is said
to have influenced the characteristics of the style of
Beethoven. . . .'[1] 'Epicure,' with a cold libretto, was

---

[1] Picchianti, 36.

not a success, being performed only thrice, and is said
to have caused a difference between its composers, each
attributing the failure to the other. They were recon-
ciled a little later through the good offices of Plantade.[2]
Pougin gives most interesting contemporary accounts of
'Epicure's' failure. The 1st act was by Cherubini, the
2nd by Méhul, the 3rd by both. Whistlings and pro-
testations were in the air. Altogether, 'extremely stormy,'
was the 'Moniteur Universel's' account. Yet there was
'elegance' in the 'poetry.' Cherubini displayed his
'original and brilliant manner,' Méhul his 'learned touch'
and 'sustained and brilliant style.' And the cause of
the 'fiasco?' Was it the subject? Not entirely. '4 in-
significant personages, opera-like scenes of magic, a
hurried ending, the love of a young girl for old Epicurus,
and the child's confession before the grave Areopagus, put
the spectators in a bad humour, and inclined them to
laughter. . . . The music is not the music for such a
subject; it belongs neither to the "buffo" nor the terrible
style, but makes an infernal noise,' etc.[8] There was no
call for the authors till the 2nd night, when the theatre
was 3-parts empty. Lastly, 'Epicure' was a work rather
for the Grand Opera. The Favart could not stage it
adequately.

On 12 Dec. 1800, a grand performance of the
'Creation' took place in Paris. Napoleon, while on his
way to attend it, was nigh being killed by the explosion of
the Infernal Machine, and a deputation, composed of the
various societies and corporations at Paris, waited afterwards on the 1st Consul to offer him their congratulations
on his escape. Cherubini, as a representative of the Conservatoire, was among the deputation, but kept in the
background, wishing to avoid any unpleasant meeting with

---

[2] De Lafage: In this year, 1800, Cherubini visited Chartres on invitation, and there wrote a march 'for the Préfet of the Eure-et-Loire.' On returning to Paris, he wrote a second march, on occasion of the Préfet's
return, after visiting his department, both founded on his Republican hymns.
[3] *Année Théatrale, Etrennes Lyriques, cit.* Pougin, *M.W.,* 1882, 772.

Napoleon; who, however, ironically exclaimed : ' I do not see Monsieur Chérubin,' pronouncing the name in this French way, in order to indicate, it is said, that Cherubini was not worthy of being deemed an Italian composer. When the composer came forward, neither said one word. Yet crowds were still rushing nightly to hear ' Les Deux Journées.' Shortly after the above incident, Napoleon invited him to a banquet at the Tuileries, given to a number of the distinguished men at Paris. After a frugal repast the company adjourned to the Salon, where the 1st Consul entered into conversation with Cherubini, both of them walking up and down the room. ' Well,' said Napoleon, ' the French are in Italy.' ' Where would they not go,' rejoined Cherubini, ' led by such a hero as you ! ' Napoleon seemed pleased, but talked now in Italian, now in French, which so confused Cherubini that he could scarcely make out what the Consul was saying. At length the latter began on the old topic : ' I tell you,' he said, ' I like Paisiello's music immensely ; it is soft and tranquil. You have much talent, but there is too much accompaniment,' and he instanced the celebrated air of Zingarelli, ' Ombra adorata,' as being the sort of thing he liked. Cherubini quietly rejoined : ' Citizen Consul, I conform myself to French taste ; " päese che vai usanza che trovi ; " says the Italian proverb.' ' Your music,' continued Napoleon, ' makes too much noise ; speak to me in that of Paisiello, that is what lulls me gently,' ' I understand : ' replied Cherubini ; ' you like music which does not stop you from thinking of state affairs.' Napoleon frowned, and the talk ended. [4]

Cherubini now found himself persistently ignored and ill-treated by the 1st Consul, and though producing masterpieces worth a fortune to the musical world, he received no honours as a composer, and hardly any income save his pay as inspector of the Conservatoire, which scarcely sufficed for his maintenance. How significant of nervous

[4] To Napoleon's charge of too many notes, Cherubini gave the 'ever-memorable reply : ' ' Not one too many.' *L. Cherubini*, Fritzsch.

prostration would seem the catalogue at this period! Hardly anything was written during 1801 and 1802 ; and, as a distraction, Cherubini occupied himself with botanical pursuits. His activity, however, in other directions as teacher ; as an unsuccessful concert promoter at the Théâtre Louvois ; as a defender of the Conservatoire against Lesueur's attacks ; as a reviewer of Catel's ' Treatise on harmony ; ' as publisher with Boieldieu of the fortnightly ' Journal d'Apollon ; ' and as a promoter of a commercial scheme to defend authors' rights by starting with Méhul, Boieldieu and others, a publishing house in the present Rue de Richelieu, is all most fully brought out for the 1st time by Pougin, and shows that Cherubini had fairly got over Napoleon's disfavour.[5]

When the Concordat with the Pope had been signed, Napoleon, who loved to return to the old ways of the Monarchy, determined to reëstablish a Consular chapel ; and, at the close of 1802, invited Paisiello, then at Naples, to come to Paris, and be director of the music. Paisiello came, and received 12,000 francs a year, lodging and a carriage.

The number of singers for the chapel was 8, besides 27 instrumentalists under Paisiello. As the old Tuileries chapel had been destroyed, the services took place in the Hall of the Council of State. All this gave umbrage to the Conservatoire. That institution, with its famous teachers, supported French taste, and Napoleon passed them all over for an Italian stranger. They resented a foreigner being preferred. At the same time, as Cherubini stood foremost among them all, they disliked him as well as Paisiello. Cherubini, indeed, might now be considered one of themselves, but, he was an Italian born, and yet thought the 1st representative of the new French music. Paisiello, anyway, pleased none but the 1st Consul. The public, stimulated by beauties of a higher order, listened with indifference to his ' Proserpine,' his Masses, his Psalms, and his

Hymns. Nor did Paisiello like his position : accustomed at Naples to be courted by artistes, and admired by the public, he found Paris a decided change for the worse. After the grand solemnity of the Coronation of the French Emperor, he asked to be released from his engagement with Napoleon, pleading as his excuse the ill-health of his wife. With difficulty he obtained his request, and returned to Naples towards the end of 1804. Napoleon then tried to get Zingarelli, but he refused all offers, wisely preferring his post at the Vatican.[6] Napoleon then told Paisiello to name his successor. He fixed on Lesueur, who accordingly became chapel-master, March 1804. Paër's secular post as ' Composer and Director of the Private Musical Establishment of the Emperor, and singing master to the Empress,' was a later distinct post as ' Court Musician.' Such was the petty contention that made Cherubini seek a distraction in the cultivation of flowers. However, 4 Oct. 1803, his ' Anacréon ou l'Amour fugitif,' a ponderous, original, unequal 2-act opera with a poor libretto by one Mendouze, aided by St. Aignan, was performed at the Grand Opera.[7]

[6] Napoleon offered Méhul the place, who, although the rival, was the friend of Cherubini, and proposed to share the office with the latter. But Napoleon would not hear of it. ' Do not speak to me,' said he, ' about that man. I want a *maëstro* who will make music, not noise.' In asking for his friend, Méhul lost the place himself. ' I can only accept the place on condition that you will allow me to share it with my friend Cherubini,' says Méhul. ' Don't mention him,' says Napoleon ; ' he is a man of snappish disposition, and I have an utter aversion to him.' ' It is certainly his misfortune,' replies Méhul, ' to have failed in securing your good opinion ; but in point of sacred musi,· he is superior to us all ; he is straitened in his circumstances, has a numerous family, and I should feel happy in reconciling you to him.' ' I repeat,' says the Emperor, ' I will not have him.' ' Well, then,' answers Méhul, ' I must positively decline ; nothing can alter my determination. I belong to the Institute ; he does not. I will not allow it to be said that I take advantage of the kindness you show me in order to secure every place for myself, and deprive a celebrated man of what he is so justly entitled to claim at your hands.'—*Musical Standard,* iii. No 416. Castil-Blaze (*Chapelle-Musique des Rois de France,* 170), assures us that Méhul's refusal of the office, because he esteemed himself less worthy of it than Cherubini, is an invention of the biographers.

[7] The caste was as follows : Anacréon, M. Lays ; L'Amour, Mdlle. Hymm ; Corinne, Mme. Branchu ; 1st Slave, Mdlle. Cholet ; 2nd Slave, Mdlle. Pelet ; Vénus, Mme. Jannard ; Bathille, M. Eloy ; Glycère, Mdlle.

'In the overture [in D] to "Anacréon" (certainly one of the finest instrumental pieces that have been written since the days of Haydn[8]) there are perhaps fewer attempts at continual imitation, fewer passages in the fugue style, and fewer laborious or abstruse modulations than may be found in the symphonies and overtures of Cherubini's admired predecessors; but to compensate for the absence of these, there is a novelty of melody, an elegance and brilliancy of effect prevailing . . . which cannot fail to rivet the attention of all who possess the least taste in our art. The 1st horns, by sustaining A and E, then moving to the chord of D, prepare the way for a very singular and effective passage, which is taken up alternately by the flute, violin, and violoncello, between each preparatory sounding of the " corni," until the movement ends with the dominant 7th in full harmony by the whole band. Nothing (to look at the score) can possibly be more simple, and certainly nothing can be more effective; it is the harbinger of good things to the " allegro " movement that follows, commencing on one note only by the bass. At the end of 2 bars there arises a very singular passage, which may be called the subject of the overture, as it is heard throughout until nearly the close, alternating from one instrument to another in a very extraordinary manner. The long continuation of the "piano," and the gradual accumulation of the " crescendo," are strikingly displayed in the 1st 50 bars; and when the climax arrives, by the full burst of the orchestra, no doubt can possibly remain on the mind of the scientific hearer that our author is a man of superior abilities. I would point out to the student a beautiful passage towards the end, marked in Bruguier's adapted duet, " Lentando," as a delightful contrast to the brilliant ones that precede and follow it. The educated musician would discover a great similarity to Mozart's style in this

Lacombe ; Athenaïs (Singing and Dancing Personage), Mme. Gardel; Male Slaves, Troupe Singers, and Instrumental Players, M. and Mme. Vestris, Mmes Taglioni and Coulon, etc.
  [8] Haydn himself survived *Anacréon's* production some 6 years.

part; it is tender, graceful, and in the true "chiar-o-scuro" of harmony, a passage bearing strong indication of the elegant mind of its author.'[9] 'Anacréon' was the 1st opera hissed at the 'Theatre des Arts.' The libretto was tiresome, though merriment was caused by some scenes, especially where Anacréon, asking his favourite attendant whether she will take anything to drink, addressed her as 'Esclave intéressante.' We are told by Castil-Blaze that the shouts of laughter stopped the actors for 5 minutes from proceeding. Lays, crowned with ivy, vine-branches, and flowers, was delighted with his 'rolê' of poet and musician. 'Anacreon' ran for 7 nights, and, out of respect for the composer, a magnificent edition of the work was printed, and eagerly bought up by connoisseurs. Cherubini, in a private letter to Bouilly, attributed the failure 'to the infernal clique embittered against all those who form part of the Conservatoire,' and asked him to avenge his defeat by getting his 'Les Arrêts' ready: in the event neither Hérold nor Cherubini availed themselves of this libretto.[10] 'Anacréon' was not much known in Vienna; the libretto being disliked. The choruses were deemed the best part, but people said that the music was generally heavy, and it was performed but once in the Austrian capital. To the critics Cherubini replied: 'Either I write everything as I choose, or not at all.'[11] Among many scenes of splendour must be noticed Corinne's air, with, according to Pougin, 'its tender melody, graceful character and forms, so often

---

[9] F. W. H., in *Quarterly Musical Magazine*. The *Revue des Deux Mondes*, 1862 (*cit.* M S. i. 59), on occasion of some Société des Concerts performances, thinks the overture scarcely merits, as a symphonic piece, the reputation it has so long enjoyed. The developments of the chief subject are excessive, and the theme itself, not a marked one (peu saillant) recurs too often. The New York Philharmonic Society gave the overture 4 times, 1845-6.

[10] Pougin, *M.W.*, 1882, 813. Miel (12) noting the non-completion of *Les Arrêts*, says: 'A resolution astonishing on the part of a man who left nothing unachieved or unfinished.' He had forgotten *Marguerite d'Anjou*, *Kourkourgi*, *Selico*, the fragments of cantatas in 1796, for inaugurating a statue of Apollo, and in 1811, for the opening of a new concert hall at the Conservatoire.

[11] *L. Cherubini*, Fritzsch.

imitated, and which has enjoyed the triple success of
theatre, drawing-room and school,' beginning 'Jeunes
filles aux regards doux;' the air, 'Je n'ai besoin pour
m'embellir ma vie,' given under Mr. Manns at the Crystal
Palace, Sydenham, 15 March 1873, the only detached air
from an opera of Cherubini that I recall hearing in any
English concert-room; the harmonious 4-tet, 'De nos
cœurs purs'; the brilliant, picturesque trio, 'Dans ma verte
et belle jeunesse;' the Bacchanalian chorus, 'Honneur au
Dieu de la Vendange; the chorus, 'Père d'Orphée;' and
the storm scene at the end of the 1st act, of which Castil-
Blaze says: 'The storm in "Anacréon" has taken rank
among the most renowned storms that have thundered on
our theatres since the "Alcione" of Marais (1706) down
to "William Tell" (1829).' [12]

Unfortunate with 'Anacréon,' Cherubini was, in some
respects, equally unlucky, from the librettist's point of
view, with the ballet of 'Achille à Scyros:' 3-4ths of the
music was his, and it was performed at the Grand Opera
18 Dec. 1804. Here, as with 'Anacréon,' the music was
simply wonderful, especially a symphonic Bacchanalian
scene, imitated in 1817 by Spontini, in a piece inserted in
Salieri's 'Les Danaïdes;' and 'superb in structure;' but
the nature of the subject, with Achilles, according to the
legend, in woman's clothes, was hardly suitable for
representation. Duport might succeed in the 'rôle' of
Achilles, but the best French feeling in the matter is
well expressed by Fétis: 'Achilles is a grand antique
figure, unendurable in a grotesque situation.' The 20th
performance of the work took place 15 Sept. 1807, with
Mdlle. Clotilde as Achilles; and the ballet-music caught
on with the public, and 'Achille' was twice revived, in
1812 and 1819. [13]

In 1805, Cherubini, to calm his mind and dissipate
his cares, undertook a labour of love in getting up a
performance of Mozart's Requiem, which the Parisians

[12] *L'Académie Impériale,* ii. 92-3.
[13] Pougin, *M. W.,* 1882, 813.

had never heard. 'Despite the disinclination of the Parisians for German music,' said German journals of the time, ' and despite the repugnance of Parisian artistes for such a difficult task, Cherubini's zeal and love for this work of Mozart enabled him to get it performed by 200 of the best singers and instrumentalists ; and performed too, in such a manner, that on the very same day he received a request to repeat it.[14] The work, in fact, made a deep sensation ; and it was thus conducted in Paris by the writer of two Requiems, that are not inferior, to say the least, to Mozart's work. Cherubini also brought out some of Haydn's compositions.

It may be imagined that, after his recent failures, Cherubini was not in high spirits. To raise them, however, there came, in 1805, through Baron de Braun, business manager of the opera at Vienna, an invitation to compose 2 operas there ; and, as the terms were liberal, he left Paris 26 June, accompanied by his wife and younger daughter Zénobie, aged 3 months, and arrived at the Austrian capital in the evening of 27 July.

Pougin cites an interesting diary of his 32 days' journey thither ; but then he did not go direct, but by way of Châlons, Verdun, Metz, Mannheim, Frankfort, Cassel, Berlin, Dresden, and Prague. At Berlin he 'experienced, in another way, a great deal of pain mingled with pleasure and very tender reminiscences. My heart was successively touched by these different feelings when I saw Sarti's family and portrait. I did not fail to visit the family every day, loving them dearly, as I do for so many reasons, and during all our interviews my imagination continually retraced my youth, my studies, and the friendship Sarti always entertained for me. But immediately the sweet illusion ceased ; sorrowful reality said to me, "You will see him no more ! " ' This is not the language of a man really deficient in feeling, as Mendelssohn and Hiller surmised.

[14] Gerber's *Lexicon der Tonkünstler,* i. 698. Otto Jahn (*Mozart,* iii. Eng. tr. 393) puts the year at 1804.

Beyond Dresden the journeyings became difficult. ' I do not think there is anything in the world so horrible as the roads from Peterswalde to Arbesau. Those I previously thought bad are nothing in comparison. If I call them roads, it is to make myself understood, and to intimate that we travelled by them, for I should be greatly puzzled had I to give them an appropriate name. Let the reader imagine a line of buildings pulled down 3 leagues and a half, and he will have a notion of the road.' The coach had to be lifted over some portions, and Mme. Cherubini and little Zénobie ' were terribly shaken and awfully frightened. The carriages would certainly have been upset ' but for being held up ' on both sides.' Again, ' It is a pity to have to travel by such abominable roads in so beautiful a country. The hills, of which it is full, offer to the eye now wild and uncultivated landscapes, though always majestic, and now delicious valleys,' and so on.

Cherubini's advent produced in Vienna a considerable sensation. The outpost of classical music in Paris, for 17 years, had come at last to a city in many respects for him a truer home ; and it is naïvely remarked that the chief Parisian musicians were glad to see Cherubini go to Vienna.[15]

He 1st of all visited Haydn, then about 73 years old. Pougin, to whom Pohl, Haydn's biographer, sent divers Viennese details, describes their interview as ' in the highest degree touching and affectionate.' Cherubini asked leave to call him father : Haydn called Cherubini son. The latter deemed he owed to him ' the fine style that did him honour,' and Haydn gave him a MS. symphony in E, with the autograph inscription : ' In nomine Domini, da me Giuseppe Haydn—padre del celebre Cherubini ; ' a gift that delighted Cherubini, who was proud of it all his life.[16]

[15] *L. Cherubini.* Fritzch.
[16] Carpani's *Le Haydine*, 268, Milan 1812, 8vo., *cit.* Pougin, *M. W.* 1883, 57. This MS. was exhibited in 1878 at the Trocadero, at the Historical Exhibition of Ancient Art. The Haydn Verein, founded by Gassman in

Cherubini also entered into a sincere friendship with Beethoven and Hummel. He 1st met Beethoven, then living at Schönbrunn, and hard at work on ' Fidelio,' in Vienna, July 1805, at the table of Sonnleithner, then secretary of the Kärnthnerthor Theatre. Cherubini met here both Vogler and Beethoven, and all extemporized on the piano.[17] Cherubini found Beethoven ' full of consideration and attention.' 'Beethoven,' said Grillparzer, in a conversation, ' was exceedingly respectful and attentive to Cherubini,' and he adds : 'I 1st saw Beethoven when I was a boy . . . . at a musical evening at the house of my uncle, Joseph Sonnleithner. . . . . Among those present besides Beethoven were Cherubini and Vogler . . . . when supper was announced, Abbé Vogler was still at the piano. . . . During his performance, the company gradually withdrew to the supper-room ; Beethoven and Cherubini alone remained. At last the latter went also, and Beethoven was left alone with the indefatigable musician. Finally . . . . Abbé Vogler, left to himself, still went on embellishing his theme . . . .'[18]

As to Hummel, Cherubini was the 1st to introduce some of his music to the Parisians, having the ' Fantasia ' in E flat, op. 18, performed at the Conservatoire, while showing marked kindness to one of Hummel's young pupils.

Cherubini was deeply gratified at the cordial reception accorded him by the Emperor Francis II., the Austrian Court, M. de Metternich, later on Austrian

---

1771, for the widows and orphans of musicians (previous to 1862 called Tonkünstler-Societät) has Cherubini on its subscription list.—*Monthly Musical Record*, 1872, i. 63.   No doubt he became a subscriber during his stay in Vienna. According to Gamucci, Cherubini presented Haydn with the medal, struck at Paris for the latter by the impresario of the Opera Theatre, as a token of admiration for the *Creation ;* but the medal in question was presented 2 or 3 years previously, in 1801 ; and a mistake to the effect that Cherubini had himself given it in person to Haydn in 1801 is refuted by the circumstance that he did not go to Vienna till 1805.

[17] Otto Jahn, and Thayer. *cit.* Pougin, *M.W.*, 1883, 64.   Dr. Frimmel in his *Neue Beethoveniana* writes that Cherubini called Beethoven's playing 'rough.'

[18] Nohl's *Beethoven depicted by his contemporaries,* tr. E. Hill, 221-2.

Ambassador in Paris, the Princes von Esterhazy, Lobko-witz and Kinsky, and the great German artists and publishers, who included Moscheles, Eybler, Weigl, Salieri, Umlauf, Streicher, Gyrowetz, Schupanzig, Czerny, Artaria, Hoffmeister, Ries, Albrechtsberger, the Abbé Gelinek, and the Chevalier von Siegfried. In 1808 Cherubini wrote a romance called ' Le Mystère ' for the above Ambassador, and an intimate correspondence was kept up between Mdlle. Metternich and Cherubini's daughter.

Among the 1st works represented under Cherubini's direction were ' Lodoïska ' 2 May, and ' Les Deux Journées ' 30 July ; 2 fresh entr'actés were written for ' Lodoïska,' as well as a new air, expressly for Mme. Campi, the 'prima donna,' when the opera was given again 27, 28 Aug. 1805, and 26 Jan. 1806.[19]

The Viennese, as might have been anticipated, became enthusiastic over ' Les Deux Journées.' As conductor, Cherubini made some changes in the ' tempi.' He took the allegro of the ' stupendous overture ' slower than usual, whereby ' this difficult piece of music gained in clearness.'[20]   Meanwhile, owing to the victory at Elchingen, and capitulation of Ulm, the war, that had broken out since Cherubini's arrival, resulted in Murat entering the Austrian capital, and in Napoleon taking up his residence at Schönbrunn.   When dictating in Vienna the terms of the treaty of Presburg, Napoleon, hearing of Cherubini's presence in the city, expressed a wish to see him.   When the composer came, he asked what cause had brought him to Vienna, and whether he had obtained permission to leave France.   Having satisfied himself on this point, the Emperor, while not forgetting his usual praises of Paisiello and Zingarelli, said in a kind tone, ' Ah, Monsieur Cherubini, I am glad you are here, and

[19] Pougin, *M.W.* 1883, 64.
[20] *M.W.* 1862. It is stated that a 4-tet, with chorus, was also added to ' Les Deux Journées ' in the 2nd act, where the pretended daughter of the water-carrier is in the water-cart. But Constance never gets inside. *L. Cherubini,* Fritzch.

since you are here, we'll have some music together.   You
shall direct my concerts.'   Thus charged with the
direction of the court-music during Napoleon's stay in
Austria, Cherubini gave 12 musical 'soirées' at Vienna
and Schönbrunn alternately.   He presided at the piano
and Crescentini sang; and each time occasions were
afforded for lively discussions on music between Napoleon
and Cherubini.   1st of all Napoleon became angry
because, as he thought, there was too much noise in the
orchestra.   To remedy this, the patient Cherubini contrived that all passages should be executed 'pianissimo,'
which satisfied Napoleon.   At another time when
Napoleon spoke about 'Faniska,' the representation of
which had been postponed on account of the troubles
of the time, Cherubini at once took the position of
assailant by saying, 'This opera will not please you.'
'And why not?' exclaimed Napoleon.   'Because,' said
Cherubini (using the same expression employed by
Napoleon at the Tuileries in 1800), 'because it has too
much accompaniment.'   'He did not understand
[music],' said Cherubini, in his old age, to his grand-
daughter Mme. Durat.   . . . . 'He asked me for
music without common sense . . . . I would not yield
to him.'[21]   The charge of 'too many notes' was
preferred against Cherubini both by the Emperor
[Francis] II. and by Napoleon.   Alluding to this,
Gerber writes : 'When such could be the opinion of
2 of the most accomplished dilettanti (?) in Vienna and
Paris, what can be the opinion of others in places where
art is immeasurably less flourishing and practised?   Unfortunately, I fear that, with all the extraordinary progress
of instrumental compositions, this would at present be the
unanimous opinion of the majority of "connoiseurs" on
hearing such music, supposing them capable of saying
what they thought with the freedom of a [Francis] II. or
a Bonaparte.   For how is it, how can it be, possible for

21 Pougin *M. W.* 1883, 142.   Cherubini attached no blame to Napoleon.

them, unprepared, to follow the artist in the expression of his multifarious ideas entwined into a whole ? Who will choose, and who will be ready to thank him for the great but unappreciated art he has employed ? [22] All this only shows, let me say again, how much Cherubini was in advance of his time. He has been far outstripped since by Wagner.

For the 12 soirées Cherubini received a large sum from Napoleon. On the other hand Cherubini was involved with Steibelt in a commercial speculation, which proved a failure. They opened a new music-printing establishment at Vienna, but owing to insufficient capital, soon found themselves embarrassed; and Cherubini, like a man of honour, sold his Florentine inheritance to pay to the last farthing his share of the debts.[23]

After signing the treaty of Presburg, 26 Dec. 1805, Napoleon at the moment of departure for Paris called for Cherubini, and, pronouncing his name in the Italian and not in the French fashion, invited him to accompany him. 'I hope very much,' he said, 'that you are here only for a holiday, and that you will return to Paris.' But Cherubini would not break his word with the Viennese, who expected at least one original work from him, and replied that he had an engagement in Vienna, and could not return before fulfilling it. On Napoleon's return to Paris, Paër became court-musician, a post that would probably have been Cherubini's had he returned with the Emperor, who seemed at this time favourably disposed towards him. Possibly he wanted to lead Cherubini on to asking a favour of him, but both were proud, and Napoleon would not take the initiative by offering, nor Cherubini by asking for, anything. 'It may easily be perceived that Napoleon did not bear any hatred towards Cherubini, but rather to that new kind of music

[22] *Vide* Gerber, under 'Cherubini' in the (later?) *Lexicon der Tonkünstler. cit. M.W.* 1862. Gerber, as cited by *M.W.* 1862, says *Joseph II.* who, dying in 1790, could have heard little of Cherubini's music. Francis II. is probably meant.

[23] Picchianti, 64.

introduced by the latter into France. Had he been averse
to him personally, there were but too many ways of
getting rid of him, as of other persons whom he disliked.
The pretended reasons as to the excessive noise of the
instruments do not seem sufficient for depreciating
Cherubini's beautiful compositions. . . . Brought up
in the midst of arms, Napoleon's hearing must have
become well accustomed to endure the greater noise of
the beating of drums, the booming of artillery and the
sharp cries of the wounded. It is rather to be believed
that in Cherubini's music . . . Napoleon discovered the
impress of an exalted spirit, and a certain Republican
austerity. . . . There perhaps arose in him some fear lest
such music should produce results that clashed with his
chief objects, which were to extinguish in the French people
cll excitement . . . and, for that very reason, he wished . . .
to maintain . . . the reputation of the old school of
Italian music, the quiet and suave style of which seemed
to him calculated to lull the popular mind. . . .'[24]
Doubtless Napoleon was accustomed to noise, and as he
had so much of it in battles, would prefer to have none in
music. 'It seemed as though the mighty ruler, warlike
hero, and man of iron will, sometimes experienced an
inward necessity of divesting himself for a period of
" everything " great, and, consequently, of the impression
produced by a grand style of art; for which reason he
preferred lighter and more catching music, perhaps considering all excitement of the mind by means of art as
unworthy a statesman and a general.'[25]

Meanwhile Sonnleithner had translated into German
'Leonora, ou l'amour conjugale,' by J. N. Bouilly, author
of 'Les Deux Journées,' who thus supplied Beethoven with
the libretto of ' Fidelio.' Beethoven's opera appeared
20 Nov. 1805, and Cherubini attended the 3 performances.

'After hearing "Fidelio," as Schindler writes, 'Cherubini arrived at the conclusion that Beethoven had not

24 Picchianti, 45.
25 *N. M. Z., M. W.,* 1862, 531.

devoted sufficient attention and study to the art of singing, and therefore "took the liberty" of recommending it strongly to his attention, for which purpose he sent for the "Method of the Paris Conservatoire," in order to make him a present of it; ' and Beethoven 'preserved in his little library, to the last days of his existence, the book he received from Cherubini.' [26]

Cherubini's 'Faniska,' with German text by Sonnleithner, the subject from a French playwright, Guilbert de Pixérécourt's 'Mines de Pologne,' was produced for the 1st time at the Imperial Kärnthnerthor Theatre, 25 Feb. 1806, before the Emperor Francis II. and all his Court, some 3 months after 'Fidelio,' with the following caste :

Count Rasinski	Herr Neumann.
Count Zamoski	Herr Weinmüller.
Faniska, wife of Rasinski	Mlle. Laucher.
Hedwige, her little daughter	Mlle. Theresa Neumann.
Oranski, Chief of the Cossacks, under Zamoski	Herr Vogel.
Moska, in Zamoski's service	Mme. B. Rothe
Rasno, nephew to Moska, and a mountain guide	Herr Ehlers.
Manoski, friend to Rasinski	Herr Rösner.
Three Cossacks	{ Herr Havermel. / Herr Urban. / Herr Kisling. }

Poles, Cossacks, and Peasants.
To commence at half-past 6.

Before and after the evening's performance, Cherubini was acclaimed. The opera was performed 28 times, the 3rd time for Cherubini's benefit. 'Faniska' vastly increased his credit, and the famous artistes at Vienna vied with one another in fêting him. 'The magnificent

[26] *Beethoven*, i. 114. Little weight is now attached to gossip chronicled by Schindler, *i.e.,* that Cherubini's criticisms on Beethoven were harsh ; that Beethoven did not always take them well ; that he found a champion, even so late as the years 1841 and 1842, in Cherubini's wife ; that when Cherubini spoke of him, he always ended by saying, ' but he is always brusque ;' that on his return to Paris his communications about *Fidelio* showed 'the slight opinion he had of it ;' that he ' was present at the earliest representation of *Fidelio* in 1805, and also in 1806,' and ' told the musicians of Paris, when speaking to them about the overture to *Leonora*, No. 3, that on account of the medley of modulations in it, he was unable to recognise the original key.' What were the above communica-

music excited the admiration of all competent judges:
Beethoven and, it is asserted, Haydn perfectly agreeing
with the opinion of the public.' [27]   An account speaks of
the 'depth, force, and rare perfection in the details—
many of those surprises that move you forcibly'—in
'Faniska;' and Pougin cites an interesting account ot
the 1st performance in the 'Allgemeine-Musik-Zeitung,'
Leipsic: 'Herr Weinmüller exhausted all the resources
of art as Zamoski. It would be impossible to act better,
or to sing the beautiful air of the 1st act with more
grace, tenderness, and expression. Mlle. Laucher
(Faniska), also, did her utmost, but unfortunately her
voice was at times exceedingly feeble. As for Herr
Neumann (Rasinski), he has no voice left at all, and it is
to be regretted that many a specimen of musical beauty
passed by in consequence unnoticed. Lastly, Herr
Ehlers proved to be as good an actor as he is an excellent
singer, and so did Herr Vogel (Oranski). The scenery,
by Herr Platzer, was perfect.' [28]   It would seem doubtful
whether Haydn, at his advanced age, still visited the
theatre; but, according to the general account, both he
and Beethoven were present at the 1st performance.
According to Miel, Haydn embraced Cherubini afterwards, saying, 'I am very old, but I am your son.' De
Lafage states that Beethoven and Haydn styled Cherubini
'the 1st musician of the century;' according to others

tions? A friend of the writer in the *Niederrheinische-Musik-Zeitung*
searched for them in vain among the Paris papers. The writer in question,
speaking of the statement about the *Leonora* overture, says: 'For this
decidedly remarkable assertion, Schindler gives no authority. What reli-
ance ought to be placed on anecdotes and statements of this kind, related
of eminent composers, and propagated by mere report, Schindler himself
has found out, often enough, in the case of Beethoven.' Cherubini is also
credited with saying of Beethoven's symphonies, 'It is impossible to
understand all this; it is a mere *dévergondage;*' and Mendelssohn was
informed that Cherubini remarked of Beethoven's later style, 'This makes
me yawn.' Now, what does all this weigh in contrast with deeds? In 1807
Cherubini led the 1st performance in Paris of Beethoven's 1st symphony,
and is seen actively forwarding at the Conservatoire, in the face of prejudices
that have long since vanished, other performances of Beethoven's works.
   [27] *M.W.,* 1862, 'You are my son, worthy of my love,' is Haydn's
alleged remark to Cherubini.
   [28] *M.W.,* 1883, 130.

Haydn called him ' the greatest of living musicians ; ' and Beethoven, ' the greatest dramatic composer of the age.' Finally, Cipriani Potter told A. W. Thayer, that Beethoven used to walk across the fields to Vienna very often. Sometimes Potter took the walk with him. . . . One day Potter asked, ' Who is the greatest living composer, yourself excepted ? ' Beethoven seemed puzzled for a moment, and then exclaimed, 'Cherubini.' [29] The German journals and Beethoven together undoubtedly called Cherubini ' the 1st dramatic composer of his time.' [30] As for the critics, they are credited with praising him as ' the most learned of dramatic composers.' Whatever were the exact words, and they may all of them be correct, there is no doubt about the general opinion meant to be conveyed. The French composers concurred in the praise of Cherubini at Vienna ; also ' Mehul, who up to this time had been considered his rival and competitor, subscribed to these praises ; but anyone who was acquainted with him knows how much such an avowal cost him ; ' Fétis adding somewhat ungenerously, ' he only made it out of an ostentatiousness of generosity, and to hide his despair.' [31] Gluck and Mozart were dead ; Weber was yet in obscurity. There was really no one to compare with Cherubini at all, unless it were Beethoven himself. Mendelssohn observes of ' Fidelio : ' ' On looking into the score, as well as on listening to the performance, I everywhere perceive Cherubini's dramatic style of composition. It is true that Beethoven did not ape that style, but it was before his mind as his most cherished pattern.' [32] The ' Athenæum ' in 1872 opines that but for ' Les Deux Journées,' we should never have had ' Fidelio.' The score of ' Faniska ' was found among

---

[29] H. E. Krehbiel's *Music and Manners,* 1898, 208, and *cit.* Pougin, Thayer's *Beethoven,* ii. 281-2.
[30] Seyfried 22, Czerny in *Cäcilia.* Thayer's *Beethoven* ii. 353, *cit. Grove* i. 184.
[31] *Biog. Univ.* vi. 60, art. ' Méhul.'
[32] Ella's *Musical Sketches.* Marx's *Music of the* 19th *Century. cit. Grove* i. 184.

Beethoven's MSS. There is a saying, too, of one of our critics touching Beethoven : 'He unites the joyfulness of Haydn with the melancholy of Mozart, while his music mostly resembles Cherubini's.' Rockstro also observes : 'We can scarcely believe it possible that the 2 great composers would have selected subjects so exactly similar in character, and bringing into play exactly the same delicate shades of emotion, passion, and feeling, had there not been a strong community of thought between them,' concluding that 'the more closely we analyse these works, the deeper will be our reverence for the genius of those who attained such splendid results by such very different means.' [33]

'It is a very remarkable fact that 2 such important dramatic compositions as Beethoven's "Fidelio" and Cherubini's "Faniska" should have been written at the same time independently ; . . . should have been in advance of their age ; . . . should display a striking similarity of style, especially in the treatment of the orchestra ; . . . should have suffered from the reproach of the music being too learned. . . . With regard to "Fidelio," . . . it was reserved for our own time to see this magnificent work appreciated in all countries. "Faniska" enjoyed at 1st a better fate. . . . In Vienna it was not often repeated, but it was performed at other German theatres. . . . Dresden and Dessau. . . . Owing to the unsatisfactory "libretto," it did not become firmly established in public favour. . . . And it might be well worth while, after modifying the book, to reproduce the opera on the stage, just as the same composer's "Medea" has been successfully revived at Frankfort-on-the-Maine

[33] *Grove* ii. 520, art. Opera. He, however, is surely wrong in saying, so far as I know, against every critic on the subject :—'yet their mode of expressing that thought was, in each case, so completely a part of themselves that not the slightest trace of similarity is discernible in their treatment even of those Scenes which most closely resemble each other as well in their outward construction as in their inner meaning. In all such cases, the most careful criticism can only lead to the conclusion that each Master did that which was best for his own work in his own peculiar way.'

and Munich.'[34]   Weber brought it out at Prague in the autumn of 1813.   Cherubini, 20 years after the 1st representation, began to meditate about having the work represented at the Opéra Comique, with another libretto. This explains the mention in 1831 of a march for that of the night patrol in the 3rd act of ' Faniska.'   De Pixérécourt began to re-adapt it to his ' Mines de Pologne ;' but Cherubini suddenly changed his mind, thinking that what pleased the Viennese would never suit the Parisians ; and he was probably right, but did not make things better by taking up ' Kourkourgi ' and writing ' Ali Baba ' instead.

The overture in F to ' Faniska ' is one of Cherubini's most finished works.   The opening is surprisingly beautiful, and the ' allegro ' exceedingly gay, but the most striking portion is a strange, weird, yet lovely subject, for the violoncellos and bassoons, that occurs later on, repeated

with a delightful persistency, and ever with an airy accompaniment for the violins, to use Macfarren's phrase, 'hovering' over it.[35]   Of the opera itself, there is a slight account in the 'Harmonicon' for 1830.   I extract therefrom the following note of the plot and of the 1st act: 'In some one of the convulsions which desolated Poland, Faniska and her infant daughter are seized and imprisoned in the castle of Count Zamoski.   The fortunate gaoler is of course, "selon les règles," deeply enamoured of his captive, and also, of course, finds her deaf to his most earnest entreaties.   As a

[34] *N.M.Z.*, *M.W.*, 1862.
[35] The New York Philharmonic Society gave this overture in its season for 1875-6.

last resource, he determines to impress her with the belief
that her husband, Count Rasinski, is dead. Rasinski, who
in disguise is hanging about his rival's castle, offers to
become himself the messenger of his own decease, and is
introduced for that purpose to the lady. . . . the infantine caresses of his daughter cause him to betray himself,
and he is forthwith consigned to a dungeon, with the
comfortable assurance of meeting, on the morrow, the fate
of a traitor. This ends the 1st act. The 2nd and 3rd acts
are occupied by the usual intrigues and expedients to work
his liberation, which is at length effected ; his party storm
the castle, Zamoski falls, and the husband and wife are
again united. It will be seen, by this short sketch, that
the story offers many good and even affecting dramatic
situations, of which the composer has not been slow to
take advantage. No. 1. The introduction opens with a
"presto" movement in B flat, ¾ time. For the 1st 10 or 12
bars the violins and basses move in 8-ves ; afterwards the
subject is continued in 8-ves by the stringed instruments,
and accompanied by chords filled in by the wind instruments. Zamoski, in great agitation, is awaiting the result
of the attempt to seize Faniska, and rapidly interrogating
the Cossacks who form his guard. At length his agent
Oranski arrives, and announces that his plan has succeeded, so far as regards the captivity of Faniska and her
child, though her husband has escaped. The satisfaction
of Zamoski is expressed in an elegant and lively "andante"
in ²⁄₄, accompanied by a chorus [of basses]. No 2. A
"scena" and "aria" for Zamoski, a bass. The recitative
is short, but marked by much beautiful modulation, of
which the following example is as delightful to the ear as
it is bold in the conception :

'The "aria" in E flat commences with an
"andantino" movement in common time, in which
Zamoski expresses the extent of his passion for Faniska.
[Here is a wonderful passage, displaying the great
Master's command of expression and modulation in 3
bars.] He then charges Oranski, an officer of his

guards, and Moska, a waiting-woman, to be most careful
of her safety, and (aside) encourages each to be a spy
upon the other's fidelity. The whole of this movement,
more particularly the parts spoken aside, is highly
characteristic. The stringed instruments throughout are
chiefly in 8-ves to a moving bass; while the wind instruments are used to mark and fill up the harmonies. It is
studded with beautiful points of imitation and singing
phrases for the wind instruments. This song requires
vast powers of voice, and also great compass, ranging
from the low F to E flat on the 2nd leger line of the bass
staff; but we venture to predict that it would well reward
any bass singer who would introduce it to a classical
audience. . . . No. 3 introduces Faniska in a recitative
"obbligato" of which it is hardly too much to say that,
for variety of modulation and just expression, it yields
only to the great scene in "Don Giovanni," where Donna
Anna mourns over the dead body of her murdered parent,
and incites her lover to avenge his death. To this

succeeds a "preghiera" in G, "molto sostenuto"
("Eterno iddio"). The principal feature is an accompaniment of 3 violoncellos "obbligati;" but occasional
phrases for the wind instruments are interspersed.'[36]

No. 4 is a "terzetto" in A, between Faniska and her 2
guards, Moska and Oranski. The latter pretends the
greatest devotion to his captive's wishes, while the former
assumes, at 1st, an air of total indifference, declaring
that she neither pities nor hates her, and is only determined to do her duty. She soon after, however, cautions
Faniska (aside) against trusting Oranski, and recommends
her to prove to him by demanding an interview with her
child. In this trio, as in all the other pieces of the opera, a
marked motion runs through the whole, and is both
original and beautiful. . . .

    'No. 5 is a chorus of villagers on a very simple vocal
subject; but the repetitions abound in variations of
instrumental accompaniment, which evince the command
Cherubini has over this branch of his art. . . .' No. 6. is
'a short melodrame and polonaise. . . .' No. 7, 'The
finale to the 1st act commences with a "larghetto" in D,
rather in a recitative style. Rasinski, disguised, is introduced by Zamoski to announce the news of his own
death to Faniska. In proof of his veracity, Rasinski
delivers a miniature of himself, which Faniska apostrophizes
in a beautifully flowing and pathetic ["andantino

[36] The whole number is given by the *Harmonicon.*

sostenuto "] in A. She shows the portrait to her child, whose infantine raptures on recognising the likeness of her father lead Rasinski to betray himself. The moment when the father seizes and bathes with involuntary tears his daughter's hand, the instantaneous burst of rage from Zamoski, is accompanied by the following bold and effective transition :

A combat succeeds, and the finale ends with a spirited "allegro," in D, . . . ' a 6-tet and chorus of Cossacks. Act II. No. 8 is an impressive orchestral introduction, 'larghetto;' No. 9, a scena for Faniska, with recitative and air, 'all of great beauty;' No. 10, a melodrama and duet between her and Rasinski, with a persistent triplet figure in the accompaniment ; No. 11, a romance, which may be compared with, and is deemed by our critic 'superior' to, that in 'Les Deux Journées,' between Rasno, Rasinski and Faniska ; No. 12 is the well-known exquisite canon, set in Italian, 'Non mi negate,' etc., and 'Dolce ne quai ristoro,' with independent prelude and an increasing variety of accompaniment as the 3 voices, Faniska, Rasinski, and Moska join in, the whole suggesting a comparison with the canon in 'Fidelio,' which may have suggested it.

It is certainly a very 'concrete melody,' and followed by a varied finale, No. 13, 'larghetto.' Act III. No. 14 is another suave and flowing instrumental prelude; Nos. 15, 19 and 20 are marches, '2 of which are superior to the general run of such compositions.' No. 16 is a brief chorus behind the scenes and an orchestral interlude ; No. 17 a fine 5-tet, variably scored, between Rasinski, Zamoski, Faniska, Rasno, and Moska ; No. 18 a short 4-tet ; No. 21 a 'vaudeville' air, sung by the chief characters, along with a spirited little 4-tet, commencing as a strict canon.

Cherubini would willingly have written his 2nd opera, as agreed upon, for the Germans, but the late war had ruined so many that he settled on returning to Paris. It is recorded that he sought Mozart's tomb, and, being unable to find the resting-place of one for whom he had a strong affection, felt that Vienna was no place for him. He would be confronting, too, Beethoven, not to say Hummel, Albrechtsberger, Preindl, Weigl, Gyrowetz, and Salieri. A permanent residence would have made him a rival. Then, too, the Parisians were already wishing him back, some saying they could not do without him. Accordingly, Cherubini, his wife and daughter, bidding good-bye to Haydn, and after a visit of considerable success, left Vienna 9 March, and reached Paris 1 April 1806. At a fête improvised for him at the Conservatoire, his entrance into the great hall was the signal for much enthusiasm from the students ; some pieces from his operas were given, and the welcome from ardent youth greatly encouraged him. Looking back now, we see clearly enough that there were no musicians then in Paris to equal 'the refined, learned and interesting Italian,' whom Schumann often felt 'tempted to compare with Dante.'

PART II.

—

SACRED MUSIC.

SACRED MUSIC.

CHAPTER I.

FRANCE AND BELGIUM.

1806—1809.

'Break forth into thanksgiving,
Ye banded instruments of wind and chord;
Unite, to magnify the Ever-living,
Your inarticulate notes with the voice of words'
WORDSWORTH.

8-part *Credo*—Spontini's *La Vestale*—Méhul's *Joseph*—Canons—Illness
—Departure for Chimay—Origin of the Mass in F—The Kyrie
and Gloria done on St. Cecilia's Day—The whole work at the Hôtel de
Babylon—Modern Church music.

A NEW period now opens out in the life of this gifted
Musician, and as presage thereof he took to finishing his
great 8-part 'Credo,' begun in Italy in 1778-9. Thibaut,
a severe critic, calls it 'incomparable.' It shows 'how
thoroughly he could adapt [Palestrina's] style to his own
individual thoughts;'[1] and it contains 'probably the finest
specimen of a quadruple fugue ever written,' with 4 subjects and 2 counter-subjects;[2] and proves 'that old art
principles and forms to a certain degree harmonize very
well with more modern resources when treated by the
hand of an experienced master to whom the dignity and
purity of his art are dearer than the frivolous success that
lasts but for a day.'[3] Only the final fugue, in the ' Treatise on Counterpoint and Fugue,' however, was published
in Cherubini's life-time.

In 1807 Spontini's ' La Vestale ' appeared. Its

[1] Maczewski, *Grove*, i. 343.   [2] Prout's *Fugue*, 211.
[3] Ritter's *History of Music*.

libretto by Jouy was written expressly for Boieldieu: so the latter tells us, and it is said that Cherubini and Méhul declined it, and Paër and others read it before Spontini came by it.[4] In competing successfully for the decennial prize institued by Napoleon, 'La Vestale' had to contend against Cherubini, Lesueur, Méhul, Gossec, Grétry, Berton and Catel: 'Les Deux Journées' and Méhul's 'Joseph et ses Frères' gaining honourable mention. But such was the strife aroused by the jury's decisions, that Spontini never received his 10,000 francs, nor Jouy his 5,000, the Emperor deeming it advisable to avoid giving further offence to the other discontented musicians. The jury, of which Cherubini was a member, for examining works for the Grand Opera, were against 'La Vestale' being put on the stage, an opera performed for 30 years, with much success, thanks, in a measure, to the Empress Josephine, who ordered the work to be represented. The further facts are these, and most interesting. Cherubini had to come to the rescue of 'La Vestale.' Hiller tells us that 'Spontini could hardly have managed the instrumentation . . . but for his aid. The parts of it had been twice written out, but still the opera would not go, and at last the composer had to take refuge with Cherubini. The bill for so much copying amounted to a most unusual sum, and Napoleon, who always looked into everything, thought it so absurd, that he decreed that the cost of copying an opera was never to exceed a certain amount. Cherubini, who might always be believed, told me this himself. . . .'[5] It was after the public had extolled to the

---

[4] Fétis (*Biog. Univ.*, viii. 2nd ed., 89) affirms that Cherubini had the 1st offer. Jouy denied this prior offering (*Grove*, iii. 666), but is here at issue with Boieldieu, whose leaving for Russia made him return the book to Jouy.—*M. W.*, 1883, 157, *cit.* Pougin's notice of Boieldieu.

[5] *Macmillan*, 1875, 271. Spontini's enemies have called his operas 'elephants;' but none deny his originality. 'It is a difficult thing to give him a fair and fit pedestal in the musical Pantheon—and one neither too high nor too low, . . . while Spontini had the dryness which, I fancy, distinguishes the pianoforte music of Clementi, and even (in a less degree) the magnificent compositions of the greater Cherubini, he has nowhere shown a science in any respect analogous to theirs. He wrote only opera. . . . A certain temperate eclecticism prevades Spontini's operas, which is often

skies what the chief Parisian composers had at 1st adjudged unworthy of musical treatment, that Méhul and Cherubini deigned to accept from poor Jouy the one 'Les Amazones,' the other 'Les Abencérages.' [6]
Cherubini, meanwhile, did little or nothing in the way of composing. Some have said that he refused in vexation the poem of 'La Vestale;' for though his popularity showed that people still had the boldness to esteem one whom the great man did not favour, yet he had been set aside, while Méhul, Gossec, Grétry, and Lesueur, lesser men, had received honours. A nervous prostration, however, not suffered for the 1st time, was the real cause of the breakdown. A few airs, an opera begun only, a collection of canons, 3 begun in 1779, and the rest finished by 1807, complete the musical record. In this last difficult form of music, Cherubini excelled and delighted. Most musical people knew at one time 'Perfida Clori,' printed in London so early as 1810, the popularity of which may be gauged from the fact of its having been set to 'God save Victoria,' and other English words. Halévy printed 3 in 'facsimile,' with remarks in the 'Gazette Musicale de Paris' of 9 March 1834. Of the volume of 63 canons in the Berlin Royal Library, one is in

insipid, rarely beautiful, never deep ; and because of this, it may justly be feared, they will sink into oblivion, with all the fine and brilliant movements which they comprise. . . .'—Chorley's *Mod. Germ. Music,* i. 204.

[6] Of Méhul's work, termed 'glorious' by Wagner, Ella observes that it ' was not received with very great enthusiasm ;' and he thinks that Cherubini's production of *Faniska* at Vienna led Méhul astray. He 'unwisely abandoned his natural style and encumbered the score of *Joseph* with bald imitations of his classical rival, which gave to his music a certain effect of mannerism. Notwithstanding this defect in *Joseph,* there are beautiful melodies, a grand dramatic sentiment, and a local colour which is excellent. Often as I have perused the touching narrative of Joseph and his brethren, its performance at the Opéra Comique in 1829, in Paris, produced a more deep and lasting impression on my feelings. . . . I do not envy the man who could witness the affecting interview of Joseph and his father, sung and acted as I witnessed it, without being moved to tears.'—*Lectures at the London Institute,* 20. Weber put Méhul next to Cherubini among the masters of the Modern French School, and conducted *Joseph* at Dresden, 30 Jan. 1817, it being the 1st opera done under his direction. It was announced in the 1910 programme of the Opéra Comique series by Thomas Beecham, at Her Majesty's, London, but not performed.

8 parts, 4 are in 4, 12 in 2 ; 3 are mixed, *i.e.*, with 2 or more subjects. Pougin deems 'his masterpiece in the burlesque line ' the canon to Sauvageot, the collector, ' vive le bric-à-brác,' and gives amusing specimens of some of the others, one founded on Cherubini's name. Meanwhile, for 18 months, Cherubini lay in a depressed state. Report in Vienna even said that he was dead.[7] For 8 hours a day he would occupy himself with drawing and botany, for months going to the ' Jardin des Plantes ' every day. ' His exquisite organization as an artist would probably have made him a great painter, as it made him a great musician. Before now, we have seen him amuse himself with drawing flowers on playing cards taken up haphazard; mastering with an uncommon skill the distribution of the different points, figures, and colours, he found means adapting all sorts of subjects.'[8] The clubs, spades, hearts, and diamonds formed the nucleus of the devices. ' On entering his rooms, the visitor beheld hung in frames against the walls a number of pictures, of all sizes. Red and black spots were more or less visible here and there . . . a sort of mania with Cherubini. They represented the most fantastic figures, groups, and scenes, produced by the aid of the hearts and diamonds of playing cards, either entire or divided, according to circumstances. There were dancers with red jerkins, singers with red hats, edifices and landscapes with strange specimens of vegetation, the cards being employed either horizontally or perpendicularly, separately, or in groups, with a greater or less number of pipes effaced.'[9] ' But it is, above all, in a set of figures drawn with the pencil, and with the hard contour of the old Florentine masters, in the profiles, that the native force of his talent is recognised.'[10] One day David the painter, Cherubini's friend, came in upon him while he was doing in ' crayon ' on a common piece of paper a landscape after Salvator Rosa, with many rocks, and traversed by a torrent that made a way for itself through a

[7] *L. Cherubini,* Fritzsch.   [8] Miel.   [9] Hiller.   [10] Miel.

From Original Drawings by Cherubini.

narrow mountain-pass. So pleased was David, that he cried out, ' In truth, admirable, courage ! ' The drawing afterwards came into the possession of Salvador Cherubini. Music being abandoned, Cherubini took to studying with assiduity the science of Linnæus, Jussieu, and Tournefort, and placed himself under Des Fontaines. He also made a herbal, 'a sad and interesting memorial of this phase of his life, which remains in the family.' [11] These pursuits somewhat improved his health, but he needed rest and change. He had become acquainted with M. de Caraman, Prince of Chimay (an enthusiastic musical amateur), and the Princess (Mme. Tallien), well known for her beauty and amiability, and had visited them in the summer of 1807. They now again invited him to their country seat in Belgium ; and so, in 1808, he set out, accompanied by Auber, for the Castle of Chimay. Cherubini arrived there safely, Rode and Lamare being also among the visitors. Bent on regaining health, he discarded laborious pursuits, and contented himself with studying botany and taking walks. Beyond a few slight pieces, music was abandoned. An amateur performance of ' Les Deux Journées ' was essayed, with Cherubini himself as Armand, who got ill during the performance. Summer wore on ; autumn came. He was left pretty much to himself. Now, it chanced that St. Cecilia's Day, 22 Nov., was coming round ; and, at the suggestion of its president, the little musical society in the village made bold to send a deputation to Cherubini, asking him to write for them a Mass that could be performed in Chimay church on the feast-day. The deputation being introduced, the president, with some trepidation, explained their object in coming. ' No, it can't be done,' replied Cherubini, and went on busying himself with his flowers. The deputation stood for a moment irresolute, and then withdrew in confusion. The sympathies of the inmates of the Castle were with them ; but nothing was said. Next day it was remarked

[11] Denne-Baron.

that Cherubini, preoccupied, took an unusually long walk alone in the park; and Madame de Chimay, perceiving that he had not made his usual botanical excursion, placed some music-paper on his table, covered with specimens of plants. Returning from his solitary walk, Cherubini began to trace out in full score a 'Kyrie.' He wrote it without apparent thought or labour, in a corner of his room, and in the intervals of repose from his labours played at pool in the billiard-room. [12] An inspiration, however, had come.

Eventually Cherubini finished writing, and, going up to Auber, showed him the MS., a piece for 3 voices, with instrumental accompaniments. Auber wished it to be tried. Cherubini assented; and, that very evening, Auber accompanied at the piano, Madame Duchambge, a visitor, took the soprano, Cherubini tenor, and the Prince bass. The former could hardly wait till the end to express their admiration. A 'Gloria' was soon added. Meanwhile St. Cecilia's Day was close at hand. The Mass could not be completed in time, but it was agreed to perform the 'Kyrie' and 'Gloria.' The village was ransacked for instruments; its resources amounting to 2 horns, 2 clarinets, a 4-tet of strings, a flute, and a bassoon. With such simple appliances, united to the voices of the village choir, were the 'Kyrie' and 'Gloria' executed. That St. Cecilia's day was marked with a white stone in the annals of Chimay. Cherubini now began to take to music more kindly, yet without neglecting his botanical studies, resumed with greater zest than before. He worked at a herbal that came into the possession of his son-in-law, Rosellini.

Cherubini had suffered in full measure at the hands of librettists, and this illness and a village choir's request had

---

[12] Miel states that the 'Kyrie' was entirely written in the billiard-room during pool, the composer only laying his pen down when told it was his turn to play, and not being disturbed by the talking going on around him. Others speak of Cherubini's writing it in his room, and playing at pool, or billiards, in the intervals of rest from his work; more probably the true account. Denne-Baron makes a statement to the effect that Cherubini took

led him to a field 1st entered in boyhood, and suited to his profound erudition, allied to imaginative genius of the 1st order; and the whilom lad of 12, who had written a 4-part Mass, was to end by producing at 76 a male-voice 3-part Requiem that remains an acknowledged classic. But as yet he was no chapel-master, and the Mass in F presents little liturgical type. It is a free essay by Cherubini on a vast scale to see what he could do on fresh ground in the maturity of his powers.

Remaining some while longer at Chimay, Cherubini returned to Paris; he completed the rest of the Mass, and in 1809 its 1st grand performance, from the MS., took place at the Hôtel de Babylon, the town-house of the Prince of Chimay.[13] The Mass in F was received with enthusiasm, and, published in 1810, made its way over Europe. 'Never shall I forget,' exclaims Fétis, 'the effect produced by this Mass confided to such interpreters. All the celebrities of Paris, of whatsoever rank, attended the performance, where the glory of the great composer shone forth with a living lustre. During the interval between the performance of the "Gloria" and "Credo," groups everywhere formed themselves, and all expressed an unreserved admiration for this composition of a new order, whereby Cherubini has placed himself above all musicians who have as yet written in the concerted style of church-music. Superior to the Masses of Haydn, Mozart, and Beethoven, and masters of the Neapolitan school, that of Cherubini is as much remarkable for originality of idea as for perfection of art.'[14] After the performance, Cardinal Caprara, Papal

a fancy to having a Mass sung in the Castle chapel; that the Princess de Chimay, after every preparation had been made, had recourse to him for the music, and that he refused her; but at length, overcome by entreaty, began a Mass.

[13] Among the violinists present were Baillot, Kreutzer, Rode, Habeneck, Libon, Mazas, and Grasset; the violoncellists included Lamare, Levasseur, Duport, Baudiot, and Norblin; the clarinet-players, Lefebvre and Dacosta; the horn-players, Duvernoy and Dominick; the flutists, Tulou; and the bassoon-players, Delcambre. Indeed, the instrumentalists mustered stronger than the vocalists.

[14] *Biog. Univ.* art. Cherubini; and *Des Manuscrits autographes de L. Cherubini* (*cit.* Girod and Pougin), giving the last sentence.

Legate, thus greeted the composer: 'Dear son, you are worthy to sing the praises of God' (Caro figlio, siete degno di cantare le lodi di Dio).[15]

The 'Kyrie,' writes Picchianti, '. . . presents an

almost continual undulation from "crescendo" to "decrescendo," as though the composer wished to express the conflicting emotions of a sinner praying. Nothing simpler or more ingenuous could be imagined than the melody of the subject given out by the soprano in the "Christe."

This seems the prayer of a pure and innocent virgin, coming forth from the innermost depths of the heart, and rising to the throne of the Almighty. The light and delicate accompaniment "obbligato" of the orchestra . . .

[15] *La Revue et Gazette musicale,* art. in *Indépendant de Bruxelles,* Aug. 1839, E. Fétis, Junr. 1843, *cit.* Pougin, *M.W.,* 1883, 173.

perfectly preserves, from beginning to end, the character
of the fugue that, owing to the learned art with which it is
elaborated, the beauty of the counterpoint, and the general
effect produced, must be reputed a perfect model in this
kind of composition. . . .'   The form of this section, with
its 2nd subject, and strict return to the 1st, is perfectly regular Would that the whole Mass were the same !   'There is
a most beautiful contrast between the brilliant theme at the
opening of the " Gloria " and the other tender and subdued

ideas expressed at the words " et in terra pax."   The
music then returning to the " Gloria " movement, passes to
an " andante con moto " of superb art, including all the
words from " laudamus Te " to the 3 " Domine's," [that
is to " Filius Patris."   This is an unusual arrangement.]
Here re-appears in its entirety the 1st subject of the
Gloria [a 3rd time], followed by a " tempo sostenuto "
consummately worked out from the " qui tollis" to the
"cum Sancto Spiritu " [another unusual arrangement]
which forms a short prelude to a superb fugue developed
on the words " in gloria Dei [Patris. Amen.] " . . . in a
long pedal point on the dominant, the chief melody of the
opening is stealthily introduced, and, uniting with the
subject of the fugue, prepares us for the grand final
cadence.'

'The Credo begins by intoning a " canto-fermo,"
the 3 vocal parts repeating it in imitation with a fugal
subject and answer.   And at the end of each verse, . . .
all the voices in unison or at 8-ves forcibly bring out, with
the word " credo," notes essential to the perfect cadence,
and this starts a new tone connecting the next verse.   This
same procedure, repeated some 7 times, before we come
to the " incarnatus," presents us with a continual assertion
of full faith in all those articles put forth, and to be pro-
fessed and believed in by the Christian.   A certain

persistent phrase in the basses of the orchestra, perfectly supported by that of the violins and other instruments, forms a most beautiful accompaniment. . . . After a slow movement with two "tempi," wherein the incar-

Allegro moderato.

nation and crucifixion of the Man-God are pathetically described [the violins in the latter portion in "arpeggio" accompaniment], the "allegro," depicting His resurrection, is reached, and, with the usual formula "credo," already employed in the 1st movement, the composer returns to emphasize the remaining articles of the Catholic Faith till he reaches the words, "et vitam venturi," allied to a fine fugue. . . . Learned harmonies and exquisite melodies are encountered in the "Sanctus" and "Agnus Dei," concluding with a very beautiful "tempo fugato" of excellent art on the words, "dona nobis pacem."' This great Mass should be heard at the Festivals, when the absent altos would have a rest.

'With the grave Gregorian melody, learnedly elaborated in rigorous counterpoint, and reduced to greater clearness and elegance without any instrumental aid, Palestrina knew how to awaken among his hearers mysterious, grand, deep, vague sensations that seemed caused by the objects of an unknown world, or by superior powers in the human imagination. With the same profound thoughtfulness of the old Catholic music, enriched by the perfection art has attained in 2 centuries, and with all the means that a composer can nowadays make use of, Cherubini perfected another conception, . . . in utilizing the style adapted to dramatic expression . . . whereby he

was able to succeed in depicting man in his various vicissitudes, now rising to the praises of Divinity, now gazing
on the Supreme Power, now suppliant and prostrate. So
that while Palestrina's music places God before man, that
of Cherubini places man before God.'[16]
As a composer for the church, then, Cherubini held
that ecclesiastical music could be both ideal and dramatic,
since prayer is objective and subjective; more of a personal
expression in a ' Miserere ' than in a ' Te Deum.' There
was nothing new in this. Palestrina himself seems to illus-
trate the distinction, but the mediæval polyphony is unaccompanied.[17] Non-accompaniment, however, is no essential principle of religious music. ' Israel played before the
Lord on all manner of musical instruments,' and these are
duly recognized by authority. Even plain-chant has
become less plain by taken very kindly to modern accompaniment, although none is ' preferable,'[18] and any is its
' death.'[19] ' Where the religious song is accompanied by
musical instruments, these must serve solely for adding
to its force, so that the sense of the words penetrate
deeper into the hearts of the faithful, and their spirit,
roused to the contemplation of spiritual things, be elevated
towards God and the love of Divine objects.'[20] Such is

---

[16] Picchianti, 48. Fétis writes the same. ' Up to this time, church
music, as Palestrina and the other great masters of the old Roman school
had conceived it, had been treated as an emanation of pure sentiment,
stripped of all human passion. Cherubini, on the contrary, wished his music
to express the dramatic sense of the words, and in the realization of his
idea he has been able to blend the severe beauties of counterpoint and fugue
with dramatic expression, sustained by every wealth of instrumentation.'
[17] The unaccompanied prevailed at Dresden Royal Chapel in 1882 from
Septuagesima to Easter, and in Advent, and is sung throughout the year at
Westminster Cathedral, whose large area demands a large choir. Clément,
formerly chapel-master of the Sorbonne, wrote in 1861 : ' Palestrina's music,
performed by very skilled artists, and directed by a learned conductor, will
be enjoyed by a select audience, prepared by a distinguished education,
and by the habitual culture of the arts, but heard in a church it will be found
cold and monotonous.'—*Hist. Gen. de la Musique Religieuse,* 328. And he
says it is ' unpopular.' but that is a variable accompaniment to music. See
also Mendelssohn's *Letters from Italy and Switzerland,* tr. Lady Wallace
1862, 167-88, praising and blaming the Roman music.
[18] Rockstro, art. Plain-song, *Grove,* ii. 769.
[19] Witt, *cit.* Taunton's *Hist. and Growth of Ch. Music,* 100.
[20] Pope Benedict XIV. Brief, 1749.

often the effect, whether of organ, or orchestra, which the psalms of praise appear to countenance. Accompaniment should not obscure the words.[21] Strange, that herein the unaccompanied sometimes compares unfavourably with the accompanied. The dangers besetting religious service from art are obvious, and have been pointed out by Cardinal Newman. Notwithstanding Palestrina's Mass of the Good Shepherd, and Weber's Mass in G, his present Holiness gives a recognized 2nd and 3rd place to mediæval polyphony, and modern concerted music. As to the latter, 'the Church has always recognized and favoured the progress of the arts, admitting to the service of worship everything good and beautiful discovered by genius in the course of ages,—always, however, with due regard to the liturgical laws—consequently modern music is also admitted in the Church, since it, too, furnishes compositions of such excellence, sobriety, and gravity, that they are in no way unworthy of the liturgical functions.' 'Motu Proprio.' The difficulty remains as to a standard in all 3 imperfect classes of music allowed by authority.[22]

Haydn, Mozart, Cherubini, Beethoven, Hummel, Schubert, Niedermeyer, Reissiger, not to name others, have shown what work Catholic composers can do in the Mass, the Hymn, and the Offertory, not forgetting Mendelssohn in the Psalm, and St. Thomas' Eucharistic Hymn.[23] 'Haydn et Mozart! C'est la foi Catholique; c'est la soumission naïve et spontanée, la dévotion vive et

[21] *Curandum est ut verba quae cantautur plane perfecteque intelligantur,* ib.

[22] Some Cecilians would exclude nearly all the Great Masters' works and instrumentation, oblivious of the fact that the highest authorities recognize both. 'It is his commentators, not the Pope, that are narrow and exclusive.'—Canon James Connelly, late Secretary to the 3rd and 4th Bishops of Southwark.

[23] Let me name Haydn's noble 1st, 3rd, 5th, 6th, and 16th Masses, with part-writing never surpassed; Mozart's in F and D, and Requiem; Hummel's 3 Masses; some of Schubert's, with corrected text; Niedermeyer's Mass in B minor; Reissiger's in E flat, No. 4; Kiel's Requiem, and Dvorak's Mass in D, etc. And in this connection it is of interest to note what even M. Ortigue feels bound to say about Niedermeyer's work, heard at Ste. Eustache, Paris. He calls it 'a masterpiece of art, style, and religious sentiment,' adding, 'for however great and frequent be the abuses that

tendre.' [24] And no wonder, if the one told his beads to
get inspiration, and the other heard daily Mass. That
they and Hummel are too light, in some of their Kyries
and Agnus Deis more especially, is a fact, but not an
invariable fact. Subject must always come 1st, singers
2nd. They left room, if not for a more beautiful, yet for
a deeper treatment felt in Cherubini and in Beethoven at
their best. Cherubini is no mere wounded traveller to be
now and again taken compassion on by a good Samaritan
in the guise of an enlightened Festival director, but such
an excelling religious genius as can never be vouchsafed
anew to each succeeding generation. Cherubini, like
Niedermeyer, can really ' conduce to prayer.' He relies
on 3, 4, 5, 6 voices, soli and chorus. Solos are brief, and
all almost invariably share in them alike ; Cherubini, too,
leans towards antiquity, amid all ' the marvellous development which musical science has undergone in the last

Music commits in churches, it would be extremely unjust to refuse to
modern art that expression, calm, elevated, contemplative, and grandiose,
of which Mozart in the *Zauberflöte,* and Beethoven in his sonatas, 4-tets, and
symphonies, have given sublime examples.' And he concludes, ' For
myself I cannot hear it without being vividly moved thereby. This work is
distinguished by the character that conduces above all to prayer ; it throws
back the soul on itself, and speaks to it a recollected language, and pene-
trates it by a 1,000 secret voices.'—*Revue et Gazette de Paris,* 27 July 1856.
  [24] M. Tonnellé, *cit.* Fr. Girod, S.J. I exclude, from the above, Bach's
Mass in B minor, Cherubini's Masses in F, D minor, G, Beethoven's Mass
in D, and Schubert's Mass in E flat, owing to over-length and development,
or too free textual treatment. To these, some, I suppose, would apply.
Spohr's words, written after abusing a Mass of Lesueur : ' But will you
believe it when I assure you that even the worthy master Cherubini has
allowed himself to be led away by this bad example, and that his Masses
exhibit in many places a theatrical style ? It is true that he makes amends
for it in those places with superior music, full of effect ; but who can enjoy
it, if he cannot wholly forget the place in which he hears it ?' He adds, ' It
would be less regrettable that Cherubini also should deviate from the true
ecclesiastical style, if in some individual parts he did not show in what a
dignified manner he can move in it. Several separate subjects in his
Masses—particularly the scientifically-conducted fugues, and, above all,
his "Pater noster" up to the profane conclusion—afford the grandest
proofs of this.'—*Autobiography* ii. 125. The E minor Mass, and, perhaps,
D minor Requiem, were never heard by Spohr ? As to repetitons, they
abound in prayer and music ; liturgy, rosary, litanies, psalters, Palestrina,
etc., and ' undue' repetitions (all that are to be avoided) become accent-
uated when fugues are set to one word ' Amen.' Plain-chant's notes, also,
to one syllable, seem at times too numerous and thus ' undue,' in the
concentus ; and in a repeat in one beautiful *accentus.*

century.'[25] Adolphe Adam, indeed, in a passage generally commended by Prout for its sound criticism, went the length of saying : 'If Palestrina had lived in our own times, he would have been a Cherubini ;' so impressed was he with the latter's devotional spirit. This is what Adam says : 'Although Cherubini's style appertains rather to the German school than to the Italian, yet you cannot rank him among the composers of the 1st of these schools. His manner is less Italian than that of Mozart ; it is purer than that of Beethoven ; it is rather the resurrection of the old Italian school enriched by the discoveries of modern harmony. I believe that if Palestrina had lived in our own time he would have been a Cherubini ; there is the same purity, the same moderation in resource, the same result obtained by causes, so to speak mysterious.' He adds, as I understand, that there are portions of his music that no mere viewing the score (ordinarily sufficient) without a hearing, can give any adequate notion of ; and continues : 'The works of this master will always serve as models, because composed on an exact and almost mathematical plan ; exempt therefore from the affected regulations of fashion, they undergo less depreciation than many works otherwise to be recommended on many accounts, but whose forms become antiquated so much the more quickly as they have been received with favour on their 1st appearance.'[26]

No verbal musical analyses of Cherubini's Masses could convey adequate notion of their expressive art, profound learning, teeming melodic variety in theme and accompaniment, Italian beauty and expressiveness, German depth of imagination and devotion. All is summed up in the 2nd Requiem, written in his old age. The liturgy inspired him as nothing else could.

Clément thinks Cherubini lacks 'one precious quality

[25] Cardinal Newman's *Idea,* disc. iv. Fétis tells us he realized the importance of studying the old Italian masters after conversations held with Cherubini in 1804 ; Pougin, that the latter re-studied Palestrina.
[26] Adam's *Derniers Souvenirs.*

—simplicity.'[27] Schlüter does not think so.[28] Simplicity is a necessary attribute of all true greatness anywhere. A Great Master is bound to be simple, or he is no Great Master at all ; and so in the most elaborate works this essential quality is seen in Cherubini. Suffice it to note among innumerable examples, the ' Et in spiritum ' and ' dona nobis ' themes of the D minor Mass, the ' Pie Jesu ' of either Requiem, the Coronation Mass in A's Communion March. In brief the music that holds the balance between variety and monotony, that expresses truthfully the sense of the liturgy, and helps the soul to devotion, that is the genuine church-music, whether Gregorian, Palestrina or Cherubini. As for declarations that 'Beethoven had not a religious soul,'[29] and that Cherubini's music ' hardly ever exhibits a religious character,'[30]

[27] 'Cherubini's church-music is imprinted with an elevated character, and in an artistic point of view, is full of beauties so exquisite, along with such an amount of science and taste, that it cannot but excite the admiration of artists. But Cherubini's works are wanting in one precious quality—simplicity. The Coronation Mass, the Ave Maria, the Ecce Panis, reveal the author of 30 operas.'—*Histoire Générale de la Musique Religieuse,* 1861, 355-6.

[28] After saying that modern church-music comes from the concert-room (or, shall I say, has been welcomed as something beautiful by the concert room, just as Wagner's operas have been), Schlüter adds : ' If (in opposition to the one-sided views of critics) we admit the lawfulness of this tendency of modern church-music, in consideration of the circumstances of the age, we must allow that Cherubini's expressive as well as brilliant Mass in D minor, and especially his Requiem in C minor, are noble and sublime conceptions. Notwithstanding the most lavish employment of orchestral and choral resources, these works are characterized by lofty simplicity, exquisite proportion, distinctness of form, and powerful imagination.'—*History of Music.* Let me add Spohr's testimony, already cited : ' But when you have once overcome the inclination to be annoyed at this frequent extremely digressive style, you then feel the highest enjoyment of art. By richness of invention, well chosen and often quite novel sequences of harmony, and a sagacious use of the material resources of art, directed by the experience of many years, he knows how to produce such powerful effects that, carried away by them in spite of yourself, you soon forget all pedantic cavil to give yourself wholly up to your feelings and enjoyment.'

[29] 'Beethoven had not a religious soul ; you would search in vain for the accents of prayer in the 2 Masses he composed, and even in his one oratorio, *Christ on the Mount of Olives.*'--Clément's *Histoire Générale de la Musique Religieuse,* 353. Cardinal Newman once expressed a doubt as to whether Beethoven's music was ' essentially religious ' much as he loved it, but this is very different from saying ' he had not a religious soul.' How does Clément know that ?

[30] Viellard, after praising Lesueur, adds : ' The music of Cherubini, otherwise full of charm and harmonic power, hardly ever exhibits a religious character.'—*Méhul, sa vie et ses œuvres.* Rather, at times, it does not.

K

I venture upon contradictories in an English church-
man's view, that 'the moral grandeur of Beethoven's genius was always present to him;'[31] a musician's
view, 'that Cherubini, by his veiled, imperceptible melody,
has known how to reach the most mysterious depths of
Christian meditation;'[32] a religious' view that, 'he possessed
a remarkable aptitude for rendering sensible, for inter-
preting religious truths;'[33] and a Prefect of Rites' view,
that his 'are choice and serious compositions, and are far
from being unbecoming the holiness of the Church.'[34]
Coming to a practical question,— one that interests the
laity, who support choirs. What are suitable for Church-
use among the 11 Masses and 2 Requiems of Cherubini?
One can but give an opinion, to be taken for what it is
worth. Some have long been sung, following lists or
traditions, to the edification of thousands. It would be
interesting to listen to the Mass written by the lad of 12,
and its two successors, and to the 7th unpublished Mass
in E flat, but at present they must be put aside, as also
the 4th Mass in F, the 5th in D minor, and the 9th in
G. There remain the 6th Mass in C, the 7th in E
minor, the 10th in B flat, the 11th in A, and the 2
Requiems (less the 1st offertory in its entirety), but not
for every Sunday, or at every funeral.

[31] 'The moral grandeur of Beethoven's genius was always present to
him, as, with less force, was also Mendelssohn's: "They believed in
God—their music showed it."' Canon J. B. Mozley's *Letters,* ed. 1885, 353.
[32] Berlioz on the Communion Prelude at Charles X's Coronation.
[33] 'Magnificent, elevated, dramatic, he strains nothing, he never
exaggerates. He offends in no case religious propriety, and never by his
music does he transport you to the theatre. . . . He can be powerful or
pathetic, severe or graceful, gay or grave, in a variety ever new. . . . He
could adapt his talent to the minutest requirements, the most complicated of
scenes, of expressions, of prophecies, of sorrows, of hopes, of holy feelings
found in the Bible and in the Liturgy. He possessed a remarkable aptitude
for rendering sensible, for interpreting religious truths, and when we hear
his music we understand that this harmonious language, so sublime, so
persuasive, is not made for the holy temples, but for our intercourse with
heaven.'—Fr. Girod, S.J. In fear of some Cecilians, I should prefer to say
that it is made for both while we are on earth.
[34] 'The compositions of Haydn, and the Masses of Mozart, of Cherubini,
and of others, are choice and serious compositions, and are far from being
unbecoming the holiness of the Church.'—Cardinal Bartolini's *Letter.* cit.
Taunton 110.

Doubtless no small part of Cherubini's success in sacred music, where he unrolls before us 'sublime visions,'[35] was owing to depth and seriousness of character, and his putting, as he did, ' Laus Deo ' to some of his church-pieces,[36] points to a faith inherited from childhood, and helping to contribute sweetness without cloying, virility without asperity, devotion without sentimentality, to an inspiration at once Italian, German and Catholic in a wondrous union.[37]

[35] Place.

[36] These words occur at the end of the French full scores of the *Sanctus, O Salutaris* (4 times), and *Pater Noster, Ave Maria,* and *Lauda Sion* (once).

[37] In this estimate I am supported by both French and German critics: ' It is in sacred music that this great musician rose to a prodigious height. There, beauty of melody, dramatic conception, the most exquisite purity of style, the most profound science, and the most novel effects are all combined ; there, by an art previously unknown, the ancient and the modern style unite to form the most perfect whole imaginable.'—Fétis.

' Nothing more tender, more soothing is there than the accents of the prayer, more touching than the cry, of suffering humanity, in the Kyrie of the Mass in F, in his Agnus Deis, and in the first strophes of his Requiem. If he represents the Passion and Death of Christ, the heart feels itself wounded with the most sublime emotion ; and when he recounts the Last Judgment, the blood freezes with dread at the redoubled and menacing calls of the exterminating angel. All those admirable pictures that the Raphaels and Michael Angelos have painted with colours and the brush. Cherubini brings forth with the voice and the orchestra.'—Miel.

' From these musical rubbish-heaps, in which so many great masters are buried, Cherubini's works rise like the Pyramids. . . . The severe studies to which he so steadily devoted himself in his youth, now made themselves felt in every voice and every bar ; whilst availing himself of all the modern licences in harmony, the spirit of his music retained a certain severity, which, like leaven, imparted a wholesome bitter to the composition. . . . An objection can hardly be raised to the assertion that Cherubini is the greatest composer of sacred music in this [the nineteenth] century.'—Hiller.

CHAPTER II.

FRANCE AND ENGLAND.

1809—1815.

'I cannot of that music rightly say,
Whether I hear or see or taste the tones ;
O ! what a heart subduing melody !'

NEWMAN.

Pimmalione at the Tuileries—Napoleon—*Le Chant sur La mort d'Haydn*—
Ode for the Emperor's marriage—Litanies for Prince Esterhazy—
Le Crescendo—The Mass in D Minor—*Les Abencérages—Bayard à
Mezières*—Honours for Cherubini—2nd visit to London—Composes for
the Philharmonic Society an overture, a cantata, and a symphony—
Offer from the Prussian Court—Return to Paris—A Cantata.

WHEN Napoleon left Vienna in 1805, he brought Crescentini, the singer, to Paris, and it was agreed that an opera should be written for him, without mention of the writer's name. In 1809, therefore, some of Cherubini's friends, who had tried to overcome Napoleon's aversion towards the Florentine composer's music, now persuaded Cherubini to write an opera anonymously. The 1-act 'Pimmalione,' with words from Cimador's ' Pimmalione,' produced in 1788 at Venice,[1] was the result. The 1st performance took place 30 Nov. 1809, at the Théâtre du Château des Tuileries, with Grassini and Crescentini as singers. ' Pimmalione!' exclaims Fétis enthusiastically, ' charming work, of a totally different character from the other productions of Cherubini, and in which you find some scenes of the happiest conception.' At the grand ' scena ' in the work, Napoleon was affected to tears ; he eagerly asked the name of its composer, yet, when told, showed more surprise than satisfaction, and said nothing ; but after-

[1] *Grove,* i. 358a

wards sent Cherubini a sum of money, and requested him
to write the music for an Ode on his approaching
marriage with the Archduchess Marie Louise, which
Cherubini accordingly did in the May of 1810.[2] The
latter also had the score of 'Pimmalione' handsomely
bound, and given to the Grand Chamberlain, who was
charged to present it to the Emperor; but Cherubini
heard nothing of the expected audience, the presentation,
or the book.

In Feb. 1810 a 'Chant sur la mort d'Haydn,' composed, according to Cherubini, in 1805, was performed at
the Conservatoire, and later on in Vienna. But Haydn
died in 1809. One explanation is that his death was
reported in that year; another that in 1805 Cherubini
wrote a hymn in honour of Haydn, which, being laid by
till after the latter's death, was, as I think Denne-Baron
hints, put to new words on its performance in 1810. 'I am
not much pleased with the poetry of the hymn,' wrote Carpani, '. . . but I know that the music was worthy of Haydn
himself . . . the audience were deeply moved.'[3] An
affecting trait in this Chant is noticed by Miel. This is a
'motivo,' which, without being actually taken from any in
the 'Creation,' recalls the section in the 3rd part,
descriptive of the creation of man. The work was a success
and it was repeated 29 April. You cannot mistake
Cherubini's intention of reflecting Haydn's inspiration
through his own.[4] Elaborate in some aspects as a composer, this made Cherubini value all the more highly
Haydn's naturalness and breadth. For though Haydn's
music is not on the whole deep, yet it is like an old friend
whose voice sounds pleasantly. What perfect part-writing!

[2] Not as stated, April 1811. *L. Cherubini,* Fritzsch.
[3] *Le Haydine,* 1812, *cit.* Pougin, *M.W.,* 1883, 189. Compare Beyle,
22 Aug. 1809, in *Lives of Haydn and Mozart, etc.,* 1818, 315, an unacknow-
ledged reproduction of Carpani by Bombet (*alias* Stendahl, otherwise Beyle).
[4] *Les Tablettes de Polymnie, cit.* Pougin, *M.W.,* 1883, 190. says that
'Cherubini has depicted the charm of Haydn's pure strains so truthfully,
that we almost believe the music to be Haydn's.' In the action 2 nymphs of
the Danube offer consolation.

How easily it all runs! It is like nature itself. There is
nothing unintelligible therein. You cannot fancy it other
than it is. You wonder, so to speak, it was not found out
before. According to Reichardt's statement in his 'Briefe
aus Paris,' Cherubini's own breadth of treatment, where
intricacy might otherwise have overmastered him, is owing
to this appreciation and study of Haydn in his symphonies.
In July 1810, Cherubini wrote his lovely ' Litanie della
Vergine' for Prince Esterhazy, who, leaving Paris then,
after having lived some years there, sent Cherubini a ring
worth 4,000 dollars.[5]

Cherubini brought out the 1-act ' Le Crescendo ' at
the Opéra Comique 1st Sept. ' Long developments
destroyed the scenic action. There was, however, . . . an
air sung by Martin, the originality of which was very
remarkable, the subject being the description of a combat,
given by a man who hates noise of any kind. The air is
sung "sotto voce," and the orchestra accompanies "pianissimo." There is nothing more piquant than this creation
of Cherubini's genius.'[6] The work is said to have failed
because of its din. ' Le Crescendo,' in fact, encountered
' a "crescendo of hisses." '[7] ' Then it was found too
noisy ; nowadays it would not be thought noisy enough.'[8]
Tchaikowsky's ' 1812 ' is noisier !

According to contemporaries, the music was masterly,
but the book weak ; the overture ' a model dialogue, a
piquant conversation,' producing ' a prodigious effect ;' the
1st air, sung by Chénard, ' supremely beautiful.' Of the
duet between him and Solié, the contemporary account

---

[5] Cherubini, Eler, Méhul, Pradher, and Catel were constituted commis-
sioners to report on de St. Pern's new instrument called the 'Organon
Lyricon,' in this year. A favourable report was sent by the commission to
the Minister of the Interior 12 Aug. 1810. This was not the only time that
our composer formed one of a commission of this kind. Thus, he reported
with Lefèvbre, Eler, Duvernoy, Méhul, Gossec, and Catel, on Müller's
clarinet ; and 20, 22, 15 July 1815, with Sarrette, Méhul, Gossec, Catel,
Rose, Jadin, Baillot, Adam, and Pradher, on Grenié's organ. Castil-
Blaze's *Dictionnaire de la Musique Moderne.*

[6] Fétis, *Biog. Univ.* art. ' Cherubini.'

[7] *Mémorial Dramatique, cit.* Pougin, *M.W.,* 1883, 207.

[8] Castil-Blaze.

CHANT

Sur la Mort

DE JOSEPH HAYDN

A TROIS VOIX, AVEC ACCOMPAGNEMENTS.

Dedié

a Son Altesse Sérénissime

Le Prince Nicolas Esterhazy de Palantha

Beau Frère d'Eléctetion, Chevalier de la Toison d'Or, grand Croix de l'ordre de S.te Étienne, Chambellan, et Conseiller actuel intime d'État, Comte Suprême et héréditaire du Comtat d'Odenbourg, Lieutenant Général, Colonel propriétaire d'un Regiment d'Infanterie hongroise, et Capitaine de la Garde noble hongroise de Sa Majesté Impériale Royale Apostolique, &c. &c.

PAR L. CHERUBINI

L'un des Inspecteurs du Conservatoire Impérial de Musique et Membre de l'Institut Royal de Hollande.

Prix

Proprieté de l'Auteur   Déposé à la Bibliothèque Impériale

A PARIS

Au Magazin de Musique, rue de Richelieu, N.º 76, vis-à-vis celle de Ménars, et en face du Petit Dunkerque.

671

A Son Altesse Sérénissime le Prince Nicolas Esterhazÿ
de Galantha.

Monseigneur

Mon admiration pour le sublime génie, et les immortels ouvrages
de Joseph Haydn, m'imposait le devoir d'offrir un tribut,
aux manes de cet homme célèbre, et généralement regretté.
Mais il manquait à ce tribut le nom du Prince qui sut
aimer, et apprécier ce rare talent, et je suis trop heureux que
Votre Altesse Sérénissime, m'ait permis de lui faire
hommage de l'hommage même que je devais à Haydn.
Daignez, Monseigneur, agréer mon ouvrage avec bonté, ainsi
que ma parfaite reconnaissance
Je suis avec le plus profond respect, Monseigneur,

De Votre Altesse Sérénissime,

Le très humble et très obéissant serviteur
L. Cherubini

observes : ' . . . the orchestra doggedly keeps to one-figured accompaniment, with an agreeable and melodious subject . . . the dialogue . . . proceeds with such clearness, the elocution is so true, and the musical logic so well observed, that we must hear it several times before we notice the magic of the accompaniment. Pieces of such merit are very rare. . . .'[9] A few compositions were composed at Chimay in 1810 on a 2nd visit thereto in the autumn.

Towards the end of March Cherubini began, and 7 Oct. finished, his 2nd Mass in D minor. Thus he spent only 6 months over probably the longest Mass extant.[10] I have found no account of it, or of a 1st performance, so I must essay to point out some of its more prominent beauties and peculiarities. Here Cherubini seems to forestall any attempt to outstrip him in developing his dramatic principle in Church Music, yet, taken as a whole, theatrical is about the last word to apply even to such a work as this. He exhibits therein a regrettable redundancy alongside an admirable succinctness, as well as certain instrumental effects seen in opera, but solemnity and devotion are comparatively seldom absent.

In largeness of design, complicated detail, and sublimity of conception, Bach's B minor and Beethoven's D major may approach it or equal it ; and Schubert's too lengthy E flat, and Niedermeyer's fine B minor, present points for comparison. While its appearance caused division of opinion in Paris as to its being superior in merit to the previous Mass in F, its forms and ideas seem more novel, and it is at some advantage as a 4-part work with the earlier Mass. Its length chiefly arises as much from repetition of text, as from number or development of themes, as is clearly seen in the Gloria and Agnus Dei. Curtailed, hardly a Mass could vie with it for devotional melodies, and a sense of this doubtless has led to its being,

[9] *Les Tablettes de Polymnie, cit.* Pougin, *ib.,* 236.
[10] Appendix II.

with good results, thus dealt with twice in England.[11]
Would that the composer had shortened it ; as the
principle of others altering his work is not one, as a rule, to
be freely encouraged.   Whole passages can certainly be
left out here without changing a bar, owing to the
independence of the different movements.   The Gloria has
5 sections and 10 different 'tempi,' and there is no
attempt at a continuous whole in the Gloria, Credo, or
Agnus Dei.[12]

   The Kyrie, after an Italian form, consists of 3 movements, only connected by the opening theme, and an agitated pendant.   It opens with a majestic prelude, followed

[11] Curtailed, it was was long in the repertory of Farm St. Church,
London (11 Feb. 1872, etc.), and was given, shortened, 8 Dec. 1887, and
26 May 1888, at the Oratory, Birmingham. 'Everybody seemed pleased . . .
the whole thing fits admirably together,' was a verdict.   It was performed
entire 5 Nov. 1865 by the then State-aided Royal Musical Institute at
Florence ; by the Bach Choir at St. James' Hall, London, under Mr. Walter
Bache, 21 April 1880 ; and at the Festivals of Worcester (twice, 1881-4) ;
Hereford (1888) ; Birmingham (1894) ; and Gloucester (1901), and it became
an established favourite with executants and audience, like his Mass in C,
and the C minor Requiem.
   [12] It is forbidden to break up into pieces, completely detached, the
versicles that are necessarily inter-connected.'—Decree Cong. Rites, 7 July
1894.

by a descending chromatic passage in syncopation that
leads to the part-vocal repetition of the opening phrase.
A crescendo culminates in a brief agitated passage, to be

again succeeded by the chromatic passage, and an instrumental reminiscence of the opening.   Without pause, the
'Christe' in ¾ time is entered upon ; a beautiful movement

ending with a 'crescendo' and 'decrescendo,' a moving
prayer.   Again is heard the agitated passage slightly
extended,—then a pause, and we enter on the 3rd movement,—a fugue with an oft-recurring refrain, the whole
soon a swelling sea of polyphony.   Yet another pause ;

the alto re-commences, and a 'crescendo' culminates in a
thrilling cry ; and then comes an after-calm, expressive of
trust in God's mercy.   Following the refrain, the violins

descend in 3rds and rise ; ' Kyrie ' is murmured, unaccompanied ; then a repetition ; and as the voices whisper
' Kyrie,' once more there comes a reminiscence of the
opening with a close, after a pause, in D major. [13]

In many composers' hands, a fugue has been made
inappropriate for a Kyrie, owing to the theme or ' tempo '
chosen. Thus Mozart's, in the Requiem Kyrie, has been
adversely criticized. Only in this D minor Mass has
Cherubini employed in the Kyrie a fugue at all, but it is
duly adapted to express supplication. In Haydn's and
Hummel's Kyrie fugues, something other than mercy,
and beyond trust, indeed a sort of triumph, seems sometimes the suggestion.

After this crushing lament, the gloom is dispersed
with Shakespearian force in the Gloria opening. Haydn

[13] To keep the pitch in this Kyrie is no light task, as festival performances
show, and it is rarely managed, owing to the fatigue of voices engaged on
too many works in 4 days.

has a like momentum, but I know nothing exactly similar
in church music for varied rhythm; and for overwhelming
grandeur we may seek a parallel in Bach's 'Sanctus.'
The sombre and subdued 'Et in terra pax' follows
instead of preceding a first 'laudamus Te,' the whole

section closing with a 2nd 'laudamus Te,' etc., to another
subject.   This is repeated with electrifying effect.

The exquisite Italian beauty of the 'Gratias agimus'
steals upon us gradually, by surprise.   Note, too, the
majestic dignity of the bass phrase, 'Propter magnam
gloriam tuam,' with the moving phrase at 'Jesu Christe.'
We may well believe that such a movement is one of the
the 'separate subjects' referred to by Spohr, as affording
one of the 'grandest proofs' that Cherubini knew the true
church style.   The stately 'Qui tollis,' with its panoply of
accompaniment, is in touching contrast with the 'miserere;'

just expressing in sound the sense of the words. None can regret its recurrence. A 'heavenly length' of joyous melody in the 'Quoniam' is succeeded by a slow affirma-

tion of the closing words of the Gloria before the great fugue, 'Cum Sancto Spiritu,' anticipated by Haydn (for example) in the Gloria of his 5th Mass, but here the theme used is the actual subject of the fugue solemnly given out in advance.

The Credo—the test of greatness as a Mass composer—opens with a chromatic passage, and then the word 'Credo' is repeated at intervals : a plan Beethoven adopted, not too successfully, in his Mass in D, and Cherubini in his Masses in F and A. The danger lies in too great an upset of the general musical idea's continuity. A master like Cherubini avoids this. The pit-falls surrounding this section are avoided where, as in some churches, the Creed is always chanted by the people and choir.

The 6-tet of the 'Incarnatus' and the 'Crucifixus' monotone for 63 bars are veritable inspirations, the muted violins wailing in an ebbing and flowing tide of

harmony.[14]   A symphonic passage conducts us to another
surprise.   In 4 pages of loveliness, the rest of the Creed
is disposed of, from the 'Et in Spiritum' down to the
final 'Amen.'   What Italian suavity and unction! what
gentle and refined accompaniment! truly 'the still small
voice' of power is here, while the tumultuous, impetuous,
Petrine expression of belief, prior to the 'Incarnatus,' is
exchanged for serenest strain as of seraphs affirming
their Faith.

Towards the close of this tender strain, the 'Et
vitam venturi' becomes even more touching with the
tearful effect of a 'tremolando' in the accompaniment.
An academic fugue, on a subject of little intrinsic interest,
but finely worked out, closes a marvel of religious art.

In the Sanctus, of due length, composed in 1822 as
a substitute for the original, the soprano's 'pleni sunt'
comes thus heralded :

and an exulting 'hosanna' reaches its climax at the cry,

[14] Mozart and Weber, in their respective Masses in G, have set an
example to Haydn, Hummel, Beethoven, and Cherubini, in not repeating
the words, 'et incarnatus est de Spiritu Sancto ex Mariâ virgine, et Homo
factus est.'   The 'Incarnatus' is the most solemn part of the 'Credo.'
Everyone kneels here except Ministers, who bow with head uncovered,
and according to strict rule, this outward Adoration lasts only during a
single recitation of the above words.   Thus either the Adoration is over
while repetitions continue, or worshippers are kneeling after the proper
time.

followed on repetition by a fine effect : the ¾ time of the
movement is changed to the accent of common time :

The well-known Benedictus for solo and chorus, with
and without accompaniment, as with Beethoven's earlier
Benedictus, opens with a prelude, and the soprano enters
alone on an inspiring phrase that forms the pivot, as it
were of a movement, like Beethoven's, too extended for
the brief time allowable between the Elevation and the
Pater Noster ; but if there be anywhere in religious music
two more devotional pieces than these from Palestrina to
the present day, it would be a matter of surprise to me.
Both, like Niedermeyer's Mass, ' conduce to prayer,' to
use M. Ortigue's phrase, and what more can poor
moderns do in their attempt, however faulty, to sing the
praises of the Eternal King ?

The Agnus Dei begins triumphantly, but the instrumental and vocal replies that succeed are full of appropriate
sorrow and pathos expressive of the text.   At the
' miserere ' the voices descend the gamut in imitation,
suggestive of the sinner's fear in God's presence, the
whole closing with a passage very expressive of supplication.   Again, what can surpass this genuine church-music?

Later on, a striking effect is produced by the reiterated burst of 'Agnus Dei,' that dies away to a whisper in the same bar, with a weird effect in a diminished 5th.

This, repeated twice a 3rd lower, is yet another of the notable effects, by 'piano' and 'forte,' with which this Mass is so full.

The devotional 'Dona nobis,' is one of the world's great melodies, I believe, in French estimation, taken up in successive sections by the different parts until the

Agnus Dei recurs; an intrusion on the 'dona' often seen, but better avoided; as much as Beethoven's drum in the Mass in D, to contrast war with peace. It would have been well, indeed, had Cherubini, as in his Mass in C, left the tender prayer of his 'dona' in undisturbed possession at the close of this Mass, which, if it had been, as the French say, more 'nette,' would have vied, both in and out of Church, with any modern Mass in the world.

In January 1813 Cherubini began 'Les Abencérages' or 'L'Etendard de Grénade,' with an uninteresting book by Jouy, from Florian's 'Gonzalve de Courdoue,' and it was produced 6 April at the Grand Opera.[15]

The characters are Almanzor, a Moorish general; Gonsalvo of Cordova, a Castilian general; Alemar, Vizier to King Mulay-Hassein (Dérivis); Oktair, Keeper of the Standards; Abderam, Chief Justice of the Senate of Elders; Kaled, a leader; Alamir, a confidant of the Vizier; Noraime, Princess of the Royal Family (Mme. Branchu); Egilone, one of the informers.

Napoleon and the Empress were present at the 1st performance, though it was the night before their departure for Germany, resulting in encounters with the Russians at Lützen and Bautzen. The 'bons-mots' of the talkers somewhat damaged its reputation, and an impression seemed to prevail that the composer had not done himself justice. Yet men of weight and influence in the Parisian musical world pronounced this work, the 1st written by him for Grand Opera, as solid, and even finer,

[15] There are 10 Nos. in the 1st Act; 8 in the 2nd; and 7 in the 3rd. The House in the Rue Richelieu was pulled down in 1820, and [in 1822] the Opera went to the Rue Le Pelletier. Sutherland Edwards' *History of the Opera*, ii. 189-9. Lafage inadvertently says *Les Abencérages* appeared in 1810.

if more laboured than the 'Médée': in brief, that there
was nothing wanting.   One Geoffroy, too, spoke a good
deal, freely distributing praise and blame.   Pougin, while
admitting its merits, refers to 'deplorably tedious passages,'
to its being 'painful and fatiguing to sit out;' and to its
reduction to 2 acts being no remedy for a bad book.
However, Spontini was not deterred from putting the
opera on the Berlin stage, and sent Cherubini a considerable portion of the proceeds,[16] an ample acknowledgment
of all he owed him in the matter of 'La Vestale.'

The overture has some notable features.   The
opening subject of the 'allegro' is certainly not very
striking, but we may note as characteristics worthy of the
master the use made of it afterwards, and of a certain
short phrase of semiquavers which occurs first of all in the

2nd bar; the vigorous theme that modulates into B flat,
and subsequently into F and A minor, the wild, weird
effect of the succeeding chromatic passage, and above all,

[16] *Grove* iii. 666-81.

the beautiful melody heralded by the contest for supremacy between D sharp and D natural.[17]

There are also two ballets, one in the 1st act, and another a long, Moorish and Spanish one, after the end of the 3rd act ; but the opera could only run 20 nights.

In the work is the scena for Almanzor ' Suspendez à ces murs mes armes, ma banniere,' sung with such success at concerts, by Ponchard and Delsarte ; and the 2 airs, ' Enfin j'ai vu naître l'aurore,' and ' Poursuis tes belles. destinées ; ' the 1st of which 3, ' full of dignity and beauty,' Denne-Baron deems, ' one of the most beautiful things that dramatic music has to be proud of since Gluck.' Many years afterwards, Mendelssohn, in a letter to Moscheles, dated from Leipsic, 30 Nov. 1837, asked : ' Has Onslow written anything new ? and old Cherubini ? There's a matchless fellow ! I've got his '' Abencérages,'' and cannot sufficiently admire the sparkling fire, the clever original phrasing, the extraordinary delicacy and refinement with which the whole is written, or feel grateful enough to the grand old man for it. Besides it is all so free, and bold, and spirited.'[18] The success of the opera was marred by the disastrous tidings from Russia of the burning of Moscow, and retreat of the French, when famine and disease did their work,— recalling the poet's words on the lost traveller whom

[17] Cherubini's overture to *Les Abencérages*, 'the least attractive of any he has written, still contains many indubitable proofs of the ability which may be found more fully displayed in the others. . . . There are several detached passages of sound modulation, several melodius streaks of light, the efforts of the sun endeavouring to emerge from the somewhat cloudy atmosphere in which it is involved ; but yet, as a whole, it will satisfy neither the critic nor the amateur, who expect from the author of *Anacréon* something superior to those ephemeral productions which are performed in England, called English operas, and to which a very considerable portion of scraping and blowing is often appended by way of overture.'—F.W.H., in the *Quarterly Musical Magazine.*

It was given by the New Philharmonic Society, 6 May 1871 ; *Lodoïska's* overture following 3 June. *Lodoïska, Médée, Anacréon,* and *Les Abencérages,* ' are replete with vigour and character ; their admirably drawn outline, exquisite finish and instrumentation, cause them to be reckoned models of their kind.'—*Schlüter.* The opera, if begun in 1812 (Cat.) was long preparing.

[18] *Letters,* ed. 1867, 177.

' The deadly winter seizes ; shuts up sense,
And o'er his inmost vitals creeping cold,
Lays him along the snows a stiffen'd corse,
Stretch'd out and bleaching in the northern blast.'
                                        THOMSON.

' Les Abencérages,' if we pass over ' Ali Baba,' largely an earlier work, re-written many years afterwards, may be deemed Cherubini's farewell to opera, although he applied for the managership of the Grand Opera in 1819, in succession to Persuis. Viotti, his old friend, says Pougin, obtained the post, and Viotti wrote to Cherubini 5 Nov. 1819 : ' I have been informed, my dear friend, that you are angry. . . . I did not seek the post. . . . I cannot help feeling extremely sorry at having been the rival of a friend whom I love, and whose genius I have always respected and appreciated, . . . of a man whom I shall never cease to love, whatever changes may take place in his heart."[19]

The French Government saw the necessity of rousing the spirits and courage of the people in so much calamity, and the opera of ' Bayard à Mezières ' appeared by order of the Duke of Rovigo 12 Feb. 1814.

Cherubini, in his catalogue, writes that it ' was composed by order of the police, the music is by Messrs. Catel, Boieldieu, Nicolo, and myself. My portion of the composition was only a trio, a concerted piece, and the war chant at the end.' [20]

Subsequently, by special request, Cherubini wrote a ' Chant guerrier,' inserted in a piece that failed, entitled ' La Rançon de Duguesclin,' or ' Les Moeurs du Quatorzieme Siècle,' represented 17 March at the Théâtre Français. Then, being appointed 2 Feb. 1814 Lieutenant of the National Guard's band, we find him producing 8

---

[19] Pougin, *M. W.* 1883, 627. In 1820, Cherubini betook himself for a new opera (unnamed) to one Biolti. *L. Cherubini,* Fritzsch.

[20] Picchianti and Gamucci mention a chorus in the opera of *L'Oriflamme* as Cherubini's ; the former telling us that it is the only piece now remembered out of *Bayard* and *L'Oriflamme,* and contains surprising effects by means of *pianos* and *fortes.* From a letter cited by Pougin, it would appear that his work in *Bayard* was engraved. *M. W.* 1883, 385.

military compositions, 'for the use of the music of the Prussian regiment, commanded by Colonel Witzleben.' How plainly this tells of the unsettled period between 1814 and 1815! Then Cherubini wrote, in quick succession, 2 cantatas for fêtes, which were given by the Etat Major and City of Paris in July and August 1814, the latter before the King.

The final restoration of the Bourbons, though depriving Cherubini for a time of his post at the Conservatoire, saved him from further neglect at Napoleon's hands; honours flowed in upon him, and besides raising from 3 to 6 the number of musicians eligible for the Institute, Louis XVIII., on 7 Dec. 1814, made him Chevalier of the Legion of Honour.[21]

In 1815, Cherubini, whose reputation was 2nd only to that of Beethoven, was again invited to London; this time by the Philharmonic Society, then in the 3rd year of its existence. At its general meeting 28 Dec. 1814, on the proposition of Clementi, seconded by Cramer, and carried by 8 votes to 6, £200 was offered Cherubini for the 3 pieces as given below. He accepted the offer, and set out for England 25 Feb. and was over here during nearly the whole of Napoleon's Hundred Days. These 3 compositions were :

1. An overture in G, begun Feb. in Paris, fin. March in London.
2. A symphony in D, begun March, fin. 24 April.
3. A pastoral cantata for 4 voices, ' Inno allo Primavera,' with full instrumental accompaniment, begun 8, fin. 19 May.

I purchased by chance a letter in Italian from Cherubini, without date, addressed to Mr. S. Vestri, 6, Rupert-street, Haymarket, and clearly written in 1815.

[21] Raoul Rochette in his *Eloge* on Cherubini before the Institute, seems to think that Napoleon had made him such not as composer, but as leader of the above band : ' Thus did Napoleon still find means of being unjust towards M. Cherubini, even in doing him an act of injustice.' Clément says that Louis XVIII. conferred this distinction ; others give the date when it was conferred as above, which, if accurate, makes Clément's statement correct, for Napoleon was in Elba from May 1814 to March 1815 ; and although the Legion of Honour was a creation of his own, the order was confirmed by Louis XVIII. in April 1814. Lastly, Cherubini says he was appointed ' by a royal decree a member,' while the chief Academies of Europe addressed him with the title of member or correspondent.

The subject-matter seems to refer to the above piece, set to Italian words:

'Friday.—Most-esteemed Signor Vestri,—Well, I shall expect your work to-morrow morning without fail. I hope you will do me the favour of coming to me, or of letting me know whether I am to go to you.   I warn you that I shall be unable to wait longer for those words, as the Philharmonic concerts are going to conclude, and this piece must be ready for the last, which will be shortly. Believe me, as I have the pleasure of signing myself, your affectionate friend and servant,

'L. CHERUBINI.'

Apparently Vestri was not in time, and this work was not performed by the Society,[22] till the next year, 1816.

Cherubini made his 1st appearance at the Philharmonic's 3rd concert of its 3rd season, 13 March 1815, which opened with the 'Anacréon' overture, and included a Beethoven symphony.   This overture, twice encored, had been the 1st piece ever given by the Society at the 1st concert, 8 March 1813, of its 1st season, during which 3 other overtures and vocal pieces of Cherubini were given. In a letter as to the 4th concert of 3 April 1815, he writes that the new overture was encored, as also the 'Incarnatus' of the Mass in F.[23]   The 'Anacréon' was also given again.   The symphony, done 1 May,[24] comparatively failed, and was not performed again till 1864 and 1870.   'The symphony,' writes Schumann, 'if I am not mistaken, pleased so little on its 1st performance in Vienna that Cherubini refused to publish it.'[25]   It was afterwards turned into a 4-tet, with a change of key to C,

[22] Philh. Soc. Progr. 1870, etc.   Pougin dates the above note Wed.
[23] The overture was given by Mr. Manns at the Crystal Palace Concerts from the printed and somewhat different German score, and I recall being greatly struck with its beauty and originality at the time.   In fact Cherubini's orchestration appeals to my sense of hearing as original and well-balanced to a degree unsurpassed by any other great Master.
[24] *M.T.* March 1908, writes 3 April, but this is an error, as the symphony was not finished till 24 of that month.
[25] *Music and Manners,* 3rd ed. 1881, *ed.* Ritter.   We shall see later on Schumann's remarks about this symphony being turned into a 4-tet.

and a new 'Lento' replacing the 'Adagio'—why, it is hard to say. There are few stranger things in musical history than this great man's supposed failure in this his one symphony. But did he fail? Were his critical Viennese audience altogether dissatisfied? One German opinion was thus expressed:—'The symphony is rich, well worked out, and nowhere marred by too much art, and recalls Haydn more than anyone else, only that it is not so humorous, and is more imaginative.'[26] The Society's analytical programme speaks approvingly of all 4 movements, calling the Minuet 'the boldest,' and the Trio 'the most original and characteristic portion of the work.'

Interesting details of Cherubini's 2nd visit to London are given by Pougin, from whom I make a few extracts.

In a letter to his wife from London, 22 March 1815, he recounts his doings: how he had 'dined at the house of Mr. Broadwood (the supposed future husband of Victorine, as Ciceri says), with Erard's son. . . . Among the party . . . were Cramer, Hullmandel, and others. . . . I went to finish my evening at the opera, where I felt thoroughly wearied, so bad was it. . . .' On Tuesday his wife's health is drunk in port wine. 'Do not be afraid, my dear, of writing at too great length. I am too eager for your letters and for news about you not to relish them deliberately, however long they may be. . . . I am now in the midst of dinner-parties and society, where I am very well received and petted. The day before yesterday I went to a grand dinner given me by Braham. . . . H.R.H. the Duke of Sussex, one of the King's sons, a great musical amateur, very affable, and altogether a good fellow, was present. He would have me placed next him at table, and was exceedingly amiable. We drank like fishes, and remained 3 hours and a half at table. At

---

[26] *L. Cherubini,* Fritzsch, 31. *M.T.* writes that there seems to be no record of Cherubini's benefit concert (tickets 10s. 6d. each. to be had of Mr. Cherubini, No. 10, Charles St., Manchester Square), &c., as advertised in the 'Morning Chronicle,' when the overture was announced again, and some selections from a new Mass (unspecified).

10 o'clock we had coffee ; we then played whist, and left
at half-past 12. . . . I embrace you tenderly, and do the
same to the children. My best remembrances to the
ladies, all our friends, and especially my dear Méhul.
Adieu, my dear. I am as good as gold. Ever and wholly
yours.'

In the foregoing and another letter of 7 April it
would appear that there had been an idea of bringing
out ' Elisa,' but it fell through. ' I foresee,' he writes,
' that my journey here will be a failure ; . . . Money
runs away here like water, and the slightest things are
proportionately dear. Already my health, which up to
now has been good, is becoming bad ; for several days
" my nerves have been ill," and I suffer from a melancholy I cannot overcome. All this troubles, consumes, and
wears me away. On Sunday I attended Mass, as I am
accustomed to do, at the Catholic Chapel [Spanish Place,
London, W.], situated next our house. . . . Adieu, my
dear, I embrace you tenderly, as well as my children. I
leave you, for my head aches a great deal with writing
this letter, though I took a pleasure in doing so.' The
climate thoroughly disagreed with Cherubini, and induced
a subsequent breakdown for 3 years. Pougin has been
the 1st to show us that, while in England, Cherubini had
a most important offer, 4 March 1815, from the Prussian
King, through Count Brühl, Chamberlain and Intendant-
General of the Prussian Theatres Royal, to be Director of
the Royal Musical Establishment at Berlin. He was
expected to write 2 operas, serious or comic, every year
for the Theatre Royal ; to conduct his own operas, and,
if needs be, alternately with the 2nd director, grand
operas by foreign composers ; to conduct, on Royal command, any Court concert, and to be a professor of any
Conservatoire that might be established. Had this come
about, we might have had no Masses, or Requiems, and
certainly no Coronation Masses—a loss, indeed, to Art.

In his reply, Cherubini, alluding to the Hundred
Days, asks whether ' it would not be better to wait till

the tempest is over before proceeding with what you propose?' Besides, he had the place of Musical Superintendant from Louis XVIII., and 'could take no other engagement if, as I hope, he is restored to the throne. Nevertheless,' he continues, 'I do not decline the flattering offer you have made me ; I simply leave it in abeyance for a moment.' He asks : Should he accept 16,000 francs a year, with extra allowance, in case he becomes professor of a new Conservatoire, since what he holds 'in a similar institution in Paris brings me in 5,000 francs with a residence?' His travelling expenses to Berlin, and an advance of 2,000 francs from his salary, conclude the terms. In the event, Napoleon's defeat and the return of the Bourbons, kept Cherubini in Paris. His journeying back thither, in June 1815, is indicated by a letter from Calais on the 5th, written at 8 a.m.

'. . . I started from London the day before yesterday, the 3rd June, . . . at half-past 5, and, after travelling all night, arrived in Dover at 9 in the morning. . . . At half-past 6 I went on board ; the weather was very favourable, but the wind extremely high. . . .' He was ill, and 15 hours crossing. After a few details this cold-hearted man (save the mark !) concludes :—' I can scarcely contain myself for joy at being near the moment of embracing you all. . . . Farewell, my darlings ; we shall soon see each other again.' [27]

He reached Paris 8th June 1815, and the turn political events had taken is shown by his writing in August a chorus and couplets for St. Louis' day and the couplets, 'Vive le Roi;' his own rapid activity by beginning 29, and completing 30 Jan. 1816, a cantata with soli, chorus, and grand orchestra, executed in the presence of the King and Royal Family, at the banquet given by the Royal Guard to the National and Body Guards at the Louvre Gallery.

[27] Diary, *M. W.*, 1883, 302, 384, 404.

CHAPTER III.

FRANCE.

1816.

'Hosannas pealing down the long drawn aisle,
And Requiems answered by the pulse that beats
Devoutly.'
                                        WORDSWORTH.

Cherubini, King's chapel-master—Mass in C—[Mass in E flat]—*Pater Noster*
—*O Salutaris*—*Lauda Sion*—*Sanctus O Salutaris*—*Ecce Panis*—*Ave
Maria*—*Le Mariage de Salamon*—Requiem in C minor.

THE year 1816 was an 'Annus Mirabilis' in the history
of this great man, and at the very outset occurred an
event fraught with consequence alike to himself, to art,
and to sacred music.

A Requiem was ordered for Louis XVI.'s anniversary,
21 Jan. 1816, at St. Denis, in presence of the King and
his Court; Martini, very ill at the time, went down to
conduct his own work. The King congratulated him
thereon, but on reaching home Martini took to his bed,
and died 3 weeks later. Cherubini had taken his duty in
the Royal Choir 2 Feb., and became, 15 Feb., Superintendant of the King's Music in his place. The
appointment was offered through his Majesty's 1st
gentleman-in-waiting, and entailed a yearly salary of
6,000 francs. Thus it was not till 55 years of age that
Cherubini ceased to be anxious about his livelihood.[1]

'The musical directors of the Royal Chapel,' wrote

---

[1] Pougin shows that Cherubini's income at this time included 1,200
francs (increased by attendance fees varying from 400 to 450 f. a year) as
member of the Institute; 2 separate pensions of 2,000 and 800 f. from the
King, and 2 salaries of 3,000 f. as Professor of Composition at the Royal
School of Music, and 6,000 f. as Superintendent of the King's Chapel, with
600 f. extra refresher. In all, 14,050 f. or £562 a year.

Spohr, from Paris, 12 Jan. 1821, 'do not conduct the music themselves, and preside only in their court uniform at the head of the vocal 'personnel,' without taking any active part in the performance. The director 'de facto' is Plantade; Kreutzer, the leading player of the 1st violin; and Baillot, of the 2nd. The orchestra is composed of the 1st artistes in Paris, the chorus is powerful and good. Every Mass is rehearsed once or twice, and under Plantade's sure and spirited direction everything goes exceedingly well.'[2]   Of the music of the King's chapel, Fétis observes: 'The ordinary service of the chapel of the Kings Louis XVIII. and Charles X. consisted of a Low Mass occupying at most half an hour, during which musicians sang various pieces, the whole duration of which was not allowed to be longer than the Mass said by the priest. This necessity was new to Cherubini, whose genius was prone to long developments. It was not without effort that he contrived to compress his ideas within such straitened limits; but his prodigious skill came in to surmount all obstacles, and each of the pieces that issued from his pen for the service of the chapel during the succeeding 14 years excited the admiration of artistes. . . . An entire Mass was rarely executed at the King's chapel; often the whole duration of the service was taken up by a 'Kyrie,' followed by a motet. It is thus that you remark 13 "Kyries," . . . 2 "Glorias," a "Credo,"' etc.[3]

[2] The conductors or 'maîtres,' as they were called, were Plantade and Valentino; the 'inspector' was Grégoire, the librarian Lefebvre, and the secretary Durais. In the choir were 3 1st and 3 2nd sopranos; 3 tenors, among whom was Ponchard; 3 basses, including Levasseur. All these were solo singers; and for the chorus there were 7 1st and 6 2nd sopranos, besides 6 boys for both 1st and 2nd, 12 tenors, and 10 basses. For the orchestra there were 7 1st violins, among whom were Baillot leader, and Habeneck; 7 2nd violins, Kreutzer leader, and C. Habeneck, 4 violas, Tariot leader, 6 violoncellos, 4 double basses, 2 flutes, 2 hautboys (Brod one of them), 2 clarinets, 2 trombones, 2 bassoons, 3 'cors,' 2 harps, and 1 drum. There were also 2 pianists and 2 organists. Such is a brief account of this perfect choir, whose equal perhaps no other place in Europe could then show.
[3] *Biog. Univ.* ii. 270.

Hiller, who spent half a day in Cherubini's study, by leave of Mme. Cherubini, tells us that the composer had carefully and characteristically noted down, at the end of the Royal Chapel scores, ' with painful exactitude,' to half and even a quarter of a minute, the time each piece should take.[4] It is said that he continued studying deeply Palestrina, as also Clari, Marcello, and Jomelli. In January was begun, and 4 March following finished, the well-known 3rd Mass in C, for 4, 5, and 6 voices. Fr. Girod knew some musicians who preferred it to Cherubini's other Masses. ' We find in it,' he says, ' striking contrasts in the " Gloria " and " Credo " between the 4-tet and the general chorus, and the 2 4-tets of soprani and men's voices. Not so grand as the Coronation Mass, there is more unction felt in it ; it is a tissue of melodic beauties united to a consummate perfection in the details of the vocal and instrumental parts. It is a music full of life, of piety and learning.' Little further has been said of this Mass, and as I have often heard it, I venture to offer a few remarks thereon. Cherubini is now a chapel-master, and we see in this Mass conciseness and liturgical

---

[4] *Macmillan*, July 1875, 271. These times have been given in the 1st volume of posthumous works issued by Richault, but not in the later volumes by Ricordi.

Most of the biographers apparently, on the authority of *Castil-Blaze* *(Chapelle-Musique des Rois de France)* have said that Cherubini shared his office with Lesueur. Seeing, it is said, that his acceptance of the post would entail the dismissal of Lesueur, who had held it with Martini under the former régime, Cherubini said to the minister : ' Monseigneur, Lesueur my friend is more worthy than I am of this high position. If I had not a young family to bring up, if I were rich, I should refuse it altogether ; but if his Majesty is willing to allow me to share with Lesueur the super-intendence of his music, I will accept it with thankfulness.' So that Cheru-bini shared the office with Lesueur at a salary for himself of three thousand francs, Lesueur's 1st term beginning in April, Cherubini's 1 July. Pougin, against Fétis and Castil-Blaze, asserts that Cherubini and Martini were *sole* superintendents, and is supported by the silence of *Le Moniteur Univer-sel*, the official Governmental organ, as to Lesueur. However, Spohr, in a letter from Paris, 12 Jan. 1821, writes : ' Lesueur and Cherubini, the 2 directors of the music of the Royal chapel, assume the duties of their office every 3 months alternately ; our arrival took place during the time of Lesueur's directorship, and Cherubini's did not begin till 1st January.' When, too, music for the Coronation Mass of Charles X. was ordered in 1825, Cherubini and Lesueur together wrote the music ; so I think it is clear that Cherubini made Lesueur his assistant.

forms.   In the Mass in C, too, may be traced some influence of Beethoven's Mass in C, written 6 years before,
and at times the form is identical.[5]

The Kyrie is one movement, only disturbed by a
recitative not altogether undevotional, but, perhaps,
preferably absent in so perfect a prayer.   After a short
introduction and recitative, the section opens with a
melodious phrase, taken up by the voices, and carried
forward by the instruments.

The figure in the accompaniment that follows is the

1st appearance of what is made so much of in this Kyrie:

[5] 'On Sunday we did (in church) Cherubini's Mass in C major.'—
Mendelssohn, from Dusseldorf, 28 March 1821, to his father.   It has been
done 30 April 1871, etc. (minus *Gloria, Sanctus* and *Benedictus*), at Farm
St. Church, London ; entire (including Offertory) 10 April 1887 and 5 Jan.
1890, etc., at the Birmingham Oratory ; and 4 July and 8 Dec. 1897 (with
30 instruments), etc., at the London Oratory ; 24 May 1887 at St. James'
Hall, London, under Sir A. Mackenzie; at Birmingham (1882 and 1909);
Norwich (1887) ; and Bristol (1888) Festivals,—a great favourite with all.

it is almost as prominent as the phrase in the pastoral

Symphony of Beethoven.   Much is made out of little.
Thus, after the simple yet grand subject beginning in
canon at the 'Christe,' the soprano takes up that figure

(before half hidden in the instrumentation), and, supported
by the full chorus and bass solo, brings it forth with
enthralling effect, the orchestra persistently repeating the
phrase in advance on the 1st beat of the bar.   The move-

ment ends on a pedal point C, with the subject in canon
already noticed.   When the voices have died away, a few
solemn chords are heard, and then the orchestra subsides
into silence.

The 'Gloria,' in one movement again without a
break, is a brilliant section for 4-tets of soli and chorus,
and its 'Qui tollis' is impressive, with violins persistently
sounding A as the moving strain of wondrous harmony
proclaims the Atonement, and implores the Divine mercy,

and violoncellos mysteriously answering the voices at
pauses in the prayer. The 'Quoniam' opens like the
'Gloria,' only to make way for the fine 'Amen' fugue,
which would have been better set to more words. But
further than this; the 2nd brief part of a not very interesting theme appears to possess somewhat less dignity
than the 1st.

The 'Credo' for 5 voices opens spontaneously and
melodiously, and not repeating the words already intoned

by the celebrant. After a movement of wonderful freedom and power, the 'Incarnatus' yields a strain of
perfect beauty for sopranos and alto, whose airy tones,
after the grave reply of bass and tenor, in sombre relief,

become still more elevated. The 'Crucifixus,' from the

et in - car - na - tus est.   et in - carnatus est.

1st entry of tenor and bass in contrary motion, is awe-
striking in its gloomy depth, with a mysterious passage

cru - ci - fi - xus,   cru - ci -

cru - ci fi - - - - xus,   cru - ci - fi -

cru - ci - fi - - - - - xus,   cru - ci - fi -

fi - - - - xus, &c.

- - - - - - xus, &c.

- - - - xus, &c.

1st sung by the bass, the whole eventually succeeded by a

Bass.

et - i - am   pro   no - &c.

low murmur at ' sepultus est.' Then follows the usual triumphant ' Et resurrexit,' and after the 8 bars of realism
at ' cujus regni non erit finis,' all in unison on the note G,
the violins sound G sharp, and the ' Et in Spiritum ' thus
preluded follows, without pause or change of time from the

'Et resurrexit.' This portion deserves attention, if only as a signal illustration of the general character of Cherubini's solos, in being neither lengthy nor monopolized by one voice. With flowing accompaniment, in character with the above, the soprano begins.

Et in Spi- ri-tum Sanc   tum Dominum et .. vi - vi - fi-

- can-tem, &c.

The bass then takes up the air, followed by the tenor.

Qui ex Pa-tre Fi - li - o-que pro- ce - dit, Qui cum, &c.

So with the 'Et in Spiritum' of Beethoven's Mass in C, the alto leading.

Et in Spiritum Sanctum Dominum et... vi- vi- fi - can-tem

qui cum Pa- tre Fi - li - o-que pro - ce   -   dit, qui cum

Pa-tre et Fi - li - o - que, &c.

Haydn and Mozart generally go through this section from the ' Et resurrexit ' to the ' Et vitam,' in chorus only ; but the later writers, for contrast's sake, sometimes treat this portion with solos and chorus intermingled. The words ' Et unam sanctam,' etc., in Cherubini's Mass, are sung in unison, as in Beethoven's : the harmony bursts forth at ' ecclesiam ' with Cherubini, and with Beethoven, and at ' confiteor.'[6] Very natural is the ' in remissionem :'

succeeded by the melodious ' Et vitam ;' a theme conceiv-

ably an attempt to describe, so far as is possible here below, eternal life. This is followed by a short subject in fugue,

significant of human life, and contrasting vividly enough with the calm ' Et vitam.' The latter gradually extends and extends itself until its whole divine beauty is unrolled ;

and then follows a magnificent passage, one which might

[6] These words are also in unison in Haydn's 1st and 3rd Masses.

fittingly have closed the Credo, with a 'rallentando' at

the 7th Amen, on the repeat? but the brief fugue
returns, with an anti-climax, and an orchestral ending
completes the dis-illusionment in a Credo otherwise
beyond praise.

The offertory, Laudate Dominum, is full of celestial
joy. 'How delightful and how beautifully scored!' wrote a
friend ; the Sanctus, and duet, O Salutaris, too, are
replete with beauty and dignity.   In the Agnus Dei there

is a 'surprise' at the 7th bar of the instrumental
introduction after a pause not easily forgotten.   The
voices now enter in unison on a stately subject, in marked

contrast to the 'miserere.'   The present 'Agnus Dei' is
a kind of miniature in form of that in the D minor Mass;

in both there is an opening instrumental prelude repeated
between each enunciation of the 'Agnus Dei,' etc., as
well as a descent of voices in imitation, at the 'miserere
nobis.'   Quite different is the 'Dona nobis pacem,' left
in undisturbed beauty, with all its delightful imitation.

How sweet and fresh it all is! How solemn and calm the ideal close! 'Peace, perfect peace,' is here, as voice, and then accompaniment, die away, 'sinking deep, deeper into the dim distance.'

Next to the Mass in C comes a Mass in E flat, only mentioned by De Toulmon, and unpublished; and the 'Pater Noster' for 4 voices, 'a grave supplication, where

the melody is severe and expressive; its beauty heightened by ingenious details. It ends with a dramatic "libera nos" of a rhythm vigorous and full of energy,'[7] otherwise a 'profane conclusion.'[8]

As to the 'O Salutaris' for contralto, the melody 'is highly censured, though its musical texture is concise.'[9] Of other works of this period, 'the "Lauda Sion," for 2 sopranos, has a very pronounced rhythm; it has some amenity and charm save in 1 or 2 melodies of rather an antiquated cast. The same can be said of the "Sanctus O Salutaris," written for tenor solo; it is holy and contemplative, but its melody is at times too spiritless, or a little common. The "Ecce Panis" [with an Iste Dies and an Ave Verum added thereto] a solo for tenor or soprano, is more novel and more melodious. In these 3 pieces, as in all Cherubini's works, there are always remarkable beauties that reveal the great Master's genius. You are especially impressed by the charm of transitions that constantly bring back with felicity the chief "motivo." '[10]

---

[7] Fr. Girod S.J.   [8] Spohr, who extols the rest.   [9] Girod.   [10] *ib.*

Schlüter ventures to call the well-known Ave Maria, written at this time, 'a piece of vanity and affectation,' while Fr. Girod observes : 'There is everything that is touching, lovely, and loving in the prayer.' Which is it for us ? I think I know.

> 'Yon pilgrim, see the " Ave Maria " shall beguile,
> And to their hope the distant shrine
> Glisten with a livelier ray.'
>
> WORDSWORTH.

An instance, anyway, is recorded as to how its merits can grow ; a good sign. It was performed 3 times at St. Michael's College, Fribourg. At the 1st performance it made little or no impression. At the 2nd, a few months later, it was generally admired. At the 3rd, the emotion of every listener might be discerned. No piece of Cherubini requires more artistic expression ; failing this, it is—anything you like.

Among these sacred works comes but one important secular composition, 'the Mariage de Salamon,' done for the 1st time 17 June, at the Royal banquet in the Tuileries, to celebrate the marriage of the Duc de Berri and the Princess Charlotte, of Naples.

Finally, in this eventful year of music, the 1st Requiem in C minor was for Louis XVI.'s anniversary, and 1st executed 21 Jan. 1817 at St. Denis' Abbey Church. It was repeated there 14 Feb. 1820,[11] for the obsequies of the Duc de Berri, murdered on the 13th. For this occasion 16 extra singers and 17 instrumentalists joined the Chapel-choir, and Castil-Blaze tells us he never knew the work make the effect it did on this occasion.[12]

[11] Castil-Blaze puts the date at 14 March in error. Halévy wrote a *De Profundis*, for full orchestra (dedicated to Cherubini), for the same occasion (Léon Halévy's Memoir). That the Requiem was produced for Méhul's obsequies in 1818 at St. Dénis is an error. It might have been for his anniversary He died in 1817. I recall 1st hearing 2 Nov. 1874 at Farm St. Church, London. In that beautiful fane, then without aisles till half way up the nave, and with an excellent organ, well played by Mr. Tilbury, and then by Mr. Archer, the 2 Requiems, the D minor part of the C major, and the *Regina Cœli*, were all heard to perfection.

[12] Hummel conducted the C minor at a Mass for Beethoven 5 April, 1827, at St. Charles', Vienna. And Mendelssohn, in a letter to Rebecca

Messe de Requiem

A Quatre Parties en Chœur

avec Accompagnement

à Grand Orchestre

par

L. CHERUBINI,

Chevalier de l'Ordre Royal de la Légion d'Honneur,

Surintendant de la Musique de S. M. Le Roi de France

Membre de l'Académie Royale des beaux Arts de l'Institut de France,

de Celle de Musique de Stockholm, associé de l'Institut Royal d'Hollande, & c.

Prix 36.ᶠ

a Paris, Chez l'Auteur, Rue du Faubourg Poissonnuere, N.º 19.

Et en Dépôt, Chez Boieldieu, Rue de Richelieu, N.º 92.

Extracts from excellent notices on occasion of performances under Herr Richter at Leipsic in 1872, and by
the London Musical Society in 1880, with a few notes of
my own, are subjoined. This Requiem (or else the
Coronation Mass in A) is the best known work of its
author, so no musical illustrations, at best inadequate, are
given.

No. 1. Introit and Kyrie. ' A happy union of
solemnity and sweetness . . . and reticent in the use of
executive means,'[13] ' while the old Italian manner of the
appearance of the 4 voices one after one . . . at the
words " et lux perpetua," " Te decet hymnus," " exaudi,"
produces charming and expressive harmonic changes.'[14]

No. 2. Gradual. An exquisite theme, 'with a feature,
which is one of the most prominent in the entire work,
namely the division of the chorus into 2 choirs, which
answer each other in the manner of a canon.'

No. 3. ' Dies Iræ.' ' True to the rule of simplicity
which, in this work, Cherubini laid down for himself, he
treats the opening verses of the great Latin hymn as
Handel might have done. Beginning with a unison of all
the brass on the dominant, followed by a " coup de tam-
tam " scarcely in keeping with the prevalent severity of
style, the master re-introduces his 2 choirs, and, for some

Dirichlet, Berlin, 23 Nov. 1834 wrote : ' I conducted Cherubini's Requiem in
the Church,' *Letters*, 1867, 5th. The 2nd season of the New Philharmonic
Society gave it at Exeter Hall, 1853. It has been given also by St.
Thomas' choir, Leipsic, on Palm Sunday 1872, under Herr Richter, a
devoted adherent of Cherubini; at Farm Street, London, 2 Nov. 1874-6;
at the Town Hall, Birmingham, under Mr. Short's direction, 22 Oct. 1877;
at the New Town Hall by the Newcastle(-on-Tyne) Amateur Vocal
Society, 24 Dec. 1878 ; at the Birmingham Festival of 1879 ; at St. James
Hall, London, 17 June 1880, by the London Musical Society, under Dr.
Barnby ; at St. James' Hall, 25 March 1881, by the Sacred Harmonic
Society under Sir Michael Costa ; the Italian Church, St. Mary of the
Angels, and St. Etheldreda's, London ; the Oratory, Birmingham ; the Pro-
Cathedral, and St. Francis Xavier's, Dublin ; St. Dominic's, Newcastle-on-
Tyne ; and St. Mary's, Barrow-in-Furness, all on Sunday, 30 Sept. 1888,
when Pope Leo XIII. ordered an universal Requiem for that day ; at St.
Joseph's, Highgate, 19 Jan. 1892 ; at St. Mary of the Angels, Bayswater,
2 Nov. 1893 ; St. Aloysius', Oxford ; St. Francis Xavier's, Liverpool ;
the Servite Church, etc.
     [13] An. Pr. 1880.   [14] *M.M.R.* ii, 1872, 71.

time, makes them sing a strict canon on the 8ve., containing nothing but tonic and dominant harmony, relieved by a restless [double-stopping, or semi-quaver] accompaniment of strings. We are accustomed to hear the announcement of the "Day of Wrath" given out with the full force of the orchestra, but Cherubini keeps the entire band silent, while even the voices are subdued.'[15] This 2-part canonic leading of the voices . . . creates the impression of the deepest fear, the most frightful consternation.'[16] Cherubini 'thus reserves himself for the "Tuba mirum," on which words the whole power of band and voices is let loose. Yet even here we have Handelian simplicity—and Handelian grandeur. In contrast, the broken "Mors stupebit," for voices alone, makes a deep impression, as does the entire following passage up to a full close in the relative major, the brass and drums being again silent. On the words "Liber scriptus," the original canonic treatment is resumed in the key just named, modulating to F and G, and emphasizing each modulation with ff chords for horns and trombones. The "Tuba mirum" passage is repeated—full orchestra as before—on the words "Rex tremendae," etc.; but with the pitiful cry, "Salva me, fons pietatis," new matter appears, a tender and beautiful cadence in C major, leading to one of the most charming episodes of the entire work. "Recordare, Jesu pie," etc. begins with broad melodic phrases for sopranos and altos in unison (observe a new figure of accompaniment in the violins), echoed by the tenors 1st, and next by the basses, the whole passage being as unpretending in structure, and yet as appropriate in effect, as any that can be conceived. After this flow of subdued emotion, the full orchestra and chorus burst wildly into "Confutatis maledictis," and here the expression of the music, dignified before, even when most emphatic, becomes almost fierce. Observe the short phrases interjected by the voices, and, on the words

[15] An Pr.   [16] *M.M.R.*

" Flammis acribus addictis," the rush of scale passages
from one extreme to the other of a diminished 7th
interval. Shortly following, comes again the cadence
" Salva me," this time to the prayer " Voca me cum
benedictis." ' [17]

'Quite wonderful is the variety and the acceleration
in expression of the most devotional praying, the prostration full of pain at the words " salva me fons pietatis,"
and " voca me cum benedictis," . . . the touching expression of the deepest abasement at the words " ora supplex
et acclinis." ' [18] The heart-shaking lament of the ' Lacrymosa,' with its pfs, not sfs, as too often sung, for the
voices, and ' semi-arpeggios ' for the strings, is one of the
most affecting passages in Cherubini. How immeasurably
greater these are, especially in the descending passage, than
any 'staccatos,' introducing the noble 'salva me,' and 'voca
me ' theme ! Here the ideal and real in sorrow soar far
above mere dramatic presentment. The ' Record ' goes
on to refer to ' the touching prayer of the " Pie Jesu," and
at the last, " dona nobis requiem " '—where 'the vocal parts
move in flowing diatonic harmony, the pf chords disappear,—and all becomes gentle and humble entreaty.' [19] In
the above setting of the ' Dies Iræ,' the one musical idea,
repeated to different words, albeit Gregorian in practice,
yet differentiates it from the later male-voice Requiem,
and from Mozart's, comparing unfavourably therewith, as
a perfect setting of words to music, as for example where
' Dies Iræ,' ' Liber Scriptus,' ' Judex ergo,' have precisely
the same notation.

No. 4. Offertory. 'Like the "Dies Iræ," this number
is scored for full orchestra, which plays a somewhat more
important part than usual in its development. Observe in
the introduction the short, graceful phrases for violins
alone, and the use to which they are put when the voices
in unison on the dominant ejaculate, " Libera-animas-om-
nium," etc. This is a case wherein the expression really

[17] An Pr.   [18] *M.M.R.*   [19] An Pr.

belongs to the orchestra, and it also illustrates what a master can do with the simplest means. The transition to tremor and restlessness at the reference to the "pains of hell," emphasized by the long, loud notes of the horns and trombones, secures another masterly contrast, while the setting of the words, "Et de profundo lacu," up to the pause, breathes solemnity and awe. Attention need scarcely be called to the prayer for deliverance from the "mouth of the lion," or the subdued and trembling utterance of "Ne cadant in obscurum." From all this the music emerges, as one passes out of the darkness of a ravine into the splendour of a sunny plain. Again, the graceful, pleading violin phrases are heard; voices and instruments stream on together in beautiful harmony, and so with a feeling of trust in infinite mercy. . . . The "Quam olim Abrahaae" follows "Tempo a capella," and appears as a 4-part fugue, with 3 short subjects. . . . If the resources of the contrapuntist be not actually exhausted in it, they are drawn upon far enough to satisfy the "proprieties," and to assert Cherubini's mastery. . . . Beginning with strings alone, which simply double the voice parts, he gradually brings forward the other instruments, at the same time allowing the strings greater freedom, and so working steadily to a climax. The Coda is undoubtedly one of the master's grandest "ensembles."

'Hostias.' 'Cherubini presents another of his exquisite musical prayers. Mark the elegance of the opening passage as the voices enter at a bar's distance from each other, and the beautifully fresh effect which the key of C [major] has upon the ear after so much of C minor. . . . The frequent response of 3 parts to the short and tendei phrases of the 4th, is likewise a noticeable feature in this truly religious movement.' It reminds me at once of the short vocal phrases at the 'Domine Deus' of the E minor and the 'Gratias' of the A major Masses of Cherubini. The fugue is then repeated, thus making the only very extended section of the Requiem.

No. 5. 'Sanctus.' 'This number, scored for full

orchestra, is chiefly remarkable for breadth of style and fulness of expression. . . . The words "Benedictus qui venit in nomine Domini" occur once, and then their "pianissimo" utterance (in "staccato" by the basses) to the soft accompaniment of bassoons, clarinets, and oboes, places them in stronger relief against the background of the rest of the movement than would be possible [with] any amount of reiteration.'

No. 6. 'Pie Jesu.' 'This is on all accounts one of the most original and affecting numbers in the entire work. As in the "Gradual," the violins are silent throughout. . . . At 1st, after 3 bars of the introduction, the number takes the form of a chorale with interludes; the sopranos leading off, attended by the strings; the tenors following, and between each strain the clarinets and bassoons continue their interludes, with only one break, to the end; and the manner in which they respond to the unison "Requiem" of the voices, must touch all sympathies. The whole movement is one of extreme simplicity, but if ever there was a case of the art that conceals art, we find it here.'[20]

'The Agnus Dei in "decrescendo,"' writes Berlioz, ' surpasses everything that has ever been written of the kind. The workmanship of this portion, too, has an inestimable value; the vocal style is sharp and clear, the instrumentation coloured and powerful, yet ever worthy of its object.' Cardinal Newman was most struck with 'the ending of the Agnus Dei—he could not get over it— the lovely note C which keeps recurring as the "requiem" approaches eternity.'[21] 'Cherubini,' said Beethoven, 'is,

[20] An Pr.

[21] *Cardinal Newman as a Musician*, 19. Two subjective, secular notices are added: 'A tone of deep lamentation, of a presentiment of death, permeates the whole composition; the strains, full of deadly sadness, and resembling sighs and congealed tears, strike the heart, and recall to the mind the end of all that is mortal. The Agnus Dei, especially, expresses a farewell to existence, to love, to all that is known under the name of happiness. We breathe in it an immense despair [?], and the soul solicits its liberation. A ray of hope bursts forth for an instant in the "Lux [perpetua] luceat eis," but dies away in the mystic obscurity of a "point d'orgue" of magical effect.' La Mara. In approved modern fashion, so we almost know what is coming, Naumann tells us that this devout work 'must be reckoned as one of the grandest creations of modern

in my opinion, of all the living composers the most admirable. Moreover, as regards his conception of the Requiem, my ideas are in perfect conformity with his, and some time or other, if I can but once set about it, I mean to profit by the hints to be found in that work.'[22] Otto Jahn refers to the Mozart Requiem's 'negative influence' in 'Cherubini's magnificent Requiem in C minor, with which the 2nd in D minor is quite in keeping.'[23] There is some positive influence, too? Thus all 3 Requiems vocally begin their 'Dies Iræ' with like notation, 2 minims and 2 crotchets, while the counterpoint of the male-voice Requiem's 'Recordare' invites comparison with Mozart's?

'Both works,' writes the critic from Leipsic, of Bach's Matthäus-Passion, and Cherubini's C minor Requiem, 'are incomparable master-works, both have been produced by, and are filled with true, faithful, religious feeling, yet they are thoroughly different in character.' He calls the Requiem 'the greatest work of Italian Catholicism,' but when he says the former 'has always appeared to us the most deeply felt and most important communication of true German art in the field of Protestant church-music,' I should have felt, having regard to the structure of the work concerned, that the

art. The master has determined his line of action ; there is no hesitation. Everything in this great poem *exists*. The listener is carried away, and becomes in spirit a co-actor in the terrible drama which is unrolled before him. What mastery does the composer display over the strict choral style ! How bold an innovator in the realm of orchestration ! Until the climax, the crash of the *tam-tam,* and the terrible blast of the trombones, depicting the destruction of the world, the composer has confined himself to the use of the viola in the place of the violin, the subdued colouring thus produced representing effectually the night of death. . . . The grandeur and passion displayed in this creation reminds us involuntarily of that wonderful work of the great Florentine painter, Michael Angelo, the last Judgment.'— *History of Music,* ed. F. Praeger and E. D. Gore-Ouseley.

[22] *Life of Beethoven,* ed. Moscheles, 313.

[23] *Life of Mozart,* iii. 393, 1882, tr. Townsend. While giving no separate notice to Beethoven, notwithstanding the Mass in C, Mass in D, and Funeral Music for All Souls' Day in Linz Cathedral, the *Catholic Encyclopædia* observes on Cherubini's sacred music : ' They are master-works of religious music, but are not available for liturgical purposes. *Some* have been for 95 years so available, to the edification of thousands.

phrase could apply to Brahms' Requiem, seeing that
Bach's 'Passion,' with its 'Christus, synagogus,' 'historicus,'
and 'turba,' is somewhat monotonously extended on
conciser Catholic forms in the Good Friday office. He
proceeds : 'Both works are treated in the polyphonic style,
but how different the counterpoint ! ' And he contrasts
Bach's ' many harshnesses ' with the ' soft, Italian, always
well-sounding, flowing melodies of Cherubini.' Moreover, while he sees ' the manifold dramatic element ' in
Bach, he finds it ' missing in Cherubini altogether. Even
in the " Dies Iræ," the broadest movement of the
Requiem, it is not to be found . . .'; a noticeable
instance of music's varying impressions on different
minds, since others would see something dramatic in 2 or
3 portions of the ' Dies Iræ ' and ' Offertory,' although
the ideal may predominate.

'The Requiem Mass in C minor,' says Berlioz, ' is
on the whole, to my mind, the greatest work of its
author. No other production of this grand master can
bear any comparison with it for abundance of idea,
fulness of form, and sustained sublimity of style.'

Hiller deems the work ' almost unique in music.'
' This great composition,' he writes, ' is truly astonishing
for the simplicity of the means employed, the colour in
the orchestra, and the purely vocal treatment of the
voices. Had Cherubini left nothing else, it alone would
suffice to make every true musician look up to him as
one of the most extraordinary and sublime of masters.'
' The Requiem in C minor commanded admiration from
the 1st as a pure example of the highest form of sacred
art. No attempt is here made at dramatic expression,
or at musical effect for its own sake. Cherubini, whose
own religious feeling was deep and sincere, seems to
have abstracted himself from all things other than the
emotions called forth by contemplation of his great
theme ; and this is the secret of the direct and irresistible
appeal which his music makes to all hearts.' [24]

[24] An. Pr.

CHAPTER IV.

FRANCE.

1816—1822.

Iste Dies, O Sacrum, Ave Verum—Tantum Ergos—Regina Cœli—Mass in
E minor—*Adjutor in Opportunitatibus*—1st Coronation Mass in G—
Blanche de Provence—Cantata for Baptism of Duke de Bordeaux
(Henry V.)—The Mass in B flat—*O Fons Amoris—Inclina Domine*—
Cherubini as Director of the French Conservatoire—His teaching.

WE are now in the flood-tide of an inspiration, as noticeable as any in musical annals. So far from the sublime
Requiem just noticed having exhausted the Royal chapel-
master, it stimulated him to as great vitality in 3 Masses
of much variety and distinction in 1818, 1819 and 1821.
Of the 'Iste Dies' of 1817, added to an 'O Sacrum
Convivium,' written in 1816, Fr. Girod writes: Its
'solemnity . . . renders it well fit for a great Benediction,
such as Easter Day's; after a grand opening comes a
very expressive bass solo, followed by the choral refrain
" Buccinate tuba." What with the calm and suavity of the
march, the "O Sacrum" in C minor contrasts admirably
with what precedes and follows it. The close is a tuneful
fugue, full of brilliancy. To this piece is joined an " Ave
verum " for 3 equal voices, of a soothing character, concise
and graceful.'[1] A 'Tantum Ergo' opening for tenor, and
closing as a majestic 4-part chorus, has the true ring of
ancient song. Fr. Girod writes of a 2nd hymn, 'the

---

[1] Fr. Girod, S.J. This last precedes *O Sacrum*. Portions of this work
are said to be from *Elisa*, but on examining the latter, I have been unable
to verify the statement.

"Tantum Ergo" for 5 voices is original and poetical, but
has not the character of fervour and solemnity that the
last piece for Benediction requires. On the whole it
produces little effect.' And of the glorious 'Regina Cœli,'
of 1818 he observes: 'It is incontestibly the most beautiful piece of its kind, and a magnificent ovation to the
Queen of Heaven,' and he adds with truth:

'Like all the author's music, it has its difficulties, but it
demands special attention to obtain an "ensemble" and
proper precision.'[2] In the variety of this noble setting,
with its jubilant opening—an Easter dawn, indeed, of
song—the rhythm of the alleluias, the awe-inspiring 'Et
resurrexit,' and the ecstatic prayer of the 'ora pro nobis,'
and jubilant return, I know of no hymn more absolutely
appropriate to words, or more inspiring to worshippers of
their risen Lord.

We now come to the Mass in E minor, 1st introduced
to an English Catholic congregation by the London
Oratory, and described by its Father Prefect of Music in
terms as enthusiastic as they are just. 'I am fast veering
to the E minor,' he wrote, '1st I regard it with a certain
fatherly fondness as having been the 1st to introduce it
into England, . . . 2ndly, as you say, it grows, and thus
shows its greatness.' The exquisite prayer of the 'Kyrie,'
'a perfect model of supplicatory song,' is in one movement;

[2] *ib.*

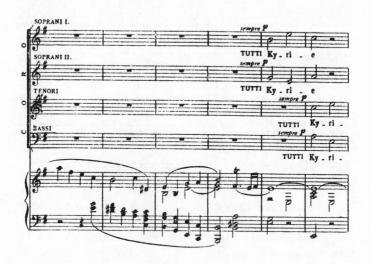

the 'Gloria,' also, is in one movement, and vivid

in its brilliancy of opening, supplicatory at the 'Qui
tollis,' and in the beautiful theme at 'Domine Deus, Rex
cœlestis' and 'Domine, Fili, Unigenite.' On recurrence at

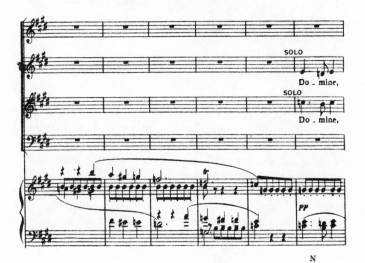

Do . mine, Fi - li

Fi - li, Do . mine, Fi - li

Fi - li, Do . mine, Fi - li

Do . mine, Fi - li

'cum Sancto Spiritu,' where the accompaniment had
previously only whispered a refrain of 6 notes on a
descending gamut, these are sung out by the chorus, as a
reply; and, like a peal of bells, it is rung out twice. The
moving theme of the 'Qui tollis' is really an 'accelerando,'
and a 'ritardino' in its accent; thoroughly Cherubini, too,
(and Beethoven) all over.

Qui tol . lis pec.ca - - - ta

The Credo,'finest of all the better known Cherubinis,'
begins in choral unison on a majestic 'canto-fermo,'
continued right down to the 'Incarnatus,'—a superb
ecclesiastical page,—and with its triumphant accompaniment, to be compared with the 'canto-fermos' of the
Mass in F (starting, as with Bach's, on the Gregorian
'accentus') and with the Mass in A, and equalling in all
respects the former, and surpassing the latter's baldness
of accompaniment in 8-ves.

One long musical strain, without pause, is mysteriously sung by successive voices throughout the 'Et incarnatus' and 'Crucifixus;' an original form and conception that I can recall in no other Mass, and to the barest accompaniment in syncopation.   Each part in turn is 'vox clamantis in

deserto;' but what saves the section from any monotony is
the wonderful change in the expression, adapting itself
to the words in that mysterious, inexplicable way referred
to by Adam, as a characteristic of Cherubini.

The 'Et resurrexit' ends with a 'pianissimo' realism
at the 'Non erit finis,' a favourite subject with Cherubini.

The theme of the 'Et in Spiritum,' 'enchanting for

its grace,' is still attended by that triumphant accompaniment, symbolizing Faith's victory at every stage, and, after the 'canto-fermo's' resumption at 'Et unam Sanctam Catholicam, et Apostolicam Ecclesiam' this itself becomes, at the close, the triumphant theme of the heavenly choir; and in the 'coda' leaves us spell-bound, though the text might well have included 'Et vitam venturi sæculi' for so sublime a conclusion of the Creed. For here we can almost imagine angels about, and, as the 'sun upon an Easter day,'[3] they seem to dance as do servers at Seville; and here joy is expressed, but no earthly joy.

The 'Sanctus' is concise, as always with Cherubini;

[3] Sir John Suckling.

the 'O Salutaris,' religioso;' while the 'Agnus Dei' 'touch-
ingly devout and soothing,' closes, perhaps, the most

lovely, and lovable, and, I should almost be disposed to
say, the most devotional of all Cherubini's Masses ; a Mass
hardly surpassable for mingled beauty, pathos and force
of expression, and a wonder for all time.

This Mass, never yet performed out of church in
England, shows Cherubini the pupil of Sarti : steeped in

older forms, it is yet musically modern for all its inimitable
touch of, and mastery over the mediæval chant.[4]

To this same period belongs the 4-part motet
' Adjutor in opportunitatibus ' a setting of the ' Gradual
and Tract' for Septuagesima. The MS., once at
Windsor, has gone to the British Museum. The
' Benedicta tu,' then referred to by Fr. Girod as a
charming trio, in which you distinguish a melody full of
unction, and fresh, novel modulation," is simply the
Sanctus of the ' Mass in F, left un-noticed by Picchianti.'[5]

In the year 1819 we have Cherubini writing his 1st
Coronation Mass in G, for 4 voices, never officially
performed, written for Louis XVIII., who was never
crowned. He now conferred the title of Chevalier of the
Order of St. Michael on the composer, although the
latter did not take the oath as such till 29 Sept. 1826,
when the 1st chapter was held after the Revolution. This

---

[4] ' It is music like this that is worthy, in an eminent degree, to claim
the place, allotted to Modern Music, in the 3-fold benediction of Pius X. :
—that Modern Music which, following its 2 great precursors, Plain Chant
and unaccompanied Polyphony, carries on to a later age, and, like them, in
an imperishable form, the devotion of consummate Art and Genius to the
service of the sacred Liturgy ; ' so writes an Oratorian choir-master at Birmingham, of long practical experience. Cherubini illustrates, too, Rockstro's
remarks in comparing the 16th and 19th centuries' styles of church-music,
albeit to the disadvantage of the latter as to stability of style. ' Yet in the
midst of the diversity which naturally ensues from this want of a common
ideal, it is instructive to notice one bond of union between the older Masters and the new. . . . Their agreement in the general distribution of
the movements is most remarkable.' And he instances the 3-fold _Kyrie_
division, the _Qui tollis_ and _Incarnatus_ as Adagios, the _Hosanna_ often ending both _Sanctus_ and _Benedictus_, and concludes : ' And in this vitality of
typical form, we find a convincing proof—if one be necessary—that the broad
aesthetic principles of Art are immutable, and calculated to survive,
through an indefinite period, the vicissitudes of technical treatment in
widely differing schools.'—_Grove_, ii. 235.

I 1st heard the work 27 June 1886 at the London Oratory, and it has
been often done there ; at St. Etheldreda's, London ; and at the Birmingham Oratory. Thus it was given 22 Oct. 1887, and 3 June 1888, 4 July
1897 ; and 20 June 1897 for the Victorian Diamond Jubilee High Mass of
thanksgiving, _coram Cardinali_ (Vaughan), and the Papal Envoy, Mgr.
Sambucetti, at the London Oratory ; and 29 June 1890, 26 May 1895,
20 July 1897, 2 Jan. 1898, etc. at the Birmingham Oratory.

[5] _Supra_, 124. Of Cherubini's hymn to Bacchus, composed April 1819,
Miel writes : ' It becomes on his lyre the noblest of drinking song..' I
have never seen it in print. It comes, strangely enough, in the Catalogue,
amidst so much sacred music.

Mass is little known in England, having been seemingly eclipsed by its rival, the 2nd Coronation Mass, but it is a work of the highest order, though requiring, from a liturgical point of view, a re-arrangement of the text in the 'Gloria,' curtailment there and in the too lively 'Credo's' close 'Et vitam,' and an omission of 'Agnus Dei' where it invades the 'Dona's' peaceful close.

The 'Kyrie' opens with a vigorous subject, which

is followed by the following apparently unpromising theme at the 'Christe,' given out by the soprano, to

accompaniment in unison by the flutes, hautboys, and bassoons. By a coincidence Dvorak's 'Kyrie' in D has a suaver treatment of a similar subject.

The whole movement is well-nigh entirely the working
out of these 2 themes. Towards the close a pedal point
is reached with a reminiscence of the 2nd subject, while
voices and instruments blend together in this sweet,
subdued strain of hope; the tenor, with the violoncellos
and bassoons, on a repetition, taking up the vocal
melody, while the other voices sing the sustaining
harmonies with enchanting effect.

The 'Gloria' opens 'majestuesement sans lenteur'

much in the manner of the 2nd Coronation Mass in A,
and sounds forth in succession the notes of the common
chord of C, and then we come to this melodious and
joyful accompaniment with a strong contrast,

which heralds in the basses chanting the opening bars of
the Gloria, and subsequently plays a conspicuous part
throughout the piece. The jubilant 'laudamus,' in a

certain freedom and breadth, reminds us of the composer
of the ' Creation,' and is a simple but striking feature in
the movement : then succeeds the ' adoramus,' ushered in
by the violoncellos 'pianissimo.' There are regrettable
repetitions, followed by a short ' Qui tollis,' solemn and
expressive ; while the ' Quoniam,' after the example of
Haydn and Mozart, is similar to the opening of the

'Gloria.' In the final fugue, 'Cum Sancto Spiritu,' the theme and words of the 'Quoniam' and 'Gloria' are introduced, a somewhat novel procedure. Cherubini brings in those of the 'Gloria' in his 'Coda' in the Mass in F, but I remember no instance of the 'Quoniam' being so used. Here occurs this brief but beautiful pedal point.

The 'Credo' begins in 2-part canon after a loud chord in the dominant, and then continues 'pianissimo.'

This canonic form is resumed at the ' Et in Spiritum,' after the impressive ' Crucifixus,' the accompaniment to which Gounod's ' There is a green hill,' albeit in common time, and so far different, seems to approve.

The concluding ' Et vitam ' is too gay, and very different from the celestial joy of the C or E minor Masses. The ' Sanctus ' is most noticeable as having no pause or break before the ' Hosanna,' while the ' Benedictus qui venit,' etc., and the ' O Salutaris ' (taking the place of the separate movement ' Benedictus,' in France, and elsewhere), are both included in the section, so that the piece may go on through the Elevation. Here all is generally, and preferably, and rubrically, silence, though in France and Italy the organ is often softly played. To the elevated beauties of the ' Agnus Dei ' in one brief movement, with its flowing accompaniment, every musician will bear testimony.' [6]

[6] The Mass has been given at the London Oratory, in part 4 July, and entire 15 Aug. 1880; at the Birmingham Oratory, 22 July 1894, etc.; at St. Andrew's, Wells St., London, Jan. 1880, etc.; the Annunziata, Florence,

Moscheles writes in his diary 28 Jan. 1821: 'At 11 A.M. I rehearsed at Paër's with Baillot for this evening; then I went, or rather ran with him, at full speed, to the court chapel in the Tuileries, where we heard a glorious Mass by Cherubini, admirably performed, as might be expected with the coöperation of such men as Kreutzer, Baillot, Habeneck. Plantade directed, and Cherubini, who talked to me, was among the audience.'

In 1821 appeared the 1-act allegorical opera of 'Blanche de Provence,' otherwise 'La cour des Fèes,' the libretto by Théaulon and Rance,' divided into 3-parts, and Cherubini composing the 3rd part. He tells us, 'This opera was ordered by the Minister of the King's Household, on occasion of the baptism of the Duke of Bordeaux [Henri V. Comte de Chambord], 1 May 1821 at Notre Dame. The 1st representation of "Blanche" took place in the evening at the Court theatre; the 2nd on the 3rd of the same month at the Royal Academy of Music, for which this opera had been composed.' On 21 May it was again performed at the Grand Opera; and Cherubini's cantata for solo voices, with choruses, to words by Baour Lormian, was executed 2 May to celebrate the same event at a fête in the Hôtel de Ville.

Moscheles writes of both in his diary. 'I drove early with Lafont to the Hôtel de Ville, where Cherubini's new cantata and the "intermède" by Boieldieu and Berton, written on occasion of the christening of the Duke of Bordéaux, were rehearsed. The 1st of these works was under the direction of the great master himself. His squeaky, sharp, little voice was sometimes heard in the midst of his conducting, and interupted my state of ecstasy, caused by his presence and composition. The whole of the magnificent and far-famed court band was in attendance. The Prefect, Count Chabrol, and his wife, whom I

etc.; and, as marked by the composer, takes 37½ minutes to execute, *i.e.* Kyrie, 5 m.; Gloria, 10 m.; Credo, 12 m.; Sanctus, etc., 6 m.; Agnus Dei, 4½ m., a somewhat lengthy Mass, but not more so than several of Gounod's that, with, may be, fewer bars but slower *tempi.*, take more time.

met at this rehearsal, offered me, in a most friendly manner, a ticket for the grand ball to be given in honour of the christening. In the evening I attended the general rehearsal of an opera which Cherubini, Paër, Berton, Boieldieu, and Kreutzer had jointly composed in honour of this same christening. The final chorus, by Cherubini, made an indelible impression on my mind. Each master conducted his own pieces, and Cherubini was loudly cheered.'[7] He writes, 9 May: 'To-day I played in the Hôtel de Ville, where the city of Paris gave a grand banquet to the Provincial Deputies. Cherubini, Boieldieu, and Berton directed the music. The chorus referred to was the exquisite cradle song, for 3 female voices, to words by Berquin, beginning 'Dors, noble enfant,' which much affected the King when he heard it for the 1st time.

In Oct. and November 1821, Cherubini wrote a Mass in B flat, 1st published in the 1st volume of his posthumous works, and performed long since at the Birmingham and London Oratories.

Its 'Kyrie' and 'Gloria' are in single movements. The latter's opening subject is resumed at 'In gloria Dei Patris,' and with a brief 'coda,' concludes the section. The 'Credo' has a beautiful 'Et incarnatus;' and the 'Et in Spiritum,' without being identical, is after the

[7] *Life of Moscheles,* i. 45, etc.

manner of the opening.   Following the 'Sanctus,' in due
proportion, succeeds a devout 'O Salutaris,' sometimes
heard at Benedictions.

The 'Agnus Dei' somewhat quaintly, to say the least,
opens with descending unisonal scale for bass, with accompaniment in contrary motion ; and the 'Dona' quietly
ends a liturgical Mass.   'We sung on 2 Feb. the B flat,
. . . wrote an Oratorian Father.   'Wingham thinks it
"very fine;" he is quite an enthusiast for the great
master.'[8]

Of the 'O Fons amoris spiritus,' written in 1822,
Fr. Girod observes: 'The motet . . . possesses a workmanship quite different from Cherubini's other religious
works [and] some persons have thought that it was not
composed by the author for the Church nor for these
words, but that it was taken from some of his abandoned
operas.   We believe that the manuscript score of this
piece, as with the "Regina Cœli," was delivered to a
German publisher. . . . The words are not extracted
from the Roman liturgy, nor from those which are used
in Germany, but entirely from one of the French liturgies.
This piece is written for soprano "concertante," with
choral accompaniment of men's voices.   The "allegro"
at the commencement and conclusion is replete with new
and brilliant ideas ; the unison of men's voices, preparing
the soloist's "crescendo," has a beautiful effect.   The
"larghetto" is sweet, but too full of organ points.'   Of
the 'Inclina Domine,' he observes : 'It is a sort of little

<hr />

[8] This short Mass takes to perform, as marked by the composer : *Kyrie*,
4 min. ; *Gloria*, 3 min. ; *Credo*, 6 min. ; *Sanctus*, 1½ min. ; *O Salutaris*,
3½ min. ; *Agnus Dei*, 2½ min.   Total 20½ min.   *Multum in parvo.*

drama of charming and varied workmanship. It comprises 3 parts; the 1st is a choral prayer of a solemn and touching effect, followed by a tenor solo of a graceful character; the answer of the chorus ends it. The 2nd is a magnificent plain chant executed in unison by the tenors and basses, and accompanied with energy and spirit by the strings. A fugal "Amen" forms the 3rd part, and closes the piece in a brilliant manner.' This hymn, written in 1823, was many years ago given in London by the excellent Henry Leslie choir, long since dissolved.

Cherubini became Director of the re-established Conservatoire in April 1822.[9] It has been regretted that he was so much occupied in this administration, being a great composer, who should rather have enjoyed much leisure for bringing out his grand ideas. As early as 1795, Grétry expressed a hope that Sarrette would occupy himself in all those duties which it was not the part of talented artistes to undertake. 'The moments of men of genius,' he says, 'are too precious to be lost in a multiplicity of duties; Méhul, Lesueur, and Cherubini are the hope of lyric theatres; to turn them aside from their talent in order to occupy them with matters of routine, would be an unpardonable fault.'[10] On his becoming director, Cherubini's compositions for the King's chapel certainly decreased in number; yet, otherwise, is there anything now to regret? It would be hard to imagine more beautiful works from him than those we possess, and we see the versatility of his power, and that conscientiousness in the discharge of public duties, that confer on him more honour than the orders and decorations received.

That great Institution of Republican origin, the Conservatoire, had, indeed, fallen on evil days. Sarrette, after successive recalls and dismissals, according as Napoleon or Bourbon was in power, was finally dismissed in 1815, and the Conservatoire, 'overthrown by a per-

[9] This old title of *Conservatoire de Musique et d'Elocution* was only restored by Royal Decree 25 Jan. 1831.
[10] *Mémoires*, iii. 372.

fidious conspiracy,' as Cherubini's diary bitterly records, was transferred from the Ministry of the Interior to the Ministry of the Royal Establishment, and became the ' Ecole Royale de Musique et Déclamation.' The classes opened in April 1816 with Perne, an able musician, as Inspector General; but the Government gave him little help. Cherubini lost his Inspectorship of Instruction, but was allowed to retain that of Composition at 3,000 francs annual salary less 3 per cent reduction (90 francs). At 1st it was proposed to reduce the school budget to 38,000 francs, but this was ultimately fixed at 80,000 francs. All who were supposed to be favourable to the Napoleonic rule, were superseded. Berton, Richer, Jadin, Grasset, Duport, Duvernoy, Sallantin, were told to go. Some of the teachers received only 500 francs as salary. There were no instruments for some of the classes. Owing to the scarcity of firewood, furniture, and especially old pianofortes, were burnt for fuel. In Jan. 1822, Perne, in despair, sent in his resignation. This roused the attention of the Marquis de Lauriston, then Minister of the Royal Household. He saw that the Conservatoire, to be kept up at all, must be reformed by able management and plenty of money. He had recourse to Cherubini, and appointed him Director, as already mentioned, with a salary of 8,000 francs, and a further 1,500 francs instead of a residence. The pay was afterwards raised altogether to 10,000 francs; but not till 1841, a year before Cherubini's death. Thus, at the age of 61, Cherubini received a tardy justice in being recognized as the ablest man to be entrusted with the important task of governing the greatest musical Academy in France. His immense experience enabled him to reform the system of all the classes. Never was there greater transformation in the conduct of an institution. Cherubini was now to show that he could be a distinguished administrator. Many can shut themselves up in the study-room, and address the world from their writing tables. Cherubini could do that, but he could govern also. Under his rule the Conservatoire rose to

its present high position ; and so long as that Institution
exists, the influence of Cherubini, once dominant in the
French capital, cannot be said to have departed thence.
That influence has been differently appraised, and with his
strict rules prevailing, his own music, it is inferred, would
never have seen the light. Genius, it may be argued,
knows no rules. In a sense this may be true. Wagner
somewhere says that what sounds right is right, but for
the ordinary run of talent anyway it is something that it
should be made to write grammatically, and I never heard
that the genius of Auber, Boieldieu and Halévy, all pupils
of Cherubini, had been fettered by his teaching. Credit
must accrue to him, whom they honoured, as having taught
them a way to true artistic success. It is easy to say that
his teaching failed to suppress bad music, but we cannot
say how much more might not have seen the light but
for his teaching.[11] My belief is that, practising what he
taught, he restrained mediocrity. Himself a genius, he was
quick to detect genius, while suppressing none. We shall
see, too, how he acknowledged merit in young and old
alike, and how they, on their part, acknowledged the debt

[11] 'Cherubini was quite incapable of making his ideals intelligible by
any means more personal than his music, and the crude grammatical rules
which he mistook for the eternal principles of his own and of all music
[were] not the smallest use as a safeguard against vulgarity and preten-
tiousness.'—Mr. Tovey, *Encycl. Brit.* new ed. art. Cherubini. The answer:
'It is necessary,' writes Cherubini of the student, 'that he should be com-
pelled to follow strict precepts, in order that eventually, when composing
on a free plan, he may know how and why his genius, if he has any, has
obliged him frequently to emancipate himself from the rigour of the 1st rules.
It is by subjecting himself at the outset to these rules in all their strictness
that he will afterwards know how to avoid prudently the abuse of licences ;'
and in his *Treatise on Counterpoint and Fugue,* he says he only followed the
same principles as Fux, Martini, and Albrechtsberger, the master of Beethoven. MS. Note *cit.* Pougin, *M. W.,* 1883, 672. But—

> 'Enough of Science and of Art ;
> Close up those barren leaves ;
> Come forth, and bring with you a heart
> That watches and receives.'
> WORDSWORTH.

When Sir Hubert Parry writes that Cherubini 'was a representative of
all that was old-fashioned and conventional in art,' judging from the
context, he must be taken to mean 'in teaching other people art.' There
is little or nothing old-fashioned in Cherubini's art.

they owed to him.   While admitting, then, that progress since his time has constructed more rapid roads to proficiency, we are bound in justice to say with Hiller, that he 'was the 1st to introduce into Paris the real, serious science of composition, and the skill that so essentially distinguishes the French composers of [the 19th] century from their predecessors is mainly due to him ;'—as witness, 'La Muette de Portici,' Auber's masterpiece, so different from his works of lighter vein, or 'La Dame Blanche,' Boieldieu's masterpiece, so superior to the lighter 'Calife de Baghdad,' or Halévy's masterpiece, 'La Juive,' so worthy of master and pupil; and all works not suppressed by Cherubini's teaching.

CHERUBINI.   [*After Jullien.*

CHAPTER V.

FRANCE.

1822.

'. . . . Strongest minds
Are often those of whom the world
Hears least. . . .
But as the mind was fill'd with inward light
So not without distinction had he liv'd,
Belov'd and honour'd—far as he was known.'

WORDSWORTH.

Cherubini's rule—Relations with masters and pupils and other musicians—
Addresses at Catel's and Boieldieu's funerals—Family correspondence
—Character illustrated.

CHERUBINI'S vast knowledge and experience were now to
be directed to training men and women[1] in all branches
of the musical profession. He engaged or continued the
services of the best men available. Under him were
Lesueur, Berton, Boieldieu, Reicha, Fétis, Dourlen, Daus-
soigne, Lays, Garat, Kuhn, Batiste, Nourrit, Plantade,
Ponchard, Blangini, Bordogni, Garaudé, Panseron, Benoist,
Pradher, Zimmermann, Kreutzer, Baillot, Habeneck, Baudiot, Levasseur, Lefebvre, Delcambre, Guillou, Vogt,

[1] Pougin thus summarizes the reform : 'a double committee of
instruction was created for music and elocution, as well as a committee of
management ; the boarding-house for male [and female] pupils . . . was
re-opened, public performances were re-established and their number fixed ;
the terms of engagement between the students and the Theatres Royal
were settled ; classes for harp, double bass, preparatory piano for women,
and reading aloud were created ; opera and comic opera and instruction in
lyrical declamation were divided into 2 distinct branches ; the schools of
music in the departmental towns of Lille, Toulouse, Marseilles and Metz,
were created as branches of the parent school ; the terms on which the
professors should retire, etc., were exactly defined.—*M. W.*, 1883, 641.

Auber succeeded Cherubini 8 Feb. 1842 ; after the latter's reign at the
Conservatoire of nearly 22 years, signalized in 1826 by his getting the opera
pitch lowered. He obtained, also, for the library, a copy of every piece of
music, or book on music, published in France.

Tulou, Mme. Wartel-Andrien, Dauprat, etc., and other artists. Perne was librarian, who was succeeded after a year by Eler. The spirit of Cherubini soon communicated itself to masters and pupils. He was a living contradiction to the notion that genius is synonymous with disorder. Probably no one more methodical and orderly ever lived. The Marquis de Lauriston thought he had got hold of the right man in Cherubini. He was right. Every professor, before opening his class each day, had to sign a book called ' le registre de présence,' to show that he had attended to his duties that day ; and this register of ' the house,' as Cherubini called the Conservatoire, the composer never failed to examine. He also saw that all the pupils were at work. But what Cherubini required of others, he exacted from himself. Strict was his rule in managing this large institution, and Cherubini set the example of being strict with himself. There he was at 10 o'clock [2] every morning, accessible to all at his office—with its walls 'covered by honourable diplomas' that came to him from all parts [3]—a large room with an anteroom separating him by double and triple doors from the pupils and their practisings, while a servant was stationed outside to answer at call the Director's bell. Here he wrote his correspondence, saw professors, pupils, or visitors, and took an occasional pinch of snuff from divers boxes, 160 in number. He was never unpunctual, and as he was never behind his time, so was he never before it. Regularity was with him a cardinal virtue, and irregularity

[2] Hiller says between 9 and 10.

[3] Miel : From Cherubini's own statement he was Commander of the Legion of Honour, Knight of St. Michael, Knight of Merit, Hesse-Darmstadt, Member of the Institute, Superintendant of the King's Music, Director of the Conservatoire, Associate of the Amsterdam Institute and Besançon·Royal Academy of Science, Member of the Milan Conservatoire, of the Stockholm Musical Academy [not given by Pougin], Cracow Philharmonic Institute, of the London Royal Academy of Music, of the St. Petersburg Philharmonic Society, of the Hague Society for the Progress of Musical Art, of the Berlin Academy of Fine Arts, of the Rouen Philharmonic Society, of the Rome Academy of St. Cecilia, and the Stuttgart Musical Union. 3 years before the knighthood of St. Michael, he appears to have received the insignia of a short-lived Order of the Lily and Fidelity.—*M. W.,* 1883-4, 609, 169.

a deadly sin. He was often looking at his watch, and counting the number of minutes wherein everything had to be done. When the Marquis de Lauriston came to distribute some prizes at the Conservatoire, Cherubini greeted him with, 'You come very late, Sir.' When the unpunctual Habeneck once rushed in to say, 'This time you cannot complain,' Cherubini looked at his watch and replied : 'No, you are not punctual ; you are 3 minutes too soon.' Never seen to laugh, rarely to smile in his intercourse with pupils, he was always in earnest, with no desire for frivolity. Never idle, when his official duties were over, he would occupy himself with etching, or botany, or with copying out his own scores for publication; or those of other masters, leaving 3,000 pages of MS. of this kind. To one who asked him why he gave himself this trouble, he replied : 'There is always something to learn.' To the same question from his wife one day he answered : 'As if one had not always something to learn,' or, according to another account, 'I learn, and were I to live 1,000 years, I should still find something to learn.' He also said to her : 'There is good to be got from them [the works of others] which remains in your mind.' His patience in writing out his scores, the pains he took, were remarkable. If a blot fell on his paper, his pen-knife helped to fit another piece of paper so neatly on to the place, that you could with difficulty see where the blot had been. His MS. scores were so beautifully written, that they rivalled printing.[4] At 12 o'clock he left his office, and proceeded on his round through the classes. His official relations with others will help us to a conclusion as to what manner of man he was. De Lafage,[5] while accounting for Cherubini's irritability, by the 20 years of vexations experienced before his worldly prospects became assured, says : 'He did not know how to accelerate progress and encourage rising talent,' the contrary being the fact. Both he and Fétis admit his scrupulous devotion

[4] *N.M.Z.*, *M.W.*, 1862. [5] Michaud's *Biog. Univ.* i. 98.

to duty.[6]   The latter says that 'he brought with him little love,' but we shall see instances quite to the contrary.   He was, indeed, inexorable in sending away those who failed to derive benefit from the classes, as also in declining to receive those whom he deemed, from any cause, unsuited to a musical or dramatic career.   'Are you the lady who wished to come out at the opera?' he said to one introduced by Halévy.   'Yes, sir.'   'It's impossible.'   'Why?'   'Why? ask your glass.'   In the same way he would show no favour in 1835 to a Mlle. Hebler, recommended through Queen Marie Amélie, because, as he wrote to her private secretary, 10 Oct., 'nature had denied her the most indispensable qualities: exterior and voice.'[7]   Again, when a man came with a powerful voice, and asked what he had better do with it, Cherubini suggests his becoming an auctioneer.'[8]   All this seems dreadful candour, but it was sincerity in the interests of those affected.   They could not have succeeded, but would never have believed it, unless plainly told so.   But Cherubini might have told them less plainly.   Had he known his compatriot, St. Philip Neri, as Palestrina did, he would probably have modified his phraseology.   The professors and pupils, on the other hand, knew their man, and thoroughly believed in him.   As Lassabathie, the voluminous Conservatoire historian, indicates, they were sure that no external influence, however exalted, would ever lead him to betray their interests.   On the contrary, he stood by them.

In 1841 a professor was appointed at the Conservatoire by the Minister of the Interior without being previously recommended to the Director and the Council of Administration.   Cherubini sent for a teacher, whom, owing to gratuitous and earlier services he deemed worthy of this extra post; and told him of his intended resignation of the Directorship if he (the teacher) were not named to a post similar to that created for the professor.   The teacher begged him to do nothing; but Cherubini wrote

6 Fétis, *Biog. Univ.* art. Cherubini.   7 Pougin, *M. W.*, 1883, 641.
8 Crowest, 99.   Pougin gives another very personal remark.

to the Minister and gained the day. The result was ' one
injustice less to deplore.'[9] His nervous, delicate organization, which could not stand even the buzzing of an insect
about his ear, was responsible for some of the defects of
his qualities. He had a good deal of the bear about him,
but as his servants would say : ' Leave him alone. When
he has acted enough of the bad man, he will become
good again. It is the good-natured churl.'[10] To continue
our illustrations : His sharp sayings became proverbial,
but there was kindness along with them now and again,
and seldom any sort of malice. A little child once came
to the Conservatoire, accompanied by a very tall father.
Cherubini was puzzled as to who was the applicant.
The father seemed too old, the son too young. ' I do not
put infants out to nurse,' he said, and passed on, but the
parent was advised to set the son to a piano in
another room, through which Cherubini must pass
on his daily round. This was done : and Cherubini,
astonished at the child's playing, asked him some
questions, which were answered. ' Bravo, my little friend,
but why are you here, and what can I do for you ? '
' Make me a member of the Conservatoire.' ' It's a
thing done,' said Cherubini, ' you are one of us.' On
leaving, he said, ' I had to be careful about pushing the
questions too far, for the baby was beginning to prove to
me he knew more about music than I do myself.'[11] One
day as he was inveighing against the parents of precocious
children, a lady came in, on an appointed interview,
bringing her son, whom she began to praise as a wonderful genius, ' a perfect child of nature.' ' Madame,' said
the maëstro, ' leave him to us. We will adopt him.
What a happiness to find a child of nature fallen on earth

---

[9] Elwart. See, too, in Pougin *M. W.*, 1883 479, a beautiful instance of
consideration for a work (to be done at the Conservatoire) by a pupil ' whose
feeble powers, he writes, ' will not be able to struggle against ' a noisy,
military overture of Berton's. He begs the latter to choose another of his
own that would be preferable.'
[10] De Lafage.
[11] Miel.

without a father, without a mother, without a sister, without a brother.'[12] On one occasion a work was brought him, generally reported to be Méhul's. 'Show it me, then,' said Cherubini to the person who brought it. At last he said, 'It is not Méhul's; it is too bad to be his.' 'It's mine,' said the other. 'I tell you it is not yours.' 'Why, dear master?' 'Because it's too good to be yours.' His son-in-law, M. Turcas, had composed a symphony, the minuet of which was performed at the Conservatoire concert of 22 April 1838, and on his informing Cherubini that he had written the symphony, the latter said, 'This will be bad.' 'And why?' 'Why? because I have done them, and Méhul also, and so I know it will be.'[13] When friends told Cherubini that they had not yet been to see Boieldieu's 'La Dame Blanche,' he replied: 'Perhaps you are waiting for her to change colour.'

When Beethoven's Mass in D was being one day given, Berlioz spoke against the fugue 'Et vitam.' Cherubini, entering the corridor, heard some discussion going on, and said, 'What is it?' Some replied, 'This fellow doesn't like the fugue.' 'That is because the fugue doesn't like him,' was Cherubini's retort. Again, he silenced one complaining of the chromatic progression from F sharp to F natural in Rossini's Prayer from 'Moïse in Egitto.' 'What do you say,' said the pedant, 'to this flagrant transgression of that libertine, Rossini?' 'What do I say?' replied Cherubini; 'I only wish I had committed it. . . .' On the other hand, Mendelssohn tells us he once took Cherubini an 8-part composition 'alla cappella,' 'Tu es Petrus.' 'The old man is really too pedantic,' he said to Hiller; 'in one passage I had employed a suspension of 3rds, simultaneously in 2 parts; he would not allow it to pass on any account.' A few

---

[12] *Ella's Musical Sketches.* He writes to his son 28 Aug. 1829, that he had 'emancipated' himself 'from the bother of receiving the pupils' papas and mammas.'—*M. W.*, 1883, 737.
[13] Elwart.

years later, Mendelssohn said to his friend, 'The old man
was right after all. They are not allowable.'[14] His
vigorous remark when asked why he no longer brought
out works at the Opera Comique, has been preserved in a
letter of Mendelssohn from Paris, 21 Feb. 1832 : 'I am
not going to give my operas without chorus, without
orchestra, without singers, and without decorations.'[15]

When Brod, the oboe-player, died in 1839, Tulou,
the flute-player, returning from the funeral, met Cherubini
and said : 'Ah, maëstro, we have lost our dear friend
Brod.' 'What! what! !' exclaimed Cherubini, then deaf.
With a loud voice Tulou repeated, 'Brod is dead,' 'Ah,'
replied the Florentine, turning away, 'Petit son, petit
son ' (little tone).[16]

Cherubini has had fathered on him the saying, 'The
only thing worse than one flute is two,' though none
have written more beautifully for that instrument than he,
as in the quarrel scene of the 'Water-Carrier.' We are
told he never lent his umbrella, not even to the kind
gentleman who, recognizing the master on the Boulevards
one day, when it had begun to rain, placed at his disposal
his own vehicle, of which Cherubini availed himself.[17]
Perhaps it was wisdom, but is the story true ?

In 1824, Adolphe Adam was called upon to serve as
a soldier. He sought out Cherubini, and after much
beating about the bush, told him that a certificate from
him attesting his (Adam's) aptitude for musical composition, might ensure him a release from the conscription.
Cherubini was fond of Adolphe Adam, and was unwilling
to refuse him any request, but did not wish to run any
risks in the matter himself. He gave him this certificate:
' I attest that the pupil Adolphe Adam follows exactly the

---

[14] Hiller's *Mendelssohn, &c.*, *cit. M. W.*, 1883, 560. He was once in
error in declaring the answer to a musical puzzle by X, a Conservatoire
professor of singing wrong when it was really right, as Benoist said, but
Cherubini had his way. See the whole incident in Pougin, *M. W.*, 1883, 672.
[15] *Letters from Italy and Switzerland*, tr. Lady Wallace, 1862, 340.
[16] Ella's *Musical Sketches*.
[17] *Once a Week*.

classes of the Conservatoire.' Adam saw that this would be of no use as an excuse to the military authorities. Remembering a finger that had been disabled for 2 years, he went to a celebrated surgeon, who had treated it, and asked him to aid him in his object. The surgeon gave him this certificate: 'I certify having operated on M. Adolphe Adam for a tumour on the finger, which has perfectly healed.' Ultimately Adolphe's short stature and bad eyesight served him in better stead, and he was enabled to continue his musical studies in peace. [18]

Cherubini was severe on those who wrote with imperfect training. Meeting Boieldieu in the theatre corridor, when the latter's 'Caliphe de Bagdad' was having a great run, he seized him by the collar and said, ' Unhappy wretch, are you not ashamed to achieve so great a success, and do so little to deserve it?' 'I remained stupefied at his words, . . . and could find nothing to say in reply. But . . . I lost no time in going to him and begging his advice. It was settled he was to take me with him to St. Just's country house . . . and there make me have an unpleasant time. I did so for 2 seasons. After that I knew what I was about. But for Cherubini, I should probably still be ignorant that science in no way detracts from expression.' And he was much pleased when Boieldieu, as the result of his studies, after 2 or 3 years, brought out the opera of ' Rien de trop.' ' Cherubini,' writes Boieldieu, 'whom my brother saw sitting the whole time in the balcony, and who never left off applauding, came up and told me before everyone that he was enchanted with the music.' [19]

Halévy, Cherubini's adopted son, once took him to hear one of his operas. At the end of the 1st act he asked his master how he liked it? Cherubini made no answer. At the end of the 2nd act, Halévy repeated his

---

[18] *Notice sur A. Adam.*
[19] *Boieldieu à Nantes, &c., Boieldieu, sa vie et ses œuvres. cit.* Pougin. *M. W.*, 1883, 499. Fétis says Boieldieu's methods never changed, but friends see much change between *Le Calife* and *La Dame Blanche.*

question. Again no reply. You don't answer me anything.' 'What should I answer? Here, for 2 hours
you've said nothing to me.' A piece of his own was once
finely given. at the Conservatoire, and a member of the
orchestra ventured to ask whether he was satisfied. 'Do
I not say nothing?' was the reply. He was in a chance
ill-humour. Another version runs: 'When I say nothing,
it means I am content,' which it did not mean in Halévy's
case.[20]

Auber at 1st only played with music, and in his
'Julie,' executed at the Conservatoire, Cherubini recognized a powerful but untrained genius;[21] but when straitened circumstances led him at 35 to seek Cherubini's
advice, he said: 'What's to be done?' 'What's to be
done?' said Cherubini, 'The matter is very simple; you
are a musician, you have ideas, work.' 'Work!' said
Auber, 'that is very easily said, but I am not accustomed
to it, and it is not much to my taste.' 'Very well, then,'
said Cherubini, 'throw yourself out of window.' Auber
didn't do that, but, making a grimace, went through a
regular course of counterpoint with Cherubini, and kept
as a precious memento the table whereat they had worked
together.[22]

Jullien encountered only encomium. 'When I was
twelve years old,' he writes, 'I played the flute and the
fiddle without having ever learned either. I then thought
I should like to become a great composer, and, to try my
hand, I wrote a Grand Mass.' Ad ed by his father to
go to the Conservatoire and study under a great master,
he repaired to the Rue Bergère and was told that M.
Cherubini consented to receive pupils on Thursdays at
3 o'clock. When he entered the composer's cabinet, he
trembled as the Florentine's eagle eye fixed itself on his
small countenance, and the following dialogue ensued:
'What do you want?' 'To learn music.' 'What is it

[20] De Lafage, Michaud's *Biog. Univ.* i 98.
[21] *Grove*, i. 102a· 1st ed.
[22] *M. W.*, 1883, 592.

you've got there?' 'Oh, a bagatelle, a Mass I've done.'
Again Cherubini looked as though he would pierce him
through, took the MS., looked at it attentively, and then:
'It's you who have done that?' 'Yes.' 'What do you
want to learn? Go away, you are music itself.'[23] Also
when Arriaga, who entered at 13 the Conservatoire,
wrote, when 15, an 8-part 'Et vitam venturi,' Cherubini
deemed it a masterpiece, and said so.[24] The opinion was
of value, coming from the author of a similar production,
it is believed, without exact parallel in modern music,
in the 8-part Credo.

In the autumn of 1825,[25] Mendelssohn, a lad at
the time, came with his father to Paris, with the
view of seeing Cherubini. 'I can well remember,'
writes Mendelssohn to his sister Fanny, 'that in my
15th year there was a question as to my studying with
Cherubini in Paris, and I know how grateful I was to my
father at the time, and often since, that he at last gave up
the idea and kept me with himself.' He might have
gained something not afterwards attained, though his
scientific training elsewhere was quite good enough. The
father particularly wished to ask Cherubini's advice as to
his son taking up music as a profession. Cherubini read
over some of Mendelssohn's works, and, with many other
Parisian artistes, heard him play the pianoforte part in
one of his 4-tets. Then the stern oracle spoke: 'This
boy is rich, will do well, but he spends too much money,
puts too much stuff on his clothes,' adding, 'I will speak
to him; then he will do well.' At his instance Mendelssohn wrote a 'Kyrie' (since, alas, lost!), which he describes
as 'bigger than anything I have yet done.' Would that
he had done as contemplated—a whole Mass. It would
have been, perhaps, a worthy complement to his 'Lauda
Sion.' Albeit admiring him, as he did musically, Mendelssohn, as will be shown, in his personal remarks on Cheru-

[23] Engel's *From Mozart to Mario,* ii. 26.
[24] Fétis, *Biog. Univ.* (1868), i. 149.
[25] Not, as occasionally stated, in 1824.

bini, displays little insight. 'What an extraordinary being!' he said, speaking one day to Hiller about him. 'You would never have imagined a man could be a great composer without possessing sensibility of heart, or any other kind of sentiment, whatever its name may be. Well, I declare to you that with Cherubini everything comes from the brain alone. Such is my conviction;' and later on he compares him to a 'burnt-out volcano, that flashes forth flame occasionally, but is completely covered with ashes and stones.'[26] Yet the 2nd Requiem burns steadily without either.

Let Liszt now recount his 1st interview. 'The day after our arrival in Paris, we hastened to Cherubini. A very warm letter of recommendation from Prince Metternich was to be our introduction. It was just 10 o'clock—Cherubini was already at the Conservatoire. . . . At last, after a quarter-of-an-hour of painful waiting, the porter opened the door of the Director's cabinet and made us a sign to enter. More dead than alive, yet urged on at that moment by an overpowering might, I sprang towards Cherubini to kiss his hand, but just then, and for the 1st time, the thought came to me that perhaps it might not be the custom in France, and my eyes filled with tears. Confused and ashamed, without again lifting my eyes to the great composer, who had even dared to confront Napoleon, my whole endeavour was to lose no word, no breath, that fell from his mouth. . . . We had already been warned that difficulties would be opposed to my reception in the Conservatoire, but until then, that law of the institution, decisively shutting out all foreigners from its instruction, was unknown to us. Cherubini 1st made us acquainted with it.'[27]

Ramann comments severely upon Liszt's exclusion.

[26] Zelter's *Letters*, iv. 35. Goethe and Mendelssohn, *cit. Grove*, ii. 257b. *M.M.R.* i, 1871.
[27] Hiller's *Felix Mendelssohn—Bartholdy.—M.W.*, 1883, 560. Mendelssohn saw Cherubini again in 1831. 'The day before yesterday,' he writes, 20 Dec., 'I paid two musical visits, to the grumbling Cherubini and the kind Herz.'—Mendelssohn's *Letters*, ed. 1868, 173.

'We see before us,' she says, 'the Italian Cherubini, the personification of a dark and inflexible law ; before him the Hungarian Adam Liszt, opposing his remonstrances, and beside the latter, with imploring, upraised hands and enthusiastic countenance, the flaming sign of genius on his brow, the boy, Franz Liszt.' As has been pointed out, however, Cherubini was not the author of the law, and to ascribe his enforcement of it to disinclination to precocious talent, and secret and instinctive fear of the boy's genius, runs counter, as we shall see, to his known conduct in dealing with pupils.[28] He spared no trouble in helping them where he could do so, as extant letters abundantly prove, of which we have seen several.

Thus one, 14 June 1821, addressed to M. le Baron De Bruyère St. Michel, shows his kind feelings towards a young musician whom, however, according to the rules, he was unable to assist. 'In answer to the letter you have honoured me with, Monsieur le Baron, I have the privilege of assuring you that I take as much interest as you do in M. Henry, whom you recommend, but unfortunately, it is no longer in my power to revoke what has been pronounced on this subject, not by me particularly, but by the assembled council of the Musical Body I preside over. This Body has been finally reduced to, and fixed at, 51 executants by the positive orders of

[28] *Franz Liszt, Artist and Man*, 1811-1840, by L. Ramann, tr. from Germ. by E. Cowdray, 1882, i. 84. Writing to Czerny from Paris, 3 Sept. 1824, Liszt's father says : 'When the programme came before the censorship, it was asked who was going to write the music ; and the poet answered, laughing, "Young Liszt." "What!" exclaimed Cherubini ; "do you think that to compose an opera is as easy as performing a piece on the piano? That cannot be passed." Some others held the same view ; Paër alone gave it as his opinion that a trial should be made. . . . Cherubini and a few others do not care to see a younger man in their circle, but that is of no consequence.' From a letter of Liszt's father, to Czerny, from Paris, 14 Aug. 1825, we learn that Cherubini, Berton, Catel, Boieldieu, and Lesueur, duly met as a jury to decide upon Liszt's opera, and accepted it.— *M.M.R.*, 1871, i. So, where was the grievance? Cherubini often had to serve on these juries. In 1799, he became one of the 'Jury de Lecture de l'Opéra,' and continued an effective member of the jury established in 1808 for the examination of works presented to the Grand Opera, as also a member, up to April 1824, of the 'Conseil littéraire et musicale,' remodelled in 1816, and re-established soon afterwards under the title of 'Jury for the Examination of Musical Works.'

Monsieur le Maréchal; you can easily assure yourself of
this, Sir, at the Etat Major. He alone can create another
place, if he likes, and so re-instate M. Henry in the corps
he belonged to before the reform.'

In another letter, written in a beautiful hand, neat
and small, and dated 8 Dec. 1832, from the Conservatoire,
and addressed to a Parisian 'impresario,' we find him
interesting himself in a Mlle. David, one of the pupils.
'Sir, Mlle. David, in whom I take infinite interest, as in
all the pupils of the Conservatoire, has told me of the
proposition she has made you to join your theatre without
receiving an appointment, up to the month of April next.
. . . I have the honour, then, Sir, to renew the request
she has made, hoping you will consent thereto without
trouble; indeed, I would beg you to do so. I can assure
you, you will be satisfied in all respects with Mlle. David,
for she is a zealous pupil, and when she gets more
accustomed to the boards, she will be able to make herself
very useful. . . . I recommend her, and beg you to believe
in my gratitude for anything you can do for her.'[29]

[29] I have also seen a 3rd letter from Cherubini (without date) to
the Duc de Richelieu, asking him to recommend M. Turcas for a
financial post in Paris; though it exhibits only a natural instance of kindness, seeing that the object of it was his son-in-law. His letter is written
in a beautiful hand, on a 4to sheet. I extract the 2nd paragraph. 'Monseigneur, . . . M. Turcas has passed the greater part of his youth in trade;
all his family follow this career, and the slender chance he possesses of
entering the new corps of Military Intendants, because of the few vacancies
and the number of competitors, has decided him to resume the career
wherein he has acquired the necessary knowledge. He is, then, attached
to a banking house and has addressed a request to His Excellency the
Minister of Finance with a view to obtaining one of the 2 places of Agent
de Change that remain for nomination for Paris. The Minister has sent
back this request to the Syndical Chamber, whose members are well disposed in favour of my son-in-law, and propose to place him on the new list
of presentation. Dare I hope, Monseigneur, that you will deign to honour
us with your high protection in a manner very important for us, since his
success will assure the prospects of my son-in-law and of my
daughter? I ask it of you earnestly, and shall be very pleased if your
Excellency would receive with some interest the request I take the liberty
of making.' The above 3 letters are preserved in the British Museum in
more or less faulty French, which Cherubini did not write very well. Thus,
in the full score of *Médée,* he will refer to 'Colchos' instead of 'Colchis;'
in the catalogue to 'solfeggo,' and 'messe solonnelle;' in the letters he
adds a 't' to 'berceau,' etc.

In 1793 Lesueur was in trouble with his opera or
'La Caverne.' Rehearsing it at the Feydeau Theatre,
he experienced all kinds of ill-will and annoyance on the
part of the artists in the orchestra, who styled him
'Monsieur l'Abbé,' because, previous to 1789, he had
worn the ecclesiastical collar at Notre Dame, Paris, when
chapel-master there. Shy novice as he was, he feared to
estrange both singers and instrumentalists by making
any observations at the rehearsal, and only dared to
address compliments. The performance, taking everything together, could not have gone worse. Cherubini,
who was present, said : 'You know how to compose
music well, but not how to execute it well ;' and there
and then he took the 'bâton,' and led a repetition of the
work, with immense success, crowning his proceedings by
hissing, not the work but the actors, during the 3
representations of the work that followed. Further, on
going into Normandy he had 'La Caverne' put upon the
Boards at Rouen, without telling Lesueur, and its success
there was as great as it had been at the rehearsal.[30]

He writes to his wife 28 April, 1797, about Méhul's
opera of 'La Chasse du Jeune Henri,' 'I shall look forward
anxiously for the news of its success. If he achieves such
success as I hope he will, and as the work deserves, he
will have a great one. The only thing that annoys me
is not being able to be present at his good fortune, so
that I may share it with him, and be the first to tell him
what gratification it affords me. But I shall have one
delight the more on my return in hearing of my friend's
new work.'[31]

Utterly unselfish, he stopped people from giving
their votes in favour of himself on the vacancy occurring
at the Institute, occasioned by Grétry's death in 1813. 'Not

[30] The above circumstances, Elwart says, took place after Cherubini's
'recent success with *Les Deux Journées ;'* if so, in or after 1800. But *La
Caverne* appeared in 1793, when the incidents at the rehearsal are by
several other writers said to have taken place, and when we know that
Cherubini was in Normandy.—*Histoire de la Société des Concerts.*
[31] *M.W.*, 1882, 622.

wishing,' he said to the Secretary, ' to oppose an artist of M. Monsigny's merit and age, I would beg those members of the 4th Class, who may intend giving me their suffrages, to unite them for the Nestor of French composers, in order that he may be elected, as he deserves to be,—that is to say, unanimously.[32] And when made King's Chapel-master, it seems quite clear that, unofficially, he let Lesueur share with him both the work and the pay.

On occasion of a performance of a piece by Cheru-bini, written for a grand religious festival, Cherubini was told the chief tenor was ill ; so, early the next morning, Begrez, a Belgian, then only a violinist, received the music of the tenor's part with a request that he would learn it, so as to be able to sing it before noon at the festival. The violinist besought Cherubini to dispense him from this heavy responsibility, for at most he was but an amateur singer. Cherubini, however, was peremptory, and assured Begrez that he had the highest trust in his musical intelligence. Begrez sang in the part, and so well, as to make a deep impression on his hearers. When the service was over, Cherubini ran to the front of the choir and embraced Begrez. This unexpected success led the latter to abandon the violin and take to singing, and he became 1st tenor at her Majesty's Theatre in this country.[33]

He thus acknowledged merit generously. Years after his predecessor Sarrette's retirement from the Conserva-toire directorship, at a banquet held in 1839 to do him honour, Cherubini, in proposing his health, said : ' May the Conservatoire for its glory and prosperity one day find a director like you.'[34] This friendship was reciprocated by Sarrette. Offered Cherubini's post in 1830 by the new Government, he declined to accept it, and his friend remained in office.

It was in 1821 that Fétis was nominated professor

[32] Quicherat's *Adolphe Nowrit,* cit. Pougin, *M.W.*, 1883, 511.
[33] Ella's *Musical Sketches.*
[34] Pougin, *M.W.*, 1883, 661.

of composition at the Conservatoire in the place of Eler, and 8 months after he had entered upon his functions, his pupils were examined by the committee of education over which Cherubini presided, with Paër, Lesueur, Berton, Reicha, and Boieldieu associated with our composer as members of the committee ; and Fétis was gratified at Cherubini thus addressing him : ' Sir, it is with much interest that the committee has passed the examination of your class, and that it has discovered in your pupils the art of making the parts sing in an elegant and natural way, an art difficult, yet so well known to the old masters, and nowadays lost ; it is with a lively satisfaction we see you labouring to revive it.' Some years later Cherubini expressed himself more explicitly as to Fétis' merits, in the report he made to the ' Académie des Beaux Arts,' on the latter's ' Treatise on Counterpoint and Fugue,' written for the Conservatoire. Cherubini observed of that work, that it was the only one of its kind wherein the rules for scientific composition, especially those for the fugue, were put forward with method and clearness.[35]   When Catel, a very young man at the time, brought out his ' Treatise on Harmony,' Cherubini wrote an article about it, praising it highly as a work possessing ' the double merit of combining in all essential points the different systems followed by the French, German and Italian schools. . . . It so reconciles them with each other, that its usefulness and merit cannot be contested ; and he declares the author ' an artist who will do his country honour.'[36]

In a letter to a friend from Paris, 15 Dec. 1820, Spohr writes : ' With a beating heart I drove through the Barrière of Paris. The thought that I should at length have the pleasure of making the personal acquaintance of the artistes whose works had inspired me in my early childhood excited the emotion which I then felt. In fancy I reverted to the days of my boyhood, in which my

[35] *Biog. Univ.* art. Fétis.   [36] *M. W.,* 1883, 531.

idol was Cherubini, whose works I had had an earlier
opportunity of becoming acquainted with in Brunswick,
at the then permanent French theatre there, than even
the works of Mozart. . . . The author, and many other
men whose works had exercised the most decided influence
on my development as a composer and violinist, I was
now soon to behold. . . . I was told of Cherubini that
he was at 1st very reserved toward strangers, even
repulsive. I did not find him so. He received me without any letter of introduction, in the most friendly manner,
and invited me to repeat my visit as often as I pleased.'[37]
Kreutzer takes Spohr on the evening of his arrival in
Paris to the Grand Opera. This leads Spohr to exclaim :
'Is it a subject for praise or blame, that the French,
notwithstanding the many excellent things with which
their operatic répertoire has been enriched during the last
20 years, still give the oldest things of all? And is it
indeed a proof of an advanced cultivated taste for art

---

[37] *Autobiography,* ii. 107. Catel died 29 Nov. 1830, and at his funeral, after
Berton had spoken, Cherubini said : 'When death carries off from society
and the arts a man of talent, whose career has been prolonged to a very
advanced age, one ought, without doubt, to regret, and be greived thereat ;
but when a premature end strikes in the prime of life the man possessing
distinguished talent, and moreover, gifted with moral virtues, characterising
the best men, one should weep the more : such was M. Catel, our loved
fellow-brother, whose loss we deplore. His musical career is remarkable
for the works he has composed, worthy to serve as models to young composers, and certainly titles that do honour to his age, and which will not be
forgotten : but what will honour his memory most are his qualities of heart
and character. It is impossible to dwell on what he has done without
ostentation ; his attachment to his friends, and the sentiments of gratitude
he· has constantly cherished, particularly towards one among them from
whom he was never separated, who had welcomed and assisted him in
youth, and who, as a father would act towards his own son, opened to him
the honourable musical career he has pursued, and wherein he has always
walked worthily ; for modest, as regards himself, admiring the talent of
his rivals, never has he been ruled by any sentiment of jealousy of their
success. After having paid a just tribute to the talent and excellent
qualities of our dear collegues, it only rests for me to address my last farewell to my friend. Adieu, for the last time, my well-loved Catel ! The
moment is not, perhaps, far off, when I shall go to rejoin you.' Halévy in
his *Derniers Souvenirs,* says that Cherubini was present at Berton's funeral
on Friday, 26 April 1830. *Read* 1844? Berton dying 22 April of that year,
this is probably correct. The above address is from the French Collection
of funeral speeches, by members of the French Institute, as also the
address at Boieldieu's funeral, in the British Museum.

when one sees them give as enthusiastic a reception (if not more so) to the oldest operas of Grétry, with their poverty of harmony and incorrectness, as to the master-pieces of Cherubini and Méhul? I think not.' Again he says, in a 2nd letter from Paris, 31 Dec.: 'The masses, the leaders of the fashion here, positively know not how to distinguish the worst from the best; they hear "Le Jugement de Midas" with the same rapture that they listen to "Les Deux Journées" or "Joseph." . . .' 'In another letter from Paris of 12 Jan. 1821, Spohr writes: 'From the frequent opportunities I had of playing before Cherubini, at private parties, I conceived a very ardent desire to have all my 4-tets and 5-tets, so far as I thought them worthy of it, heard by that master so highly esteemed by me, and to introduce them by degrees to his notice, in order to ask him his opinion of them. But in this I succeeded with very few only; for when Cherubini had heard the 1st 4-tet (No. 1 of the Op. 45, written at Frankfort), and I was on the point of producing a 2nd, he protested against it, and said: "Your music, and indeed the form and style of this kind of music, is as yet so foreign to me, that I cannot find myself immediately at home with it, nor follow it properly; I would therefore much prefer that you repeated the 4-tet you have just played." I was very much astonished at this remark, and did not understand it until I afterwards ascertained that Cherubini was quite unacquainted with the German masterpieces of this kind — of Mozart and Beeth-oven—and, at the utmost, had once heard a 4-tet by Haydn at Baillot's soirées. As the other persons present coincided with Cherubini's wish, I consented the more readily, as in the 1st execution of it some things had not gone altogether well. He now spoke very favourably of my composition, praised its form, its thematic working out, the rich change in the harmonies, and particularly the "fugato" in the last subject. But as there were still many things not quite clear to him in the music, he begged me to repeat it again when we should next meet.

I hoped he would think nothing more about it, and there-fore at the next music party brought forward another 4-tet. Before I could begin, however, Cherubini renewed his request, and I was therefore obliged to play the same 4-tet a 3rd time. The same thing occurred also with No. 2 of Op. 45, excepting that he spoke of it with more decisive praise, and said of the " adagio : " " It is the finest I ever heard." He was equally pleased with my pianoforte 5-tet, with the concerted accompaniment of wind instruments, and I was frequently obliged to play it on that account.' Moscheles was in Paris at this time, and tells us he met Spohr there. 'At Baillot's house, who had got up for Spohr and myself a genuine soirée of artistes, he was greeted with real enthusiasm. I also played and improvised. He played, I played, and we each shared in a brotherly way the applause of this select audience, which included Cherubini, Boieldieu, Auber, Hérold,[38] Adam, Viotti and Lesueur.

On 20 March 1821, Moscheles wrote : ' I spent the evening at Ciceri's, son-in-law of Isabey, the famous painter, where I was introduced to one of the most inte-resting circles of artists. In the 1st room were assembled the most famous painters, engaged in drawing several things for their own amusement. In the midst of these was Cherubini, also drawing. I had the honour, like every one newly introduced, of having my portrait taken in caricature. Begassé took me in hand and succeeded well. In an adjoining room were musicians and actors, amongst them Ponchard, Levasseuer, Dugazon, Panseron, Mdlle. de Munk, and Madame Livère of the Théâtre Français. The most interesting of their performance, which I attended merely as a listener, was a vocal 4-tet by Cherubini, performed under his direction. Later in the

[38] Mdme. Moscheles adds : ' Applause in this instance means no ordi-nary recognition,' namely, there were present, Cherubini, Boieldieu, Auber, Hérold, Adam, Lesueur, Pacini, Paër, Mazas, Habeneck, Plantade, Blangini, Lafont, Pleyel, Ivan, Müller, Struntz, Viotti, Ponchard, Pellegrini, Nadermann, Garcia, Martinville, Mangin, Bertin, Schlesinger, Lemoine, Pape, Petzold, Erard, Freudenthaler, the brothers Bohrer, and others.

evening the whole party armed itself with larger or smaller " mirlitons " (reed-pipe whistles), and on these small mo- notonous instruments, sometimes made of sugar, they played, after the fashion of Russian horn music, the over- ture to " Démophon," 2 frying-pans representing the drums. On 27 March there was another " mirliton " concert at Ciceri's, in which Cherubini took an active part.' [39]

At 2 o'clock it was Cherubini's custom to go home, and then his day's work at the Conservatoire was over. He lived in an unpretending set of rooms on the 3rd floor of the house No. 19 Rue du Faubourg Poissonnière. Visiting him in 1835, Eugène Gautier notes that ' articles of furniture belonging to different epochs proclaimed the advanced age of the occupants. Tables with spindle legs stood near sideboards by Jacob, ornamented with gilt brass.' [40] ' Cherubini's wife,' Hiller writes, ' a stately and wise matron, who bore unmistakeable traces of former beauty, . . . always spoke of him as Monsieur Cherubini, but with the greatest tenderness. The eldest daughter . . . was a most lively and active woman, and had a lovely little daughter. . . . " Here in this room," she said to me one day, " Papa wrote ' Les Deux Journées.' He sat at a litttle table in the window, and there in the corner of the wall I played with my companions. Beyond a certain fixed line we might not go, but within that space we might make as much noise as we liked." ' Pougin's ac- count goes to corroborate Mme. Turcas : ' Cherubini, leaving his wife to look after his guests,' now and again, and ' absorbed and abstracted in his inspiration, . . . would write without a single erasure or correction . . . it mattered nothing to him that . . . 20 persons went on talking, laughing and arguing, provided they did not sing.' [41]

Hiller writes of Cherubini's only son, Salvador, as ' a

[39] *Life of Moscheles*, i. 45.   [40] *cit.* Pougin, *M. W.*, 1883, 539.
[41] *M. W.*, 1883, 705.

handsome, agreeable and accomplished man;' of his
younger daughter as a 'beautiful and charming girl.'[42]
Before a window was his writing table. Opposite the
fireplace in his bedroom was a small piano (happy instrument!) of 5 and a half octaves (from the workshops of old
Sebastian Erard), which he had used for many years
whilst composing. Cherubini greatly prized it, and always
took it with him when visiting his friends out of Paris, at
Chimay, Chartres, Gaillon, Breuilpont, Malabri, Montlignon, etc. After his death his widow gave it to Pierre
Erard, for the latter's collection of historically interesting
instruments. It now stands by the side of the pianos of
Piccinni and Gluck.[43]

'Hiller tells us that he had asked leave to take home
a couple of volumes from the Conservatoire library, and
received the answer: "That cannot be; it's forbidden."
It was no use insisting, so I changed the conversation, but
as I was taking leave, he said: "What was it you wanted
to borrow from our library?" And when I answered that
it was a volume of Palestrina's "motets," the old man
replied in an almost confidential tone, "I shall send for
them for myself and then you shall have them." My last
Sunday in Paris he invited me to join his family dinner,
and before we sat down he presented me with 2 scores,
begging me to choose one. . . . I seized the thickest and
was about to pocket it, when the well-known, "That cannot be," sounded in my ears. It seems that these manuscripts had their appointed places, according to number
and letter in his library, and could not upon any condition
be withdrawn. However, on the following Tuesday I
received a copy of the score I had chosen (a beautiful
"Agnus Dei"), which the indefatigable old man had accomplished in the 2 days with a trembling hand, but the
utmost clearness and neatness. Some letters I afterwards
received from him are written in terms of such tender
kindness that it is impossible to recognize in them the

stern Director with his "That cannot be!"'[44]   Boieldieu,
knowing how 'no' was always Cherubini's 1st word, said
to him one day, 'What a pity your 2nd impulse never
precedes your 1st! It would be so much more agreeable
for those who have business with you if it did.'[45]

The relations between Cherubini and Rossini were
truly fraternal. When 'Guillaume Tell' came out in
1829, the artistes serenaded him after the performance,
and Cherubini placed a wreath upon his head. Writing
to his son Salvador, 28 Aug. 1829, he says: 'Your mother
has, of course, told you of the success of "Guillaume Tell."
The music is marvellously beautiful, but the book is too
long, and badly constructed. No matter; the work is very
fine!'[46]   The 1st interview between the composers was
narrated by Rossini himself to Pougin. Ushered into
Cherubini's drawing-room, he went straight to the piano
and sung by heart an air from 'Giulio Sabino,' one of
Cherubini's earliest operas. 'So you know that air, do
you?' said Cherubini. 'Yes, I do, maëstro, as you perceive!' 'And when did you hear it, for it's a very long
time since it used to be played?' 'Oh, I heard it in the
streets, where it is still sung, and having a good memory,
I have retained it.' They became henceforth fast friends.
When Cherubini made objections to losing his younger
daughter, and to her marrying Rosellini, a distinguished
archæologist, Rossini told him he must consent. 'You
will kill me if you talk like that.' 'You have nothing,'
said Rossini, 'you find an idiot ready to take your
daughter without dowry, outfit, anything.' 'I will not
allow you to speak to me like that,' said Cherubini. 'You
possess,' said Rossini, 'more talent than I do, that is well
known, but my "pizzicati" are worth more than all your
fugues.' And Cherubini at last consented.

Cherubini's love for Halévy was well reciprocated.
The latter became his pupil, at 12 years of age, in 1811,
and finished his 'Pygmalion' in 1827, which he feared to

[44] *Macmillan,* July 1875.   [45] *M. W.,* 1883, 500.   [46] *ib.* 1883, 737.

bring out, though Cherubini praised it. When Cherubini tried him, he would exclaim : ' O, M. Cherubini, how can you talk like that to me, who would do everything in the world to save you the shadow of an annoyance ! ' and so the tiff was soon at an end.[47] Cherubini essayed to get Halévy into the Institute on Boieldieu's death in 1834, by trying to delay the election till ' La Juive ' had appeared, but in the event Reicha obtained a few more votes. The latter, however, dying within the year, Halévy was then elected.[48]

To Boieldieu, as to Halévy, Cherubini was a 2nd father. He wrote an ' O Salutaris ' for his marriage in 1827, and the following hitherto unpublished letter further illustrates their intimacy : ' I had formed the project this morning of seeing you on leaving the Conservatoire, my dear friend, but the rain, to my regret, has prevented me. I wished to know first of all for myself, how you are, and to talk to you afterwards of the poem read to the jury. I avail myself this evening of my son, who is going to see you, to write to you, and send my letter by him. I have charged him to give me news which I hope will be still better than what you gave me yourself yesterday. I am now going to talk to you of " La Cour d'amour du Roi Réné ! " It is a very pretty piece by him, which we have listened to with much pleasure ; it will gain much with some slight corrections that Lubbard will be directed to make known to the author. The subject is musical, and will ensure your charming and fine talent displaying itself. All I fear, and this is my sole doubt, is whether the style be according to the present taste, which is no longer accustomed to the Troubadours and their amours ; further, my fear is perhaps not well founded. For your amiable music can warm and quicken what is too cloying in the character of the piece. It is for you, dear friend, to consider it. I repeat again, the poem is pretty, and the conclusion

[47] Pougin, *M. W*, 1883.   [48] *ib.*

happy. Good-day. My wife sends you many messages, as well as to yours. I do as much, and embracing you, I am ever yours, L. CHERUBINI.'[49]

On Boieldieu's death in 1834, after Garnier and Berton had spoken, Cherubini spoke at the grave:—
' Gentlemen, it is not long since we accompanied hither the remains of our colleague ; to-day we have to weep over the premature death of Boieldieu, my very dear friend, whose fine talent and excellent character will be for us all an inexhaustible source of regret. Friendship long united me to this amiable man and distinguished composer. I saw him commence his musical career, which he worthily pursued, going from success to success. I will not now mention all the works he has composed, for all the world knows them, and will not forget them. It was the value and reputation of his productions that took him to St. Petersburg to be at the service of the Emperor of all the Russias ; it was these same successes that opened to him the portals of the Institute. He was Professor of Composition at the Conservatoire of Music, a post he had quitted some time, and to which he was called anew ; but he was already smitten with the malady which has taken him from us. I have no need to enlarge here on the praises he merits, for who did not love Boieldieu ? Who did not admire and cherish his talent ? But I cannot refrain from noting what his death makes me experience. My chagrin is inexpressible. I have lost a friend, a brother. I have only a sorrowful remembrance of him. I, who weep, must console his companion, his son ! Alas ! their affectionate attentions assuaged his sufferings, but could not prolong his days. Farewell, Boieldieu ! Farewell ! I preceded you in life in the career you so nobly followed, and it is I who regret you ! I that weep to-day over the earth that is about to close over you ; for God has willed to call you to the end before me.'

In addresses and anecdotes, in personal details and

---

[49] *MS.* in British Museum.

characteristic sayings such as the foregoing, we seem to get a little nearer to the man himself, and Cherubini's letters, for which his admirers must ever be grateful to Pougin and the composer's family, complete the picture of one who is seen to be in many respects very much like other people, capable of affection and of inspiring it in others. We have seen how his 'heart was successively touched' at seeing Sarti's family at Berlin in 1805, and how he 'visited them daily, loving them dearly.' He writes to his wife, 28 April 1797: 'I have at length received a lettter from you, my darling, and hope to receive another to-morrow. I thank you for the pleasure you have procured me, for it is a pleasure to hear about you and my little Cocotte. Pretty dear! So she often asks after me, does she? . . . Give my dear Victorine, who writes like a little angel, a 1,000 kisses from me.'

'Paris, 1827.

'My good Salvador,—My dear son! you are going away for a year, and I have not been able to embrace you once more before you leave! . . . I wish you all the happiness we all desire for you. Receive my blessing, and if, unfortunately, I should not see you again, I recommend your mother to your care. . . . Farewell, my good son; love me always. . . .'[50]

To M. Rosellini (his son-in-law) :—

'Paris, 16th November, 1829.

'. . . From the day I decided on letting you have my daughter, I had to prepare insensibly for her departure. But the grief I feel will be eventually mitigated, if, as I am firmly convinced, you continue to make her happy. . . . I like to think we shall come together again some day, re-united and content, if I live long enough. . . .'[51]

[50] *M. W.*, 1883, 737.   [51] *ib.* 1883, 738.

To M. and Mme. Rosellini (son-in-law and daughter).

'Paris, 23rd January, 1835.

'My dear children, Hippolyte and Zénobie,—The proverb says: better late than never! . . . I desire you may not experience so mournful a loss as that you suffered last year. . . . Have you not as a consolation a handsome, good, and charming "bambino," who will cause you to forget the one you did not know. I am anxious to see him, to embrace him, and to go through with him my military drill; but Heaven knows when that will be! . : . tell Eugène that if he is always good and obedient, I shall always be fond of him, and send him more soldiers and other nice things. . . .' [52]

To Mme. Cherubini :—

'Saint Cloud, Sunday, 26th August, 1836.

'. . . My darling wife! . . . as I was coming back from the Château after the Mass of St. Louis, I was taken to the little pavilion in the park, . . . and there I found Mme. Tiron and her children, . . . all dressed up as peasants. Directly I arrived, they began singing a kind of refrain, and mowing some hay, which they had spread out on the ground. On removing it, they discovered some scores of Rossini and others ; they had put upon them the titles of my operas and of the Coronation Mass. Then they sang some verses ; then they placed the scores, whereon Mlle. Esther had placed a wreath of flowers, in a heap, round which they danced. Then each came and kissed me and presented me with a bouquet. It was very pretty ! It was thus they 'fêted' me. . . . Long live Saints' days, especially when they are celebrated by one's good friends. . . .' [53]

Such is the man, of whom Hillier, too hastily following Mendelssohn's lead, said: 'I never could gather that he possessed the depth of feeling we naturally

[52] *ib.* 15 Dec. 1883, 781.
[53] *M. W.*, 1883, 781, which see for further details.

associate with a great composer,' and whose family
affection was solidly proved by the excellent education he
gave his 3 children.[54]

'Cherubini in society was outwardly silent, modest,
unassuming, pleasing, and obliging, and possessed the
finest and most engaging manners. At the same time
he who did not know that he was with Cherubini would
think him stern and reserved, so well did the composer
know how to conceal everything, if only to avoid ostentation. He truly shunned brag or speaking of himself;'[55]
a singularly marked point in one highly gifted as he was,
and by no means too common among such, as witness
Berlioz and Wagner. I cannot recall reading of one
single word of self-praise. But see, as an example, the
very opposite, as when, during a concert he attended,
a piece by Beethoven being followed by his own overture to 'L'Hôtellerie Portugaise' (certainly, apart from the
introduction, not an important composition), he remarked
quite naturally : 'I am now going to appear a very small
boy.'

Adam says : 'He was worshipped by those around
him. The veneration his pupils held him in reached to
fanaticism. MM. Halévy and Batton lavished on him
in his last moments a truly filial care. Boieldieu never
spoke of him save with respect and tenderness ; and
Cherubini bestowed on his pupils all the affection they
had for him. . . . Hardly a month has yet passed
since, when speaking to me of that cherished pupil
[Halévy], he put forth so much earnestness in describing
to me the love he bore him, that I was moved to
tears.'[56]

On making his last journey to England, in 1826,
Weber went by way of Paris, and visiting Paër, Auber
and Rossini, 'was far more deeply touched and delighted
when old grey-headed Cherubini, whom he greatly

---

[54] *Macmillan*, 1875.
[55] *L. Cherubini*, Fritzsch.
[56] *Derniers Souvenirs.*

reverenced, twice visited him in his hotel.'[57] Bellini, Donizetti, Mercadante, Chopin, Spohr—most German musicians, in fact, coming to Paris—made their pilgrimage to this truly great man. Meyerbeer sends Cherubini his 'expression of homage and devotion,' and Dessauer, the Bohemian composer, writes, 'I kiss those hands that have given us so many immortal works.'[58] 'The sensations that you experienced approaching Cherubini,' continues Adam, 'were so strange that it would be hard to define them, much more to understand them. The veneration you had for his great age and fine talent was suddenly altered by ridicule excited by little trifles to which he clung with a persevering obstinacy. Then at the end of a few minutes, as though he understood that he had acted the disagreeable too long, his face relaxed, that smile, so refined and shrewd, came to animate the fine head of the old man, good nature resumed the ascendant, little by little the faults of a spoilt child disappeared, he became a good man in spite of himself; his heart opened out to yours, and then you could resist him no longer ; you left him charmed and altogether surprised at having felt towards this extraordinary man, in so short a time, senti- ments so different—repulsion, admiration, enthusiasm.'[59] There was a Cherubini who had lost all his ruggedness ; smiling, because he had thrown off the last trace of his official position ; attentive to every one, and ready to enter into friendly conversation.'[60]

At my request, conveyed through Mme. Hillebrand at Florence, Mme. Rosellini, from Pisa, sent me 4 para- graphs in answer to queries, and the 4th as being the most material, and corroborating Adolphe Adam, is here recorded in her own simple words : 'Mon père a eu beaucoup d'amis de cœur, et aussi parmi ses admirateurs

[57] *Carl Maria von Weber*, the Life of an Artist, tr. from the German of his Son, Baron Max Maria von Weber, by J. Palgrave Simpson, ii. 425.
[58] Pougin, *M. W.*, 1883, 577.
[59] *Derniers Souvenirs.*
[60] Pougin, *M. W.*, 1883, 703.

les plus fervents, de très hauts personnages, mais excepté les périodes dans sa vie, où la découragement et sa santé nerveuse et délicate l'empêcherènt de travailler, il s'absorbait tellement dans ses travaux et ses devoirs qu'il ne lui restait guère de temps à donner à la correspondance. . . . Tout ce qui a été dit sur la caractère de mon père, ses habitudes si exactes, minutieuses même, a été rapporté dans ses diverses biographies avec assez de vérité, surtout si ce qu'on a dit de lui n'a pas été rapporté par des personnes qui n'avait pas en affaire à lui dans un de ses moments un peu trop vifs. Etant fort distrait de nature, s'il devait sortir de ses préoccupations intimes pour porter un jugement, ou répondre sans avoir bien compris, son prémier mouvement était souvent d'irritation, mais comme il était bon, et sans préjugé aucun, il se remettait facilement, et ses manières devenaient aimables, à moins qu'on voulût les faire transiger sur des choses que ne lui semblaient ni honnêtes ni justes—Il fuyait l'intrigue, et plutôt que de solliciter, il supportait la gêne—Il était sobre, il avait des goûts simples. Ayant une santé délicate il était très sévère pour tout ce qui pouvait l'altérer, l'écartant de son régime ; il pouvait assister à de somptueux diners, mais jamais il n'y prenait plus que ce qui lui était strictement nécessaire—Il était si nerveux qu'un son, une note qui n'était pas juste, le mettait hors de lui et l'agaçait au dernier point—voilà tout ce que je puis dire.'

This is corroborated by Adam : 'Extremely nervous, brusque, irritable, absolutely independent, his 1st movements almost always appeared unfavourable. He easily returned to his natural disposition, which was excellent, and which he would conceal, under appearances the least flattering.'[61] 'My own recollections of him,' wrote Mme. Moscheles to me, 'are anything but pleasant. He looked a dry, screwed-up, little man. Ingres' portrait

[61] Halévy, about 1835, the year when his *La Juive* appeared, suffered from an excitability and nervousness that alarmed himself and his friends, and Cherubini, to reassure him, reminded him how he himself had been at times a sufferer in the same way, and yet had recovered from the same.

gives the most accurate conception of his outward appearance. He had a finely-shaped head, with thin lips, keen eyes and grey locks. His remarks were generally satirical.'

Miel writes that ' this irritability did not last long. It left too little traces for it to be ascribed as a result of organization. The phantasmagoria of Sarti : might it have over-excited that youthful imagination and impressed on too sensitive organs a too durable shock, or ought we descend to the superstition of names, and accord to that of Professor Bizzarri a mysterious influence on the pupil's future ? '

' His voice had a touch of dryness,' observes Hiller, only 17 years of age when 1st introduced to him. He adds : ' Though he had lived in Paris for 50 years, his pronunciation of French had not lost certain Italian peculiarities. His conversation was full of vivacity, interspersed with short, cutting sentences, often thrown out in an ironical manner ; his remarks were generally to the point, and he thoroughly understood the virtue of silence.' [62] ' His voice was feeble, probably from narrow-chestedness, and somewhat hoarse, but was otherwise soft and agreeable. His French was Italianized. . . . His head was bent forward, his nose was large and aquiline, his eyebrows were thick, black, and somewhat bushy, overshadowing his eyes. His eyes were dark and glittered with an extraordinary brilliancy that animated in a wonderful way the whole face. A thin lock of hair came over the centre of his forehead, and somehow gave to his countenance a peculiar softness.' [63]

As to Cherubini's general appearance, Hiller says that he ' gave one more the impression of a distinguished statesman than a musical composer.'

Finally, let me cite the eloquent Halévy, in whose, alas ! incomplete critical writings on his great master, his adopted father, we see an ardent affection, sometimes

---

[62] *Macmillan,* 1875.   [63] *L. Cherubini,* Fritzsch

conspicuous on the page, sometimes lurking beneath in
that restraint of a fierce reserve that Hope-Scott ascribes
to John Gibson Lockhart's love for his own.[64] 'Whether
it be devotion, filial affection or artistic conviction,
I avow that Cherubini's renown is dear to me, and
I would preserve it from all attack.' He says, with
a certain bitterness, 'Men do not easily accord their
admiration; you are not inscribed without a contest on
the golden book of posterity. The mere lustre of a
name is, then, for an artiste one of the most glorious
of testimonials, a certain indication of high influence, the
proof of an eminent position. It is a heritage to leave
after you, often acquired at the expense of a whole life's
repose, by works and incessant combats—the right to the
respect of all. It is now-a-days most especially that this
right is often contested; now-a-days that strong [or
weak] hands, pulling off [or vainly trying to pull off] the
mantle of purple, effacing those acquired suffrages, ruffle,
tear and trample it to tatters at the will of caprice and
passion. It is even this peril, especially, which makes the
possession of a blessing, though won with difficulty, and
however precious it may be, in one moment or another,
liable to be attacked by a whole army.' Once more,
before opening that fine biographical fragment on his
master, he says: 'Whatever opinion you may have of
Cherubini's genius, whatever may be the degree of
sympathy that you feel with his works, you cannot deny
that his name is great and illustrious. Among the names
written in the sanctuary of the arts, this is one of the most
venerated. He took little care of it when he was alive;
it is only a pious duty to seek to make it popular after his
death. We shall strive to follow him in his works, to set
store by their importance, to measure the influence they
have exercised on contemporary works; we shall see what
place they are worthy of occupying in the history of art.'

---

[64] Abridged *Life of Sir Walter Scott* by Lockhart. Introductory Letter
by J. R. Hope-Scott, Q.C., D.C.L., addressed to Mr. Gladstone.

I have quoted thus from Halévy's words, for Cherubini's sake. A man loved by no one is clearly not lovable, but Cherubini was no such man. Angularities and idiosyncracies, however great, do not hide any real personal worth, and 70 years after his death that worth continues to be attested by the record of his relations at home and abroad, in public and private life, with great and small people, and, on the whole, by the consistent and honourable career that he so long and so faithfully pursued, in that beautiful art and profession which he so conspicuously adorned.

Cherubini

Membre de l'institut, compositeur de musique

CHAPTER VI.

FRANCE.

1822—1835.

'. . . the high-embow'd roof
With antique pillars massy proof . . .
There let the pealing organ blow,
To the full-voiced quire below ;
In service high and anthems clear. . . .'

MILTON.

The Concerts d'Emulation and Société des Concerts—Beethoven's Mass in
D, and Letters to Cherubini—*Adjutor et Susceptor*—*Lætare Jerusalem*—
2nd Coronation Mass in A—*Confirma hoc*—Communion March—3 *O
Salutaris*—*Sciant Gentes*—Officer of the Legion of Honour—*Treatise on
Counterpoint and Fugue*—4-tets and 5-tet—Introduction to *La Marquise
de Brinvilliers*—*Ali Baba.*

CHERUBINI re-established Aug. 1822, along with the
'Pensionnat' of the Conservatoire, the public Competitions
in vocal and orchestral works by the pupils, wherein all
who had gained the 1st prize since 1816 could be
candidates. These were a step towards the 'Société des
Concerts du Conservatoire,' founded by a decree of 15
Feb. 1828, and both may be considered together.

Habeneck invited his musical friends to dinner on St.
Cecilia's day, 22 Nov. 1827, telling them to bring their
musical instruments with them. Among those who
responded were Guillou, Tulou, Vogt, Brod, Dacosta,
Buteux, Dauverné, Bulk, Dauprat, Blangy, Meifred,
Mengal, Dossiou, Henri, Barizel, Tilmant (the elder),
Battu, Tolbecque, St. Laurent, Amedée, Seuriot, Claudel,
Guérin, Urhan, Norblin, Vaslin, and Chafft. The
'Eroica' symphony was tried, and not liked! After
several essays, at Duport's manufactory, Rue Neuve des
Petits Champs, and at Habeneck's house in the Rue des
Filles St. Thomas, discontent at the symphony was

succeeded by admiration. Cherubini being informed of this, and of Habeneck's idea of having concerts, agreed that they should take place in the great hall of the Conservatoire. Since 1815 the public exercises of the pupils had not been resumed. Through his desire to restore these, Cherubini agreed to ask the king's minister, M. Sosthène de Larochefoucault, for the authorization desired by Habeneck, who himself agreed to find the funds for the expenses.

The government, however, granted 2000 francs a year towards the latter, and the decree founding the Society was communicated by Cherubini to the professors and a number of the chief pupils. Amidst general approbation an engagement to abide by the decree was signed by those present, 24 March. A provisionary committee of the new Society, composed of Cherubini (president), Habeneck (vice-president), Guillou (secretary), Dauprat, Brod, F. Halévy, Kuhn (chef-du-chant), Meifred, Amedée, A. Bonet, A. Dupont, and Tajan Rogé, convoked an assembly of all those who had signed the adhesion to the regulations of the decree; and Guillou, in the name o' the committee, made known the proposed rules of the committee, and an adhesion to them was signed.

On Cherubini's and Méhul's recommendation, Habeneck was chosen conductor of the concerts, and between 1828 and 1862 there were 359 performances of works by Beethoven.[1] And Cherubini's whole action as director of

---

[1] Elwart's *Histoire de la Société des Concerts.* The 1st symphony was given 13 times ; the 2nd 26 ; the 3rd 28 ; the 4th 24 ; the 5th 53 ; the 6th 51 ; the 7th 52 ; the 8th 14 ; the 9th 19 ; the overtures to *Fidelio* 7 ; *Leonora* 4 ; *Coriolanus* 9 ; *Ruins of Athens* 2 ; *Egmont* 6 ; *King Stephen* 1 ; *Prometheus* 7 ; in C, 2 ; 4-tets, Op 18, 3 ; 9th 4-tet fugue, 2 ; 7-tet 27 ; trio for 2 oboes and *cors anglais* 4 : Total, 359.

'Yet Berlioz (*Mémoires*, 74), when saying that the musicians of Paris were indifferent to Beethoven, actually dares to include Cherubini among the number. He speaks of the Florentine as one ' who concentrated his bile and dared not expend it on a master (Beethoven) whose successes irritated him profoundly and sapped the edifice of his most cherished theories.' This charge is directed in vain against the man who, in the teeth of opposition, had Beethoven's 1st symphony performed in Paris (for the 1st time) in 1807, and now followed this up by co-operation with Habeneck's scheme. Elwart tells how ' When Cherubini was informed of Habeneck's plan, he

the Société des Concerts shows his regard throughout for Beethoven; and it is recorded how one day Cherubini, becoming impatient with a pupil who, while describing to him the performance of one of Beethoven's symphonies, said nothing about the merits of the composition, thus addressed him : ' Young man, let your sympathies be 1st wedded to the creative, and be you less fastidious of the executive ; accept the interpretation, and think more of the creation of those musical works which are written for all time, and all nations—models for imitation, and above all criticism.' [2]

A number of concerts took place every year. No solos were allowed, and at Cherubini's order the movable platform, rising step by step, just as it now stands, was built. At the 1st concert 9 March 1828, the ' Eroica ' symphony was performed, and found great favour among the pupils. The ordinary concerts took place on Sundays at 2 o'clock ; others that might now and then take place on week-days were called ' concerts spirituels.' At the 1st concert for 1829 (Feb. 15), ' Chant sur la Mort de Haydn ' was sung by Ponchard, Nourrit, and Maillard ; at the 4th concert in 1830 (4 April), the celebrated introductory Chorus from 'Elisa,' the solos sung by Prévot and Hurteaux ; and on 1 Feb. 1835, Clapisson's ' Voici la

agreed to the request that the latter should obtain the authority of the Minister with a degree of warmth that does honour to his memory.' Again : ' The Minister, M. de Larochefoucault, assented to Cherubini's proposals.' The very decree begins : ' At the request of the Directors of the " Ecole Royale de Musique," we have resolved,' etc. ; and art. 9 charges Cherubini with the execution of the decree. The statutes of the ' Société des Concerts ' begin thus : ' With the agreement of the Director of the " Ecole de Musique." ' Lastly, Cherubini was chairman of the administrative and executive committee. ' Cherubini knew very well that Habeneck's object was the performance of the works of Beethoven. Had he entertained so poor an opinion of the latter as he is reported to have held, he certainly would not have promoted and arranged the whole affair with the zeal he did.'— *N.M.Z., M.W.,* 1862., 559. But, according to Berlioz, Berton was one who pitied German music ; Boieldieu, one who was ignorantly surprised at the least harmonic combinations ; Paër, one who told unfavourable anecdotes of Beethoven ; Catel, one who cared more about his rose trees than music ; Kreutzer, one who disdained all that came from the other side of the Rhine ; Lesueur, one who was deaf, and not attending the Conservatoire concerts. All these, according to Berlioz, were enemies to Beethoven.

[2] Ella's *Musical Union* papers.

Nuit,' recommended to Habeneck for performance by
Cherubini himself. At the extra concert at the Conservatoire, 30 May 1830, a rather unfortunate circumstance
occurred. Cherubini, before beginning, always waited for
Royalty, and the only Royal princess who loved and
patronized music, coming 10 minutes late, some hissing,
forerunner of the storm in July, began, and was not
sufficiently drowned by the voices to prevent her hearing
the salute from a pit that did not respect the mark of deference on Cherubini's part in delaying the performance.
Besides these great concerts were, as stated, the smaller
ones, 'Concerts d'Emulation,' given by the pupils themselves. Cherubini did not allow the young ladies of the
Conservatoire to take part either in solos or choruses. They
were only allowed to perform in public on the harp or the
piano, while the orchestra played the pupils' compositions.
In spite of all the representations of the most eminent
professors, Cherubini strictly adhered to these rules. The
chief box was reserved for Cherubini, D'Henneville,
Delavigne, and Lambert, and competition was stimulated
by the presence of the great director. Cherubini, then,
encouraged these concerts, conducted by Elwart from
1822, as warmly as the great ones initiated in 1828.

In 1823 Beethoven finished his Mass in D, offering
a copy in MS. to divers European sovereigns for 50
ducats. The Emperor of Russia, the Kings of France,
Prussia and Saxony accepted it. In presenting the MS.
to Louis XVIII., Beethoven appears to have written a
letter to Cherubini, then the French Royal Chapel-master,
to use his influence for the acceptance.[3] It was dated from

---

[3] There are various versions of it. I give Lady Wallace's translation
from Nohl's Collection of Beethoven's *Letters*, 1790-1826, Engl. ed. 1866. It
is independently translated also in Schindler's *Life of Beethoven,* so strangely
edited by Moscheles, 1841, ii. 205-8. A 3rd translation appears in *Beethoven's Letters,* ed. Kalischer, 1841, *tr.* J. S. Shedlock, 1909, 234-5. The
letter also appears in Schindler's *Life,* ii. 352. The paragraph beginning
'My critical situation,' etc., and half of the next, from 'and you will
always,' etc., and the rest of the letter to the end, is in French, or other
copies give these parts in English and German. A copy is in the Berlin
Royal Library. See also *M. W.,* 1883, 576.

his country house just outside Vienna, and Schindler
received the draft from Beethoven with instructions what
to do with it. A French translation of the letter was,
presumably, sent to Cherubini, but it seems doubtful if it
were sent at all, and it was followed by a 2nd. Anyway,
on Schindler visiting Cherubini in Paris in 1841, he said he
had never received it, nor had he ever heard of its existence
till after Beethoven's death.[8] The letter ran as follows,
according to the draft sent by the writer to Schindler:

'March 15, 1823, Vienna.

' Highly-esteemed Sir,—I joyfully take advantage of
this opportunity to address you.

'I have done so often in spirit, as I prize your
theatrical works beyond others. The artistic world has
only to lament that in Germany, at least, no new dramatic
work of yours has appeared. Highly as all your works
are valued by true connoisseurs, still it is a great loss to
art not to possess any fresh production of your great
genius for the theatre.

' True art is imperishable, and the true artist feels
heartfelt pleasure in grand works of genius, and that is
what enchants me when I hear a new composition of
yours; in fact I take greater interest in it than in
my own ; in short, I love and honour you. Were
it not that my continued bad health stops my coming to
see you in Paris, with what exceeding delight would I
discuss questions of art with you ! Do not think that this
is merely meant to serve as an introduction to the favour
I am about to ask of you. I hope and feel sure that
you do not for a moment suspect me of such base sentiments.

' I recently completed a grand solemn Mass, and
have resolved to offer it to the various European courts,
as it is not my intention to publish it at present. I have
therefore asked the King of France, through the French
embassy here, to subscribe to this work, and I feel certain
that his Majesty would at your recommendation agree to
do so.

'My critical situation demands that I should not solely fix my eyes upon Heaven, as is my wont ; on the contrary, it would have me fix them also upon earth, here below, for the necessities of life.

'Whatever may be the fate of my request to you, I shall for ever continue to love and esteem you ; and you will always remain of all my contemporaries the one whom I esteem the most.

'If you wish to do me a very great favour, you would effect this by writing to me a few lines, which will solace me much. Art unites all the world ; how much more, then, true artists, and perhaps you may deem me worthy of being included in that number.

'With highest esteem, your friend and servant,

'BEETHOVEN.'

Besides accepting a copy of the Mass, Louis XVIII. sent Beethoven a heavy gold medal.

In a letter to Louis Schlosser, chapel-master at Darmstadt, 6 May 1823, from Vienna, Beethoven would appear to have sent a 2nd letter to Cherubini, for he writes : 'You receive here, my dear Schlosser, a letter to Cherubini and one to Schlesinger. . . . Say to Cherubini all the good things you can think of; tell him that I most ardently wish to receive soon a new " opera " from him ; that altogether I have the greatest respect for him above all our contemporaries, and that I hope he has received my letter, and ardently desire to receive a few lines from him. Inquire also of Schlesinger whether he has delivered the letter to Cherubini. . . . I beg you very much indeed to write to me at once from Paris about both it and regarding Cherubini and Schlesinger.' Beethoven gave this 2nd letter for Cherubini, in May 1823, to Schlosser, who received a call from Beethoven himself the day before his departure for Paris. Beethoven attributed Louis XVIII's. acceptance of the Mass to Cherubini's influence. Anyway, the King's chapel-master would have been favourable in the matter beyond question.

In May 1825 appeared Cherubini's own Mass, perhaps the most celebrated.   Charles X. had succeeded to
the French throne in the previous year, and Cherubini, as
King's musician, had to write the music for the Coronation
in that month.   He settled to write the Mass, the
Offertory, 'Confirma hoc,' and the Communion March,
leaving the rest to Lesueur.   The King entered Rheims
Cathedral at 8 o'clock in the morning of 30 May to the
strains of a March by Lesueur.   Approaching the officiat-
ing prelate, Mgr. Latil, Archbishop of Rheims, in the
sanctuary, his Majesty kissed his ring, the Archbishop
handing him his sword.   Here Lesueur's anthem
'Confortare' was sung, and during the preparation for
the anointing, his anthem 'Gentem Francorum.'   During
the 7 stages of the anointing, the chorus, 'Unxerunt
Salamonem' was heard, followed by the Coronation
March, while as soon as the 'Veni Creator' had been
sung, the Archbishop advanced toward the King and
placed the crown on his head.   The Princes of the Blood
Royal then approached his Majesty, crying 'Vivat rex in
æternum.'   'Vive le Roi' resounded for a quarter-of-an-
hour through the building, and the chorus 'Vivat rex'
was sung, accompanied by the full organ; a number of
doves and other birds were let loose in the cathedral; 3
discharges of musketry followed; the cathedral doors
were opened; the people poured in; infantry and cavalry
bands struck up outside; and then came a short 'Te
Deum' by Lesueur.   Cherubini's Mass followed, a work
'endowed with such a character of grandeur, that it will
evermore remain a lasting monument of art, on account
of the greatness and loftiness of its ideas, the depth of its
conception, the nobility of its expression, the richness and
magnificence of its harmony and tone, and its brilliant
clearness in all that relates to polyphony and harmonics.'[4]

[4] *N.M.Z., MW.,* 1862. *Queen Marie Amélie's Journal,* etc.   The
number of artists was 198 :—20 1st sop. ; 20 2nd ditto ; 28 tenors, 28 basses
(96) ; 36 v., 30 violas, 'cellos and double-basses, 28 wind, and 8 percussion
instruments (102).   The whole ceremony took 3 hours.

'The Mass,' writes Fr. Girod, '. . . is the most known, and to my mind the most beautiful, of Cherubini's Masses. Written for the large area of Rheims cathedral, the acoustic power of which was enfeebled by hangings and decorations, as well as by the immense concourse of all classes of people, it required a vast increase of executive power; and it was for this reason that Cherubini availed himself of the modern full orchestra, with 4 horns, 3 trombones, the ophicleide, etc., and wrote for 3 voices, since he despaired of finding enough contraltos for the formidable choir such an orchestra required, and, moreover, did not wish for any vocal or instrumental solo.[5] Such are the elements of this colossal Mass in the grandest style . . . it is all novel, inspired. . . . In the "Kyrie," the melody, at once simple and touching, is well characterized, with the strains at 1st calm and soothing; then, in modulating from A major into C major and E, the orchestra becomes animated, the tone of supplication more pressing, more energetic; afterwards the calm returns with the resumption of the 1st theme, while the predominating sentiment seems to become more loving and confiding. . . . an admirable model of prayer, . . .' In one movement, it yet has 4 brief subjects, the last on a pedal point. 'The "Gloria" is designed in large and salient forms; you find in it the triumphal hymn 1st heard at the commencement of the piece, and then at the close; it opens with an "andante" in unison for the voices, and is continued by the grand "allegro" of the "Laudamus te," in which a "crescendo," admirably introduced, seems to rouse the faithful to redouble their transports of praise and adoration. The "andante" on the words, Gratias agimus, admirably depicts the Christian soul in ecstasy before the presence of Divine greatness.' This opening somewhat resembles the 'Hostias,' and 'Gratias' of the C minor Requiem and E minor Mass respectively, the

---

[5] The Mass in A had a 4th (alto) added to it by one Haydn Corrie, it is believed, in Ireland, and is thus published by Messrs. Novello of London.

characteristic being in all 3 a brief, but lovely phrase, that
once heard haunts the ear, a brevity so often seen with
Beethoven, as in a phrase in the 'Mount of Olives' march
of soldiers.   That such brevity should ever be mistaken
for poverty of invention would be a strange mistake.   On
the contrariwise, it is indicative of the reserve of elastic
strength.   Cherubini is both Italian and German.   His
melodies can be as long as those of any Master, and also as
short, at command.   Here the theme is varied by 'pizzicati'
for strings in contrast with the broad, vocal strains, at times,
with touching effect, entirely unaccompanied.   But there
is here one elaborate instrumental interlude, the purport
of which seems somewhat difficult to understand in a section
otherwise entirely characteristic of the best in his sacred
music.   'In the slow movement that succeeds it, the
sense of the "Qui tollis" is given in all its reality. . . . Most
composers take here the tone of sorrow and repentance,
while in truth the subject is the triumph of the Lamb over
sin ; this glorious victory is celebrated in a chant both
severe and forcible, followed by the grave supplication,
full of hope, " miserere nobis." . . . You secretly acknowledge the author must be a Catholic by conviction, to be
able to compose in a style so truthful and feeling.'   The
' Quoniam ' duly repeats the opening with a ' coda,' but
without fugue.   ' The " Credo " is a creation apart, . . .
a complete and varied whole; . . . a model of truthfulness,
of grandeur, and dramatic interest.   In it every mystery
has, so to speak, its appropriate colouring. . . . expressed
alternately by the basses and tenors, in a solemn melody
that resembles plain-chant.'   The bold 8-ves of skipping
quavers and semi-quavers, but agreeably varied by crotchets
instead, cannot compare for effect with those attending
the canto-fermos of the Masses in F and E minor.   ' Each
mystery is in a different tone, but diatonic to the one that
has preceded it ; as soon as a mystery is announced, some
wind instruments summon the whole choir to the profession
of faith, and the word " credo " is given twice. . . .
The touching mystery of the Incarnation is confided to

the sopranos. It is the outburst of the purest faith and
charity.' The instrumental prelude leading thereto, as in
the Masses in D minor and C, is distinctly suggestive of
an angel's descent to announce our Lord's birth. ' The
"Crucifixion" is, in truth, admirable ; its pathetic tone is
very expressive. A delicious harmony, that gradually
dies away, conveys the idea of "sepultus est ; " and to
show that death has but a transient empire over the Body
of its conqueror, the phrase of "sepultus" does not finish ;
it is intercepted by the entry of the horns and trumpets,
that announce the surprise of all nature, and proclaim the
miracle of the Resurrection. The style here takes a new
character of elevation and magnificence, which it sustains
to the end. Throughout the entire section, the composer's
idea of making the chorus renew its profession of faith is
carried out at each mystery. Among the most noticeable
passages must be cited the "decrescendo," so striking in
its realism, on the words "cujus regni non erit finis "'—a
favourite text with Cherubini, as in the E minor Mass,
and with what simplicity of means does he express it !—
' the broad strain of the "et unam sanctum," the
"crescendo" at the "expecto," that brings back the
triumphal theme of the "Et resurrexit" for the "et vitam."
The offertory, "Propter veritatem," is a perfect type of
its kind ; and soft melodies, relieved by imitation, are
found therein, as well as felicitous modulations. The
"Sanctus" is a short but magnificent hymn of praise,
both majestic and animated. The "O Salutaris" requires
more care and precision in execution than the rest of the
Mass. It is a fresh and delicate composition. It would
have been better to give it as a trio than in chorus,
although the author equally allows both methods. The
prayer in it assumes quite a celestial tone, very suitable to
the awful mystery that at that moment takes place ; you
will remark therein the moaning and touching plaint of
the accompaniment at the "bella premunt." The
"Agnus Dei," at 1st in A minor, is the soothing expression
of humble and resigned supplication ; when it goes into

the major it indicates, by the sweetness of its music, peace and repose—" dona pacem.'' '[6] This might have

been signed by Haydn.   Prout truly observes of one aspect of Cherubini's genius: ' The statuesque coldness and reserve, the severe simplicity of style to be found in much of his sacred music seem admirably in keeping with the service of the church. . . . In his most jubilant work, the great Coronation Mass in A, we never lose the impression that it is " sacred " music to which we are listening.'[7]   It is a Mass, however, for nothing less than ' a double of the 1st class.'   ' I enjoyed it much,' wrote the late Fr. Garnett, of the London Oratory, of this Mass; 'knowing every note, it grows on me more and more, and even the rehearsal of the band melted me to tears [it was the same with Fr. Girod].   One feels so absolutely safe with the great master—he knows exactly where to go next, and how to get there, and his vitality seems to support one and give strength to one's faith; no one ever yet approached him in Mass music.'

Of the celebrated Communion Prelude in this Mass, Berlioz observes: ' It is mystical expression in all its

[6] *De la Musique Religieuse,* 245.   The *Sanctus,* I noticed, was given during the removal of the Blessed Sacrament to the High Altar in Antwerp Cathedral, on the eve of the Assumption 14 Aug. 1878.   The next day Beethoven in C was given.

[7] *Academy,* 21 Aug. 1875.

purity, contemplation, and Catholic ecstasy. . . . Cherubini, by his veiled, imperceptible melody, has known how to reach the most mysterious depths of Christian meditation. This piece breathes only of Divine Love, of faith without doubt, of calm, of the serenity of a soul in presence of its Creator; no earthly sound comes to mar its heavenly quiet, and it brings tears to the eyes of those who listen to it; tears that flow so gently, that the hearer of this seraphic song, carried away beyond mere ideas of art and a remembrance of the actual world, is unaware of his own emotion. If ever the word " sublime " has had a true and just application, it is with respect to Cherubini's Communion March.'

In another place, when complaining that the orchestral works were played on a pianoforte before the Academy, previous to the decision as to who had gained the prize, he says : ' Take, for example, the Communion March, from the Coronation Mass of Cherubini ; what becomes of those delicious holding notes for the wind instruments, that plunge you into a mystic ecstasy ; that ravishing interlacing of flutes and clarinets, whence results nearly all the effect ? They disappear completely, because the piano can neither hold nor swell a note.' [8]

---

[8] *Autobiography,* i. 116. M. A. Guéroult (art. *Revue Encyclopédique*) wrote as follows : ' During Cherubini's Mass you will listen as a connoisseur, and be altogether in a dream. After hearing the Credo of the Coronation Mass, you will say : There is a powerful composer ! How he handles the vocal and instrumental forces ! What felicity in the return of the word "credo," which recurs incessantly after each musical period ! how energetic and how solemn an affirmation ! what force, what meaning in effects ! Meanwhile you have had time to remark that the chorus has slackened, and a trombone sent forth a blast of questionable appropriateness. . . . As to the symbol of Nicæa, the Sacrifice of the Mass, and the great event it recalls, you hardly think of it more than after a representation of *William Tell.* You go out a *dilettante,* and not a Christian.'

Fr. Girod, S.J., in a long and able reply, ends by saying that this Credo ' has called forth from more than one auditory tender emotions that have almost brought tears. . . . Let only this music,' he adds, ' be executed under the conditions established in the body of this work, and it will be impossible not to draw from it effects that are profoundly religious.' As to M. Guéroult himself, Girod does not hesitate to say that ' of all the theorists who have striven *to elevate plain chant at the expense of concerted music,* he is the most adroit, and the one whose arguing is the most captious.'—*De La Musique Religieuse.*

How simple and how great! How appropriate for
a ' Quarant Ore! '

'The Confirma hoc Deus,' Fr. Girod says, 'is written
for the same orchestra as the Coronation Mass; it is rich
and grand, but in the fugal style, and consequently less
acceptable to the ordinary public, in spite of its brilliancy
and spirit.' I do not know what the Father means here
by a fugal style, nor did another connoisseur who read
the passage, but I do know that, set to the Offertory's
words for the Mass on Whit-Sunday, it is one of the most
magnificent of all Offertories.

At one of the performances of the Mass in a hall of the
' Menu-Plaisirs,' Paris, Hummel was present, at this
period welcomed in the French capital with open arms by
Cherubini.[9] At the end of the concert that great master

[9] Fétis, *Biog. Univ.* i. art. 'Cherubini.' The Coronation Mass in A
was given 26 May 1872, 2 April 1878, 26 May 1880, 29 May 1887, 20 May
1888, 8 Dec. 1892, etc., at the London Oratory; once the wind band parts
only were heard, and with good effect. The Mass was given at the Italian
Church, Hatton Garden, London, *coram* Mgr. Sambucetti, the Papal Envoy,
29 June 1897, and at other times, being long stock pieces both there and
at the Birmingham Oratory, and at Our Lady's, Grove Road, London, etc.

of church music turned to Cherubini in a transport of enthusiasm, and said, 'Your Mass is golden.' At another time, when it was given in the same place, the entire hall resounded with universal acclamation. As a mark of his appreciation of this, the 11th and (if the 2nd Requiem be excluded) the last Mass of Cherubini, Charles X. raised him to the grade of Officer in the Legion of Honour.[10]

The Mass in A was preceded in 1823-4 by some motets. 'There is only praise,' writes Fr. Girod, 'to be awarded to that essentially religious piece, the delicious 4-tet of "Adjutor et Susceptor;" it is felicitously tinged with a sweet gravity, and a firm and well-marked vigour.' 'Lætare Jerusalem,' 'Inclina Domine,' already noticed, and ' Exaudi Domine,' were the others. These were followed in 1826 by 2 'O Salutaris,' one a bass solo, the other a 4-part chorus, with accompaniment 'ad libitum;' and in 1827 by a 3rd for 2 tenors and bass, for Boieldieu's marriage. In 1828 came an 'O Filii,' for solo and chorus, and in 1830, as complements to the ' Adjutor in Opportunitatibus ' for Septuagesima, 2 motets, ' Sciant Gentes ' with tenor and 4-part chorus, and ' Esto mihi,' a 4-part chorus, for Sexagesima and Quinquagesima respectively. These 1826-30 hymns, save the ' Esto ' and 'O Filii,' have all appeared as posthumous works, with other pieces already published. To the 1st volume issued by Richault, Salvador Cherubini appended this notice : ' Lovers of religious music have kept in reminder works composed by Cherubini . . . for the ancient Chapel Royal.

' Since the Author's death, these compositions, gathered together, have, for the greater part, remained in MS.

---

[10] In Sept. 1825, the King of Prussia, writes the *Biographie Universelle des Contemporains,* sent Cherubini a diamond ring, accompanied by an autograph letter, in token of satisfaction at a Mass composed for him by the latter. What was this Mass, unless the *Petite Messe de la Ste. Trinité,* of which there is no mention in Cherubini's catalogue? I think it all a mistake. The King sent him such a ring on receiving the score of *Ali Baba.* In 1826 Cherubini was further gratified by the Grand Duke of Hesse Darmstadt sending him his Order of Merit.

'In view of the musical movement in France and abroad, that tends to grow apace, these works, so set store by from the 1st, could not remain any longer for the sole use of a few. I deem it, then, a duty to publish them.

'In the enterprise of this edition, which will form several volumes, I rely on the friendly and devoted co-operation of M. Edward Rodrigues, to whom are already due praiseworthy efforts for the propagation of classical music. . . . As to the revision of arrangements for piano and organ, and orchestral accompaniments, and the perfect conformity of the impression with the original manuscripts, I have had recourse to the learned good offices of M. Vaucorbeil.

'I am happy to proffer here this testimony of my gratitude for these honourable friendships, whose devotion unites itself with my own in the accomplishment of the work consecrated to the memory of my father. Salvador Cherubini, Paris, 1 May, 1867.'[11]

When the Royal Chapel choir had sung its last Mass, 25 July 1830, and at St. Cloud its last vespers, all the artistes belonging to it were discharged on reduced pensions. Truly, as Castil-Blaze observes, the cannon of the 27 July was as sad for music as that of 10 Aug. had been. The official recognition of Louis Philippe, the citizen King, was made at the Chamber of Deputies 30 Aug., but Charles X. had seen what was the last French and Catholic Coronation: at least, there has been none since. The July revolution abolished the King's Chapel, and Cherubini lost the post of King's musician, held by him for 14 years, with such rare and conspicuous distinction. He also seemed likely to lose his post at the Conservatoire, the penalty for being under so many successive and such very

[11] Among the subsequent work: issued by Ricordi were the great E minor Mass, and the noble motet of 1818, 'Adjutor in opportunitatibus,' which must not be confounded with the 'Adjutor et Susceptor' of 1824.

different masters—Louis XVI., the Mountain, the Republic, Napoleon, Louis XVIII., and Charles X. But
Sarrette declined to take Cherubini's place.

Five years later Cherubini, Director of the Conservatoire, printed at his own expense the famous ' Treatise on
Counterpoint and Fugue,' the letterpress, as alleged, being
by Halévy, Cherubini not being good at oral teaching,
and unable to explain himself with a fulness equal to his
knowledge; so we are told. He had never meant to
publish a regular treatise, and his exercises were put in a
regular form only by the special desire of his friends. In
support of these facts we have the express and reiterated
assertion of Fétis, while G. A. Macfarren brought in a
counter theory.

' Admirable as are its rules, and lucid as is their
explanation,' he writes, ' there is not one of them which is
not violated in some or other of the illustrative examples—
a fact to induce the supposition that the principles may
have been taken from his oral teaching, and examples
supplied by one of his pupils, who had a better memory
for the rules than capacity for their application ; and this
at a period when the infirmity of advancing age disinclined
the master for the work.'

But Pougin will have none of this : ' Cherubini's
probity as an artist was too complete and absolute to
allow him to commit a fraud of this kind,' and he cites a
note of Cherubini in connection, wherein the latter seems
able to express himself in print as well as anybody else.
I extract the following : ' It is an error to believe that
there are 2 kinds of counterpoint, viz., the German and
the Italian. . . . Counterpoint is one and the same in all
countries. . . . Counterpoint is, so to speak, the veritable
grammar of musical science. It is by counterpoint that
the faculty of composing purely and vigorously is acquired.
. . . I here, therefore, make my profession of faith,
by declaring that in this treatise on counterpoint
I carefully follow the same principles as the Fuxes,
the Albrechtsbergers, the Martinis, and innumerable

others. . . .'[12] Pougin is probably right, in the main, although Halévy may have helped his master, so busy almost to the last with the innumerable details of administration.

Baillot, about the year 1829, was famous for his 4-tet parties; amongst those who assisted at them we find Guynemer (2nd violin), Tariot, St. Laurent (tenors), Lamare, Norblin (violoncellos), as well as Mendelssohn, Vidal, Schumann, Lipinski, Kummer, Bohrer, Sauzay, Urban, Mialle, and Vaslin. He now drew out from the shelf Cherubini's 4-tet in E flat, composed in 1814, but never performed. It was universally admired. In Germany many 4-tet parties were formed, and Cherubini's work was performed with applause before distinguished audiences of 'connoisseurs.' Mendelssohn took to it, playing the tenor part. It was the signal for Cherubini's entrance upon a new field of composition. Fétis observes : 'These compositions are of a very high order ; Cherubini has here a style of his own, as in all his works; he imitates neither the manner of Haydn, nor that of Mozart, nor that of Beethoven.' We learn from Spohr that Cherubini knew nothing of those masters' similar works in 1821 save one 4-tet of Haydn,[13] when writing the 4-tet in E flat. Schumann, in his review of the Leipsic winter musical season of 1837-8, remarks : 'We closed with the 1st of the already long published 4-tets by Cherubini, regarding which a difference of opinion has arisen even among good musicians. The question is not as to whether these works proceed from a master of art—about this there can be no doubt—but whether any are to be recognised as models of the genuine 4-tet type. We have grown accustomed to 3 famous German masters as models in this branch, while, with just recognition, Onslow, and then Mendelssohn,

[12] *Biog. Univ.* ii.; *Imp. Dict. Biog.; M. W.*, 1883, 672. When Baillot in 1834 edited *Les Méthodes de Violon et Violoncello,* Cherubini kindly added bass parts to the various musical examples that are admirable studies for young *virtuosi* on those instruments. Cherubini had interested himself at a much earlier period in the *Singing School Tutor* of Mengozzi, Garat, Gossec, and Méhul, aiding those musicians in their work.

[13] *Autobiography* ii.

have been admitted to the circle of followers in the path of the first 3. And now comes Cherubini, an artist who has grown grey in his own views, and in the highest aristocracy of art; and even now, in spite of age, the best harmonist among his contemporaries; the refined, learned, interesting Italian, whom I have often compared with Dante for his firm exclusiveness and strength of character. I must confess, however, that even I experienced an unpleasant impression on hearing this 4-tet for the 1st time, especially after the 1st 2 movements. It was not what I expected; many things seemed to me operatic, overladen, while others appeared small, empty and opinionated. It may have been the result of a youthful impatience in me that did not at once discern the significance of the grey-beard's often wonderful discourse, for in many ways I traced otherwise the master commander to his finger tips. But then came the "Scherzo," with its enthusiastic Spanish theme,

etc.

the uncommon "Trio."

and lastly the "Finale," that sparkles like a diamond

whichever way it is turned, and there could be no doubt
as to who had written this 4-tet, and whether it was
worthy of its master.   Many will feel like me ; we must
1st become acquainted with the peculiar spirit of this,
"his" 4-tet style.   This is not the well-known mother
tongue we are so familiar with ; a polite foreigner speaks
to us ; but the more we learn to understand him, the
more highly we must respect him. . . . For performance
it needs much—it needs artists.'

Cherubini now turned to his symphony in D, and
altered it this year into a 4-tet in C, with a new 'Lento,'
to replace the 'Adagio,' written in March 1829.   This was
introduced into England in 1852 by the 4-tet Association.
Schumann writes : 'A few dry bars, the work of the
intellect alone, there are, as in most of Cherubini's works ;
but even in these there is always something interesting in
the passage, some ingenious contrivance or imitation,
something to think about.   There is most spirit in the
"Scherzo" and last movement, both full of wonderful
life.   The "Adagio" has a striking individual A minor
character, something romantic and Provençalish.   After

hearing it several times, its charms grow, and it closes in such a manner as to make you begin listening again, though knowing the end is near at hand.' He thinks it was 'written long before the 1st 4-tet [really in fact a year after, as a symphony] . . . the symphony, if I am not mistaken, pleased so little on its 1st performance in Vienna that Cherubini refused to publish it . . . a double failure has arisen, for if the music as a symphony sounded too much like a 4-tet, the 4-tet is too symphonic. I am opposed to all such remoulding; it seems to me an offence against the 1st divine inspiration . . . it would be impossible for anything of the kind to be produced by any writer who had not earnestly studied, thought and written for a long series of consecutive years.'[14]

The 1st 3 were dedicated to Baillot in 1835, and along with 3 others and the 5-tet in E minor, complete the list of Cherubini's chamber music. He writes: 'I feel so deeply honoured by your dedication and by being called your friend . . . the reflection of your name will cast too much splendour on mine not fully to satisfy the dearest ambition by which I am animated. How pleased I am once more to express my respectful and tender devotion.[15] 'In the winter of 1838,' writes Fétis [perhaps it was 1837], Cherubini 'invited a few musicians to his house, and laid before them the 5-tet which he had just completed. Though the composition

14 *Music and Musicians*, 1st series, 209-11-22 ed. Ritter, 1881. G. A. Macfarren had an unfavourable opinion of the 4-tets, and I give his opinion for what it is worth. He has greater men who think otherwise, however, about them, and who, as players, ought to know. 'Their merit entitles them to no distinction, and it is scarcely to be supposed that his several subsequent works of the same class . . . can possess any greater interest, since these prove the author's entire want of feeling for the style, and aptitude for the form of instrumental chamber music.'—*Imp. Dict. Biog.*, 1013. I much prefer Schumann's careful opinion and appreciation, and I always enjoyed No. 1, especially when played by Joachim, Lady Hallé, Straus, Ries and Piatti. The 4 tet in E flat was 1st introduced to the Monday Popular Concerts, 27 Feb. 1853, by Herr Becker, Ries, Doyle and Piatti, and subsequently, on more than one occasion, by Joachim ; and the other 5 have also been given in London, Nos. 4. 5, 6 being introduced by Sir C. and Lady Hallé in their 1889 season of Chamber Music Concerts at St. James' Hall.
15 Letter of Baillot, 12 Feb. 1835. *cit.* Pougin, *M.W.*, 1883, 511.

was admitted to bear signs of his very advanced age, yet all acknowledged it to be characterized by a freshness of ideas which no person could possibly have believed to be possessed by a man who stood, so to speak, with one foot already in the grave.'[16]   Cherubini writes: 'I have just finished, 22 Nov. 1837, my 6th 4-tet, and a 5-tet.   It occupies me, and amuses me, for I have no pretentions in the matter.'

'My very dear Master,' wrote Baillot feelingly, 14 Dec. 1834, 'I was exceedingly sorry not to see you yesterday at my 1st "Soiree;" we executed your 4-tet and made a profession of faith; the work was admired and praised to the skies by all the artists and enlightened amateurs; the others felt it and will like it more each successive time.   We reckon on performing your 2nd, that in C, next Saturday, when we hope very much to see you, as well as Mad. Cherubini, and our good friend Salvador.   Do not trouble yourself about our rehearsal; we shall hold it more freely without you, your presence intimidates us, because we feel all the wrong we do you in consequence of our criminal errors, but when once a piece is well understood and well rehearsed, we see you, whether present or absent, at the end of every note, or rather, we feel your presence in our hearts, and give ourselves up to all the sentiments that your admirable works inspire.   Let me beg you to continue enriching us with beautiful things, and completing our repertory which we began with Haydn and Mozart, and are bound to carry on with yourself and Beethoven. . . . We shall never render your inspirations as well as they ought to be rendered, but be assured that nothing which issues from your soul can be rendered by us save with the profoundest feelings of respect, affection, and gratitude.'[17]

In 1831 Cherubini finished 29 Sept. the Introduction to ' La Marquise de Brinvilliers,' an opera founded on the story of the poisoner, 'distinguished by a vigour of

---

[16] *Des Manuscrits Autographes*, etc. ; and *Biog. Univ.* art. Cherubini.
[17] *M. W.*, 1883, 511.

colour, an elegance of style, and a flower of melody, which does Cherubini great honour.'[18]   But although Batton, Berton, Carafa, Auber, Cherubini, Blangini, Boieldieu, Hérold, and Paër coalesced to write the rest, with a despairing effort to revive the fortunes of the Opera Comique, this extraordinary assemblage of talent could not write a popular work.   The public had set itself against 'pasticcios' and operas in collaboration. This work, 1st performed 31 Oct., ran till 9 Dec., when the doors of the house were closed.

Cherubini gives us the following account of 'Ali Baba :' 'An opera I began long ago, in 3 acts, and which I finished in 4 acts, with a prologue, for the Royal Academy of Music.   It was represented at that theatre 22 July in this year (1833).'

On 28 Aug. 1829, 4 years before, he wrote : 'You imagine, do you, my son, that "Ali Baba" is getting on ?   You are mistaken, I stopped it altogether. I shall certainly not jeopardize my reputation, at least now, by giving a work at a theatre which has not a better company than that of the Opera Comique, and no good chorus singers ; at a theatre where, in a word, everything is going from bad to worse, though there are, at present, two managers.'   And Pougin cites another letter of 15 July 1830, to Mélesville, descriptive of 'Ali Baba' from a 'precis' in a Sale Catalogue, 26 May 1877.   'Those who have talent,' runs the 'precis,' 'and are still young, can afford to experience a defeat ; but he who is old, and looks upon this score as his last dramatic effort, cannot terminate his career by a failure, which he deems certain.'[19]

During the revolution he had written a 3-act opera, 'Kourkourgi,' but the 'libretto' by Duveyrier Mélesville the elder was ridiculous, and the work was never performed.   His friends, knowing the many beauties the music contained, urged him to set it in order.   Scribe and Mélesville the younger had both heard a very original

[18] Castil-Blaze.
[19] *M.W.*, 1883, 737, 673.

trio of sleepers in the work, and had wished to make it known to the public. But through Auber's mediation, an entirely new libretto from the tale in the Arabian Nights was now written by the 2 authors. So vigorously did Cherubini set himself to work, that in a short time the score reached 1,000 pages, and little of the original work remained; but, in its remodelled state, the veteran composer had not much confidence in its success, and suspected that M. Véron, the manager of the Grand Opéra, had only accepted it out of respect and deference to himself. He had never been at home in Grand Opera, and it has been remarked how few of Cherubini's and Méhul's operas were brought out therein. His feelings of impatience and anxiety were clearly seen; for after the last general rehearsal, he left for Versailles, having carefully calculated beforehand the duration of the acts and 'entr'actes.' When the clock of the palace at Versailles struck 8 o'clock in the evening, Cherubini pulled out his watch, and said, 'Now they commence the overture.' Every hour, or rather at every act, he looked at his watch. At half-past 11 'Ali Baba' was over, according to his watch, 'which,' said he, 'went very well and marked the time of the Opéra.' The old man then went to bed and slept peacefully, but did not return to Paris until he had received a reassuring despatch, and never once went to see 'Ali Baba' performed—never even spoke of it, except in order to say, 'It is too old to live long; it has taken 40 years to come into the world.'[20] Some said: 'Cherubini has outlived himself;' and hundreds of people were driven away by the big drum and cymbals, which drowned all the beauties of the piece.[21] 'Poor Cherubini,' said Rossini to Dr. Hiller, 'how they murdered his lovely score! how they cut and mutilated it! his heart must have turned round in his body.' 'I assisted in the pit of the Opera-house,' writes Berlioz, 'at the 1st representation of his work, "Ali Baba." This score, all the world then

[20] Halévy's *Derniers Souvenirs,* etc., 165-6,
[21] *L. Cherubini,* Fritzsch.

agreed, is one of Cherubini's tamest and emptiest. Towards the end of the 1st act, fatigued at having heard nothing striking, I could not restrain myself from saying loud enough to be heard by my neighbours : " I give 20 francs for an idea ! " In the middle of the 2nd act, always beguiled by the same musical " mirage," I went on with my bidding by saying : " 40 francs for an idea ! " The " finale " over, I got up, exclaiming these last words : " Ah, my faith, I'm not rich enough—I give it up ! " and I went away. 2 or 3 young people, sitting near me on the same bench, looked at me indignantly. They were Conservatoire pupils, who had places there in order to admire profitably their director. They did not fail—I knew a little later—to go the very next day and tell him of my insolent bidding at a price, and my discouragement, still more insolent. Cherubini was so much the more outraged that, after having said to me, " You know how I love you," he should, without doubt, have to find me, as was to be expected, horribly ungrateful. This time it was not a question of snakes ; I tallied more with one of those venomous asps whose bites are so cruel to self-love. He avoided me.'[22]

M. de Boigne gives us an amusing account of it.[23] 'The representations of " Ali Baba " were less gay. In " Ali Baba " everything was wearisome and soporific— poem, music, and ballet ; the airs of which, however, were composed by Halévy. Those fastidious 40 thieves had better rested eternally buried in their jars, and in the works of Galland. Cherubini, demanding hospitality at the opera for " Ali Baba," has the same effect with me as Belisarius holding out his helmet to the passers-by. " Ali Baba " is one of those fossilised operas which a director only accepts when they are thrust down his throat by illustrous old age ; and for fear of being declared a Vandal, the director had to pass it off for a masterpiece, and with a loss of 50 to 60,000 francs. But the public,

[22] *Mémoires*, i, 111.   *Autobiography*, i. 297-8.
[23] *Petits Mémoires de l'Opéra.*

who were not bound by the same considerations as M. Véron, yawned so much and so widely, under " Ali Baba's " very nose, that real hissing would have spoken less eloquently. The public condemned without appeal, and executed pitilessly those 40 thieves who had not stolen anything. Cherubini could not recover from his surprise ; he sought everywhere for the cause of " Ali Baba's " failure, everywhere except in his music, and he finished by discovering the key to this mystery full of horror. "With miserable choruses like these of the opera," said he, " there is no success possible. Never have I been able to get them to sing, or even to march to time, one of my 40 thieves." In fact, during the rehearsals, the march of the 40 thieves had completely absorbed him. He did not cease to tap the floor with his bâton, and to cry : " Keep time, sirs ! . . . sirs, keep time ! " '

Mendelssohn says in a letter from Dusseldorf, dated 7 Feb. 1834: 'I have just looked through Cherubini's new opera, and though I was quite enchanted with many parts of it, still I cannot but deeply lament that he so often adopts that new Parisian fashion, as if the instruments were nothing, and the effect everything, flinging about 3 or 4 trombones, as if it were the audience who had skins of parchment, instead of the drums ; and then, in his "finales," he winds up with hideous chords, and a tumult and crash most grievous to listen to. Compare with these some of his earlier pieces, such as " Lodoïska " and " Medea," &c., &c., where there is as much difference between brightness and genius as between a living man and a scarecrow ; so I am not surprised that the opera did not please. Those who like the original Cherubini cannot fail to be provoked at the way in which he yields to the fashion of the day, and to the taste of the public ; and those who do not like the original Cherubini find far too much of his own style still left to satisfy them either, no matter what pains he may take to do so—he always peeps forth, the very 1st 3 notes. Then they call this " perruque, rococo." ' In a letter to Devrient, intendant of the Berlin Opera, dated 5 Feb. 1834, he says: 'If I were you, I would push forward just now the "Ali Baba" of the old gentleman, and tease the directors till they put it on the stage, where it would fail, as it has done in Paris.' [24]

'This opera affords the spectacle full of interest of an old man of 73 letting an astonished public hear songs full of grace and freshness, choruses above all praise, instrumental details new and ingenious, and showing everywhere a verve of talent which is rarely found in youth. However, . . . the subject was cold, and beneath the reputation of its authors, and the nature of the beauties of the score made it, like all those of Cherubini, more worthy of esteem in the eyes of connoisseurs than those of the public, who found it beyond their capacity to understand.' [25]

The overture to 'Ali Baba' in F, performed under Mr. Manns, 19 Oct. 1872, at the Crystal Palace, has always appeared to me one of the finest examples of Cherubini's mastery of orchestral effects; in this respect ranking with the overture to 'Medea,' 'Les Deux Journées,' 'Anacréon,' and 'Faniska.' It is scored for the fullest Band; a circumstance which alone gives it a unique place among his overtures, and is full of genius. The opening subject is vigorous and broad; the clash of

cymbals and pause has something Turkish in it, the triplet

[24] *Letters,* tr, Lady Wallace, etc.
[25] de Lafage.

passages for the violins are striking, and the melody of
the 2nd subject captivating. The whole is skilfully

worked up to an effective, if somewhat noisy climax.
Towards the close, a long ' coda ' begins with accelerated
time in a ' pianissimo ' passage for the strings that never

fails of effect. It should be heard, at least, sometimes at
our concerts. The great master appears therein at once,
as usual in anything orchestral.

The success of the work in Paris, indeed, was not
great ; in Berlin ' brilliant.' It was played there, Cherubini
tells us, 27 Feb. 1835, at the Grand Theatre Royal ; the
King, who had attended the last rehearsal, ' contrary to
his custom,' remaining till the end ; and sending the
composer a diamond ring, besides the £100 given on
Cherubini forwarding him the MS. score.[26] Fétis, who
heard it, assured us that ' Ali Baba ' is full of beauty, and
that many pieces are worthy of the composer, who introduced therein a march from ' Faniska,' and the fine
bacchanalian scene from the ballet of ' Achille.' Clément
tells us that one verse—' Au moka surtout je songeais ! '
excited scandal among the purists.

[26] Cherubini's Diary and *Moniteur Universel*, cit. Pougin, *M. W.*, 1883,
689.

Quicherat blames the book for any failure, and refers to the opening air sung by Nourrit, one of a pleasing and melancholy character, to a powerful and melodious robbers' march, and delicate sleepers' trio. We may be quite sure there were many fine things by the ' old hand.' The chief parts were sustained by Nourrit (Nadir), Levasseur (' Ali Baba '), Mdlle. Falcon (Morgiana), and Madame Damoreau (Delia). It was played 4 times, the receipts on the 4th night being 9,000 francs. Nourrit went for his holiday, and, on his return, it was played a little while longer.

' All competent judges were lost in astonishment at the fact of a composer, whose 1st works bore the date of 1771, being able, 60 years later, to produce another of such extraordinary freshness and such glowing fancy. Cherubini was 72 years of age, but both his head and his heart had remained young, and his latest dramatic production displayed, in conjunction with the maturest knowledge and the most beautiful form, the loveliest blossoms of profound feeling and youthful passion. That the work did not retain its place in the repertory was not astonishing, in the case of a public who were intoxicated by the perfumes arising from the flowery path which Rossini and his imitators had forced the opera to take.'[27]

' On the production of Cherubini's last opera,' wrote Riehl, the able German critic in 1860, ' people in France regretted that the old master came 200 years too late, while German musicians . . . glanced at the finely written score, as though they had a presentiment that the creations of such a man as Cherubini would 1st be neglected as unfashionable, to rise up again, at the expiration of a few years, as imperishable works of art,'[28]

[27] Quicherat's *Adolphe Nourrit*, cit. Pougin. *M. W.*, 1883. 689; *M. W.* 1862.
[28] *Musikalische Charakterkopfe*, 90, 2nd series. The theme of Halévy's 1st article in the *Gazette Musicale de Paris* was an ingenious fiction, entitled *Ali Baba et Sainte Cécile*, which served to show the thoughtlessness and injustice of the musical editors of Paris, not one of whom would consent to publish the score of *Ali Baba*. ' This article' in turn felicitous and elegant, depicts well the sentiments of devotion, admiration, and almost filial affection with which the author was animated for his illustrious master;

a presentiment well founded, as subsequent history
proves, so far as some of his secular, and more of his sacred
music, are concerned.

Cherubini had a great wish to see his native land
once more. He was to have brought out 'Ali Baba' at
Marseilles. It would have been his opportunity for
sailing to Italy, seeing at Pisa his daughter Zenobia,
revisiting at Florence the scenes of his childhood—
the street, the house where he had been born—and
calling upon Dr. Nesti, son of one of Cherubini's sisters.
But it was not to be; just as he was on the point of
leaving Paris, cholera broke out at Marseilles, and
frustrated this plan.[29]

---

sentiments he preserved for him during his whole life.'—Pougin's
F. Halévy.

[29] Fétis, when mentioning Cherubini's leaving Italy in 1788, writes that
he never saw Italy again, except once, in a voyage made long afterwards.
I infer that Fétis thought the composer carried out his project in 1831.
Cherubini writes 28 Aug. 1829, to his son : '. . . Such a journey is an utter
impossibility, unless I resign my position in the school. . . . Thus, my dear
boy, I am forced to renounce what my heart and affections most desire.
Do not let us talk about it any more, for I suffer if I only think of it.'
Again, to M. Rosellini, 24 Aug. 1834 : 'All this year I thought I should be
able to go to Marseilles, but my project could not be carried out. Let us
hope that next year we shall be more fortunate.'—*M. W.*, 1883, 737, 765.

CHAPTER VII.

FRANCE.

1835—1842.

'A voice to Light gave Being,
To Time and Man his earth-born chronicler,
A voice shall finish doubt and dim foreseeing,
And sweep away life's visionary stir.'
WORDSWORTH.

Requiem in D minor—Resignation of Conservatoire Directorship—
Made Commander of the Legion of Honour by Louis Philippe—
Portraits—Ingres—A Canon in his honour, the last composition—
Death of Cherubini.

BETWEEN the production of his 25th opera, and of the
2nd Requiem, some 3 years, there is so very little to note
by way of composition, that it looked as though Cherubini's
career as a composer were at length virtually over. Even
the revision of his 'Counterpoint and Fugue,' a work not
formally planned by him at 75 as a regular Treatise, had
been too much for one who was still at the helm as a
teacher, judging from the assistance of Halévy, who wrote
upon its 'Errata' in the musical 'Gazette de Paris' of
5 June, 1835. So long as the direction of the Conservatoire
continued in his hands, Cherubini might fairly have claimed
a repose from the labours involved in further production
and publication. Nevertheless the 'burnt-out volcano'
was to exhibit to a wondering musical world, in the
following year, 'signs of life'[1] as unmistakeable as they
were unexpected and unprecedented, in the appearance
of one of the most beautiful compositions of any age.

On 24 Sept. 1836, Cherubini's 2nd Requiem in D
minor, for 3 male voices, which had been begun Jan. or
Feb., lay completed at Montlignon. We have Verdi

---

[1] Berlioz's *Mémoires*, 183.

By Z. Belliard.

L. Cherubini

(1830).

writing at his best in old age, Zingarelli as usual at 87; Handel writing 'Jephtha' when 66 years old, and Haydn the 'Seasons' when 68; but the production of such a masterpiece as this, from a man of 76, is surely a circumstance without a parallel in musical annals.[2]

It was 1st executed at the 5th concert of the Conservatoire, 19 March 1837. On the 24th it was repeated by desire. On 25 March 1838, the whole work, with Beethoven's 4th symphony and Weber's 'Euryanthe' overture was done in 2 parts, and, strangely enough, with a violin solo between, by Habeneck, played by Lecointe, a pupil.[3] 'That is a beautiful Mass,' said Cardinal Newman, on hearing it for the 1st time in 1885, and deemed it not wanting in effect through the absence

[2] It owed its origin to a difficulty about doing Cherubini's 1st Requiem, with female voices, for Boieldieu's obsequies, Mgr. Quelen, then Archbishop of Paris, interposing in the interests of stricter rubrics. Hiller found Cherubini 'at work on a large score,' and on enquiring what it was, the master replied : 'After [Boieldieu's] death in 1834, it was proposed to execute a Requiem for him at the Madeleine, but the clergy would admit no female singers, and thereby caused great annoyance. I do not wish the same thing to happen at my death, so I am writing a Requiem for men's voices— and then they will not have occasion to quarrel on my account, at least.' According to Fétis (*art.* Boieldieu)—the 1st Requiem was done after all, *i.e.*, at the chapel of the Invalides (which was not strictly under his Grace's jurisdiction?) However that may be, it looks as though the obsequies were originally to have taken place at the Madeleine, over which the Archbishop would have full jurisdiction, it being a parish church. 'Very well, then, since they have resolved that women's voices shall not be heard in a church, I shall do one for my own funeral, which will play them a good turn, and to which there will not be any objection,' Cherubini is reported to have said, half in raillery, half in vexation.—Miel 21 ; Pougin *M. W.*, 1883, 461.

[3] Halévy wrote a review of it in the *Gazette Musicale de Paris* 7 May 1837. It was 1st executed, it is believed, in this country 2 Nov. 1872, with organ accompaniment, and also at the Requiem for Mr. J. R. Hope-Scott, of Abbotsford, Q.C., D.C.L., 5 May 1873 ; on both occasions at Farm Street Church, London, and 3 Nov. 1884 ; as well as 30 Sept. 1888, and 7 Nov. 1889, at the Carmelite Church, under M. Noyer, a very skilful organist, who performed marvels on a Cavaillé-Coll organ there. The 2nd of the 3 latter dates was the occasion of a general Requiem, ordered by Leo XIII. on a Sunday, throughout the world. It was given at the Birmingham Oratory, with Mr. Langston as organist and Mr. Stockley as conductor, 13 Nov. 1885 ; with a few instruments 1 Dec. 1888, and, for the 1st time in England with full orchestra, at the Birmingham Midland Institute, under Mr. W. Sewell, A.R.A.M., 28 Jan. 1909, a red-letter day in English musical annals. Generous notices of a devotional performance appeared from Mr. E. Newman (*Daily Post* 29J n.), Mr. O. Pollack (*Daily Mail*) and Mr. R. J. Buckley (*Daily Gazette*).

of soprani and contralti, and said to Mr. Stockley, who conducted, 'There is magic in your stick!'

Mendelssohn wrote to the Hon. Committee of the Lower Rhine Musical Festival, in a letter dated from Leipsic, 18 Jan. 1838: 'With regard to the 2nd day, I may 1st enquire whether you intend to apply to Cherubini for his grand Requiem; it must be translated, and is entirely for men's voices; but as it will only last an hour, even less, that would not much matter, and, according to the universal verdict, it is a splendid work.'[4]

'Cherubini,' writes another, 'was endowed with manly genius; his strain is broad, round, and soaring heavenward, leaving the earth at an immeasurable distance. This manliness of style and freshness of creation did not abandon him even when near to his grave. His 2nd Requiem, which was his last great work, ranks among his masterpieces.'

Hiller might think it ranked far beneath the 1st Requiem, but would probably find few now-a-days to agree with him. He admits the score to be astonishing, while in Naumann's view the darker colouring afforded by tenors and basses seems more suitable for a Requiem. It is, perhaps, superior to No. 1 in continued textual appropriateness in the sequence. The music, as it should be, is ever subordinate to the text. So it is in the 1st Requiem, save in the 1st part of the 'Dies Iræ,' down to the ' Recordare,' where, as has been already noticed, one great idea almost entirely dominates the text, whether it be ' Tuba merum,' ' Liber scriptus,' or ' Rex tremendæ,' or 'Judex ergo,' that is sung. I subjoin a loving appreciation by the late Rev. William Maher, S.J., the composer of an exquisite Pastoral Mass, and two widely known tunes, to a rhymed translation of the ' Anima Christi,' and to Fr. Albany J. Christie's ' To Jesus' heart all burning.' This unpretending notice was furnished at my request, without instruction to give his name, but from affection to his

4 *Letters,* tr. Wallace, etc.

memory I venture now to do so, adding further musical examples and some few words of my own where they seemed called for.

'It is impossible to hear or study this almost un-approachable composition without feeling how intimately impressed the author must have been with the whole spirit of prayerful, earnest, mournful supplication implied in the idea of the Christian sacrifice for the dead.

[No. 1, Introit]. 'The 1st notes he employs have been consecrated by the usage of centuries to the word "Requiem."

'These notes have breathed a prayer of rest for the departed ever since the day when the 1st Gregorian Mass for the dead was sung. The succession of the 4 opening notes cannot fail to recall a host of associated memories to all who have become familiarized with the grand strains of the older music. Thus there is a kind of awe-inspiring solemnity in the way in which Cherubini opens the Mass [of Requiem]. After 12 bars of symphony, the deep bass voices supply the subject, which is taken up in fugue by each of the succeeding parts, and what may be called the 1st period ends with a long swelling chord on A, the instruments piling up "arpeggio" upon "arpeggio" till the close. Then the light of hope breathes gradually upon the subject, the words "et lux perpetua" being

heralded in by the 2nd tenor, and, as it were, reflected
and intensified by the other voices in succession. "Te
decet hymnus" is a prayerful subject in which the
meaning of the words is as nearly represented by the
music as music is capable of representing the meaning of
words. "Exaudi orationem meam;" the passionate
intensity of this cry is well expressed by the short sharp
demi-semiquaver which initiates each repetition, and the
minim and quaver leave room for—nay, almost force—
the deep drawn sigh from the singer between each
repetition.

'In the Kyrie each of the parts comes, as it were, in
turn before the Lord to supplicate for mercy, the way

being led by the 1st tenor. Towards the close of this
movement the hearer cannot fail to be struck by the
emphasized repetition of the word "Kyrie" by all the
voices.

[The 'pianissimo' continues during a brief chromatic passage, and then comes a reminiscence of the Kyrie theme, starting on as brief a pedal point.]

'No. 2.   The Gradual is a lovely movement in ¾

time [one of the most perfect pages of inspired Church music ever written], the voices unaccompanied, full of flowing melody, intended doubtless as a foil and contrast to the whirlwind of sound with which the Dies iræ, No. 3, commences.

'If this sublime Sequence[5] had never found a worthy interpreter until Cherubini's time, he would most certainly have removed the stigma from his art. Perhaps of all worthy interpreters he has proved himself by this matchless piece the worthiest of all. The 3 bars of symphony, beginning as they do "piano," end in a very hurricane of sound as all the voices crash forth the words "Dies iræ" in almost despairing cry [as at "Liber scriptus"]. "Solvet sæclum" is sung by the bass, and immediately followed

by the tenors, who repeat every 4 syllables after they have been pronounced by the bass in ascending scale, till the "tuba mirum" [itself an inspiring 4 bars].

[5] The *Dies Iræ* hymn, by Thomas de Celano, O.S.F.(1255) a recognized part of the Requiem in 1385, is generally called a Sequence, like the 3 established hymns—*Victimae Paschali, Veni Sancte Spiritus,* and *Lauda Sion.* Sequences date from at least the 9th century, and arose as an amplification of the alleluias of the Gradual by the choir, sung afterwards by the people and then the choir again. They agreeably varied the strict ritual, though the Council of Trent, on their becoming too numerous, restricted their use.

'Here, too, the whirlwind of sound reappears, and the same artifice of short and sharp repetition between tenor and bass, this time in the key of B flat, occurs in the words "cum resurget," almost presenting to the eye the opening of the graves and the rising of their dead to judgment.' [The 'coget omnes ante thronum' and the 'mors stupebit' are expressed with the condensed force and sublime simplicity of genius.]

'A melodious symphony, beginning in unison for the violin
and violoncello, and taken up by the oboe, prepares the
way for the wonderful piece of declamation confided to

the basses, "Judex ergo cum sedebit" [repeated at
'Quidquid latet apparebit']. Almost the same phrase
occurs before the words "nil inultum remanebit," which

are followed by that cry of agony, "quid sum miser tunc
dicturus" [with an accompaniment perhaps less appro-
priate]. The movement, "Rex tremendæ majestatis,"

"mäestoso," is very descriptive; it opens with 3 "arpeggio" notes by all the stringed instruments, which prepare the ear for the opening chord of A, sustained by all the voices, who, after pronouncing the word 'Rex' *ff*, as it were, give place to the basses to proclaim the advent of the King of immense majesty,

whose presence is acknowledged and done homage to by all in a passage of great power and grandeur. The act of faith is 1st proclaimed by the leading tenors, and then taken up with shouts of acclamation by all the other parts, "Qui salvandos salvas grâtis," and the supplication

which naturally follows as its logical outcome . . . is one of the loveliest pieces of modulation in the whole work.

'In the next movement, $\frac{3}{4}$ time, one of indescribable pathos, the parts each take a separate verse as if each had its own petition to present,

its own plea for pardon to urge. The 1st tenors sing, " Recordare, Jesu pie ;" the 2nd, " Juste judex ;" the basses, " Quærens me." And, curiously enough, with such consummate art is this managed, that they seem not to interfere with each other ; each succeeds the other at short intervals, one beginning its petition whilst the other parts take breathing time, and are silent. The whole is sustained by a flowing melody of surpassing grace, given chiefly to the violoncellos and basses. All unite in praying to be on that dreadful day admitted into the fold of Christ; "inter oves locum præsta, statuens in parte dextra," ends the movement, each of the parts ceasing in turn, the bass being the last to leave off with those wonderful 4 notes.

dex - - tra.

['This 'Recordare' as will be seen, in its truly affecting beauty, runs Mozart's very close.]

'Then, as if the consummation of all had come upon the world, the "presto" begins with a violin passage which brings before the eyes of the imagination the surging flames springing up from the abyss, and forms a prelude to the raging, despairing cry, in unison, of all the parts, "Confutatis maledictis," which breaks off and is again repeated in unison, 1st by the tenors, then taken up by the bass, mounting at every repetition by a major 3rd;

Con-fu - ta-tis ma - le - di-ctis, con-fu-ta tis male-
- di-ctis, ma-le - di-ctis, ma-le - di-ctis.

the whole sentiment culminating in a climax of descriptive writing with the words "flammis acribus," the torturing, searching nature of the flames being brought to the sense of hearing in a way which baffles description. Agonized rage, despair, confusion, are all concentrated in those few

flam-mis a - cri - bus,..................... flam - mis
flam-mis a - cri - bus, flam - -
flam-mis a - cri - bus, flam - -

a - cri-bus ad - di - ctis, flam-mis a - cri-bus, &c.
- - - mis, a - cri-bus ad - di - ctis, &c.
- - - mis a - cri-bus ad - di - ctis.

bars. The word "maledictis" is repeated thrice, as the self-pronounced doom of those who are without hope.

ma-le - di-ctis,   ma-le - di-ctis,   ma-le - di-ctis.

After a pause the saved are heard to pray—to rise, as it were, before the throne of the Judge in prayer—in an unaccompanied song of lovely calm and peace, "Voca me cum benedictis." The "andantino," which follows

the old figure, noticed in the last "andantino," "quærens," etc., is again introduced, the movement being given to the violoncellos; it is the heart-broken wailing of a crushed and contrite supplication, "Oro supplex, cor contritum quasi cinis" [twice repeated a 3rd higher in each case], and presents a striking piece of modulation, most expressive of the sentiment intended to be conveyed.

'The "lacrymosa dies illa" is a most plaintive

melody [beginning in unison], ending with a moving supplication for mercy to be shown to the departed. The "pie Jesu," which concludes this masterpiece, is full of

calm hope that the prayer for the absent one shall be heard. The sorrow of the bereaved, however, is abiding to the end.' [The 2 penultimate Amens *ff* are abrupt and disturbing in this peaceful close, and would scarcely be missed were they left out].

'No. 4. The Offertory. The march-like triumph of the opening is quite in keeping with the sentiment conveyed in the prayer. This is addressed to Jesus Christ the conqueror, the " Rex gloriæ," the King of

glory, who triumphed over death; its import is to obtain the deliverance of captives from the prison-house of flame.' The lake, the lion, and the outer darkness, in a few brief bars, are all imaged forth, while ' piano,' ' sforzando,' and ' forte ' play their wonted part in the expression of Cherubini's inspiration. ' The prayer that the standard-bearer, Michael, may take them into the holy light is accompanied by clarinets, oboes, and flutes, treble instruments, in a strain of wonderful beauty, which continues for 23 bars.

' The " allegro moderato," which immediately succeeds, is a specimen of earnest passionate pleading, " Quam olim Abrahæ promisisti," being repeated in [a brief] fugue by

T

all the voices; the idea is dwelt upon and expanded still
further in the movement which succeeds the intervening
peaceful "larghetto," "Hostias et preces" [the latter
closing with this exquisite passage descriptive of transition
to eternal life]. Each group of voices seems to vie with

 all the rest in enforcing its claim for
mercy for the departed [on the
repeat of the fugue, shortened, and
a variation of part of the original
subject, not over lengthy, and an effective coda, with the subject inverted

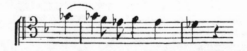

and an accelerated 'tempo.'] "Promisisti"—Godis held,
so to speak, to His word—"Thou hast promised,"
being repeated over and over again, as though in literal
fulfilment of the injunction of our Lord that we were
to succeed by our importunity in prayer.

'No. 5. The Sanctus. No one who has ever heard
the melodious phrase of symphony which ushers in the
voices in the Sanctus can ever forget it. Its value

and beauty seem to be enhanced as it is repeated in
various forms, while the voices have their own independent
work in a passage of great power and majesty. The
" Hosanna," the 1st syllable of which is sung to a demi-
semiquaver, and the 2nd to a minim, is an outburst
which never fails to electrify the hearer.' Yet strains,
whether immediately before or after the most solemn
part of the canon, namely, the Elevation, would seem
better ' piano ' than ' forte '—such as the ecclesiastical
Sanctus openings of Beethoven's Mass in C, and of
Hummel's Mass in D, or, Gounod's ideal Benedictus
of the ' Messe Solennelle,' or Cherubini's ' O Salutaris '
of the Mass in E minor. But the modern Sanctus is
generally a loud ' hosannah,' and sometimes too long.

' The words of the Benedictus having been already
sung in this movement, the piece after the Elevation is
set to the concluding words of the Dies Iræ, " pie Jesu ; "
this (No. 6) is a charming movement in $\frac{6}{8}$, written for
voices without accompaniment, except here and there,
where the clarinet and other wind instruments are
introduced between the various phrases to support the
intonation of the voices and keep them up to the proper
pitch.

'No. 7. The Agnus Dei. The introduction which prepares the way for the voices consists here, as elsewhere in other parts, especially in the Dies Iræ, in a piling up of sound, as it were, which reaches its climax on the 5th bar, the bar during which the voices are pronouncing the holy name of God. The intensity of sound gradually subsides,

leaving the voices quite to themselves in the exquisitely tender passage, " Dona eis requiem." This treatment of the words occurs 3 times; the long-drawn-out sweetness of the notes in which ' sempiternam' is sung is very striking. The Communion, " Lux æterna," immediately succeeds, and is ushered in by the bass with 3 notes at

the end of the bar.
It is a passage of won-
derful force. The light
which seems to burst
in upon the eye is

almost too dazzling to bear.   Then the motive for hope
is beautifully given, "Quia pius es," by the 3 parts in
succession, accompanied severally by the oboe, clarinet,
bassoon, each singing the notes of the common chord of
B flat, the first tenor commencing on F and ending on D,
the 2nd tenor taking up the D and descending to B flat,
the basses beginning with B flat and concluding on A.
The whole terminates with the words, "Requiem æternam
dona eis, Domine," slowly and solemnly chanted by
tenors and bass, the bass leading on D, the tenors
answering on A.

The persistence of the open 5th for 18 bars, accompanied,
as it is, at intervals by the rolling of muffled drums, has an
inexpressibly mournful and solemn character.   On the

19th bar the major chord is heard once more, and the tenors, with the cheerful ringing tones of hope and anticipation of answered prayer, once more implore light for the departed spirit. The bass in contrary motion

repeats the chord—the cadence lengthens out, swells, and dies away—and then the last notes are heard like the subsidence of a great storm; the descending chromatic passage, with D for the pedal note, may be almost said to be sobbed out by the instruments; one more prolonged roll of muffled drums; a flute in an ascending " arpeggio " is answered by a bassoon with descending " arpeggio; " and all is at rest.'[6]

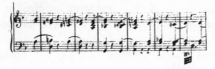

Few more perfect works of modern art and devotion than this Requiem

in Introit, Kyrie, Gradual, Offertory, Agnus Dei, and

[6] With reference to the above critique, Fr. Coleridge, S.J., when Editor of the *Month*, wrote in 1874, that while it did not settle the vexed question of church musical style, yet, that what struck him was 'that those who . . . find themselves incapable of appreciating the devotional treasures which are here pointed out, might at least believe that there are others who can interpret them, and find their souls raised nearer to heaven by the process.' This for the benefit of those who, more papal than the Pope, see little Church music later than the 16th century, which may be a prejudice, arising from abuses, and a premiss believed to be unsound, and a playing upon 2 words, ' ideal ' and ' dramatic.'

Communion exist, whether considered vocally, instrument-
ally, or liturgically. Cherubini now retired more and
more to the peace of a happy home, where the loving
care of his devoted wife, son and eldest daughter, lightened
his last years. He is thus described by one who saw
him then : ' Although his body was bent under so great
a weight of years, his eye was full of fire, his face full of
majesty, his forehead full of brightness. It was delightful
to behold his waving, silvery hair, which thickly covered
his head, and played beautifully around his ears and
temples.' Moscheles, who saw him in 1839, writes :
' Cherubini, never the most courteous of men, was very
friendly ; we had a good hour's earnest conversation on
art matters. He said that, with the exception of his
Directorship at the Conservatoire, he had nothing more
to do with music ; he couldn't write another note ; he
wasn't strong enough to hear and enjoy musical impressions. I think I might have assured him, without
flattery, that he belongs to the few who even in their
lifetime have already earned immortality. As for my
poor Lafont, I saw him lying in his coffin whilst the
funeral service was being held in the church of St. Roch ;
the music was Cherubini's, but without organ accompaniment, to my taste an indispensable adjunct.'[7]

The Minister having insisted on some new Conservatoire regulations, to which the Director at length
reluctantly consented, the latter took occasion to resign
4 Feb. 1842, a decision noted on the 5th in the
' Courier des Theâtres,' which said, ' It is believed that
considerations of health have something to do with this
new resolution ; the fact is M. Cherubini feels the need
of repose, earned by a long course of work and a
multiplicity of cares. It was reported yesterday that he
would return to Italy.'[8]

[7] I was told by Mme. Moscheles that Cherubini was always particularly
kind to her husband, at whose house in Paris he heard for the 1st time the
latter's pianoforte ' Sonate Symphonique' (dedicated to Louis Philippe) for
4 hands, and bestowed the greatest encomiums upon it.—*Life of Moscheles.*
[8] *M.W.,* 1883, 782.

King Louis Philippe, bent on bestowing a signal mark of his appreciation of such lengthened services in the cause of music, for the 1st time made a musician Commander of the Legion of Honour. The results of that great administration have already been considered ; the wonder is that he could carry it on so long, despite much annoyance from authority, including a position offered over the heads of all his French professors to his countryman Rossini, and grandiloquently entitled 'Inspector General of Singing in France.[9]

At length, in due course, to quote Halévy's eloquent but not altogether pleasing account, written 3 years after Cherubini's decease : ' He succumbed, bowed down by years, but struggling against death, as, up to that supreme day, he had struggled against old age, which had in consequence respected him. He had preserved all his energy of will, all his distinctness of judgment, all his clearness of intelligence. Strong, and possessing a young and vigorous mind, the octogenarian felt himself the equal of the men about him who had not, in most cases, attained or passed maturity. He would scarcely acknowledge their right to be younger than himself, and, in his pride, the term old man was distasteful to him. . . . He accepted nothing of old age save the deference it brings with it ; for him years meant authority. . . . "I am beginning to get old," he said to me one day. He was then more than 80. These words, that would have been commonplace coming from other lips, struck me grievously as coming from his, and filled me with sadness. . . . I saw in them the presentiment and symptom of approaching dissolution . . .'[10] And Halévy ends with an idle fancy

[9] See Cherubini's generous and masterly memorandum on this subject. *M. W.*, 1884, 120-1. 'Although he may be reproached for having been too minute in the details of his direction of the Conservatoire, it is no less true that he raised that school, fallen from its ancient splendour, when it was in M. Papillon de la Ferte's province, as superintendent of the King's Menu-Plaisirs. The respect which the great talent of Cherubini inspired exercised its influence on the professors and pupils ; the glory of his name was reflected on the establishment that he directed.'—Fétis, *Biog. Univ.*, art. Cherubini.

[10] *M. W.*, 1883, 593, *cit.* Pougin.

about Ingres' Polymnia being of some avail as a support
and preservative against death—wherein a false note is
sounded by an undoubtedly sincere and devoted admirer
of Cherubini.   That sleepy-looking muse could, alas! do
nothing for anybody at any time.

A blow had come to Cherubini in the death of his
son-in-law, M. Turcas.   It was some time before he
regained his cheerfulness.   One day, when laid up by
some slight illness, he was complimented by Halévy on
his looks.   He replied, ' I have not 10 years more to live.'
It was a safe prediction for an octogenarian.

On 11 June 1841, Cherubini wrote to Schlesinger: ' I
thank you very much for your goodness in sending me
the Programme of the great Festival at Cologne last
Whitsuntide, at which they executed my 4th solemn Mass,
with the Latin words.   I do not believe I merit, Sir, all
the compliments you have been willing to address me on
the subject of that work, and I repeat my thanks for the
kind and amiable things you have had the goodness to
say to me.   Mme. Cherubini has been very sensible, Sir,
of your remembrance and the promise you have been
willing to make in her regard to obtain an autograph of
Beethoven.   We shall be charmed, she and myself, to see
you again in Paris next winter, as much as yourself in
giving us this expectation.   Accept, Sir, the most distinguished assurance with which I have the honour to be
your devoted servant, LUIGI CHERUBINI.' [11]

By well before the close of 1841, Ingres, the celebrated
French artist, had painted a portrait of Cherubini, which
Hiller deems ' not so much painted as actually chiselled
in colours.'   It was bought by the King and subsequently
found a place in the Luxembourg Gallery.   It is now in
the Louvre, and established the painter's reputation, after an
article by Mme. d'Agoult had called attention to its merits.

[11] *Beethoven's Letters,* ed. Kalischer, 234-5, 1909.   The above is given in
French.   Wagner also refers to a Mass of our composer given in 1832 at
Vienna.   ' A very poor students' rehearsal at the Conservatoire, at which
they performed a Mass by Cherubini, seemed to me like an alms paid
begrudgingly to the study of classical music.'—*My Life,* i. 77.

Miel thus describes Ingres' great picture : ' While seated on a fauteuil, and dressed in the modern fashion, Cherubini directs a glance forwards—that is a preoccupied one, but wherein genius shines. Polymnia, invisible to him, standing upright behind the seat, robed in the severe majesty of ancient costume, with a crown of laurel on her brow, the fingers of the left-hand resting on the strings of the lyre, is stretching out the right-hand over her favourite, and overshadowing him with her protection, expressing by her authoritative mien that this man belongs to her. Original and mysterious composition, unexpected but natural contrast between the real world and the ideal world, an individual portrait that has become a sublime historical picture.'[12]

Pougin tells us that the portrait mentioned above had been begun in Rome in 1837, Finberg says 1839. The idea of the added white Muse standing beside this dark seated

[12] Miel, 28 ; De Beaufort's *Abbé Liszt,* 203. A magnificent print from Ingres by P. Sudre in 1843 was printed by Lemercier and published in Paris by H. Gache, 58 Rue de la Victoire, and in London by J. Bouvier, 70 St. Martin's Lane. My own copy, 'avant les lettres,' marked No. 110, was received from Felix Moscheles 16 Jan. 1874 for 50 francs. In the original picture the composer's right elbow rests on a table, thereon a quill pen, an open music-book, and, beyond it, 2 closed volumes labelled 'Les Deux Journées,' 'Ali Baba.' In Sudre's print, however, he rests by a ledge at the foot of a column, which looks more artistic. Anyway, there are, we know, 2 portraits, one with and one without the rather sheepish-looking Polymnia, which may account for this difference in the background. The figure certainly contributes a fine *chiar-o-scuro,* but otherwise there would probably be an agreement with the judgment of A. J. Finberg (*Ingres* 48, in Series, *Masterpieces in colour,* ed. T. Leman Hare) that it is 'doubtful whether this addition is an improvement.' The figure of Cherubini only was photographed for the *Musical Times* of March 1908. A fair lithograph, somewhat after Ingres, is in Clément's *Musiciens Célèbres.* And there is an old engraving in an oval, with 'Cherubini' inscribed below, and beneath this a lyre between 2 pages of an open music book. Portraits by Z. Belliard ; E. Hader (photographed by Sophus Williams, Berlin); R. Grüner(Haslinger, Vienna, and Schlesinger, Paris); Vigneron (Rocca, Berlin, and Peters, Leipsic); and others issued by Artaria and Witzendorf, Vienna ; Heckel, Mannheim ; by the French press of Aubert and Junca, and by Champlin and Apthorp's *Cyclopædia of Music and Musicians* (Jan. 1889), are to be noted. A caricature of Cherubini and some of his MSS. were among the late Mr. Julian Marshall's collection. Eugène Gautier, visiting Cherubini at his rooms in 1835, writes : ' A rather large portrait of middling merit, but broadly painted, represented a lady still young. This was Cherubini's mother, a Florentine of the middle of the 18th century, who, 100 years before, had, when she sat for her portrait, put on her best gown of white *gros de Naples,* embroidered with various-coloured silk. Her hair

A. Cherubini

|After Ingres.

figure was an after-thought. The 1st sketch without the Muse, according to Pougin, 'a marvellously beautiful design,' came into the possession of Ambroise Thomas, successor to Auber as Director of the Conservatoire.

'When the picture was finished, Ingres, taking care to place it in a favourable and mysterious light, invited Cherubini to come and see it, but did not choose to be present at the scene of astonishment and outburst of gratitude that he foresaw. Mme. Ingres alone awaited the composer as the witness of his surprise and rapture. Seated before the representation of his apotheosis, Cherubini contemplated it a long time with discouraging tranquillity, while preserving a silence that quite overwhelmed Mme. Ingres. . . . At last he rose, and murmuring a few polite words, withdrew. The painter, who was on the watch, hastened to appear after Cherubini had left, and asked his wife what had been the effect produced by the surprise they had arranged. "It produced none," said Mme. Ingres, "absolutely none! No mark of astonishment or joy, no trace of emotion!" Ingres was dumbfoundered. He could not understand such insensibility on the part of a man of genius in the presence of his deified portrait. A few days afterwards Cherubini, having come to pay Ingres a visit, was, in his turn, coldly received, and scarcely any attention was paid to a roll of paper he gave his host, though he did so with an air of solemnity. It was a piece of music composed by Cherubini, a canon to the glory of Ingres. After glancing at it, the painter gave it to Mme. Hittorf, and his illustrious colleague and friend, Auguste Couder, who made out the parts, and found the music to be majestic and of rare beauty. It was arranged by M. Couder and Mme. Hittorf that they should prepare a surprise for Ingres by singing him the canon one evening at the house of the lady who agreed to

was powdered, and she wore on her slightly discoloured lips the amiable smile with which she used to greet her husband's pupils.'—*Journal Officiel,* 17 July 1877, *cit.* Pougin, *M.W.,* 1883, 539. I may add that a medal, with Cherubini's effigy thereon, by M. Prudhomme, made its appearance in July 1834.

give a grand party on purpose. It was 15 March 1842. Ingres kept them waiting, and, when he came, wore a sad and sombre look. "What is the matter, my dear friend?" said Couder. "I am deeply grieved," replied Ingres; "Cherubini died this morning." On receiving this news, the guests tacitly gave up the plot they had formed to sing unexpectedly the canon they, had learned and rehearsed. After dinner, however, they changed their mind, and, while Ingres appeared absorbed in thought, they suddenly aroused him by the fine phrases of the music composed in his honour. He burst into tears.'[13] Such is Blanc's touching narrative.

Cherubini had grown weaker by 12 March, and on the 15th, after uttering some words, indistinctly heard by those about him, and surrounded by his wife, son, elder daughter, Halévy, Batton, and other intimate friends, he expired, being in his 82nd year.[14] I have not ascertained whether he received the Last Sacraments, but he appears to have practised his religion in life. He was not mystical in religion, his daughter said, but broad-minded. His music is both. May he who hymned Our Lady's praises; who was probably born on her Nativity, and certainly christened by her name on her octave, and who died in the month of St. Joseph, her spouse, have received the reward of those that use their talent while yet it is day.

[13] *cit.* Pougin, *M.W.*, 1884, 29. Blanc was told by Mme. Rosellini, that painter and composer had interchanged drawings and music, and that in Montauban Museum are some of Cherubini's gifts to Ingres.

[14] He is reported to have said 'Je ne veux pas mourir,' a somewhat ordinary remark, and one also ascribed to Spontini by Berlioz, who was present at the latter's death.—*My Life,* by R. Wagner, i. 350-1. Hiller also notes among the last incidents, that Cherubini asked for a handkerchief, and that they gave him one marked No. 8. 'You have made a mistake,' he said, 'you have given me No. 8, and I have not had No. 7.' 'That is true, but a drop of Eau de Cologne has been spilt on No. 7, and knowing you detest scent I————' 'No matter, order before everything.' No. 7 was brought and used. 'Now I have used it,' he added, 'you can give me No. 8.' *Macmillan,* July 1875; Pougin, *M.W.*, 1884, 184, *cit.* Revue de Paris in *Siècle,* 25 March 1842.

CHAPTER VIII.

FRANCE.

1842.

'. . . Then in melodious swell
Inviting Requiems for the faithful dead. . . .
O Sanctuary rare of all creation . . .
Soothing the soul with hope . . .'
                                        CASWALL.

Cherubini's Obsequies—Halévy's Address—Monuments at Père-la-Chaise
and Santa Croce, Florence—Honours to his memory—The Cherubini
Society—Conclusion.

As Cherubini was a Commander of the Legion of
Honour, the funeral took place with much ceremony and
with military honours 19 March 1842. The procession,
joined by no less than 3,000 persons, started from the
gates of the Conservatoire, and passing along the Boulevards, amidst the grand strains of Cherubini's own funeral
march for General Hoche, directed its solemn course to
the church of St. Roch. Cherubini's 2nd Requiem was
performed here, by his own dying wish, and ' with thrilling
effect ; ' so wrote a writer, who was present, to the
' Athenæum ' in 1874.[1] ' At one blow ' Halévy ' lost a
master, a father, and a friend. I can still see him bending
beneath the weight of his 3-fold grief, holding with Auber
one of the corners of the pall as they proceeded from the
Rue de Faubourg Poissonière to the church of St. Roch.
Tears were streaming down his face, and at each roll of
the funeral drum, at each plaint of the instruments . . .
he staggered as though struck to the heart.'[2]

When the ceremonial was over, the ' cortège ' proceeded to the cemetery of Père-la-Chaise. Here Raoul

---

[1] An event recalling Mozart's Requiem for Weber's funeral 21 June
1826 at St. Mary's, Moorfields, London.

[2] *M.W.* 1883, 593, Pougin's *V. F. Halévy, sa vie et ses œuvres.*

Rochette, in the name of the Institute, of which Cherubini was a member, Lafont the younger, who read an address for Zimmermann, whose emotion prevented him delivering it himself, and Halévy, representing Cherubini's friends, said successively a few touching words over the deceased ; a deluge of rain and hail happened to fall at the time, but so absorbed was each person in listening with religious silence to the various addresses, that no one left the scene.

Halévy's words were as follows : ' Gentlemen, it is a sad duty to come to this still open tomb, to bid a last farewell to one who was my master, my guide, and my friend. In the name, then, of all who loved you, receive, Cherubini, this eternal farewell. Before the earth closes for ever on your remains, listen once more to the voice of those who for 30 years have venerated and cherished you. God permitted that, at the end of your long and laborious career, in the struggle you maintained with disease and death, that your strong reason should never waver. Your noble intelligence kept watch to the end in the exhausted body you beheld dying day by day. At the supreme moment, those who had the privilege of sharing with your family the task of paying the last sad attentions that soothed your dying moments, wished on your account for the arrival of death, which you yourself prayed God to send you, for no illusion was any longer possible, neither for them nor yourself ; your sufferings spoke only too clearly. When death struck you down still erect, and still animated by your strong will, they almost thanked God for putting an end to your pains by calling you to Himself. But now the picture of those sufferings is growing fainter, and we feel only the immensity of our loss. We look for you near us ; near the hearth around which we used to gather. Only a few days have elapsed, and in the profound sorrow of the period of mourning, now beginning, we perceive what a void there will be for ever about us. Once more do I bid you farewell, in the name of those who will endeavour to follow you in the path you have marked out for them. You loved them as

TOMB OF CHERUBINI

MONUMENT AT PÈRE-LA-CHAISE, PARIS.

if they had been your children, and they weep for you as
they would weep for a father. Your venerated and
glorious name will ever be for them the symbol of all that
is noble and renowned.   Farewell, Cherubini, farewell.'

Under the presiding care of the Duc de Coigny, a
commission was instituted, with the object of raising a
monument to him. Through subscriptions received by
the Conservatoire, the present handsome tomb, by Leclerc,
with marble medallion and bas-relief of the head of the
Florentine master by Dumont, was erected at Père-la-
Chaise. The Muse is crowning his head with a wreath,
and on the pedestal is inscribed, under the heads of
'Musique Religieuse' and 'Musique Dramatique,'
Cherubini's chief works, such as the 'Messes de Requiem,'
'Messe du Sacre de Charles X.,' 'Lodoïska,' 'Elisa,'
'Médée,' 'Les Deux Journées,' 'Faniska,' 'Les Abencé-
rages, etc.; followed by 'Musique Instrumentale' and
'Œuvres Theoretiques.' By a Royal Order of 11 June,
the Paris Municipal Council's resolution, granting the
ground for it gratuitously, was approved.[3]

On 7 April 1842, a Requiem was sung for Cherubini
at Pisa, and on the morning of 22 April 1842, the faithful
saw suspended to the main door of the church of St.
Michael and St. Cajetan at Florence, the following
inscription :

A

LUIGI   CHERUBINI

FIORENTINO

COMMENDATORE DELLA LEGION D'ONORE

DIRETTORE DEL CONSERVATORIO MUSICALE DI PARIGI

OVE OTTUAGENARIO IL XV MARZO MDCCCXLII.

TERMINÒ LA SUA LABORIOSA ED ILLUSTRE CARRIERA

UOMO DI ANTICHE VIRTÙ ED INTEMERATI COSTUMI

PROFONDISSIMO NEI MISTERI DELL' ARMONIA

IL. QUALE NELL' ARTE DI CHE FU MAESTRO

E MASSIMAMENTE NELLA MUSICA SACRA

[3] *Revue et Gazette Mus. de Paris*, 20 Aug. 1843, *cit*. Pougin. *M.W.*
1884, 29.

SPIEGATO GENIO POTENTE

PER MAESTOSI CONCETTI E SUBLIMITÀ DI STILE

A NESSUNO SECONDO

PRESSO GLI STRANIERI LA GLORIA ITALIANA SOSTENNE

SUOI CONCITTADINI[4]

'While the faithful were invited thither by the church-bells to pray for the repose of the illustrious deceased, between 200 and 300 members of the Musical College made the vaulted roof of the magnificent temple resound with the last inspired strains of music, wherein this perfect composer had depicted the terrible day of tremendous wrath, and had earnestly begged of the Divine Judge to number him among the blest. And of that immense crowd assembled together, perhaps, there was not one man old enough to remember having seen him amongst us, or in a position to recall the affectionate acclamation he had received from his fellow-countrymen, more especially on the occasion of the representation of his opera of "Idalide," at the great theatre in 1784, with which, without its being foreseen, he bade a last farewell to his native place. From that period Cherubini was but an historical name for Florence, a title of glory that will endure for ages.'[5]

No sooner did Cherubini's death become known than a general anxiety prevailed to do him honour. The municipality of Paris bestowed his name on a new street running into the Place Louvois, and to the great Opera-house, and that of Florence did the same on a street in the new quarter of Maglio, and proposed to call the large and elegant Theatre Pagliano after his name.[6]

---

[4] 'His fellow-citziens to Luigi Cherubini, Florentine, Commander of the Legion of Honour, Director of the Conservatoire of Music at Paris, where, an octogenarian, he ended, 15 March 1842, his laborious and illustrious career, a man of antique virtue and spotless character, most profound in the mysteries of harmony, in the art whereof he was a master, and especially in sacred music, displaying a powerful genius, in majesty of conception and sublimity of style 2nd to none, the upholder among strangers of the glory of Italy.'

[5] Picchianti, 5.

[6] Gamucci.

Bartolini, some time back, had executed a bust of Cherubini, an acknowledged masterpiece. Pierre J. David also executed a medallion of him; and a bronze statue was raised to his memory at Florence, with the inscription that had been affixed to the door of St. Michael and St. Cajetan. A revival of ' Les Deux Journées ' at Paris no less honoured its composer; and, by a strange coincidence, Bouilly, the writer of the book, also an octogenarian, died 26 May, a month or so after Cherubini; so that Emile Vanderburch—who, along with both, was member of the old Society ' d'Enfants d'Apollon,' could now, in the society's name, offer homage to Cherubini, and say in his elegy that the authors of ' Les Deux Journées ' had died hand in hand.[7]

Kalkbrenner, too, composed a piece in our composer's honour, and Baillot wrote to his brother-in-law, M. Guynemer, from Paris 9 April 1842 : ' I was well assured that you would share in our sorrow on the occasion of the loss we have sustained in the venerable Cherubini. I can say nothing in addition to what you already think and feel on this subject : the loss to the musical world is immense ; but it falls yet heavier on those who had the opportunity of knowing, under a somewhat rough exterior, the genuine intrinsic worth of him who was also, perhaps, the " last and noblest Roman " in the purely classical style of art. All the principal artistes of Paris attended his funeral, and it was not without considerable emotion that I beheld amongst them M. Ingres, to whom we are indebted for the faithful portrait of our lost friend, a work which is the " chef-d'œuvre " of his pencil, because inspired by his heart.

' We followed him to his last abode—but no! his abode is no longer on this earth ; heaven has, ere this, received him whose sacred compositions seemed to forestall the harmonies of a better world, and to invite us to render ourselves worthy of being admitted into it.

[7] *N.M.Z.*, *M.W.*, 1862.

'Two days ago, April 7, "Les Deux Journées" was performed at the theatre. It was only announced by the bills in the morning, yet the house was crowded. I could not withold my assistance. The success—a strange expression after 40 years of success—was perfect. It was very well acted, and the music was executed with that "ensemble" which cannot be equalled when it proceeds from the unanimity of sentiment and respect, of which we find so few instances in social life. Nothing languished; the actors and the musicians excelled themselves, and the 3 acts were finished in 2 hours and 20 minutes. The curtain was afterwards raised to exhibit the bust of Cherubini, by Bartolini, upon an elevated pedestal, with the actors from the principal theatres ranged around it in costume. The 2 chief performers of the evening recited some appropriate and very touching verses from the pen of the octogenarian author of "Les Deux Journées," M. Bouilly. The whole passed off in a style worthy of the occasion, and must have interested even those most indifferent to the beauties of the art, or the triumph of genius. And what music! I longed for you beside me, even while the pleasure, regret, and a tumult of deep emotions had taken such total possession of my poor heart that I tried in vain to stifle them; and you, I know, would have felt as acutely. . . .'[8]

Lines by Emile Deschamps were also given, and the cradle song from 'Blanche de Provence,' writes Theophile Gautier, 'more than feebly,' in sarcastic vein at an attempt to make amends when a man is dead for the neglect of his works when living.[9]

[8] Letter sent to Guynemer for insertion in *Mainzer's M.T.* i, 26. Moreau-Sainti took Armand; Henri, Mikeli; Mme. Mélotte, Constance. The latter part was superbly rendered by Mme. Parepa-Rosa in Boston, New York, U.S.A., and elsewhere under M. Rosa's direction and in his admirable company, and it is pleasing to record another performance of the *Water-Carrier* by the pupils of the Royal College of Music, *Daily Graphic*, 22 Nov. 1911.

[9] With regard to Cherubini. writes Pougin, '. . . the ingratitude had been so glaring, that a writer who certainly could not pass as an enthusiast in music, Theophile Gautier, was unable to restrain a cry of indignation on the subject,' and he wrote in *La Presse* of 19 April 1842: 'Of a certainty,

Rossini felt deeply the loss of his great countryman, and by kindness and sympathy strove to assuage the grief of those who felt their bereavement the most keenly. He had found, about 1855, at a dealer's, a beautiful Louis XVI. attired portrait of Cherubini, executed, it was supposed, about 1780, probably later, 'his fresh young face, full of distinction, surrounded by an abundance of powdered hair,' and he sent Mme. Cherubini a half-size photograph of it with this note: 'Here is the portrait of the great man, who is still as young in your heart as he is in my mind. Kindly accept it as a tender memento. From yours affectionately, G. ROSSINI.' On 7 Oct. 1843, Raoul Rochette read Cherubini's 'éloge' at the Institute. Lastly, must be mentioned the raising of the monument to Cherubini in the church of Sta. Croce, Florence.[10]

On 22 Dec. 1861, the great hall of the Conservatoire was crowded with artists and amateurs to listen to a concert given to aid ways and means, and conducted by Tilmant, with the following items :

Overture to 'Anacréon' . . .	Cherubini.
Chorus, 'Dors, noble enfant' from 'Blanche de Provence'	Cherubini.
'Chant des Titans' . . .	Rossini.
Fragment from 'Prometheus' . .	Beethoven.
Introduction and Chorus from 'Elisa' . .	Cherubini.
Symphony in C minor . . .	Beethoven.

respect for the dead is a fine thing, but respect for the living would be something finer. . . . To-day you are dead, and, without any intermediate stage, the voices which abused you yesterday simply form an elegiac chorus. What a loss art has just suffered! Irreparable disaster! Sun for ever concealed below the horizon! What a great nature, and what a great genius! . . . a number of dithyrambics which, had they come a little sooner, would have gently delighted the old man's heart. M. Ingres, at least, did wait till the illustrious maestro was laid in his coffin to have him crowned by the Muse. The revival of Cherubini's " Deux Journées " will add nothing to his glory.' *M. W.,* 1882, 731.

[10] Pougin, *M. W.,* 1883, 560. This portrait has since been lost. Morini seems to have taken the initiative with zeal and energy. A committee was formed, with the Marquis Pompeo Azzolino as President, and the Duke di San Clemente, Professors Cav. L. F. Casamorata, O. Mariotti, A. Marini, Cav. O. Fantachiotti (sculptor), L. Picchianti, Cav. T. Mabellini, Cav. G. Maglioni, Cav. G. Sbolci, A. Biagi, V. Meini, and Cav. F. Morini as members. In Italy 3000 lire were subscribed, of which King

The 'Chant des Titans' was expressly written by Rossini for the concert, as a homage to Cherubini, and at a time, too, when he had given up composition. On 8 Dec. 1865, a concert took place at Florence.

Overture to 'Faniska' . . .	Cherubini.
'Da nobis pacem,' from . . .	Mendelssohn.
Symphony in G minor . . .	Mozart.
'Kyrie,' 'Gloria,' 'Credo,' Mass in D, No. 2 .	Beethoven.

Cav. F. Morini had placed on the exterior wall of the house in the Via Fiesolano, where Cherubini had been born, the following inscription, by L. Venturi :

QUI NACQUE IL XIV. SETTEMBRE MDCCLX
LUIGI CHERUBINI
CHE SOMMO NEL MAGISTERO DELL ARMONIA

CREATORE DI SUBLIMI MELODIE RELIGIOSE

RESTAURÒ OGNI MANIERA DI MUSICO STILE

E NELLE RAGIONI DELL' ARTE

SERBÒ PEREGRINO FRA GLI STRANIERI LA GLORIA

DEL PRIMATO ITALIANO [11]

Victor Emmanuel gave 500, Prince Carignano 200, and the Minister of Public Instruction 200. The municipality of Florence also gave 500 lire towards the completion of the work. Through the deaths of the Marquis Azzolino and Professors Marini and Biagi, Morini became president, and nominated Professor A. Basevi to the Committe, and subsequently the Marquis L. Niccolini, the Marquis L. Torrigiani, and Professors Cav. C. Mussini and A. Biagi. Morini, associating with himself the Duke di San Clemente and Cav. Casamorata, formed an executive committee, with the Duke as treasurer, Casamorata as collector. Meini was secretary. A sub-committee was formed at Paris by Prince G. Poniatowski, Auber being vice-president, the Prince and Halévy vice-presidents ; and Berlioz, Carafa, Clapisson, Kastner, Meyerbeer, Reber, Rossi, Ambroise Thomas, and O. Monnais (secretary), members. Monnais, the French treasurer, 6 March 1862, announced the result of the French subscriptions—5212 lire. In the meantime C. Ciardi, the flutist, had collected a further sum at St. Petersburg, and 200 lire were received from the King of Portugal, besides other subscriptions from distinguished persons in Italy, England, France, Russia and Germany. Gamucci, *Alcune Notizie storiche sul Monumento in S. Croce a L. Cherubini.*

[11] Here was born, the 14th September 1760, Luigi Cherubini, who, supreme in the mastery of harmony, creator of sublime religious melodies, restored every kind of musical style, and, though a wanderer among strangers, preserved in all that concerned his art the glory of Italian supremacy.

MONUMENT AT SANTA CROCE, FLORENCE.

Meanwhile, Fantacchiotti, who was to execute the monument, and had declined to receive any sum for his services, was tracing on marble the form of the monument, already sketched out in chalk, and modelled in plaster. The work was approved, and the contract settled with Fantacchiotti by Casamorata, Oct. 1869. The inscription, by Venturi, runs:

LUIGI CHERUBINI

N. IN FIRENZE IL DI XIV SETT. MDCCLX.

M. IN PARIGI IL XV. MAR. MDCCCXLII.

SCRITTORE INSUPERATO DI MELODIE RELIGIOSE

ARRICCHÌ DI NUOVE BELLEZZE OGNI MANIERA DI MUSICO STILE

E SALUTATO DA TUTTA EUROPA

SOMMO NEL MAGISTERO DELL' ARTE

EBBE A PARIGI

OVE RESSE IL CONSERVATORIO MUSICALE

GLI ONORI DOVUTI ALL' INGEGNO ED ALLA VIRTÙ

E DA' SUOI CITTADINI

QUESTO MONUMENTO FRA LE GLORIE ITALIANE

NELL' ANNO MDCCCLXIX [12]

Gamucci goes on to describe the monument at Sta. Croce. Over the inscription, on a ribbon entwined with a crown of laurel, is sculptured the 1st musical phrase of his 'Ave Maria.' Above the base of the monument is an urn, while there are 2 figures, larger than life, 1 representing Music, placing a crown on the head of Genius, personified as the winged youth, leaning against a column, upholding a medallion, whereon in 'bas relief,' is sculptured Cherubini's effigy. 'Beautiful, noble, yet sad is the figure representing Music, that quietly holding the lyre in her right hand, crowns Genius with the left. . . . The bashful and modest expression of the counten-

---

[12] 'Luigi Cherubini, born in Florence 14 Sept. 1760, died in Paris, 15 March 1842; unsurpassed writer of religious melodies, he enriched with new beauties every kind of musical style, and, hailed by all Europe as supreme in the mastery of the art, received in Paris, where he directed the Musical Conservatory, the honours due to genius and virtue, and from his fellow-citizens this monument, amidst Italy's glories, in the year 1869.'

ances, with nothing earthly or pagan about them, the quiet demeanour of the figures, undoubtedly symbolize religious music, wherein Cherubini was unapproached. . . . Professor Fantacchiotti's conception is beautiful, delicate, tender, with the imprint of novelty. . . . The repose, order, and harmony that reign in every portion, make it worthy of admiration.'

Finally, with regard to the Cherubini Florentine Choral Society, founded at Florence by Mme. Laussot it gave admirable concerts under her direction, at the Corsini Palace, Florence, one of which I was happy to attend 16 May 1881, Signor G. Buonamici conducting.

On the 17 Nov. 1877, Mme. Laussot (née Jessie Taylor), afterwards Mme. Hillebrand, wrote to me from 50 Lung'Arno Nuovo, Florence, as Foundress and Honorary Directress of the Society, forwarding a communication from Count de Cambray-Digny, ex-Minister of Finance, and President of the Society. She said of the Society: 'Though till now only partially developed, it is our earnest desire and hope that this institution will in time contribute to make known the works of the great Florentine composer, under whose patronage it has placed itself, and we are anxious that all true musicians who, like yourself, take an especial interest in Cherubini, should not ignore, but rather sympathize, if possible, with the efforts we have not ceased to make for years, to attract and promote greater attention to, and study of, that master's productions in his native city.' [13]

'Cherubini,' exclaims Adolphe Adam, 'has just

---

[13] She continued : 'I have been informed by my friend Dr. Hans von Bülow, that he has had an interview with you on the subject of a slight rectification to which . . . I thought both you and our Society were entitled, and which . . . could only be made by a musical authority well acquainted with the Society. . . . It will give me great pleasure to be able to transmit the acceptance on your part [of the Membership] . . . as I own it did . . . to find that . . . an addition to musical literature in a subject of such vital interest to me was the production of a countryman not a professional musician.'

In my reply to his Excellency 22 Nov. 1877, accepting the membership, I expressed a hope of doing in a new edition justice to the Society, and my thanks, too, for his kind notice of *Memorials*.

breathed his last! He whose works have been the admiration of all Europe is no more! Immortality has commenced for this illustrious man. Few careers of musicians have been so admirable, so well fulfilled. During the 2nd half of the last century, and the 1st of this, his name has ever been pronounced with respect, his works have been cited as models, and accepted as such by all composers, of whatever school they were; their purity, their classicism, have placed them outside and beyond all the frivolities of fashion, all the concessions made to the taste of the public. . . . In fact, compare the 1st works of Mozart with those of Cherubini, composed nearly at the same period . . . and you will be surprised to see how much certain passages of Mozart will appear to you old-fashioned, while nothing in Cherubini's works will betray the period at which they were written.[14]

'Cherubini,' writes Georges Kastner, 'has given proof of a fecundity and a universality indeed surprising. It is true to say that during his long career he never knew repose. And why repose, when science and inspiration are your humble slaves, and at every hour await your commands?'[15] On the other hand, 'it is certain that the great artist never worked hurriedly or negligently. If all his works are imprinted with the mark of genius, they are none the less remarkable for the pains with which they are elaborated.'[16]

'Cherubini's position is unique in the history of his art; actively before the world as a composer for 3-score years and ten, his career spans over more vicissitudes in the progress of music than that of any other man. Beginning to write in the same year with Cimarosa, and even earlier than Mozart, and being the contemporary of

---

[14] The above opinion may refer to the early religious music, though no details are to hand, but if to the early secular, as is more likely, it may be considered, along with Hiller's, that they resembled the works of their day, and with Halévy's view (*supra*) that there was nothing to reveal the later genius, which developed slowly, till *Ifigenia* in 1788, and still more *Lodoïska* in 1791, showed the great Master, hitherto in *embryo*.

[15] *Sur les Manuscrits Autographes de Cherubini, cit.* Fr. Girod, S.J.

[16] Girod.

Verdi and of Wagner, he witnessed almost the origin of the 2 modern classic schools of France and Germany. . . . His artistic life was indeed a rainbow based upon the 2 extremes of modern music, which shed light and glory on the great art-cycle over which it arched.'[17]

Ulibicheff's praise of Cherubini began these 'Memorials;' at their close, I would fain cite Hauptmann, who is in agreement to a noticeable extent with him and Hiller. 'Who ever wrote more finely for the orchestra than Cherubini? He is full of animation and brilliancy, and he, at all events, did not learn it of Mozart.' And of 'Lodoïska' in 1854, at Leipsic: . . . 'I was interested from beginning to end. It was refreshing, once in a way, to get rid of that disgusting, boneless pulp of emotion, out of which modern operas are made. . . . Cherubini feels every subject deeply, but his emotion is so chastened, so beautifully subdued by artistic form, that we never suffer the pain of oppressive realism, which is the aim of modern musicians to inflict. . . . In spite of the utter absurdity of the libretto, I listened with unflagging spirits and complete enjoyment to every note of "Lodoïska." The "Cantilena" is never prominent, though the music, as we should expect of an Italian, is vocal throughout ; but the orchestration supporting it is marvellous. The harmony is not lumped in chords, it hovers about, it is woven of various and consonant figurations, each of which seems to exist solely for itself ; it never becomes an inert mass, there are no clammy, thorough-bass accompaniments, filling the middle parts, and stuffing and developing the chords into "those interesting harmonic progressions." "Interesting harmonic progressions" there are, however, and plenty of them, the fact being, that the most interesting of such things date from Cherubini, their virtual founder. But to be able to write like Cherubini, is equivalent to saying

[17] G. A. Macfarren.

that one can play with the most difficult tasks, as he did. It is not born in a man to do this; it takes any amount of hard work to acquire the capability.'

And again in 1845: ' Spohr probably got his tendency towards what he calls "interesting harmonic progressions," from Cherubini,[18] but Cherubini, happily for himself, remained Italian, and his "interesting harmonic progressions" are invariably saturated with pure melody, which makes them more transparent and less compact; they are never introduced, except when they can be appropriately used, and they occur more frequently in the instrumental than in the vocal part, to which latter chromatic passages do not easily accommodate themselves, as his vocal music is more diatonic in style.'[19] And finally, apropos of the sacred music, and the 8-part Credo, ' a noble and effective work,' he observes: ' None of the musicians that we remember could have produced such music. . . . So even are the style and the workmanship that you cannot detect the join. He is as full of feeling as he is free from sentimentality; it is this which makes his music last. Fifty years, more or less, do not affect him; he is his own counter-balance. Formal he may be, but never dry; nay, much of the charm of modern Harmony originated with him. As an Italian, he had 2 privileges to start with; his classical form (*i.e.*, his large and regular construction), and his independent melody. The consequence is, that his full harmonics never obscure the transparency of his art. Though too intent on over-refinement in Harmony, the main division of his form is not affected; its movement is always healthy and natural.'

[18] The Introduction to *L'Hôtellerie Portugaise* overture *(supra* 74*)* had seemed to me, in 1874, ' extremely quaint and mysterious—something, too, perhaps, in the manner of Spohr;' and Hauptmann thinks ' much of his harmony has become common property—like Cherubini's.' *Letters,* tr. A. D. Coleridge.

[19] For the ' effects' learnt from Cherubini, and referred to by Hiller *(supra,* 42*)*, the signs of decadence in *Faniska* and *Ali Baba,* and for the ' absence of scenic instinct' noted by Fétis, see Hauptmann's *Letters,* Appendix iv., and Lavoix's *Histoire de l'instrumentation,* 1878.

' The sound is like the rushing of the wind—
The summer wind among the lofty pines ;
Swelling, and dying, echoing round about.' [20]

' Such was Cherubini ; a colossal and exceptional nature, an incommensurable genius, an existence full of days, of masterpieces, and of glory.'[21] The high place he holds in the history of his art is undisputed, and his admirers may justly claim for him the distinction of being the greatest contrapuntist and most learned musician of his day, while the originality, depth and pathos of his inspiration put him among the foremost composers,—and this at an epoch that looks likely to shine in the annals of an etherial art as the golden age of music.

[20] Newman.   [21] Miel.

THE END.

APPENDICES.

I.

BIRTH.

CHERUBINI gave 8 Sept. as the date of his birth in 1809 for Choron's 'Dictionnaire Historique,' and in the Biographical Notice, dictated by him to his secretary De Beauchesne in 1831; and for myself I strongly incline to think this was the correct date. Pougin tells us that 8 is the original date, which has been subsequently scratched out for 14, but not effaced, and the latter still thinks it possible that the registrar of baptism may have assumed the birth to have been the previous day; and that there must have been some ground for this earlier date, 8. Baptismal registers are not always correct as to births. Lafage thinks that 14 is a mistake, and 8 has been followed by Arnold in 1809, Rochette in 1834, Place in 1842, Adam in 1859, Clément in 1868, etc. The 1843 catalogue gives 14 according to the baptismal register and corrected Biographical Note. In 1834, Castil-Blaze invented a solution of the problem; 8 was the date of birth, 14 that of baptism! and Miel in 1842, and Denne-Baron in 1862, actually follow him here, although the latter seems to have been aware that Cherubini was not baptized till 15th.[1] Cherubini, he writes, corrected the catalogue error in some notes that he left behind him, and Nisard cannot explain to what notes

---

[1] Picchianti avers that many followed Gervasoni, a Milanese professor, who, according to Gamucci, originated the error of the 8th, corrected from the registers by the *Rivista Musicale* of Florence; and he further states that Miel's error of the 14th was corrected by himself in a note to the life appearing in the *Rivista* in April 1842, translated from a preceding March number of the *Revue et Gazétte de Paris*.

Denne-Baron alludes, but he may refer to De Beauchesne's original 1831 entry. In his 'Lexicon der Tonkünstler,' Gerber duly assigns Cherubini's birth to 1764. One consideration is presented for the date 14. If the composer were so weakly at birth that his life was despaired of, his parents might have had him baptized next day. It is as likely that they would have looked to his getting stronger and delayed baptism, as recorded at the Baptistery. To conclude, it would, in my opinion, be best for the biographer to follow Fétis, and record both dates, while favouring the earlier date, 8 Sept., which happens, also, to be the Feast-day of the Nativity B.V.M. Hence the name given to our composer, Mary, is well accounted for, and he is baptized on her 8ve day, the 15th. The following are copies of the official certificates of Cherubini's birth and baptism, for which I am indebted to Picchianti :

'Certificasi da me infrascritto ministro delle fedi di nascita che si conservano nel reggio uficio dell' Opera di Santa Maria del Fiore, della città di Firenze, come nei registri di battezzati dell' Insigne Oratorio di San Giovan Battista, della sudetta città fra gli altri nomi apparisce l'appresso Luigi Carlo Zanobi (*sic*) Salvadore Maria, del signor Bartolomeo di Marco Cherubini, e della signora Verdiana di Filippo Bosi, nato il dì quattordici settembri mille settecento sessanta, il primo minuto della mattina,' &c.

'Io infrascritto battezziere dell' insigne Basilica di San Giovan Battista di Firenze attesto essere stato battezzato a questo sacro fonte, il dì quindici settembre mille settecento sessanta, un bambino figlio del sig. Bartolomeo di Marco Cherubini, e della signora Verdiana di Filippo Bosi, del popolo di San Pier maggiore, con i nomi di Luigi Carlo Zanobi (*sic*) Salvadore Maria,' &c.

More recently Gamucci obtained the following, confirming the above :

'Opera di S. M. del Fiore, Firenze,

30 Giugno 1869.

'Fede per me Ministro nell' Uffizio dell' Opera suddetta qualmente ai Registri dei Battezzati nell' Insigne Basilica di San Giovan Battista di questa città, che si conservano in questo Uffizio : apparisce essere stato battezzato a quel fonte, il dì 15 settembre mille settecento sessanta, un bambino figlio del signor Bartolomeo di Marco Cherubini, e della signora Verdiana di Filippo Bosi, nato il dì 14 settembre detto 1760, al primo minuto della mattina, nel popolo di San Pier Maggiore, a cui sono stati imposti i nomi di Luigi Carlo Zanobi (*sic*) Salvadore Maria.

(*Bollo o secco.*)   'Il ministro, L. Bocci.

II.

LENGTH OF MASSES.

Cherubini notes how long his Mass should take, (thus the Mass in G, 37½ minutes; that in B flat, 20½); a more important point than the number of bars. A Gounod Mass may take longer than a German Mass, though it have fewer bars, and this owing to slow 'tempi' predominating, as compare the above Mass in G and the 'St. Cecilia,' taking some 52 minutes.

CHERUBINI.						
D minor, 5.	F. 4.	G. 9. A. 11. Coronation.		C. 6.	E minor 8.	B flat 10.
	Bars	Bars	Bars	Bars	Bars	Bars	Bars
Kyrie ... 437	220	101	117	133	117	67
Gloria ... 895	602	503	339	279	325	144
Credo ... 668	632	435	400	348	403	192
Sanctus ... 66	53	28	31	23	24	23
Benedictus 130	151	26	43	28	24	15
O Salutaris ——	——	50	79	64	44	80
Agnus Dei 367	371	61	92	158	78	111
Totals 2563	2029	1204	1101	1033	1015	632

BACH.	BEETHOVEN.		SCHUBERT.	HUMMEL.		
B minor.	D. 2.	C. 1.	E flat 6.	D. 3.	E flat 2.	B flat 1.
	Bars	Bars	Bars	Bars	Bars	Bars	Bars
Kyrie ... 270	225	131	164	85	133	72
Gloria ... 775	567	380	463	324	271	190
Credo ... 835	468	370	541	405	273	339
Sanctus ... 315	78	48	86	62	33	65
Benedictus 207	158	145	177	123	186	138
Agnus Dei 95	433	182	256	118	165	144
Totals 2497	1929	1256	1687	1117	1061	948

NIEDERMEYER.		HAYDN.		VER-HULST.	REIS-SIGER.	GOUNOD	PALES-TRINA.
B Minor.		B flat 1.	D. minor Imperial.	G minor.	E flat 4.	St. Cecilia.	Pope Marcellus
	Bars	Bars	Bars	Bars	Bars	Bars	Bars
Kyrie ...	119	157	160	75	48	117	77
Gloria ...	486	300	245	252	305	221	135
Credo ...	321	332	245	597	220	279	200
Sanctus ...	48	45	56	52	97	108	80
O Salutaris	37	—	—	—	—		
Benedictus	73	116	161	53	92	36	60
Agnus Dei	121	152	118	76	82	69	107
Totals	1205	1102	985	1105	844	830	659

It would seem from the above that Cherubini has written the longest Kyrie and Gloria; Bach the longest Credo, Sanctus, Benedictus; Beethoven the longest Agnus Dei. Cherubini's C and A include Offertories. Six of the above are not suitable, as they stand for Church use—Bach (B), Beethoven (D), Cherubini (D, F, G,) Schubert (E flat). The Sanctus is sometimes of due length for the short period from the Canon's opening to the Elevation, sometimes not, as Palestrina (80), Reissiger (97), and Gounod (108), etc. The latter's Benedictus (36) is a model in every way. There is little more room here for extended movements, between the Elevation and the Pater Noster, than before the Elevation. The same applies to the Agnus Dei, unless many Communions were being given, which is not now the case: consequently most of the above are too long, including Palestrina's, and are usually curtailed. Cherubini (G, E, A,) Verhulst, Reissiger, are models herein, and so would Gounod be but for the intrusion of 'Domine, non sum dignus.' Cherubini's E minor O Salutaris is perfectly placed. Palestrina sings 'Agnus Dei,' etc., twice before singing any 'miserere nobis.' Bach happily wrote 4 short Masses.

REQUIEMS.

Dvorak's fine, but unequal, work is the longest.

Jomelli's, Dvorak's, and Verdi's each include a 'Libera.' Portions of these only seem liturgical.

| | DVORAK. | BERLIOZ. | VERDI. | CHERUBINI. | | GOUNOD. (Mors et vita). | JOMELLI. | MOZART 2. |
				1.	2.			
	Bars.	Bars.	Bars.	Bars.	Bars.	Bars.	Bars.	Bars.
Introit -	127	71	77	99	106	129	32	49
Kyrie -	24	38	63	43	71	29	129	53
Gradual -	97	—	—	28	47	—	—	—
Dies Irae -	808	688	699	325	303	706	392	352
Offertory -	694	203	221	517	196	162	258	167
Sanctus -	91 ⎫	203	40 ⎫	21 ⎫	19 ⎫	57	103	38 ⎫
Benedictus	46 ⎭	—	99 ⎭	16 ⎭	23 ⎭	—	100	76 ⎭
Pie Jesu -	106	—	—	78	67	76	—	—
Agnus Dei	70	78	74	162	71	60	114	49
Communion	75	122	105	38	72	39	110	51
TOTALS	2138	1403	1378	1327	975	1258	1238	835

As to curtailment, often possible without artistic loss from 'undue repetitions,' shortening merely to shorten what is of reasonable length is not the notion, nor cutting out of all fugues, often the most ecclesiastical portions. High Mass is not a *Missa Cantata*. In an age of scurry, art, 'improved and shortened,' may descend to the dead level of some forgotten propers. The Pope's wishes are to be interpreted as favourable to true art, subject to liturgical rule.[2]

[2] *Notes of Cherubini relating to Copies of his second Requiem, etc.*

"Je, soussigné, reconnais avoir reçu la somme de *mille francs* pour le prix de cinquante exemplaires, *à vingt francs* chaque, de ma deuxième Messe de Requiem pour voix d'hommes [here follow some words scratched out].

'Paris, ce 12 Octobre, 1837, pour acquit L. CHERUBINI,

'Compositeur, membre de l'Institut, &c.

'Mon cher et ancien Ami,—J'avais été quelque temps sans vous envoyer ce que je reçois à l'Institut, comme j'avais fait jusqu' à présent, pour faire un échange des annales des voyages que vous avez eu la complaisance de m'envoyer. Or comme j'ai une bonne recolte de piece de l'Institut, je m'empresse de vous les adresser. Agréez, mon cher ami, la nouvelle assurance des sentiments d'estime et d'attachement de votre devoué.

'L. CHERUBINI.

'Paris, 10 Aug. 1836.'

III.

BERLIOZ.

In 1826 Berlioz entered the Conservatoire and found a friend in Lesueur, but, from his own account, not one in Cherubini. Berlioz has told us a good deal about his relations with Cherubini; but if he throws light on weak points in the latter's character, he does not shine as a pattern of discretion and good sense himself.[3] 'Another feather in the cap of this turbulent youngster,' writes the 'Edinburgh Review,' '. . . was his quarrel with Cherubini. . . . The anecdote here told only makes the scholar's insolence, not the master's punctiliousness, ridiculous. Berlioz rejoices in detailing the revenges with which, in after-life, he was able to commemorate this petty quarrel. But, from 1st to last, he was more willing to provoke than disarm opposition. His father, who bore his absurdities and violences with wonderful patience, was in the end disappointed, and wearied into leaving him to his own resources.'[4]

Cherubini was aware that Berlioz had not followed the usual routine at the Conservatoire before entering Lesueur's class for composition, and so made him first of all enter that of Counterpoint and Fugue under Reicha, which, in the Conservatoire studies, preceded the class of composition. Berlioz did not wait long before he had his 1st interview with the Director, and who had made a rule that the men should enter by the door in the Rue du Faubourg Poissonnière, and the women by that in the Rue Bergère, at 2 opposite extremities of the building. Berlioz entered by the door in the Rue Bergère, and, when a servant stopped him in the middle

---

[3] *Memoires,* 32, 38, 47, 60, 68, 74, 80, 86, 111, 183, 199-200, 204-5, 265; since translated 1874 by R. and E. Holmes, 1884, as the *Autobiography of Hector Berlioz,* is 40-2, 47, 68, 95-8, 111, 119-26, 156-7, 183, 204, 262, 287-8, 291, 296-7, 304.

[4] Jan. 1870, 47. Berlioz is frequently making Cherubini 'avaler des couleuvres,' swallow adders: [freely] to have vexations thrust upon you without you daring to complain, to be forced to pocket affronts.

of the court, declined to return and enter the other way. The servant, accordingly, went to tell Cherubini, on whose arrival an acrimonious dispute ended in Berlioz, who declined to give his name, being chased out of the room. Whether Cherubini remembered the incident 12 years later when, 'pleasant enough,' he received him in 'a more official manner,' Berlioz could not say. He became ultimately the librarian.

A year after this Berlioz entered Lesueur's class, and the latter 'seeing that my studies in harmony were advanced enough . . . wished to set my position right in the Conservatoire. He spoke about it to Cherubini . . . and I was admitted. Very fortunately he did not propose on this occasion to present me to the terrible author of "Médée."' However, he was received well some years later.

At the 'concours' or competitions among the pupils, which were under the direction of the Institue, on one occasion the following subject for illustration was given from Tasso: Hermione, leaving Clorinda, but disguised in the latter's dress, goes out from Jerusalem, to carry to the wounded Tancred the care and attention of her faithful but unfortunate love. Berlioz essayed this subject, and at the words,

> 'Dieu des Chrétiens toi j'ignore,
> Toi que j'outrageais autrefois,
> Aujourd'hui mon respect t'implore ;
> Daigne écouter ma faible voix,'

which were marked, to be set to music as an 'air agité,' he thought that the music should include a solemn prayer, and added one accordingly. On the day of the decision as to the successful candidates, Berlioz went down to the Institute, anxious to know what had been the fate of his composition, or, as he expresses it, 'to know whether the painters, sculptors, engravers of medals, and engravers on copper-plate, had declared me a good or bad musician.' Pingard, the porter, gives him a long narrative, the upshot of which is that discredit is thrown on a system

X

whereby others than musicians could vote on the merits of musical compositions, and intimating that votes were obtained by unworthy personal considerations animating the voters.[5] It was pointed out that the piano could not bring out a certain good effect in the instrumentation. This Cherubini made light of as an 'incomprehensible medley.' Further, Berlioz had not conformed to the programme, but written 2 airs 'agités' instead of one and added a prayer in the middle. By 2 votes Berlioz was short of getting the 1st prize, but he got 2 or 3 years later the 1st prize. Altogether his complaint is not a very serious one on the score of non-success.

Berlioz says of his own attacks on the Institute : 'The liberty I have used on this subject has led Cherubini to say that, in attacking the Academy, "I was beating my nurse." Had I not obtained the prize, he could not have taxed me with this ingratitude, but I should have passed with him and many others for an unsuccessful candidate taking vengeance for his defeat.'

As to the above instrumental effect, perhaps there was little in it. Cherubini knew best about that, and Berlioz admits that he had not followed the instructions laid down. Berlioz at another time tells us that he determined to give a concert entirely of his own compositions. There was no difficulty in procuring instrumentalists, since so many of them were his personal friends, and it was agreed on all hands that the best place for holding the concert was the chief concert-hall of the Conservatoire. The authorization of the superintendent of the Fine Arts, M. Sosthène de la Rochefoucault, Minister of the king's household, had to be obtained, and also, as a matter of courtesy, the concurrence of Cherubini. The one was obtained without difficulty, not so the other, and all sorts of difficulties were unreasonably raised, inclusive of a Sunday for the concert, etc.

[5] Castil-Blaze comments severely on the ignorance of a director of the 'Beaux-Arts,' who, addrsssing the author of *Démophon, Lodoïska, Elisa, Médée, Les Deux Journées, Anacréon, Faniska,* and *Les Abencérages,* said : 'Monsieur Cherubini, you who do so well Masses, Vespers, should you not at last try to compose an opera ?'

In 1832, Berlioz returned from Italy, having been away but 18 months.

'On arriving in Paris, one of my first visits was to Cherubini. I found him excessively aged and enfeebled.' He admits he received him with affection, but this is only the occasion for more banter.

Each year 3,000 francs were given out to the French composer who in competition should be most successful in a musical work. M. Gasparin, Minister of the Interior, secured the performance of Berlioz's Requiem, written for the obsequies of General Damremont, which was eventually executed in the church of the Hôtel des Invalides 5 Dec. 1837, and, according to Berlioz's rambling statement, every obstacle was put in the way, down to Habeneck's attempt to wreck the performance by taking a pinch of snuff while conducting, and all because it 'had been for a long time the custom, on similar occasions, to execute one of his 2 funeral Masses.' It could only be the case of the 1st in the past, as the 2nd had only been composed in 1836, the year before. But Pougin, at any rate, shows that Berlioz wrote this letter to Cherubini :—

Sir,—I am deeply touched by the noble abnegation which has led you to refuse your admirable 'Requiem' for the ceremony at the Invalides; kindly believe I am profoundly grateful. As, however, the determination of the Minister of the Interior is irrevocable, I now earnestly beg you to think no longer of me, and not to deprive the Government and your admirers of a masterpiece which would throw so much lustre on the solemnity.

I remain, with profound respect,

Your devoted servant,

H. BERLIOZ.[6]

Berlioz mentions a little later that a professorship of harmony at the Conservatoire was vacant, and one of

[6] *M. W.* 1883. 626.

Berlioz's friends managed to get him on the list of candidates for the appointment. Berlioz also wrote to Cherubini, as to what looked like an unreasonable difficulty, that the applicant must be a pianist, and Berlioz failed to get the post. 'You know how I love you,' said Cherubini, and the place was given to one Bienaimé, who played the piano no better than Berlioz, or Cherubini himself. The latter's readiness to carp is shown by Habeneck (so far from jeopardising Berlioz's success on another occasion), writing him a note on the success at Lille of his *Lacrymosa,* along with a Credo of Cherubini, and the note appeared in the *Gazette Musicale.* When Habeneck told Cherubini that his Credo had also gone well, the latter said drily, 'Yes, but you did not write to me.'

Cherubini must have been close upon his last days, if this circumstance occurred, as stated, after the previous incidents in 1837. Berlioz is not strong in chronology. His Memoirs have few dates. He relates the Requiem's execution in 1837, before his application in 1833 for the vacant post for harmony. He leads us to suppose that the post was refused because of spite, owing to the performance of his own Requiem instead of Cherubini's in 1837. But there could be no spite in 1833 about an event in 1837.

Such, in brief, is Berlioz's record of relations with Cherubini, showing faults on both sides. Berlioz, it may be added, was a very great admirer of Cherubini as a musician, none more so.

IV.

HAUPTMANN.

Hauptmann remarks of the effects learnt from Cherubini, and referred to by Hiller ('supra,' 42), that their influence over modern opera has been 'undue,' though how they are 'actual imperfections,' it is less easy to understand. 'We have enough and to spare,' he writes, ' of the romantic solos for the violoncello, of the general pause to excite expectation, and similar devices in the shape of anatomical preparation of sentiment, of harmonic progressions without any sort of ' cantilena,' etc. Only there is this difference, that in Cherubini the music never quite ceases to be musical ; as an Italian, he cannot change his skin.' Of ' Faniska,' at Leipsic, he says : ' The crystal clearness of Cherubini was a thing of the past when he wrote that opera ; it is stiff with peculiarities—to such an extent, indeed, that he has an unwholesome influence on the geniuses who imitate him.' Again: ' The libretto is irredeemably bad, . . . a palpably ridiculous effort to outbid " The Water-Carrier," and what a clumsy device is that poor puppet child.' [7] And as to 'Ali Baba' at Cassel, in 1835, 'the overture is nothing but a draped skeleton, though the drapery is rich enough,' and the opera ' remarkable.' ' I am satisfied that it is a pasticcio of both Cherubini's styles, and I am interested in watching the changes which age has brought upon him. There are numbers in which he appears at his best, and there are others almost more dry and glassy than the dry parts of " La Dame Blanche." The introduction [as with " Démophon" and " Médée"] to the 1st Act is lovely from beginning to end, but it is followed by a Romance which, though carefully and

---

[7] The reviewers, he writes, ' were very high and mighty about the *Water-Carrier* the other day, quite condescending, in fact . . . for 60 years the best judges have thought it a fine work. Down comes the *Wiener Musik-Zeitung* and says there is nothing in it, or very little, at all events. So the many hundreds of thousands who have enjoyed it hitherto . . . knew nothing about it ? Well, it does not much matter ; the opera holds its own [The Review] . . . will not prevent our enjoying what we know to be good.' He excepts this opera from a certain 'hardness' he finds elsewhere. Hauptmann admits that such music as the *Water-Carrier* is written *con amore*, its ' melo-dramatic character,' bearing, however, ' evil fruit later on in the works of other composers.' Spohr, he says, heard and liked one of the 4-tets, playing 2nd violin in it in Paris, and asked one Wiele what he thought of them, who replied, ' I found several very pretty passages in my part.' *Letters* I. 13, 52, 65, 78, 119, 134, 206 ; II., 26, 91, 126, 155, 203, 227, 258. A pause of 43 bars in the violoncello part of No. 1's slow movement is rather trying for the player.

elaborately orchestrated, is thin and poor and dry in
effect.' The 'absence of scenic instinct' is thus ably
described : ' The music [of ' Faniska '] is here and there
very beautiful, but at times mere rubbish, forcibly adapted
to the situation, but not arising out of it. We take it
quite calmly in Italian Operas. . . . Cherubini, however,
after accentuating every detail, every movement of every
character in " Faniska " leaves them all " suspendus "
on the stage, putting into the mouth of one alone an
un-naturally long solo at the expense of others, in whom
we are equally interested.'

V.

FLORENTINE CHORAL CHERUBINI SOCIETY.

Société Chorale Florentine Cherubini,
Rue Gino Capponi Num. 28,
Florence, 17 Novembre, 1877.

Monsieur,

L'œuvre remarquable que vous avez récemment
publié sur notre illustre compositeur Chérubini, la meilleure
qui a été produite de nos jours à ce sujet, ne pouvait
manquer de vous donner des droits à la reconnaissance
de tous les admirateurs de cette puissante intelligence.

C'est ainsi que la Comité dirigeant la Société Chorale
Florentine Cherubini est sûr de se rendre l'interprète des
vœux de tous ses administrés en vous nommant Membre
honoraire d'une société qui fut placée dés sa naissance
sous ce haut patronage par sa digne Fondatrice, Madame
Laussot.

En m'aquittant avec impressement, Monsieur, du
devoir de vous faire part d'une résolution qui honorera
notre Société bien plus qu'elle ne vous honore, et que

vous voudrez, j'espère, bien accueillir, avec bienveillance, je vous prie d'agréer l'expression de ma haute considération.

Le Président,

(Signed) L. CAMBRAY-DIGNY.[8]

à Edward Bellasis, Esq.

[8] I may add that in a letter of 6 Nov. 1877 Mme. Laussot wrote that she had heard from Mme. Rosellini, who promised to send some of the answers to my questions, and as to the possibilities of finding any correspondence of her father's, which she thought would be most valuable. She then hoped to see Mme. Rosellini soon, but did not think she herself had a notion of the magnitude of her father's importance to the musical world. She had several times invited her over to the Society's concerts when compositions of her father's were being done. Mme. Rosellini refers to the 1862 biography in the *Ménéstrel.*

SOME CORRIGENDA AND NOTANDA.

p. 5. de Lafage observes that Ugolini is not mentioned as a master of Cherubini ; nor was he such.

,, 43, note 18. *For* H. Jenks *read* W. S. Rockstro.

,, 48, ll. 26-7. *Erase* quotation marks.

,, 55. A treble clef should come before the chords.

,, 60. *Reference* 10 *after* Garde Nationale.

,, 61, l. 3. *Read* was sung.

,, 68, note 25. For Adam's *read* Halévy's.

,, 95. *i.e.* 'Père d'Orphee' chorus here must be *Démophon's* opening, perhaps used again, as with a scene of *Achille* in *Ali Baba.*

p. 116. I have seen no corroboration of the *M.W.'s* 1862 statement as to the 2 prizes not being given. *Re* 'La Vestale.' Spitta, in this matter of confusion, notes Jouy's assertion as to his libretto being for Spontini, and Fétis' as to its being originally for Cherubini (who returned it after a long delay), but discredits all the rest. See *Grove* 666, as cited.

p. 138. The Mass in F''s Kyrie has also a fugue.

,, 149, note 25. *Read* Music and Musicians.

,, 161, l. 7. *Erase* 2nd and.

,, 165. *Erase* [with an Iste Dies, etc.]

,, 166, note 11. The day after death seems soon, but funerals are within 24 hours. *Insert* it *after* hearing.

p. 167, note, l. 2. *Read after* 1867, 56.

,, 178. *Read* ritardando.

,, 207. *Reference* 27 *at end of 1st paragraph,*

,, 235. *i.e.* the "Vivas" outside were heard within.

,, 336. Add Kalisch and St. Ange to Editors.

A CHRONOLOGICAL CATALOGUE OF CHERUBINI'S WORKS.

1773—1841.

THIS has been compiled, in the 1st instance, from Cherubini's own Chronological Catalogue and Supplement, issued in 1843 by Bottée de Toulmon, Librarian of the Paris Conservatoire. Five pieces [noted in square brackets] have been added on the authority of Cherubini's MS. Memorandum Book; and in an Addenda such other works are given as have been ascribed to him on lesser authority, or in error. The numbering of works in the original Catalogue, following their amount and their distribution in MS. lots (the MSS. lost not being numbered), has been discarded. A cross before a work indicates such loss at the time of projected sale in 1843, or its inclusion in a prior sale made of all his music by Cherubini's father; an asterisk that a work has been published. Some 150 publishers of works and arrangements are added, and information from Clément, Pougin, etc., a contribution to the subject only. Only the chief publisher's name, where more than one is put on a work, is given.

Various firms are not now existent, or survive under new names. Thus Schonenberger became Lemoine; Diabelli became Spina, Schreiber, and Cranz successively; Choron became Canaux, Regnier-Canaux, Graff, Graff-Parvy, Parvy, Perigally-Parvy, and Heugel; and so on.

Cherubini's Italian nationality of birth, German affinities in style, and French residence as composer and teacher, seem to account for the fact that no one country has taken up the publication of his chief works in any uniform edition.

NAMES OF PUBLISHERS OF COMPOSITIONS BY CHERUBINI.

ALSBACH.
ANDRE.
ARNOLD.
ARTARIA.
ASCHERBERG.
ASHDOWN.
AUGENER.
AUGUSTIN.
BACHMANNN.
BAYLEY.
BAUER.
BELLMAN.
BENOIT.
BERRA.
BERTARELLI.
BESSEL.
BEYER.
BIRCHALL.
BLANCHI.
BOHME.
BOOSEY.
BOSWORTH.
BOTE (BOCK).
BRAINARD.
BRANDUS (DUFOUR).
BREITKOPF (HAERTEL).
BREWER.
BURNS.
CAPRA.
CARISCH.
CARY.
CHAPPELL.
CHORON.
CHOUDENS.
CHURCH.
CIANCHETTINI (SPERATI)
CLEMENTI (COLLARD).
COCKS.
COLOMBIER.
COSTALLAT.
COTTRAU.
CRAMER (BEALE).
CRANZ.
DAVIDSON.
DETERVILLE.
DIABELLI.
DIDOT.
DITSON.
DONAJOWSKI (see
          PAYNE).
DURAND.
ECK.
ELLIS.
EULENBERG.
EVETTE.

FALKNER.
FALTER.
FASANOTTII
FISCHER.
FORBERG.
FREY.
FUERSTNER.
GALLET.
GARNIER.
GAVEAUX.
GIROD.
GORDON.
GOULDING (DALMAINE
          & POTTER).
GRAFF (PARVY).
HAMMEL.
HANSEN.
HASLINGER.
HAWKES.
HECKEL.
HEINRICHSHOFEN.
HEUGEL.
HIRSCH.
HOFFMANN.
HOFFMEISTER (KUEHNEL)
HOPWOOD.
HOSICK.
IMBAULT (NADERMANN)
JENSON (KLAUWELL).
JUNNE.
KAHNT (NACHTFOLGER)
KATTO.
KISTNER.
KLEIN.
KLEMM.
KNIGHT.
LAPINE.
LATTE.
LE ROY.
LEBLANC.
LEDUC.
LEMOINE.
LEONARD.
LEUCKART.
LITTOLFF.
LONGMAN (BRODERIP).
LONGMANS (GREEN).
LONSDALE.
LOSE.
LUNDQUIST.
MARIANI.
MECHETTI.
MEYER.
MICHOW.
MILLS (LONSDALE).

MOLLO.
MONRO (& MAY).
MORI (LAVENU).
MURAILLE.
MUSTEL.
NAGEL.
NOVELLO (EWER).
PACINI.
PAEZ.
PATEY (WILLIS).
PAYNE.
PEREGALLY (PARVY).
PEROSINO.
PETERS.
PETIT.
PITMAN.
PORTHMANN.
RECLAM.
REGNIER (CANAUX).
RICHAULT.
RICORDI.
RIETER.
ROBERTSCHEK.
ROSZAVOLGYI.
RUEHLE (WENDLING)
SCHIRMER.
SCHLESINGER.
SCHONENBERGER.
SCHOTT
SCHREIBER.
SCHWEERS.
SENFF.
SHEARD.
SIEGEL.
SILVER.
SIMON.
SIMROCK.
SINE.
SONZOGNO.
SPEHR.
SPINA.
STEINER.
STEINGRAEBER.
STOLL.
THIEME.
TRAUTWEIN.
TROUPENAS.
WALKER.
WEEKES.
WEISS.
WEISSBERGER.
WHITE.
WILLIAMS.
WITZENDORF.
ZUMSTEEG.

Year.	Description of Work.	No. of pp. MS.
1773.	Mass in D, I., 4tet, acc.; Florence ·	146
	†Intermezzo for a 'theâtre de société'	—
1774.	Mass in C, II., 4tet, acc. ·	166
	†La Pubblica Felicità, cantata for sev. voices, ex. in side-chapel of Duomo for fête in honour of Peter Leopold II., Grand Duke of Tuscany	—
	†Dixit, psalm, 4tet, acc.	—
1775.	Mass in C., III., *ib.*	143
	Dixit, psalm, solo and chorus ; organ acc. ·	19

Cherubini says, 'See No. 1, year 1773.' On turning to No. 1, the Mass in D, we are referred to No. 4 (the psalm below). These cross references are numerous in the original Catalogue.

	†Il Giuocatore, intermezzo for 'theâtre de société'	—
	†Magnificat, 4tet, acc.	—
1776.	Lamentations of Jeremiah, 2 duets, acc.	—
	†Miserere, 4tet, acc.	—
	†Rondeau	—
	†Duet	—
	†Comic Air ·	—
1777.	Motet, 4tet, acc., from Mass, I	36
	†Oratorio, ex. at St. Peter's, Florence	—
	†Te Deum, 4tet, acc.	—
1778.	Montes et Colles, do., Bologna	3
	Angelus ad patrem, 5tet	2
	Venit Dominus, 6tet	2
	Lauda Jerusalem	1
	Lauda Jerusalem (treated differently)	1
	Beati omnes	1
	A viro iniquo libera me	1
	Expectabo Dominum. (This and 4 above, 4tets)	1
	Petrus Apostolus, 6tet	4
1779.	Vox clamantis, Milan	1
	Non confundetur	1
	Salva nos, Domine ·	1
	Lumen	1
	Ipse invocabit me	1
	Leva, Jerusalem	2
	Venit Dominus. (This and 6 above, 4tets)	2
	Expectabo Dominum, 5tet ·	2

Above unacc. 17 antiphons on plain chant, à la Palestrina.

1780.	†Litanies, 4tet	
	Sonata, 2 organs ; copy	17

Cherubini, throughout his Catalogue, makes a distinction between 'MS.' and 'copie,' the 1st, no doubt, meaning his own autograph MS.

Year.	Description of Work.	No. of pp. MS.
1780.	Ad cultum fidei, 4tet.	1
	Regnavit, exultet, do.	1
	Parasti, 2 choirs	3
	Above 3 unacc. antiphons from previous ones.	

†*Sonatas (6), clavichord ; printed at Florence . —
†Airs in Sartis' operas, mentd. in Cherubini's notice to
Catalogue . . . . . —
†IL QUINTO FABIO, 1st opera, 3 acts, ex. for autumn
fair, Alessandria della Paglia . . . —

	Tu quella vita in dono, air	18
	Vado a morir, ben mio, rondeau . . .	24
	Padre, deh ! resta, recit., air . . .	23

Above 3 pieces in ' Il Quinto Fabio.'

1781.	Amato padre, addio ! recit. air for lady, Milan .	42
	Se vi giunge il tristo avviso	24
	Caro consorte amato	22
	Distaccati al primo cenno	27
	Questa è causa d' onore	34
	Agitata tutta io sono	28

Above 5 airs in comic opera ex. at Milan.

†Motet, solo, acc. for Marchesi . . . —

	Nemo gaudeat, motet, 2 choirs, 2 organs ; copy .	41
	Caro padre, air in opera begun for Venice .	27
	Morte, morte fatal, recit. duet in same . .	52
1782.	ARMIDA, 2nd opera, 3 acts, ex. during carnival, Florence	456
	ADRIANO IN SIRIA, 3rd opera, 3 acts, ex. in spring for opening hall, Leghorn	400
	Saprò scordarmi ingrata, air to above for Crescentini .	29
	*Solitario bosco ombroso, Florence . . .	2
	*Compagni, amor lasciate	2
	*Il pastor se torna aprile	4
	*Io rivedrò sovente	2

Above 4 nocturns are duets, pfte. acc.

†*Nocturns (10), 6 ded. to Signor Corsi, Grand Chamberlain to Peter Leopold II. ; pfte. acc. 1786, 12pp. ;
Cianchettini & Sperati; *Longman & Broderip*;
Frey; *Novello*; It. Ger. *Peters* ; etc. Other
nocturns appear in Cat. ' Hark, the village maids,'
4-tet, from C.; words by Oliphant. *Longmans,
Green* ; (*Novello*) . . . . —

Year.	Description of Work.	No. of pp. MS.
1782.	Io che languir, solo	2
	E mentre dolcemente, solo	2
	Above 2 nocturns, pfte. acc. set to 'ottava rima' of Marino,	
	Ella dinanzi al petto, solo, set to 'ottava rima' of Tasso, solo	2
	Bella rosa porporina, canzonet, solo . . .	1
	Above 4 pieces, pfte. acc. See 1782 duets.	
	Il. MESSENZIO, 4th opera, 3 acts, ex. in autumn at Pergola, Florence, 8 Sep. . . .	540
	Duet in above opera not ex. as here . .	24
	†Duets (2) with acc. 2 'cors d'amour' for George Nassau Clavering, 3rd Earl Cowper, Florence .	—
	Non bramo il merito, air for Babbini, in pasticcio, 'Semiramide'	12
1783.	Il. QUINTO FABIO, 5th opera, 3 acts, ex. Jan. at Argentina Th., Rome	520
	Forza è pur bell' idol mio, comic tenor air, Florence .	20
	Pensate che la femmina, do.	16
	†Comic bass air	—
	Ninfa crudele, 5tet, canon, fig. bass, copy . .	24
	LO SPOSO DI TRE, MARITO DI NESSUNA, 6th opera (buffa), 2 acts; entitled, by Picchianti, 'Lo Sposo di tre Donne;' by 'Harmonicon,' 'Lo Sposo di Tre Femmine,' ex. Nov. at St. Samuel's Th., Venice .	658
1784.	Choruses (2), in oratorio from pieces in Cherubini's operas, ex. in winter at Jesuits' Church, Florence ; copy	69
	Tutto d'orror m'ingombra, tenor air, in oratorio as above, de Toulmon ; copy . . .	45
	L'IDALIDE, 7th opera, 2 acts, ex. in winter at Pergola Th., Florence	400
	L'ALESSANDRO NELL' INDIE, 8th opera, 2 acts, ex. at spring fair, Mantua	420
1785.	In questa guisa, oh Dio ! recit., duet ; London. copy	51
	Non fidi al mar che freme, air . . .	16
	Va cediamo al destin, recit. . . .	15
	Che mai feci ! finale	28
	Se tutti i mali miei, air ; copy . . .	20
	Frà cento affanni e cento, air ; copy . .	24

Above 6 pieces in pasticcio, 'Il Demetrio,' ex. 22 Jan. in London, one for Crescentini ; another sung by Mme. Ferraresi ; 2 of above in a 2nd opera, acc. to de Toulmon.

Year.	Description of Work.	No. of pp. MS.
1785.	LA FINTA PRINCIPESSA, 9th opera (buffa), 2 acts, ex. at King's Th., Haymarket . . .	528
	Chaconne ; copy	60
1786.	Al mio bene, al mio tesoro, tenor air ; copy . .	27
	Nobile al par che bella, duet ; copy . .	19
	Per salvarti, oh mio tesoro ! rondeau ; copy . .	20
	Madamina, siete bella, tenor air ; copy . .	23
	Assediato è Gibilterra, bass air ; copy . .	30
	Cosa vuole il marchesino, addn. to 1st finale ; copy .	40

Above 6 pieces in Paisiello's ' Il Marchese Tulipano,' ex. in London.

| | A tanto amore, air ; MS. in British Museum ; noted by Cherubini as lost . . . . . | — |
| | †Another air . . . . . | — |

Above 2 airs in Cimarosa's 'Giannina e Bernardone,' ex. 13 Jan., 1787, in London.

	IL GIULIO SABINO, 10th opera, 2 acts, librettist, Metastasio ; ex. at King's Th., Haymarket . .	417
	Amphion, 2nd cantata, for concert of 'Loge Olympique,' Paris, never ex. ; copy	153
1787.	†*Romanzas (18), on Florian's ' Estella,' duets, pfte. acc., 45 pp. in print ; Paris See 1782 duets . .	—
1788.	IFIGENIA IN AULIDE, 11th opera, 3 acts, ex. at carnival, Royal Th. Turin.* Air, A voi torno, sponde, amate, London, 1789 (piccolo, flute, oboe, viola, horns in A & D, trombone in D), acc. ; trio, &c. .	502
	Misera Ifigenia, recit. obblig. in above, not ex. as here	21
	Sarete alfin contenti, recit., air for, sung by Mdme. Todi at ' Loge Olympique,' Paris ; copy . .	82
	Ma che vi fece, oh stella, scena, air for Mdlle. Baletti ; de Toulmon ; copy . . .	50
	*DEMOPHON, 12th opera, 3 acts, 31 sc. librettist, Marmontel, ex. 5 Dec. full sc. Paris ; pfte. sc. Ger., Fr., *Peters* ; ov. arr. Mezger ; copy . .	770
1789.	Circe, 3rd cantata, words by J. B. Rousseau, ex. at concert of ' Loge Olympique ; ' copy . .	76
	Ti lascio, adorato mio ben, recit., rondeau . .	56
	Non sò più dove io sia, recit., air ; copy . .	41
	Capriccio, pfte. study ; copy . . .	38
	D'un alma incostante	16
	Mi stà nell' anima	11
	Vedrai nel suo bel viso . . .	35
	Piano, piano . . .	34

Year.	Description of Work.	No. of pp. MS.
1789.	Scritti addio	31
	Ah ! ho male al cuore	24
	Del caro ben che adoro	23
	Or m' accorgo dell' errore	23
	Viva amor, last finale ; copy . . .	34

2 of above airs and finale for Mme. Raffanelli, 2 for Mandini, 1 each for Mme.
Mandini, Viganoni, Scalzi, all in Paisiello's 'La Molinara,' or 'Molinarella,'
ex. by ' Bouffons ' at Tuileries Th.

	[Air for Mme. Galli in Cimarosa's 'Il Fanatico Burlato.]	
	Se del duol che il cor m' affanna, air in Guglielmi's	
	'La Pastorella nobile' ex. 12 Dec. at Tuileries	
	Th.; copy	36
1790.	'Marguerite d'Anjou,' act I. of opera begun for	
	Louis XVI. and Court at Tuileries, *i.e.* :	
	Respires-tu ? air	26
	Tout doucement, trio	31
	O reine infortunée ! air	26
	Couplets, air	3
	Non ce n'est pas, do.	32
	Princes et rois, do. · . . .	32
	Ne jugez, pas, chorus . . .	14
	Finale	51
	O Salutaris, trio, bass ; Breuilpont . .	7
	Domine Salvum, do., do. . . .	7
	Adoremus, do.. do. · . . .	5
	Regina Cœli, do., do. . . .	9
	O Filii, do., do. · . . .	7
	D'un dolce amor la face, air ; Paris · . .	29
	Che avenne ! che fu ! duet , . .	42

Above 2 pieces full sc., placed in Paisiello's or (acc. to Pougin), Salieri's 'La Grotta
di Trofonio,' ex. at Tuileries Th.

	Di valore armato il petto, air . . .	16
	Mirate ! oh Dio, mirate ! do. . . .	24

Above 2 pieces full sc., for Viganoni and Mme. Barchielli, in Guglielmi's 'Le Due
Gemelle,' ex. at Th. de la Foire St. Germain.

	Fà ch' io veda il dolce aspetto, air ; copy . .	32
	Perdonate mio signore, do., do. . . .	16

Above 2 pieces, for Mengozzi and Mlle. Nebel, in Paisiello's 'La Frascatana', ex.
at do.

	Volgi, o cara, amorosetto, air . . .	32
	Cara da voi dipende, 4tet . . .	48
	Evviva amore, finale	20

Above 3 pieces in (Anfossi, Piccinni, and Parenti's) 'I Viaggiatori Felici,
ex. at do.

Year.	Description of Work.	No. of pp. MS.
1790.	Al par dell' onda infida, air . . .	24
	Senza il caro mio tesoro, do. . . .	26
	*Lungi dal caro bene, do.; Ger.; *Mechetti*; *Cranz* .	15
	Son tre, sei, nove, trio	36
	Van girando per la testa, air . . .	42
	Ah generoso amico, recit. obblig. . . .	17

† of above 6 pieces for Mme. Mandini, 3 for Viganoni, in Cimarosa's ' Italiana in Londra,' ex. at do.

> [2 'Allegros' of airs for Mme. Baletti in Sarti's ' La Gelosie Villane' and Guglielmi's 'La Bella Pescatrice.']

1791. †*Rom. (6) 15 pp.; Paris	—
*Dors, mon enfant, rom.; Paris . . .	2
*Le portrait de Thémire, do. ; copy . . .	2
*Le veuf inconsolable, do. ; copy. See 1782 duets .	2
Moro, manco, air	30
Fuggite, o donne, amore, air	23

Above 2 pieces, for Mandini and Mme. Mandini, in Paisiello's ' Il Tamburo Notturno,' ex. at Feydeau Th.

> Choruses (3) in ' La Mort de Mirabeau,' or more correctly by Pougin : ' Mirabeau a son lit de Mort ;' words by Pujoulx, aft. in 'Lodoïska,' ex. 24 May at Feydeau Th.

> *†LODOISKA, 13th opera, 3 acts, 17 Nos.; librettist, F. Loreaux ; ex. 18 July at Feydeau Th.; full sc., *Imbault*, fol., cherubs playing harps; ov., *Breitkopf*; *Brandus* ; *Simrock* ; *Payne* ; pts. *Bellmann* ; *Leonard* ; op. pfte.sc., Fr., *Heugel* ; Ger., *Peters* ; *Reclam*; *Schlesinger*; *Haslinger*; *Hoffmeister*; op., pfte., *Diabelli* ; *Haslinger*; *Peters*; ov., pfte., solo or duet, *Breitkopf* ; *Hoffmeister* ; *Pacini* ; *Simrock* ; *Losé* ; *Artaria* ; *Nagel* ; *Peters* ; *André*; *Witzendorf*; *Arnold*; *Diabelli* ; *Bauer* ; *Cranz* ; *Furstner* ; *Leuckart* : *Litolff* ; *Rosza-volgyi*; *Schott* ; *Siegel* ; *Hirsch*; *Ricordi* ; *Weissberger* ; *Ashdown* ; *Bénoit* ; *Lemoine* ; *Capra*; pfte. double duet, *Latte*; *Klemm* ; pfte., v., *Diabelli* ; pft. duet, fl., v., 'cello, *Mills* ; 2 guitars, *André* ; 4-tet, *Peters* ; *Cranz*; 7-tet, 2 v., fl., 2-ten ; 'cello, bass or 2 celli, *Lavenu* ; 2 v., *Bénoit* ; harm., pfte., v., *Cranz* ; *Mustel* ; fl., v., cello, harm., pfte., *Lemoine* ; pfte., duet, v., 'cello, *André* . . . . , . .

Year.	Description of Work.	No. of pp. MS.
1791.	A ces traits je connais ta rage, duet in above, altered	—
	Cette indigne barbarie, air in above, not used	—
	Penso, rifletto, air in Martini's 'Il Burbero di Buoncore.'	—
	Ti rasserena oh cara, added to 6tet in Gazzaniga's 'Le Vendemmie.'	44
	Quest' è l'ora, recit. obblig., in Paisiello's 'La Pazza d'Amore,' all 3 ex. at Feydeau Th. . .	20
	[†Finale of 6-tet in Gazzaniga's 'Il Finto Cieco'] .	—
1792.	†L'Amitié, air for Mdlle. C. T. (Mme. Cherubini) .	—
	Non ti fidar, o misera, 4tet, in Gazzaniga's 'Il Don Giovanni tenorio'; ex. at do.; copy . .	64
	†Di qual rigido marmo, recit., duet (recit., air; C's MS. Mem. BK.) for Mdlle. Baletti, in Martini's 'La Cosa Rara,' ex. at do.	—
	Le Dolci sue maniere, air	38
	Ma se tu fossi amore, do.	17
	Io mi sento un non sò che, do. . . .	18
	Il core col pensiero, trio	47
	Compassione ad una donna, duet . . .	26
	Above 5 pieces in Salieri's 'La Locandiera.'	

[Air in Cimarosa's 'Giannina e Bernardone' for Mme. Morichelli.]

1793.	*La Libertà (13) canzonets, Metastasio; duets for Mme. Ethis; Chartreuse de Gaillon, Paris; *Birchall*; *Clementi*, etc. . . . . . } *La Palinodia a Nice (13) do., do., duets for do. }	114
	Trios (2), v. and pfte., acc. for fête of M. Louis, architect	8
	Berenice che fai, recit. air for Mme. Ethis; copy .	78
	L'Exil, rom. for same; copy, pfte. acc. . .	2
	KOURKOURGI, 14th opera, 3 acts, without ov., and part of last finale; librettist, Duveyrier-Mélesville, elder	497
	*Hymne à la Fraternité, sung in Tuileries gardens 1st Ven., An II (22 Sep.), and at Gr. Op. (Castil-Blaze); Paris; (rare) and also 'Musique des Fêtes et Cérémonies de la Révolution,' etc., 1899. Cherubini mentions this and 7 other Republican pieces in Cat. section 1795, saying he cannot recall their dates, but that they were written between then and 1798. Clément dates them from 1793; *Siné*; copy .	13
1794.	*Le Salpêtre Republicain, chorus, sung Pluv. [An II. (Jan.), at fête for opening saltpetre works; Pierre, *Au Mag. de Mus., etc.* Paris; ed. 1899, copy .	3
	Clytemnestre, 4th cantata, solo, for Mme. B. of Havre.	31
	Rom. in 'Selico,' opera begun . . .	30

Year.	Description of Work.	No. of pp. MS.

1794. *Elisa, ou le Voyage aux Glaciers du Mont St. Bernard, 15th opera, or ' Elisa, ou le Metz,' ' Elisa, ou le Mont St. Bernard,' 2 acts, 13 nos. ; librettist, R. St. Cyr, ex. 13 Dec. at Feydeau Th. ; full sc. 2 vols. *Le Roy*: ov. *Breitkopf* ; op. pfte. sc. Fr. Ger. *Breitkopf*; *Berra*; Ger. *Reclam*; Fr. *Heugel*; *Hoffmann* ; *Litolff* ; *Capra* ; *Ricordi* ; ov. pfte. solo or duet, *Breitkopf* ; *Hoffmeister*; *Peters*; *Nagel*; *Bohme*; *Cranz* ; *Leuckart* ; *Ricordi* ; intr. *Lemoine* ; pfte. double duet, *Klemm* ; *Latte* ; ov. 4tet. *Breitkopf* ; *Diabelli* ; ov. 7tet, 2 v., fl., 2 ten., 'cello, bass or 2 'celli, *Mori* ; air, *Bellmann* 520

1795. †*Hymne du Panthéon, chorus; 45 pp., Paris; and ed. 1899 —

*Chant pour le Dix Août (1792 anniv.), chorus ; words by Lebrun, of Institute. Paris ; clarinets, horns, bassoons, acc., and ed. 1899 ; copy . . 13

*Solfeges (65) for all keys, for 1 to 4 voices, begun this year, and continued up to editing of complete work in 2 parts of Conservatoire solfeges (fol.) issued, An VIII., IX. (1799, 1802), as ' Principes élémentaires de Musique,' etc. 4 to fig. basses (262 pp. MS.). Solfeges for different voices, fig. bass (35 pp. MS.) appear in Cat. under 1805, & continue from 1820 to 1841 (114 pp. M.S.), in autograph or copies, for the Jan., May, June, July, Nov., Dec. vocal & instrumental competitions, 38 are given by de Toulmon. See 7th & 8th books of Conservatoire Solfeges ; ' Méthodes de Chant,' etc. with 67 solfeges (1822-41) by Cherubini ; *Mustel*; *Heugel*, 1865. Solfeggien Paris Conserv, etc. Ger., Fr. ed. *Paez ; Schlesinger ; Jensen*, ed. 1896. Precise dates given, *Memorials* 1874 . 411

1796. Fragment of Cantata for Apollo statue in concert hall . 25

1797. *†Médée, 16th opera, 3 acts, 14 nos., librettist F. B. Hoffmann, ded. to Méhul, ex. 13 Mar. at Feydeau Th., full sc., 1 vol. fol. 300 pp. Paris, with alterations in author's hand, in Brit. Mus.; ov. *Breitkopf*, *Hoffmeister*; *Peters*; *Simrock*; *Payne*; op. pfte. sc. *Breitkopf* ; Ger. Lachner's recits., 2 versions of duet, end Act 1. Fr.,Ger.,*Peters* ; Ger. *Reclam* ; 4tet, *Witzendorf* ; pfte. duet, *Haslinger* ; pt. op. *Junne* ; *André* ; *Hammel* ; *Schott* ; *Mustel* ; *Breitkopf* ; pt. op., pfte. duet. *Diabelli* ; ib. pfte.

Year.	Description of Work.	No. of pp. MS.
1797.	*Simrock* ; *Witzendorf* ; Vous voyez, *Lemoine* ; ov., 4 airs, *Breitkopf* ; ov. & intr. Mass in F, Kyrie, 7tet, 2 v., fl., 2 ten., 'cello, bass, or 2 'celli, *Mori* ; ov. 4tet, *Witzendorf* ; *Cranz* ; *Diabelli* ; *Artaria* ; ov. pfte. double duet, *Latte* ; *Klemm* ; 5-tet, 2 v., 2 ten., 'cello, *Breitkopf* ; pfte. solo or duet, *Diabelli* ; *Peters* ; *Hoffmeister* ; *André* ; *Arnold* ; *Berra* ; *Diabelli* ; *Heckel* ; *Hansen* ; *Siegel* ; *Litolff* ; *Simrock* ; *Capra* ; *Ricordi* ; *Fürstner* ; *Leuckart* ; *Losé* ; *Witzendorf* ; mch. impr. pfte. *Breitkopf* ; *Augener* ; It. Eng. lib. *Davidson* ; recits. Arditi	—
	*Ode, 18th Fruct. (4 Sep.) conspiracy of poignards, sung at Gr. Op. (Castil-Blaze), Paris, and ed. 1899; copy	54
	*Hymne et Marche funèbre pour la mort du Général Hoche, words by M. J. Chénier, ex. 10th Ven. An VI. (1 Oct.) at State fun.; & 11 Oct. at Gr. Op. as 1-Act. piece. Pompe funèbre du Gén. H. ; *Haslinger* ; *Schott* ; *Heugel* ; ed. 1899 ; Trauer-Marsch, *Berra* ; *Breitkopf* ; Fun. mch. *Augener* ; org., *Patey* ; pfte.	55
1798.	Viens voir sur l'écorce légère	2
	Blessé par noire perfidie . . . ,	2
	Une chanson pour une fête	2
	Voyez cette naissante rose	2
	Above 4 rom. pfte. acc. See 1782.	
	*Collection of 39 fig. basses . . .	73
	*Hymn for Fête de la Jeunesse, 10th Ger. An VI (30 Mar.) words by Parny ; Paris ; and ed. 1899 ; copy .	6
	*Hymn for Fête de la Reconnaissance, 10th Prair., An VI. (29 May) words by Mahérault ; Paris ; copy .	7
	*L'HOTELLERIE PORTUGAISE, 17th opera, 1 act, librettist, St. Aignan ; ex. 25 July at Feydeau Th., full sc., ov. *Breitkopf* ; *Ricordi* ; *Costallat* ; op. pfte. sc. pt., *Senff* ; Ger., Treitschke : *Breitkopf* ; ov. pfte. solo or duet, *Breitkopf* ; *Hoffmann* ; *Litolff* ; *Costallat* ; *Lepine* ; *Ricordi* ; *Peters* ; *Leuckart* ; *Cranz* ; *Peters* ; ov. string 4tet, *Diabelli* ; *André* ; ov. 7tet, 2 v., fl., 2 ten., 'cello, bass, or 2 'celli, *Lavenu* ; trio, Que faire, *Girod* ; pfte. double duet, *Latte* ; *Ricordi* ; *Costallat*, 2 fl. ib. .	334
1799.	LA PUNITION, 18th opera, 1 act, librettist, Desfaucherets ; air, *Lemoine* ; ex. 23 Feb. at Feydeau Th., *ov., Paris	374

Year.	Description of Work.	No. of pp. MS.

1799. La Prisonnière, or Emma, opera, 1 act, by Cherubini
and Boieldieu ; librettists, Jouy, Longchamps &
St. Just ; ex. 12 Sep. at Montansier Th. ; ov. by
C., *Simrock ;* ov. pfte. *Breitkopf : Witzendorf* ;
Ashdown ; duet, 2 v. (or v., bass), *Cranz* ;
Paez ; ov. 7tet, 2 v., fl., 2 ten., 'cello, bass, or
2 'celli, *Lavenu* ; pfte. v. 'cello   .   .   56
†*Odes (2) solo, set to Greek, of Anacreon ; *Didot*   —

1800. *Les Deux Journées, 19th opera, 3 acts, 14 nos. : in
England, ' Water-Carrier ' ; in Germany, Wasser-
träger,' or ' Graf aus Armand,' ' Die beiden
Gefahrvollen Tage,' ' Die Tage der Gefahr ' ; in
Italy, ' Il Portator d'acqua,' ' Le Due Giornate ;
librettist, J. N. Bouilly ; ded. to Gossec ; ex. 26 Niv. An
VIII (16 Jan.), at Feydeau Th., full sc., frontispiece
(Armand about to get in water-cart, soldier look-
ing away), 1 vol., fol. ; *Gaveaux* frères ; Fr. Ger.,
Peters ; ov. *Breitkopf* ; *Peters* ; *Payne* ; *André* ;
Bellmann ; and parts *Cranz* ; op. pfte. sc., Ger.
Breitkopf ; *Simrock* ; *André* ; *Artaria* ; *Bote* ;
Litolff ; *Heugel* ; *Peters* ; *Reclam* ; Eng., Fr.,
Ger., *Boosey* ; It. *Sonzogno* ; Fr., *Schlesinger* ;
op., pt. op., arr. v., ten. 'cello, fl., (4,-5-tet), cornet,
guitar, harm., pfte., *Bachmann ;   Artaria ;
Eck ; Cranz* ; *Diabelli ; Simrock ; Steiner ;
André* ; *Ricordi* ; *Forberg* ; *Schott* ; *Lemoine* ;
Steingräber ; *Simon* ; *Eulenberg* ; *Schweers* ;
Klein ; *Schlegel* ; *Haslinger* ; *Weiss* ; *Novello* ;
Mustel ; *Augener* ; *Peters* ; *Paez* ; *Diabelli* ;
Ashdown ; *Hoffmeister* ; *Breitkopf* ; *Heugel* ;
Cranz ; *Artaria* ; *Bohme* ; *Witzendorf* ; *Fischer* ;
Evette ; (Am. Org.), *Brewer* ; Fr., Ger., *Bote* ;
Ger. *Hansen* ; (Mus. Lib. 1. 96), *Knight* ; op.
pfte. duet, *Hoffmeister* ; *Peters* ; ov., 5tet, 2
v., 2 ten., 'cello, *André* ; *Weiss* ; *Breitkopf* ; 5tet,
fl., 2 v., alt. 'cello, *Bohme* ; str. 4tet, *Witzendorf* ;
4tet, fl., v., ten., 'cello, *André* ; 2 v. (fl.), *Paez* ;
Cranz ; *Artaria* ; 2 v., fl., ten., 'cello, bass,
Lavenu ; pfte. double duet, *Haslinger* ; *Klemm* ;
Simrock ; pfte. solo or duet, *Breitkopf* ; *Peters* ;
Mustel ; *Bauer* ; *Haslinger* ; *Hirsch* ; *Hoff-
mann* ; *Litolff* ; *Michow* ; *Rozsavolgyi* ; *Ruhle* ;
Schott ; *Cocks* ; *Leuckart* ; *Ashdown* ; *André* ;
Arnold ; *Artaria* ; *Augener* ; *Berra* ; *Cranz* ;
Diabelli ; *Eck* ; *Heckel* ; *Meyer* ; *Nagel* ;

Year.	Description of Work.	No. of pp. MS.
1800.	*Peters* ; *Simrock* ; *Witzendorf* ; *Hoffmeister* ; lib. *Bote* ; *Brietkopf* ; Eng. Carl Rosa progr. version. The dialogue in French Opéra Comique is put to recitative if a work be given as Italian Opera in Italian. Thus when ' Le Due Giornate ' was executed at Covent Garden, London, in 1872. Sir Michael Costa put the dialogue to recitative of his own. Separate portions have been set to other words, i.e., ' Tardar non ponno,' (Mikeli's air), ' Sweet are the banks,' etc. See Vienna and other General Catalogues for preciser details as to instrumental arrangements, of a varied kind, from this, the most perfect example of the composer's operatic style, and a classic work despite the libretto's inferior literary style	471
	Epicure, opera, 3 acts, by Méhul & Cherubini ; librettist, Demoustier ; ov., pt. 1st, 3rd acts by C., ov. 7tet, 2 v., fl., ten., 'cello, bass, or 2 'celli, *Lavenu* ; pfte. double duet, *Latte* ; *Cranz* ; *Klemm*	305
	Marche du préfet d'Eure-et-Loire Chartres : Marche pour le retour du préfet après sa tournée dans le departement ; see Republican Hymns ; Paris .	9
1801.	Morceau d'ensemble, act 2 of ' Deux Journées ' ; copy .	
	*Solitario bosco, (2 pt., nocturns, *Ditson* ; *Lundquist* ; tr. Gillington, *Williams* : pfte., or harp acc., see 1782)	2
	*L'Echo, rom., pfte.	2
	*Un Jour échappé de Cythère, do. . . .	1
	*Tu les brisas, ces nœuds charmants, do. . .	1
	*La cintura d'Armida, nocturn, from Tasso's ' Jerusalem Delivered,' do. ' ottava rima,' Paris ; Ger. *Peters* ; etc.	2
	Above pieces placed in Nos. of Fr. mus. journal successively.	
1802.	Duet and chorus of un-named, unfin. comic opera .	33
1803.	*ANACREON, ou L'AMOUR FUGITIF, 20th opera (ballet) 2 acts, 12 sc. ; librettists, Mendouze, St. Aignan ; ex. 4 Oct. at Gr. Op., and styled by Fétis, ' Anacréon chez lui ;' by Picchianti, ' Anacreonte in sua Casa ;' full sc.; 1 or 2 vols., fol., *Garnier;* ov. *Breitkopf* ; *Ricordi* ; *Peters* ; *Simrock* ; *Payne* ; op. pfte. sc., *Breitkopf* ; *Reclam* ; *Peters* ; *Litolff* ; pt. op. Eng., Ger., Fr., It., guitar acc., *Diabelli* ; *Schott* ;	

Year.	Description of Work.	No. of pp. MS.

1803. *Cramer; Augener;* 2 airs, *Costallat;* 3 *Breit-kopf;* 2 *Schonenberger*; ov. 7tet, 2 v., fl., 2 ten., 'cello, bass or 2 'celli, *Lavenu* (fl.,) 5-tet, *Bachmann*; str. 4tet., *Diabelli*; fl., v., and 'cello, *Cramer*; fl., v., harp, *Goulding*; pfte., harp or v., *Artaria*; pfte., double duet, *Latte*; *Breitkopf; Simrock; ib.* 4tet, *Schmidt; Siegel*; pfte. solo or duet, *Breitkopf; Cranz; Leuckart*; *Siegel; Simrock; Ashdown; Hirsch; Ricordi; Costallat; Ascherberg; Litolff; Hoffmann; Sheard; Ricordi; Hoffmeister; André; Berra; Nagel; Peters; Witzendorf; Walker;* ballet, duet, *Breitkopf; Peters;* pfte., fl., 'cello, pfte., v. or fl., 'cello; harp, fl., 'cello, or viola; harp or pfte., fl., 'cello, pfte., str., arr., *Schmidt;* fl., pfte., *Simrock;* 2 v., *Leonard;* 2 fl., *ib; Ashdown;* pfte., fl., v., *Simrock;* ballet, *Breitkopf,* etc.   .   607

Fragment of above not used   36

1804. Air, couplets treated 2 ways, unfin. opera, ' Les Arrets,' librettist, Bouilly   13

Sonatas (2) or studies, ' cor.,' pfte. acc.   .   16

*Achille à Scyros, pantomimic ballet, 3-4ths by Cherubini; librettist, Gardel younger; ex. 18 Dec. at Gr. Op., pfte., arr. by C., *Hoffmeister; Peters*   383

1805. *Chant sur la mort d'Haydn, Trauergelang, etc., 3 part, sop. & 2 ten.; ded. to Prince N. Esterhazy, orig. to words in honour of Haydn (Denne-Baron), or, on report of Haydn's death (Pougin), ex. in winter 1810 at Conservatoire exercises; *au Mag. de Mus.* Paris; *Frey*; pfte. sc. Fr., Ger. *Kühnel*; It., Eng., *Cianchettini; Peters; Schott;* & v , *Schlesinger,* etc.   .   .   .   63

Entr'actes (2) for ' Lodoïska,' Vienna .   .   .   18

Air for Mme. Campi to same   .   .   34

March wind instr., for Baron de Braun; copy .   .   14

Sonata for cylinder organ of do.; copy   .   .   8

1806. *FANISKA, 21st opera, 3 acts, 21 nos. librettist, Sonn-leithner, ex. 25 Feb.; at Imperial (Kärnthnerthor) Th.; Vienna, 1 vol., fol. full sc. *Troupenas*; ov. *Breitkopf; Peters; Payne*; pfte. sc. It. *Troupenas; Peters; Andre; Artaria*; It., Ger. *Haslinger*; abridged, op., 4tet. *Breitkopf; Cranz;* It., Ger. *Breitkopf; Bachmann; Reclam;* pt. op. pfte., 2 fl., *Steiner;* ballet air,

Year.	Description of Work.	No. of pp. MS.
1806.	*Losé*; Tanze; *Spehr;* pol. *Diabelli;* ov., 3 mches, pfte. duets, *ib. Cramer;* mch., *Artaria; Augener;* 3 mches., *Falter* ; ov., 7-tet, 2 v., fl., ten., 'cello, bass or 2 'celli, *Mori;* str., 4-tet, *Diabelli;* pfte. double duet, *Fasanotti; Bachmann; Costallat; Ricordi;* pfte., harm., *Bote; Mustel;* harm., pfte.., *Novello;* pfte. solo or duet, *Fürstner; Leuckart; Siegel; Breitkopf; Hoffmeister; André; Arnold; Artaria; Cranz; Diabelli; Heckel; Nagel; Peters; Witzendorf; Capra; Ricordi; Simrock*, etc.	462
	†*Credo (8-part) unacc., fin. in Paris, begun in Italy 1778 or 1779 ; fugue in 'Treatise on Counterpoint & Fugue' as *ricerca* ; rest not pub. in C.'s lifetime, pfte. acc. ad libitum, *Peters* ; Lo stretto della Fuga, *Novello* -	—
	Air to Echo for cylinder organ, Panharmonicon, 4tet acc.	6
	Credimi si mio sole, recit., air for Crescentini, 4tet. .	10
1807.	Chorus, melodrama for unfin. opera. . .	12
	*Canons, 2, 3, 4 part, 1779-1807. Cherubini does not date them prior to 1811. MS. of 63 in Berlin Lib.: 1, 8-part ; 4, 4-part ; 12, 2-part ; 3 mixed. 3 in MS. 'fac-simile,' 'Gazette Musicale de Paris,' 9 March, 1834, with remarks by Halévy. 10, It. Eng., words by Gianni, Crotch, and D.L., ded. to Duke of Sussex, pfte. acc. *Cianchettini; Cramer;* 10 in 1821, *Clementi;* 12, *Frey;* 12, It., Ger. ; 24, *Schott;* 12, *Schirmer;* 12, *Lemoine;* Perfida Clori (Go, faithless Clori), *Novello;* Non mi negate, or Dolce ne guai ristoro (Faniska), Fior di Aprile, etc., Absence is over (Perfida), etc. Perfida Clori, set to God save Victoria, by Bartholomew ; Lo! morn is breaking, *Chappell;* Borne on the night, *Ashdown; Fischer; Silver; White: Leonard;* org.; Am. Org., *Brewer* . .	76
1808.	Le Mystère, rom. by Bernard, 17 June, for Count Metternich	2
	†March for wind instr., 8 Oct. . . .	—
	†Country Dances (6)	—
	†Minuet	—
	†Dance air	—
	†Rom. (2)	—

Above 11 pieces composed at Chimay Castle.

Year.	Description of Work.	No. of pp. MS.

1808. †*Mass in F, IV, 3-part, Kyrie, Gloria at Chimay, begun
23 Nov., fin. in Paris, 1809 ; ex. Mar., 1809, at
Hôtel de Babylon, Paris ; full sc. *Frey; Heugel;* 1
vol. *chez l'auteur; au Conserv.* pfte. sc. *Peters;
Heugel; Hoffmeister;* Incarnatus & Benedictus,
Birchall; Lonsdale; Benedictus (as Benedicta tu
inter mulieres), *Canaux;* Incarnatus, as motet, Ad te
levavi, *Novello; Cary; Cocks; Falkner.* The
numbering of the Masses has been incorrect.   Even
if the 1st 3 Masses, written in 1773 and 1774, be
left out, the Mass in A is not No. 3, nor the Mass
in C No. 4.   Various other Masses, too, are omitted.
Gauntlett calls the D minor No. 4 ; and if the
E flat (de Toulmon) be omitted, the E minor becomes
No. 7.   The D is the 4th 4-part Mass   .   .

1809.   March for wind instr. ; 12 July ; Chimay   .   .   17
La Rose, rom. ; 12 July, do.   .   .   .   2
Rom. ; 16 July, do.   2
Country dances (3) ; 21, 23 Sep., 1 Oct., do.   .   6
Pimmalione, 22nd opera, 1 act, ex. 20 Nov. before
Napoleon I. & Empress, at Château des Tuileries
Th., Paris   424

1810·   Fantasia, org. or pfte., Jan.; *Augener; Richault;
Ricordi*   4
Ode for Napoleon's Marriage, May ; copy   .   .   24
*Litany of Our Lady, 4tet, instr. acc. July, for
Prince N. Esterhazy; (16 min.) pfte. sc., *Richault*;
Ricordi   47
Le Crescendo, 23rd opera, in 1 act ; librettist, Sewrin,
ex. 1 Sep. at Op. Com. ; ov. ; air, *Costallat*; copy   57
March for wind instr., 22 Sep. ; Chimay   .   .   2
Dance air, 24 Sep. ; do.   .   .   .   4
Country dances (2), 6, 13 Oct. do., ms. & copy   .   4
Trios (2) for fête, 9, 12 Oct. do.   .   .   .   27

1811.   Rom. of M. de Nivernois, 6 Mar., Paris   .   .   2
Stanzas for Isabey's album   .   .   .   2
Rom. on a child, by Mme. de Genlis, for her album,
14 May ; copy   4
See Rom. 1808.
Fragment of Cantata for opening New Conservatoire
Concert-hall ; fin. 27 May   .   .   .   60
Le Mystère, rom., for M. Guérin's album, 12 June ;
see 1808   2
*Mass in D Minor, V, begun end of Mar., fin. 7 Oct.
full sc., *Chez l'auteur*, etc. (*Richault*) ; *Heugel*;

Year.	Description of Work.	No. of pp. MS.
1811.	1 vol. fol., *Frey*; pfte. sc., *Peters*; *Simrock*; *Novello*; Amen, Credo, org., *Novello*; No. 2 of Series from C.'s works, *Cramer*; 'Cum Sancto,' fugue, pfte., *Augener*; *Leonard*; *Williams*; *Pitman*	263
	Madrigal, 4tet, Nov., fig. bass . .	27
	Canon, 8-part, for Neukomm's album, de Toulmon .	2
1812.	'Pour la Goulette,' Cantata (5); ex. 15 Dec. at reunion; 4tet	55
1813.	*Les Abencerages, ou L'Etendard de Grenade, 24th opera, ballet ; 3 acts ; librettist, Jouy ; ex. 6 Ap., at Gr. Op. Begun end Jan. 1812 ; full sc. Ov. *Breitkopf*; *Peters*; *Payne*; op., pfte. sc., *Peters*; *Reclam*; ov., pfte., v., 'cello, *Paez*; pfte. double duet, *Schmidt*; *Simrock;* solo or duet, *Breitkopf;* *Schlesinger;* *Peters;* *Hoffmeister;* *Siegel;* *Simrock;* *Ricordi;* *Bote;* pt. op., *Siegel;* *Simon;* *Girod;* *Heinrichshofen;* *Lemoine;* Balletstücke ; *Trautwein;* MS. Spontini & Brissler, Berlin Royal Lib. 25 nos. . . .	357
	La Ressemblance. rom., for Mme. Louis, 9 May ; pfte. acc.	2
1814.	March for National Guard music, 8 Feb. . .	4
	*†Trio, 'morceau d'ensemble,' 'chant guerrier,' in 'Bayard à Mezières,' comic opera, 1 act, by Cherubini, Catel, Boieldieu, and Nicolo Isouard ; librettists, Dupaty & Chazot, ordered through Duke of Rovigo by Govt. ; C. says, 'by the police.' ex. 12 Feb. at Feydeau Th.; C.'s work printed .	
	Pas redoublé for National Guard music, 13 Feb. .	4
	'Chant guerrier,' air, couplets, in 3-act opera 'La Rançon de Duguesclin, or Les Mœurs du Quatorziéme Siècle,' librettist, Arnault; ex. Mar. or Ap, at Th. Fr.	6
	Pieces (8) for wind instr., for Prussian Regt., under Col. Witzleben, pas redoublé, 24 May ; do., 27 May ; do., 28 May ; do., do., 30 May ; do., 2 Mches, 31 May	16
	Cantata (6) 3-part, 20 July, for fête by Etat Major and Superior Officers of Paris garrison, to National & Body Guards of Louis XVIII. . . .	42
	Cantata (7) sev. voices, with choruses, ex. 29 Aug. before Louis XVIII. during fête by City of Paris .	81

Year.	Description of Work.	No. of pp. MS.

1814. *String 4tet, in E flat 1; ded. to Baillot, sc. *Payne*;
Kistner; Peters; pfte. duet, *Kistner; Peters*;
scherzo, trio, v., pfte., *Schott* ; *Eulenberg*;
Costallat ; *Ricordi* ; pfte. v. *ib.* 'cello ; *ib.* solo ;
ib. duet, *Leuckart* ; pfte. *Rieter* . . 28

1815. *Overture in G, for Philharm. Soc., begun Feb. in Paris,
fin. Mar. in London ; ex. 3 Ap. ; full sc. ed.
Kahnt (not same in few details as Society's work.
Progr. Crystal Pal. Concerts; Grove); duet pfte. *ib.* 39

Symphony in D for same, begun Mar. fin. 24 Ap., ex. 1
May (see Society's progr., 16 Mar. 1870, etc.) . 102

Cantata (8), Inno alla Primavera, Die Frühling, Le
Printemps ; words by Vestri; 4tet for same, begun 8,
fin. 19 May, ex. 1816; Ger., It.; pft. sc.,
pfte duet, *Kistner* ; Fr., It., *Petit* ; *Bayley* . 32

English air for Mme. Chinnery, end May, London . 2

Chorus & couplets, St. Louis' day, Aug. Paris . . 35

Vive le Roi! air, couplets, Aug. ; pfte. . . 2

One of above, transl. Ger. (Girod).

1816. Cantata (9) sev. voices, chorus for banquet by Royal
Guard to National and Body Guards in Museum
Gallery, ex. in presence of Louis XVIII. and Royal
family. Begun 29, fin. 30 Jan. . . . 62

*Mass in C, VI; 4-5-6tet, and chorus, begun Jan.
fin. 14 Mar. ; and Off. Laudate Dominum,
full sc. *Chez l'Auteur (Richault)* ; *Heugel* ;
Frey ; pts. *Schlesinger;* O Salutaris, *Novello* ;
Diabelli ; *Peregally* ; Laudate, *Diabelli* ;
Schlesinger ; *Schirmer; Novello* ; *Haslinger* ;
pfte. sc. *Haslinger* ; *Diabelli* ; *Peters* ;
Kyrie, Credo, Agnus, abr. *Burns*; pfte. duet,
Novello ; *Diabelli* ; pfte. solo *Diabelli* ; O
Salutaris, after the Elevation, is set to 1st quatrain
only, the Sanctus including ' Benedictus ' and 2
' Hosannas ' ; Credo, org., *Novello* . . 65

*Short Kyries (3) Paris 38

†Laudate, recit. chorus . . . —

†Short Sanctus . . . . —

*O Salutaris, for mezzo sop. solo; 5tet, v., ten, 'celli,
bassi, ex. by Malibran at Birm. Fest., *Petit* ;
Colombier ; pfte. sc., *Novello*; *Ashdown* ; set
as, Deus, ego amo Te, *Schott* ; *Diabelli* ; Rossini
introduces it into his ' Messe Solennelle ' . 3

Year.	Description of Work.	No. of pp. MS.
1816.	Kyries (2) duet, in chorus and 4tet, short . .	3
	†Kyrie, trio (Gloria, same as Mass in F, 4); de Toulmon	—
	Kyrie 4tet (Gloria, same as Mass in D minor, 5); de Toulmon	44
	Kyrie, 4tet (Credo, same as Mass in D, 5); de Toulmon. The Credo, Cherubini says, was published in 4th ' Messe Solonnelle' (*sic*) for 4 voices; and de Toulmon, following a misleading enumeration, means the Mass in D. The term ' messe solennelle' is used so indifferently by C. (for he thus speaks of the Mass in D minor but once) that it has been here discarded. The ' Missa Solemnis,' or High Mass, is such as, on account of fulness of ceremonial with music, is appropriate to the more solemn festivals, the celebrant being assisted by deacon and sub-deacon	36
	Kyrie, 4tet (Agnus Dei, same as Mass in D minor 5); i.e. ' deuxième messe à 4 voix,' de Toulmon .	19
	(MASS IN E FLAT, VII.; de Toulmon; Gloria, see that in B flat below; not named by Cherubini) .	62
	*Kyrie in C, trio 2 ten., bass; pfte. sc. *Ricordi* .	3
	Crux Alma, hymn, trio 2 sop., ten., arr. from air in ' Faniska;' de Toulmon . . .	7
	*Pater Noster, 4tet, chorus, full sc. org. or pfte. acc., *Petit*; *Diabelli*; *Regnier*; *Alsbach*; *Peregally*; pfte. sc. *Schott*; arr. org., arr. harm. *Novello*; *Leduc*	9
	*O Salutaris in C, trio, 2 sop., contra.; pfte. sc. *Ricordi*.	3
	*Ecce Panis, tenor solo; full sc. *Petit*; *Diabelli*; *Canaux*; *Cranz*; pfte. sc. *Novello*, in 3 keys; *Peregally*; *Durand*; Eng., Lat.; *Augener* .	8
	*Ave Maria, sop., full sc., with clar. or ' cor Anglais;' *Petit*; *Canaux*; *Diabelli*; *Novello*; pfte. sc., & other arr. *Parvy*; Lat., Ger., *Bote*; *André*; *Spina*; *Schlesinger*; *Diabelli*; *Schott*; *Goulding*; *Boosey*; *Chappell*; *Cramer*; *Novello*; Eng., Lat., *Augener*; It. *Ricordi*; *Forberg*; *Hansen*; *Haslinger*; *Ashdown*; *Brainard*; *Fischer*; *Gordon*; *White*; *Durand*; *Leduc*; *Blanchi*; *Cottrau*; *Thieme*; *Bessel*; *Hösick*; *Augustin*; *Cranz*; *Forberg*; *Costallat*; *Perigally*; *Bosworth*; *Hawkes*; *Evette*; *Leonard*; *Williams*; *Simon*; *Mustel*; *Rühle* *Bellman*; *Ditson*; *Hopwood*. . .	4

Year.	Description of Work.	No. of pp. MS.

1816. *Lauda Sion, 4 verses, 2 sop., *Petit*; *Regnier-Canaux* ;
Diabelli ; *Schott* ; pfte. sc. *Schott* ; *Novello*,
etc., org. arr. *Brewer* ; (Am. Org.) Above 20
pieces, omitting Crux Alma, for King's Chapel . 11

Le Mariage de Salamon, cantata, (10), solo, chorus,
words by Dureau de la Malle, ex. 17 June at Tuileries royal banquet after marriage of Duc de Berri . 38

†Gloria in B flat, 4tet . . . . —

Credo in D., 4tet 36

†*Requiem in C minor, I, 4-part chorus, written for
anniv. Louis XVI.'s death, ex. 21 Jan., 1817, at
Abbey of St. Denis ; full sc. 1 vol. fol., *chez l'auteur
et chez Boïeldieu,* Paris ; *Frey* ; *Brietkopf* ;
Peters ; with org., *Simrock* ; pts. *Schermer* ;
pfte. sc. *Simrock* ; *Church* ; *Brietkopf* ; *Peters* ;
Lat., Eng. *Novello* ; pfte., harmonium arr.,
Bote ; *Mustel* ; duet, *Brietkopf* ; *Ricordi* ;
Pie Jesu, org., *Gordon* ; *Augener* ; req. off.,
Simon 81

†*Ave Verum, trio 3 sop., O Sacrum Convivium, chorus,
acc., full sc. *Petit* ; *Colombier* ; pfte. sc. horn,
Schott ; *Novello* ; *Gallet* ; *Muraille* . . —

1817. *Iste Dies, 4tet, fragment for above to make motet of
usual length (½ hour) for Low Mass, full sc. *Petit* ;
Colombier ; pfte. sc. *Schott* ; org. arr. *Novello* ;
Gallet ; *Katto* 29

*Tantum Ergo, 5tet, 2 sop., alt., ten., bass, full sc.
Diabelli ; *Colombier* ; *Schott* ; pfte. sc. *Schott* ;
Novello 8

*Tantum Ergo, ten. solo and 4tet., full sc. (4½ minutes)
Petit ; and org. acc. *Diabelli* ; pfte. sc. *Diabelli* ;
Richault ; *Ricordi* . . . 6

Kyrie in C, to be found, writes Cherubini, in ' Messe
Solennelle ' for 3 voices (Mass in F or A) . 4

*O Salutaris, trio, ten., bass, *Ricordi* . . . 3

*Agnus Dei, 4tet, pfte. sc. *Ricordi* . . . 7

*Sanctus O Salutaris, ten. or sop. solo, full sc. *Petit* ; do.
and pfte. acc. *Canaux* ; *Novello* ; *Schott* ;
Haslinger ; as Lauda anima mea, etc., *Diabelli* ;
O Salutaris only, pfte. sc. *Perigally* ; *Novello* ;
Ditson 5

Gloria in F, solo, chorus. Above 13 works for King's
Chapel 18

Amour, amour, new air, not yet ex. for ' Lodoïska ' . 8

Year.	Description of Work.	No. of pp. MS.
1818.	*Regina Cœli, 4tet, full sc. *Schonenberger*; *Simrock*; *Diabelli*; pfte. sc. *Diabelli*; *Simrock*; *Choudens*; Lemoine; *Heugel*	46
	O Filii, hymn, 4tet, *Heugel*	37
	*Mass in E minor, VIII., with O Salutaris, 1st quatrain, 4tet, pfte. sc. *Ricordi*; *Ditson* . . .	73
	O Salutaris, 4tet, soli and chorus. Above 4 pieces for King's Chapel	8
	¦Pieces (2) for Conservatoire competition, 1 hautboy, 2 bassoon	—
	Je ne t'aime plus, rom. 2-part, 29 Oct., pfte.; Malabri .	2
	*Adjutor in opportunitatibus, Septuagesima motet, grad. and tract. Ps. ix, 9·10; 18-9; cix. 144, full sc. *Haslinger*; pfte. sc. *Ricordi*; ms. at Windsor, now (1912) at Brit. Museum . . .	42
	Kyrie, 4tet; de Toulmon	8
1819.	Kyrie, above 3 works for King's Chapel, 4tet . .	19
	Hymn to Bacchus, chant de table, trio, unacc.; 21 April	2
	*Mass in G (Coronation), IX, 4tet, for crowning of Louis XVIII.; with Sanctus, Benedictus, O Salutaris, (1st quatrain) and 3rd Hosanna, full sc. *Frey*; pfte. sc. *Richault*; *Ricordi* . . .	104
1820.	Scène de table, duet, pfte. acc. ad. lib. Jan. . .	5
	Marche funèbre, gr. orch., Mar. . . .	7
	*In paradisum, 4tet, pfte. sc., (9½ m.), *Richault*; *Ricordi*	10
	Litany of our Lady in C, 4tet, Dec. . . .	47
	Domine, Dominus noster, sop., hautboy acc.; air from 'Elisa,' with alterations. Above 4 works for King's Chapel	10
	†Canon, 2-part, for Cherubini's Album, 19 Dec. .	—
1821.	' Blanche de Provence or La Cour des Fées,' 1-act opera, by Cherubini (3rd part). Berton, Boieldieu, Kreutzer, Paër; ordered by Minister of King's Household, on occ. of Duke of Bordeaux's baptism, 1 May 1821, at Notre Dame; librettists, Théaulon and Rancé, ex. at Court Th., and 3 May at Gr. Op.; lullaby, trio, sop., pfte. sc.; Dors noble enfant, words by Berquin, *Peters*; *Augener*; *Blanchi*; *Schirmer*; Sleep, Royal Child, words by Oxenford, *Novello*; Sleep, baby, sleep, etc. .	83
	Cantata, (11) for sev. voices, and chorus; librettist, Baour-Lormian, ex. 2 May, at Hôtel de Ville fête, on occ. of Duke of Bordeaux's baptism . .	90

Year.	Description of Work.	No. of pp. MS.
1821.	*O Salutaris, 4tet, Aug. ; *Heugel*, 1st in 'La Maitrise'	
	15 June 1857, same as that in 10th Mass · ·	17
	Agnus Dei, in G, 4tet, August · ·	13
	*Mass in B Flat, X, O Salutaris, 1st quatrain, 4tet, Oct.-Nov. ; ex. 6 Jan. 1888 at London Oratory ; pfte. sc., *Richault* ; *Ricordi* · ·	50
1822.	Litany of our Lady, 4tet ; de Toulmon ·	35
	*O Fons amoris spiritus, hymn, tenor or sop. and chorus, Jan.; above 5 works for King's Chapel; *Haslinger*; *Schonenberger* ; pfte. sc., *Simrock* ; *Lemoine* ·	26
	*Sanctus in A, and Hosanna in ¾ time, to replace that in D minor Mass, 5 · · ·	6
	Chant for harmony in score; 2. Air for hautboy; 3. Air for Clarinet ; pfte. for Conserv. competition ·	16
1823.	†L'Amant trompé, rom. for Mdlle. C.'s album, 10 July	—
	Bassoon piece, for Conserv. competition 18 July ; fig. bass, taken from solfeges of 1823 · · ·	2
	Le bon Médor, rom. for M. Bérat's album, 2 Sep.; pfte. C. says: 'forme recueil avec le No. 276' (some misprint) · · · · ·	2
	Kyrie in C minor, 4tet · · · ·	15
	Lætare Jerusalem, Mid Lent motet, recits. & ch., 16 Nov. ; both for King's Chapel · · ·	62
	Stanzas for Duke of Angoulême's return, 27 Nov.; from 'Il Quinto Fabio' No. 1 ; pft. acc. · ·	2
	*Inclina Domine, introit, 4tet, full sc., 16 Dec. ; full sc. *Schonenberger* ; pfte. sc. *Simrock* ; *Amen*, org. *Novello* ; *Lemoine* · · · ·	21
1824.	Exaudi Domine, introit, 4tet, recit, chorus; de Toulmon; both for King's Chapel · · · ·	17
	*Adjutor et susceptor meus, chorus : de Toulmon ; pfte. sc., *Simrock* ; *Costallat* · · · ·	10
	†*Adoremus, hymn, trio, tenors, *Colombier*; pfte. sc., *Simrock* ; 4tet, org. acc., *Galle* ; *Heugel* ·	—
	Clarinet piece for Conserv. competition, 20 July : fig.. bass · · · · · ·	2
1825.	*Mass in A, XI, 3-part, sop., ten., bass & ch., for crowning of Charles X, at Rheims, 30 May, fin. 29 Ap., including Sanctus (with Benedictus), O Salutaris, 1st quatrain, 3 Off., Christum, pts., *White* ; Propter veritatem ; Confirma ; Communion March ; full sc. ; Mass, 2nd Off., Propter, O Salutaris, *chez l'auteur Heugel* ; Confirma, *Schonenberger*; pfte. sc. Mass, 2nd Off., *Simrock*; *Peters*; *Novello*; *Witzendorf*;	

Year.	Description of Work.	No. of pp. MS.
1825.	*Bertarelli*; and with 4th alto pt.; Strengthen, (Confirma) & Benedictus, *Novello*; *Williams*; *Ashdown*; *Ditson*; pfte. sc. Benedictus, *Simrock*; *Evette*; Comm. mch., pfte. duet, pfte. solo, *Witzendorf*; pfte. or org. solo, *Novello*; O Salutaris, *Cranz*; *Ditson*; *Gallet*; org. arr. Cum Sancto, O Salutaris, etc.	80
	Christum sempiternum, Off., 3-part; de Toulmon, same as that of Mass in A	17
	Trio for Mme. M., fête, St. Charles' Day, 4 Nov., unacc.	2
1826*	O Salutaris, bass; for King's Chapel; (5 min.); pfte. sc., *Richault*; *Ricordi* . . .	5
	In Memorials 1st ed. p. 404, No. 406; for 1827 *read* 1826, *and, under* 1827, *for* 494 *read* 404.	
	*O Salutaris, 4tet, 1st quatrain (4½ minutes), 2 sop. or ten., mezzo-contr. or bass, contr. or bass; acc. ad. lib.; fin. 30 Mar.; *Richault*; *Ricordi* .	3
1827.	*O Salutaris, 2 ten., bass, unacc.; 9 Jan., for Boieldieu's marriage, 23, ex. with bassoons, 3 celli, org. acc, at King's Chapel, *Ricordi*; *Ashdown* . .	4
1828.	Piece for Baillot's album, 4tet; 9 Sep. . .	5
	O Filii, hymn, solo, chorus; de Toulmon . .	2
1829.	*String 4tet in C. (2), with New Adagio, March, rest on symphony in D of 1815; ded. to Baillot; sc. *Payne*; *Costallat*; *Eulenberg*; *Kistner*; *Peters*; arr. pfte. duet, *Kistner*; *Peters* . . .	26
	†Canon, trio, 4 July, given Dr. C., Bologna, 4 Aug. .	—
1830.	*Sciant gentes, Sexagesima motet, 4tet; pfte. sc., *Ricordi*	36
	Esto mihi, Quinquagesima motet, 4tet; both for King's Chapel	42
1831.	New March, for that of night patrol in 3rd act, 'Faniska,' 15 May; 4tet . . .	2
	†Introduction to 'La Marquise de Brinvilliers,' opera by Cherubini, Auber, Batton, Berton, Boieldieu, Blangini, Carafa, Hérold, and Paër; librettists, Scribe, Castil-Blaze; ex. 3 Oct. at Opéra Comique, fin. 29 Sep.	—
1833.	*ALI BABA, OU LES QUARANTE VOLEURS, 25th opera, 4 acts, 24 nos.; prologue; pfte. sc., Fr., Ger., portrait, Paris; fol. Partly founded on 'Kourkourgi'; librettists, Scribe and Mélesville, younger, ex. at Grand Opera 22 July; ov., full sc. *Breitkopf*; arr. harm., wind instr., etc., *Breitkopf*; op., pfte. sc., Fr. or Ger., *Litolff*; *Hoffmann*; pfte. duet, *Diabelli*; pfte.	

Year.	Description of Work.	No. of pp. MS.

1833.   solo, *Breitkopf*; ov. pfte. duet, *Peters* ; *Breitkopf*;
ballet music, pfte. duet ; 2 v. (or v. & bass) duets,
Breitkopf ; pfte., v. or fl. ; 5tet, fl. & str., *Augener* ;
Breitkopf; *Williams* 1000

1834.   †Chansonette for M. A. de B.'s album, 20 Jan. . —

*String 4tet in D minor, (3); ded. to Baillot; fin. 31 July;
sc., *Payne*; *Eulenberg*; *Costallat* ; *Peters* ; arr.
pfte. duet, *Kistner* ; *Peters* . . . 39

1835.   Vive le bric-à-brac, canon, 2-part, for Sauvageot, 15 Jan. —
String 4tet in E., (4); begun Sep., 1834, fin. 12 Feb.,
sc. *Payne*; *Eulenberg* 32

Marches régulières d'harmonie pratique dans la composition ; de Toulmon ; no precise date in Cat.,
probably in Treatise on Counterpoint & Fugue ; pub.
this year, Paris; tr. Ger., Stöpel ; *Kistner* ;
Schlesinger; tr. Engl. Hamilton, 1841 by subscription (650), ded. to Duchess of Kent, *Cocks* ;
tr. Cowden Clarke, 1854, *Novello* ; Clarendon
Press, 1866 ; Halévy's errata, ' Gazette Musicale
de Paris,' 5 June 1836; Lo Stretto della Fuga,
Novello . : . . , —

Italian arietta, for album, 16 Apr. ; pfte. . . —

*String 4tet in F., (5); begun 25 Feb., fin. 28 June ; sc.
& pts. *Payne*; *Eulenberg* . . . 23

Italian arietta, for Mme B.'s Album, 20 Sep. ; fig. bass
copy, Montlignon 2

1836.   *Requiem in D minor II, 2 ten., bass, begun Jan. or
Feb., fin. 24 Sep. at Montlignon ; including Sanctus
(with Benedictus) & 'Pie Jesu ' ; Dies Iræ, ex. 19
Mar., 1837, at 5th Conservatoire concert ; whole
work, 25 Mar, 1838 ; with org. acc., full sc. Au Conservatoire ; *Schlesinger* ; *Frey* ; without do.,
Peters; pfte. sc., *Breitkopf* ; *Ricordi* ; *Novello* . 88

1837.   *String 4tet in A minor, (6) ; begun 4 July 1835, fin. 22
July ; sc. *Payne*; *Eulenberg* . . . 30

*String 5tet in E minor, (1); begun 30 July, fin. 28 Oct.;
sc. *Payne* ; *Breitkopf*. C. terms it a ' 1st 5tet,' so
intended to do others ? MS. Note-book, *cit.* Pougin. 50

1839.   Arietta for Album, 1 Jan. . . . . —
[Cherubini's record ends ; de Toulmon adds :—]

1842.   Canon, words & music, by C., early in Jan., for Ingres,
fac-simile, Blanc's ' Ingres.' . . . —

SOME MUSICIANS WHO HAVE EDITED OR ARRANGED
WORKS OR PIECES OF CHERUBINI.

ARDITI.	ELLIOTT.	LANGER.	ROTH.
BARRY.	ENGEL.	LEVI.	SALAMAN.
BATISTE.	EYKIN.	LICKL.	SCHAAB.
BERTONCINI.	FESSY.	LINCOLN.	SCHIRMER.
BEST.	FASANOTTI.	MARZIALS.	SCHMIDT.
BIEREY.	FUMAGALLI.	MATAUSCHEK.	SCHNEIDER.
BIZET.	GAUNTLETT.	MAZZINGHI.	SCHUBERT.
BOCHSA.	GEVAERT.	MEZGER.	SEIBT.
BONN.	GOLTERMANN.	MEFINER.	SMALLWOOD.
BOOM, VAN	GOPFERT.	MOCKWITZ.	SMITH.
BOYNEBURGH.	GROSJOHANN.	MOFFAT.	SOYKA.
BOYSE.	HADDOCK.	MOORE.	SPARK.
BRISSLER.	HATTON.	MULLER.	STARK.
BROWN.	HECKER.	NEVILLE.	STEIBELT.
BRUGUIER.	HEMY.	NODNAGEL.	STOCKHAUSEN
BUEHRER.	HERMANN.	NOVELLO.	TOURS.
BURGMUELLER.	HILES.	PAUER.	TRAVIS.
CALLCOTT.	HOCH.	PITT.	ULRICH.
CAVALLO.	HUMMEL.	PIXIS.	VIARDOT-GARCIA.
CHWATAL.	HUSSLA.	POPP.	WAHLFAHRT.
COOPER.	KELLER.	PROUT.	WALDECK.
CORRIE.	KLAGE.	REICHA.	WALTHER.
COSTA.	KLEINMICHEL.	REINECKE.	WATTS
CRAMER.	KLINGENBRUNNER.	REINHARD.	WESTBROOK.
CZERNY.	KREMSER.	RICHARDSON.	WITTEMANN.
DENEAUX.	KRETSCHMER.	RIELS.	WODEHOUSE.
DIETSCH.	KREUTZER.	RIMBAULT.	WUSTROW.
DORN.	KRUG.	RITTER.	ZOELLER.
DREILER.	LACHNER.	ROSSINI.	ZULEHNER.

SOME COLLECTIONS WHERE PIECES OF OR FROM
CHERUBINI MAY BE FOUND.

Alliance Musicale.
Amateur Organist.
Andamenti d'Armonia.
Aurora.
Cäcilia.
Cole's Exercises in Sight-seeing.
Ecclesiasticon.
Echos d'Italia.
Ecole Classique du Chant.
Gemme d'Antichità.
Hullah's Part-Music.
Hummel's Twelve Select Overtures.
Knight's Musical Library.
Lyre Sacrée, La.
Mèlodies Célèbres.
Musical Bouquet.

Musica Sacra.
Musikwoche.
Organist's Anthology.
Oratoriensatze.
Pianiste, Le.
Popular Choruses.
Procuro Generale.
Rêpertoire Classique.
Schirmer's Choruses.
Scuola Corale, La.
Select Compositions for the Organ.
Select Sacred Songs.
Singer's Library of Concerted Music.
Società Musicale, Naples.
Vocal Library of Popular Classics.

ANALYSIS OF CATALOGUE.

The above, some 446 works, or sets of works, may be divided into two parts—secular and sacred music—of which the first part takes 335, the second 111. The numbers in Cherubini's Catalogue reach 230, and 446 should be a far higher number for an exact total. Of the whole, some 135 have been published. Cherubini composed 65 Airs, 48 Romanzas, 47 Duets, 35 Hymns, 25 Operas, 25 Psalms, 14 Kyries, 13 Masses (with or without Offertories and O Salutaris, and including 2 Requiems), 13 Dances, 11 Cantatas, 10 portions of Operas, 10 Marches, 9 Sonatas, 9 Nocturns, 8 Choruses, 8 Trios, 7 Pas redoublés, 6 Instrumental 4tets, 6 single or sets of Canons, 4 Litanies, 4 Anthems, 4 Operatic Finales, 4 Recitatives, 4 sets of Solfeges (in all over 160), 4 Rondeaux, 3 Odes, 3 Sanctus, 3 vocal 4tets, 2 portions of Cantatas, 2 Intermedes, 2 Lamentations, 2 Madrigals, 2 Credos, 2 Agnus Dei, 2 Glorias, 2 Hautboy pieces, 2 Bassoon pieces, 2 Table pieces, 2 Clarinet pieces, 2 Funeral Chants, 1 Oratorio, 1 vocal 6tet, 1 Chaconne, 1 Canzonet, 1 Capriccio, 1 Offertory, 1 Instrumental 5tet, 1 Overture, 1 Symphony, 1 Ballet, 1 portion of an Oratorio, 1 Organ Air, 1 Minuet, 1 Pianoforte fantasia, a Course of Harmony, a Collection of 39 figured basses, Airs in Sarti's operas, a piece for Baillot, and Stanzas (2) set to music for Isabey and the Duke of Angoulême. Total, 446.

ADDENDA.

5 Operas ascribed to Cherubini :

1. 'Artaserse,' by Fétis ('Biog. Univ.' ii., 390, art. Cherubini), & Grove ('Dict. Music & Musicians,' art. Crescentini).

2. ' Didone Abbandonata,' by Riemann ('Dict. Music,' art. Cherubini), who names Brescia (1787-8) as the place of production.

3. ' I Viaggiatori Felici,' by the writer of 'L. Cherubini,' Fritzsch, in

reality a collaboration by Anfossi, Piccinni and Parenti, to which Cherubini contributed.

5. ' Isabelle,' in connection with performances of ' Les Deux Journées,' in Paris. Grétry (and others) wrote ' Isabelle.'

Fétis also writes of ' several operas ' among Cherubini's juvenile works, whereas there are none, and Denne-Baron of ' religious pieces ' to some of Sarti's works; this, too, in the year (1784) when both master and pupil almost simultaneously quitted Italy for Russia and England respectively. Other compositions and arrangements not located in the catalogue for certain, or wrongly ascribed to Cherubini, are subjoined, with authorities :—

1795? Hymne à la Victoire, words by Carbon de Flins, sung at the Grand Opera. Castil-Blaze. ' L'Académie Impériale de Musique.' i. 15.

1796. ' Il Perruchiero,' adaptation from old intermezzo? 'Niederrheinische-Musik-Zeitung' notice, *M.W.* 1862.

1799. ' Hymne funèbre sur la mort du Général Joubert,' words by Chaussard, sung at Grand Opera. Castil-Blaze, 'L'Académie.' i., 15.

1805. An air for Mandel, C.F. Pohl. Pougin thinks this an error, *M. W.* 1883, 64.

1813. Chorus in ' L'Oriflamme,' 1 act opera, by Méhul, Paër, Berton, Kreutzer, ex. at Gr. Op. 31 Jan., 1814. Picchianti and Gamucci.

' Nausicaa,' librettist, Toug. 1st act sketched. Letter, 12 Dec. 1810, of Cherubini, cit. Pougin, *M.W.* 21 Ap. 1813.

' Tantum Ergo,' (' Crown of Jesus ' Hymn-book), arr. Hemy, *Richardson.*

1816 *Petite Messe de la Sainte Trinité sur les chants de l'Eglise, en Contrepoint mesuré à trois voix avec acc. d'orgue. Words from the Psalms. Simrock.

*Sonata in B flat. In coll. 17th & 18th century music. See Cat. 1780, *Breitkopf.*

Instrumentation of 'Adagio' in E of Viotti's 22nd Concerto in A minor, ascribed to Cherubini.

' Salvum Fac,' arr. from C., *Cranz.*

Romance, Essex to Elizabeth, Tilly ' A l'abaissements des prières.' Brit. Mus. Catalogue.

Serenata, *Mariani.*
' Spirit of Mercy,' *Fischer.*
Thanksgiving Anthem, *Gordon.*
' Veni, Jesu,' *Ditson; Ellis; Fischer.*
A Cherubini Album has been edited by Reinecke; *Breitkopf.*
Reports on Conservatoire, on Instruments, by Cherubini and others; Brumaire An V. *Porthmann;* 1815, *Déterville;* reprint, *Leblanc,* 1819, etc.
V'cello arrangements from Cherubini by Fény.

MUSIC COPIED BY CHERUBINI.

1. Marcello's Psalms, i. 446 pp.; ii. 336; iii. 420; iv. 338.
2. Collection of Lotti's madrigals, with Tantum Ergo by Sacchini, and Salve Regina, solo, by Majo.
3. Latin pieces by various authors, with explanatory table, 446 pp.
4. Pergolese's Salve Regina and Cantata, 120 pp.
5. Three motets, by Pergolese, Jomelli & Durante, 172 pp.
6. Clari's Duets and Trios, i. 92 pp; ii. 102; iii. 124.
7. Pieces by Handel, Leo, Palestrina, &c., (with biographical notice of Handel, by Cherubini), 193 pp.
8. Jomelli, 3; Durante, 2 pieces. One of last 24 pp. copied by Cherubini, others doubtful. *Duets by Durante (ed. Cherubini).
9. *Oblong ms., with table, of Père Martini's canons, with Cherubini's solutions; 90 pp.; Paris.
10. Jomelli's ' Miserere ' for 2-part ; 104 pp.
11. Sarti's ' Saggio superficiale sopra il principio della musica,' 24 pp.
12. Sarti's ' Compendio scientifico del canto fermo, o sia dei toni ecclesiastici,' 17 pp.
13. ' Esempii di Contrappunto rigoroso di varii autori,' oblong m.s. 61 pp.

DUPLICATE MSS.

Ov. ' Crescendo,' 25 pp.
Ov. ' Faniska.'
Separate parts of the 6th 4tet in A minor, 43 pp.
1825. 1. Gradual, Propter veritatem, Offertory, Mass in A, 11 pp.
  ,,   2. Confirma hoc Deus, do. 21 pp.
  ,,   3. Marche Religieuse, with instr., do.
  P.S.—' Démophon' full sc., *André* ; ov. pfte. double duet, *Leuckart* ; chorus, *Zumsteeg* ; air, ' Ah, che forse,' by *Ricordi;* ov. ' Deux Journees ' str. 5-tet, *Mollo* ; ov. ' Anacréon ' pfte. duet, *Monro.*

NOTE.

We read in Cherubini's Catalogue, 'Les personnes qui desirent devenir acquéreurs pourront s'adresser à M. Petit, ancien éditeur, demeurant Rue St. Thomas du Louvre No. 13.'

A notice from Cherubini's widow also appeared in the 'Musical Times' with reference to the sale. Fr. Girod, S.J., expresses his regret at the dispersion of the MSS. (1853). See account of the same 11 years after the composer's death in Hiller's 'Aus dem Tonleben unserer Zeit' and 'Musikalisches und Persönliches' (originally appearing in the 'Cologne Gazette,' Breitkopf & Härtel, Leipsic, 1876). The latter work contains the article on Cherubini, in 'Macmillan's Magazine,' for July 1875, by Ferdinand Hiller. 'The treasures collected in his library,' he writes, ... 'might adorn and enrich the greatest National Library.' This, in part, they now do.

In connection with apparently a further sale of MSS., I insert the following from *M.W.*, 1860, xxxviii. 172.

'Those artistes and amateurs who have a passion for works not printed, or published, of a great master, will learn with pleasure that the compositions of the renowned composer, Cherubini, the greatest contrapuntal writer that ever lived, are now for sale at Paris, by his widow, in MS., consisting, in his own handwriting, of overtures in score, masses, operas, sacred pieces, cantatas, orchestral pieces, 4tets, 5tets "solfeggi," etc., etc., comprising nearly 300 works, composed between the year 1773 and 1841. Here is a field for musical societies, students and directors of music, to produce novelties, and study one whose works hitherto known and printed, are patterns of excellence in every point of view, and held up as models of perfection to the student. The directors of the Philharmonic Societies, Musical Unions, and Sacred Harmonics, etc., should look after the works. They will find overtures, chamber-music, oratorios never produced before the public,' etc.

Napoleon III. was in treaty for a large collection when the war of 1870 broke out, and, on a better offer for the same than that of the French Republican Government being made, this was purchased in the summer of 1878 by the German Government for the Royal Library at Berlin, where it is now located and valued.

On enquiry, the publishers of the posthumous works, Messrs. Richault & Ricordi, did not possess the full scores. It is to be hoped that, at least, the score of the incomparable E minor Mass will be given to the world, and rejoice the admirers of this consummate Master and Teacher of the 1st rank in a great art. While it is futility to say of all Cherubini's sacred works that they ' are not available for liturgical purposes,'[1] all of them lose much without their instrumentation, although a good organ and organist do well, as an engraving may give a good idea of an original picture. But to attempt, without a trained choir, either Palestrina or Cherubini, is to be unfair to both; and the Missa de Angelis, and simple chants, as beautiful, in their way, as either, are the alternative, and one specially pleasing to Authority.

With regard to the Gregorian, I had learnt from childhood the Mechlin; was later on introduced to the Ratisbon, and finally to the Solesmes. It is clear that a theoretical question as to the best form of plain-chant must raise a problem of difficult solution for the learned,

---

[1] The ' previous career in the theatre ' is hazarded in an earlier Addenda, as ' one of the causes' why some of the Masses are not so available, and it is said : ' The originality of the later style will largely account for any exaggerated views about its general character, but to say that no portions of the later school's work are open to animadversion would be as unreasonable as to deny that the Kyrie of Beethoven's Mass in C, and the *Pie Jesu* of Cherubini's Requiem in C minor, are as devotional as Plain Chant or Palestrina. The recitatives in Cherubini's Kyrie in C were better away [?] and Orlando di Lasso can be as lively in a *Sanctus* as Rossini in a *Tantum Ergo.* The sixteenth music can be, and is, as defective in ecclesiastical style as that of the nineteenth, but we do not condemn it wholesale on that account. The Holy Father condemns neither the one nor the other in his *Motu Proprio.* . . Dulness may be tolerable to the ears of some, who find liveliness not to be endured. This is a matter of temperament. It would be well, however, while the repetitions of words in the concerted chant were being lessened, if the notes to one syllable in some of the Gregorian could be diminished,' a retort prompted by occasionally unfair treatment of Masters.

and this suggests caution in accepting any indiscriminate condemnations of Great Masters, such as the above. Gregorian, Palestrina, Cherubini, can all be trying at their worst: taken at their best, they can all be approved.

With respect to Cherubini's secular music, when it is said in the Preface that he has written 'little or nothing' apart from the overtures and larger Masses, for drawing and concert-rooms, this is safely said only as to instrumental music published—1 symphony, 6 sonatas, etc. For when the amount unpublished is surveyed, it would be hard to say that Cherubini did not cover a considerable vocal field for drawing and concert-rooms. But, probably, a great deal is ephemeral, occasional, else it would have found its way ere now into print: it does not seem likely that one so actively engaged, and for so many years, as teacher and director of the chief Musical Academy in France, would be so favourably situated for compositions of generally sustained excellence, as other Great Masters, who were neither teachers nor directors.

As an instance of disproportion in 'Grove,' it is noticed in a previous Preface that $5\frac{1}{2}$ columns are devoted to Cherubini and $113\frac{1}{2}$ to Mendelssohn: 'probably a far lesser Master,' is added. In his 'Lauda Sion' and 'Psalms,' Mendelssohn is so beautiful that I should feel indisposed to depreciate such a Master; so romantic, too, in the 'Hebrides' and the 'Midsummer's Night's Dream;' so genuine, too, in the 'Greek' music, and in other portions of his work, symphonic and vocal; still, he never seems to be of the calibre that Cherubini can be; and $5\frac{1}{2}$ columns seemed as inadequate as $113\frac{1}{2}$ seemed excessive. A rebuke to a critic's veiled sneer at Cherubini was given in a 'Pall Mall Gazette' No. of Jan. 1899 by R.W., who indicated that native composers were not made his 'equals' thereby (a tone they themselves would be the last to countenance, but rather one of admiration, not unmixed with veneration and wonder.)

P. 66. Dirce's air is accused by Chorley of
'dryness' and 'insufficient' vocal interest (Act. 1.,
Sc. 1.—'Médée'). Apart from its sequel, however,

the air's opening ('Memorials,' p. 66), promises well, and
seems free from aridity. Hauptmann sees no dryness in
Cherubini's sacred music, but it is not absent from his
operatic.

P. 119. Fétis, in 1843, was the first to give the
account of the origin of the Mass in F in the ' Revue et
Gazette Musicale de Paris.' 'Cherubini,' he says ' was
seated near a cheerful fire, engaged in placing his day's
harvest in his herbarium, when a servant entered and
announced the members of the Harmonic Society.' 'Des
Manuscrits Autographes de L. Cherubini,' *M.W.* 1883,
157. The same writer observes of the fugue in the
8-part Credo : ' The dread of wounding M. Cherubini's
modesty prevents my giving utterance to all the eulogy
that this fine production deserves. I can only urge all
those who study the art of composition to examine it
attentively, returning to it again and again.' (' On
Counterpoint and Fugue ').

Note 23, p. 126, the Mass in D referred to is
probably Dvorak's finest work.

P. 166. The Requiem in C minor was 1st given in England 28 Mar. 1834, in London, at Alsager's Private Concerts by the Queen Square Select Society, Mrs. H. R. Bishop taking soprano, M. Spagnoletti 1st viola. *Grove* i. 57[b.]

Hummel, the composer of the Masses in B flat, E flat, and D, that rank so highly (especially the last), is the author of variations on the march in the 'Water-Carrier' and of an arrangement of the overture to 'Lodoïska' for pianoforte; and of the overture to 'Anacréon' for pianoforte, and flute or violoncello.

HUMMEL.

POSTSCRIPT.

IN a 'Book of Oratorios,' London 1902, with a Prefatory Letter by the present Archbishop of Birmingham, Cherubini's music—Dies Irae in C minor; Gloria in E minor; Regina Cœli; Agnus Dei in C; Confirma hoc, Deus; Sanctus in A; Credo in C; Domine Jesu in C minor—illustrates the following: The Creator and Creature; Our Lord's Incarnation, Life, and Passion; God's Church; His House; Our Blessed Lady; Christ's Kingdom, and Life after Death: i.e. some of the best in ancient and modern church music is here varied by a brief discourse dividing the selections,—the whole religious 'pasticcio,' an extension of Palestrina's and Animuccia's 'Laudi,' in St. Philip Neri's time at the Chiesa Nuova, Rome; the Naples Oratory, etc. The Oratorian 'music' and 'voices' at Rome are described by Evelyn in Nov. 1644, and Jan. 1645, as 'rare.' The oratorio is more suitable for church than concert-room, and should have a new life there in the 20th century, just as it flourished in the 16th at the Chiesa Nuova, adapting itself to St. Philip's Apostolate. The Oratory, St. Paul's, and other churches, where the conditions are favourable, accordingly favour the oratorio to-day.

NOTANDA, ETC.

p. 26, *for* Lodoïska *read* Dirce; p, 68, below l. 5 bass clef sign; pp. 70, 146, *read* melodious; p. 74, 'Les Follies,' etc, by Corelli; p. 111, treble clef sign before notes; p 118, *add* for *after* means; *read* pips; p. 126, *read* cantantur; p. 129, *read* Vielliard; p. 169, *read* fps; p. 170, *read* Abrahæ; p. 222, *read* Hiller; p. 229, *read* Blangini; p. 242, 'Esto mihi' published by Heugel; 259, note 3, *erase* semi-colon; p. 260, *read* mirum; p. 288, *read* citizens; p. 291, *read* not *before* wait. Appreciations in Brief.—*For* Emile Deschamps *read* Bouilly. p. 51. *Kourkourgi's* libretto is taken by Duveyrier from Metastasio's *Olimpiade.*

INDEX.

354   *Index.*